Children's Literature Review

Guide to Gale Literary Criticism Series

For criticism on	Consult these Gale series
Authors now living or who died after December 31, 1999	*CONTEMPORARY LITERARY CRITICISM (CLC)*
Authors who died between 1900 and 1999	*TWENTIETH-CENTURY LITERARY CRITICISM (TCLC)*
Authors who died between 1800 and 1899	*NINETEENTH-CENTURY LITERATURE CRITICISM (NCLC)*
Authors who died between 1400 and 1799	*LITERATURE CRITICISM FROM 1400 TO 1800 (LC)* *SHAKESPEAREAN CRITICISM (SC)*
Authors who died before 1400	*CLASSICAL AND MEDIEVAL LITERATURE CRITICISM (CMLC)*
Authors of books for children and young adults	*CHILDREN'S LITERATURE REVIEW (CLR)*
Dramatists	*DRAMA CRITICISM (DC)*
Poets	*POETRY CRITICISM (PC)*
Short story writers	*SHORT STORY CRITICISM (SSC)*
Literary topics and movements	*HARLEM RENAISSANCE: A GALE CRITICAL COMPANION (HR)* *THE BEAT GENERATION: A GALE CRITICAL COMPANION (BG)*
Asian American writers of the last two hundred years	*ASIAN AMERICAN LITERATURE (AAL)*
Black writers of the past two hundred years	*BLACK LITERATURE CRITICISM (BLC)* *BLACK LITERATURE CRITICISM SUPPLEMENT (BLCS)*
Hispanic writers of the late nineteenth and twentieth centuries	*HISPANIC LITERATURE CRITICISM (HLC)* *HISPANIC LITERATURE CRITICISM SUPPLEMENT (HLCS)*
Native North American writers and orators of the eighteenth, nineteenth, and twentieth centuries	*NATIVE NORTH AMERICAN LITERATURE (NNAL)*
Major authors from the Renaissance to the present	*WORLD LITERATURE CRITICISM, 1500 TO THE PRESENT (WLC)* *WORLD LITERATURE CRITICISM SUPPLEMENT (WLCS)*

ISSN 0362-4145

volume 89

Children's Literature Review

Excerpts from Reviews,
Criticism, and Commentary
on Books for Children
and Young People

Scot Peacock
Project Editor

Detroit • New York • San Diego • San Francisco • Cleveland • New Haven, Conn. • Waterville, Maine • London • Munich

THOMSON

GALE

Children's Literature Review, Vol. 89

Project Editor
Scot Peacock

Editorial
Justin Karr, Rebecca J. Long

Research
Sarah Genik

Permissions
Shalice Shah-Caldwell

Imaging and Multimedia
Dean Dauphinais, Robert Duncan, Leitha Etheridge-Sims, Mary K. Grimes, Lezlie Light, Dan Newell, David G. Oblender, Christine O'Bryan, Kelly A. Quin, Luke Rademacher

Composition and Electronic Capture
Carolyn A. Roney

Manufacturing
Stacy L. Melson

LIBRARY OF CONGRESS CATALOG CARD NUMBER 76-643301

ISBN 0-7876-6782-X
ISSN 0362-4145

Printed in the United States of America
10 9 8 7 6 5 4 3 2 1

Contents

Preface vii

Acknowledgments xi

Literary Criticism Series Advisory Board xv

Preface

Literature for children and young adults has evolved into both a respected branch of creative writing and a successful industry. Currently, books for young readers are considered among the most popular segments of publishing. Criticism of juvenile literature is instrumental in recording the literary or artistic development of the creators of children's books as well as the trends and controversies that result from changing values or attitudes about young people and their literature. Designed to provide a permanent, accessible record of this ongoing scholarship, *Children's Literature Review* (*CLR*) presents parents, teachers, and librarians—those responsible for bringing children and books together—with the opportunity to make informed choices when selecting reading materials for the young. In addition, *CLR* provides researchers of children's literature with easy access to a wide variety of critical information from English-language sources in the field. Users will find balanced overviews of the careers of the authors and illustrators of the books that children and young adults are reading; these entries, which contain excerpts from published criticism in books and periodicals, assist users by sparking ideas for papers and assignments and suggesting supplementary and classroom reading. Ann L. Kalkhoff, president and editor of *Children's Book Review Service Inc.,* writes that "*CLR* has filled a gap in the field of children's books, and it is one series that will never lose its validity or importance."

Scope of the Series

Each volume of *CLR* profiles the careers of a selection of authors and illustrators of books for children and young adults from preschool through high school. Author lists in each volume reflect:

- an international scope

- representation of authors of all eras

- the variety of genres covered by children's and/or YA literature: picture books, fiction, nonfiction, poetry, folklore, and drama

Although the focus of the series is on authors new to *CLR,* entries will be updated as the need arises.

Organization of the Book

A *CLR* entry consists of the following elements:

- The **Author Heading** consists of the author's name followed by birth and death dates. The portion of the name outside the parentheses denotes the form under which the author is most frequently published. If the author wrote consistently under a pseudonym, the pseudonym will be listed in the author heading and the author's actual name given in parentheses on the first line of the biographical and critical information. Also located here are any name variations under which an author wrote, including transliterated forms for authors whose native languages use non-roman alphabets. Uncertain birth or death dates are indicated by question marks.

- A **Portrait of the Author** is included when available.

- The **Author Introduction** contains information designed to introduce an author to *CLR* users by presenting an overview of the author's themes and styles, biographical facts that relate to the author's literary career or critical responses to the author's works, and information about major awards and prizes the author has received. The introduction begins by identifying the nationality of the author and by listing genres in which s/he has written for children and young adults. Introductions also list a group of representative titles for which the author or illustrator being profiled is best known; this section, which begins with the words "major works include," follows the genre line of the introduction. For seminal figures, a listing of major works about the author follows when appropriate, highlighting important biographies about the author or illustrator that are not excerpted in the entry. The centered heading "Introduction" announces the body of the text.

- **Criticism** is located in three sections: **Author Commentary** (when available) **General Commentary** (when available), and **Title Commentary** (commentary on specific titles).

The **Author Commentary** presents background material written by the author or by an interviewer. This commentary may cover a specific work or several works. Author commentary on more than one work appears after the author introduction, while commentary on an individual book follows the title entry heading.

The **General Commentary** consists of critical excerpts that consider more than one work by the author or illustrator being profiled. General commentary is preceded by the critic's name in boldface type or, in the case of unsigned criticism, by the title of the journal. *CLR* also features entries that emphasize general criticism on the oeuvre of an author or illustrator. When appropriate, a selection of reviews is included to supplement the general commentary.

The **Title Commentary** begins with the title entry headings, which precede the criticism on a title and cite publication information on the work being reviewed. Title headings list the title of the work as it appeared in its first English-language edition. The first English-language publication date of each work (unless otherwise noted) is listed in parentheses following the title. Differing U.S. and British titles follow the publication date within parentheses. When a work is written by an individual other than the one being profiled, as is the case when illustrators are featured, the parenthetical material following the title cites the author of the work before listing its publication date.

Entries in each title commentary section consist of critical excerpts on the author's individual works, arranged chronologically by publication date. The entries generally contain two to seven reviews per title, depending on the stature of the book and the amount of criticism it has generated. The editors select titles that reflect the entire scope of the author's literary contribution, covering each genre and subject. An effort is made to reprint criticism that represents the full range of each title's reception, from the year of its initial publication to current assessments. Thus, the reader is provided with a record of the author's critical history. Publication information (such as publisher names and book prices) and parenthetical numerical references (such as footnotes or page and line references to specific editions of works) have been deleted at the discretion of the editors to provide smoother reading of the text.

- A complete **Bibliographical Citation** of the original essay or book precedes each piece of criticism.

- Selected excerpts are preceded by brief **Annotations,** which provide information on the critic or work of criticism to enhance the reader's understanding of the excerpt.

- Numerous **Illustrations** are featured in *CLR*. For entries on illustrators, an effort has been made to include illustrations that reflect the characteristics discussed in the criticism. Entries on authors who do not illustrate their own works my include photographs and other illustrative material pertinent to their careers.

Special Features: Entries on Illustrators

Entries on authors who are also illustrators will occasionally feature commentary on selected works illustrated but not written by the author being profiled. These works are strongly associated with the illustrator and have received critical acclaim for their art. By including critical comment on works of this type, the editors wish to provide a more complete representation of the artist's career. Criticism on these works has been chosen to stress artistic, rather than literary, contributions. Title entry headings for works illustrated by the author being profiled are arranged chronologically within the entry by date of publication and include notes identifying the author of the illustrated work. In order to provide easier access for users, all titles illustrated by the subject of the entry are boldfaced.

CLR also includes entries on prominent illustrators who have contributed to the field of children's literature. These entries are designed to represent the development of the illustrator as an artist rather than as a literary stylist. The illustrator's section is organized like that of an author, with two exceptions: the introduction presents an overview of the illustrator's styles and techniques rather than outlining his or her literary background, and the commentary written by the illustrator on his or her works is called "Illustrator's Commentary" rather than "Author's Commentary." All titles of books containing illustrations by the artist being profiled are highlighted in boldface type.

Indexes

A **Cumulative Author Index** lists all of the authors who have appeared in *CLR* with cross-references to the biographical, autobiographical, and literary criticism series published by the Gale Group. A complete list of these sources is found facing the first page of the Author Index. The index also includes birth and death dates and cross-references between pseudonyms and actual names.

A **Cumulative Nationality Index** lists all authors featured in *CLR* by nationality, followed by the number of the *CLR* volume in which their entry appears.

A **Cumulative Title Index** lists all author titles covered in *CLR*. Each title is followed by the author's name and corresponding volume and page numbers where commentary on the work is located.

Citing *Children's Literature Review*

When citing criticism reprinted in the Literary Criticism Series, students should provide complete bibliographic information so that the cited essay can be located in the original print or electronic source. Students who quote directly from reprinted criticism may use any accepted bibliographic format, such as University of Chicago Press style or Modern Language Association style.

The examples below follow recommendations for preparing a bibliography set forth in *The Chicago Manual of Style,* 14th ed. (Chicago: The University of Chicago Press, 1993); the first example pertains to material drawn from periodicals, the second to material reprinted from books.

Frederick, Heather Vogel. "Cynthia Rylant: A Quiet and Reflective Craft." *Publishers Weekly* 244, no. 29 (21 July 1997): 178-79. Reprinted in *Children's Literature Review.* Vol. 86, edited by Scot Peacock, 124-26. Detroit: Gale, 2003.

Strong, Pauline T. "Playing Indian in the Nineties: *Pocahontas* and *The Indian in the Cupboard.*" In *Hollywood's Indian: The Portrayal of the Native American in Film,* edited by Peter C. Rollins and John E. O'Connor, 73-81. Lexington: The University Press of Kentucky, 1998. Reprinted in *Children's Literature Review.* Vol. 86, edited by Scot Peacock, 124-26. Detroit: Gale, 2003.

The examples below follow recommendations for preparing a works cited list set forth in the *MLA Handbook for Writers of Research Papers,* 5th ed. (New York: The Modern Language Association of America, 1999); the first example pertains to material drawn from periodicals, the second to material reprinted from books.

Frederick, Heather Vogel. "Cynthia Rylant: A Quiet and Reflective Craft." *Publishers Weekly* 244. 29 (21 July 1997): 178-79. Reprinted in *Children's Literature Review.* Ed. Scot Peacock. Vol. 86. Detroit: Gale, 2003. 124-26.

Strong, Pauline T. "Playing Indian in the Nineties: *Pocahontas* and *The Indian in the Cupboard.*" *Hollywood's Indian: The Portrayal of the Native American in Film.* Eds. Peter C. Rollins and John E. O'Connor. Lexington: The University Press of Kentucky, 1998. 73-81. Reprinted in *Children's Literature Review.* Ed. Scot Peacock. Vol. 86. Detroit: Gale, 2003. 124-26.

Suggestions are Welcome

In response to various suggestions, several features have been added to *CLR* since the beginning of the series, including author entries on retellers of traditional literature as well as those who have been the first to record oral tales and other folklore; entries on prominent illustrators featuring commentary on their styles and techniques; entries on authors whose works are considered controversial; occasional entries devoted to criticism on a single work or a series of works; sections in author introductions that list major works by and about the author or illustrator being profiled; explanatory notes that provide information on the critic or work of criticism to enhance the usefulness of the excerpt; more extensive illustrative material, such as holographs of manuscript pages and photographs of people and places pertinent to the careers of the authors and artists; a cumulative nationality index for easy access to authors by nationality; and occasional guest essays written specifically for *CLR* by prominent critics on subjects of their choice.

Readers who wish to suggest new features, topics, or authors to appear in future volumes, or who have other suggestions or comments are cordially invited to call, write, or fax the Managing Editor:

Managing Editor, Literary Criticism Series
The Gale Group
27500 Drake Road
Farmington Hills, MI 48331-3535
1-800-347-4253 (GALE)
Fax: 248-699-8054

Acknowledgments

The editors wish to thank the copyright holders of the excerpted criticism included in this volume and the permissions managers of many book and magazine publishing companies for assisting us in securing reproduction rights. We are also grateful to the staffs of the Detroit Public Library, the Library of Congress, the University of Detroit Mercy Library, Wayne State University Purdy/Kresge Library Complex, and the University of Michigan Libraries for making their resources available to us. Following is a list of the copyright holders who have granted us permission to reproduce material in this volume of *CLR*. Every effort has been made to trace copyright, but if omissions have been made, please let us know.

COPYRIGHTED EXCERPTS IN *CLR*, VOLUME 89, WERE REPRODUCED FROM THE FOLLOWING PERIODICALS:

ALAN Review, v. 29, Spring-Summer 2002. Reproduced by permission. —*American Libraries,* v. 33, March 2002. Copyright © 2002 by the American Library Association. Reproduced by permission. —*Best Sellers,* v. 38, January, 1979. Reproduced by permission. —*Book Report,* v. 11, September-October 1992; v. 13, January-February 1995; v. 15, September-October 1996; v. 19, September-October 2000; v. 20, September-October 2001. © copyright 1992, 1995, 1996, 2001 by Linworth Publishing, Inc., Worthington, Ohio. All reproduced by permission. —*Booklist,* v. 71, April 15, 1975; v. 77, January 15, 1981; v. 78, June 15, 1982; v. 81, May 15, 1985; v. 84, September 15, 1987; v. 85, March 1, 1989; v. 86, May 1, 1990; v. 88, September 15, 1991; v. 88, February 15, 1992; v. 88, April 1, 1992; v. 88, May 1, 1992; v. 89, September 15, 1992; v. 89, December 15, 1992; v. 89, February 15, 1993; v. 89, April 15, 1993; v. 90, September 1, 1993; v. 90, September 15, 1993; v. 90, November 15, 1993; v. 90, February 15, 1994; v. 90, April 1, 1994; v. 90, April 15, 1994; v. 90, May, 1994; v. 91, January 15, 1995; v. 91, April 1, 1995; v. 91, June 1, 1995; v. 92, September 1, 1995; v. 92, October 1, 1995; v. 92, December 1, 1995; v. 92, February 1, 1996; v. 92, February 15, 1996; v. 92, March 1, 1996; v. 93, September 1, 1996; v. 93, November 15, 1996; v. 93, March 1, 1997; v. 93, April 1, 1997; v. 94, October, 1997; v. 94, April 1, 1998; v. 94, May 15, 1998; v. 94, June 1, 1998; v. 94, July 1, 1998; v. 94, August, 1998; v. 95, September 15, 1998; v. 95, November 1, 1998; v. 96, September 15, 1999; v. 96, October 15, 1999; v. 96, November 1, 1999; v. 96, June 1, 2000; v. 97, November 1, 2000; v. 97, December 15, 2000; v. 97, February 1, 2001; v. 97, February 15, 2001; v. 98, March 15, 2001; v. 98, May, 2001; v. 98, August 2001; v. 98, September 15, 2001; v. 98, October 1, 2001; v. 98, February 1, 2002; v. 97, August 2001; v. 98, April 1, 2002; v. 99, September 15, 2002. Copyright © 1975, 1981, 1982, 1985, 1987, 1989, 1990, 1991, 1992, 1993, 1994, 1995, 1996, 1997, 1998, 1999, 2000, 2001, 2002 by the American Library Association. All reproduced by permission. —*Books for Keeps,* n. 45, July 1987; n. 51, July 1988; v. 66, May 1992; v. 240, November 1992; v. 4, September 1993; v. 4, November 1993; v. 18, July 1994; v. 22, January 1996; v. 244, March 1997; v. 71, September 1997; v. 124, January 1999; v. 246, September 1999. © School Bookshop Association 1987, 1988, 1992, 1993, 1994, 1996, 1997, 1999. All reproduced by permission. —*Books,* n. 10, January 1988. © 1988, Washington Post Book World Service/ Washington Post Writers Group. Reproduced by permission. —*Books for Your Children,* v. 12, 1977. © Books for Your Children 1977. Reproduced by permission. —*British Book News Children's Books,* Autumn 1980; December 1987, March 1988. © The British Council, 1980, 1987, 1988. All reproduced by permission. —*Bulletin of the Center for Children's Books,* v. 22, January 1969; v. 23, June 1970; v. 26, November 1973; v. 27, March 1974; v. 28, January 1975; v. 28, July 1975; v. 29, March 1976; v. 30, April 1977; v. 33, October 1979; v. 34, January 1981; v. 44, June 1991; v. 45, December 1991. Copyright © 1969, 1970, 1973, 1974, 1975, 1976, 1977, 1979, 1981, 1991 by The Board of Trustees of the University of Illinois. All reproduced by permission. —*Catholic Library World,* n. 62, July, 1990. Reproduced by permission of Commonweal Foundation. —*Childhood Education,* v. 350, October, 1973; v. 78, Winter 2001. Copyright © 1973, 2001 by the Association. Both reproduced by permission of the Association for Childhood Education International, 17904 Georgia Avenue, Suite 215, Olney, MD. —*Children's Book Review,* v. 1, June, 1971. Copyright 1971 Children's Book Review Service Inc. Reproduced by permission. —*Children's Book Review Service,* v. 2, September, 1972; v. 1, November, 1972; v. 3, December, 1973; v. 4, October, 1975; v. 3 December, 1975; v. 4, April 1976; v. 5, May 1977; v. 6, January 1978; v. 6, June 1978; v. 7, July 1979; v. 13 July, 1983; v. 25, September 1996. Copyright 1972, 1973, 1975, 1976, 1977, 1978, 1979, 1983, 1996 Children's Book Review Service Inc. All reproduced by permission. —*Children's Literature in Education,* v. 16, Spring, 1985. Reproduced by permission. —*Christian Science Monitor,* v. 92, May 25, 2000 for a review of "The Wanderer" by Enicia Fisher. © 2000 The Christian Science Publishing Society. All rights reserved. Reproduced by permission of the author. —*Commonweal,* v. 90, May 23, 1969; v. 97, November 21, 1969; v. 99, November 23, 1973. Copyright © 1969, 1973 Commonweal Publishing Co., Inc. All reproduced by permission of Commonweal Foundation. —*Growing Point,* v. 4, July, 1965 for a review of "The Grange at High Force" by Margery Fisher; v. 8, October, 1969 for a review of "War on the Darnel" by Margery Fisher; v. 12, May, 1973 for a review of "Dunkirk Summer" by Margery Fisher; v. 13,

COPYRIGHTED EXCERPTS IN *CLR,* VOLUME 89, WERE REPRODUCED FROM THE FOLLOWING BOOKS:

COPYRIGHTED EXCERPTS IN *CLR*, VOLUME 89, WERE REPRODUCED FROM THE FOLLOWING WEB SITES:

Gerald Hausman, From *Gerald Hausman.* ⟨http://www.romanceweb.com/ghausman/message.html⟩ (January 29, 2003). Copyright © 1997 Romancing the Web. All rights reserved. Reproduced by permission of the author. —Winthrop, Elizabeth. "Holding On to the Right Memories." ⟨www.elizabethwinthrop.com⟩ (June 2003). Reproduced by permission of the author.

PHOTOGRAPHS AND ILLUSTRATIONS APPEARING IN *CLR*, VOLUME 89, WERE RECEIVED FROM THE FOLLOWING SOURCES:

Aylesworth, Jim, photograph. Jim Aylesworth. Reproduced by permission. —Hausman, Gerald, photograph by Bobbe Besold. Reproduced by permission. —Lawson, Julie, photograph. From a jacket of her *Blown Away.* Reproduced by permission. —Lingard, Joan, photograph by Gunnie Moburg. Reproduced by permission of Joan Lingard. —Schwartz, Alvin, drawing by William Bourne. Gale Research. —Winthrop, Elizabeth, photograph by Ellen Warner. Reproduced by permission.

Literary Criticism Series Advisory Board

The members of the Gale Group Literary Criticism Series Advisory Board—reference librarians and subject specialists from public, academic, and school library systems—represent a cross-section of our customer base and offer a variety of informed perspectives on both the presentation and content of our literature criticism products. Advisory board members assess and define such quality issues as the relevance, currency, and usefulness of the author coverage, critical content, and literary topics included in our series; evaluate the layout, presentation, and general quality of our printed volumes; provide feedback on the criteria used for selecting authors and topics covered in our series; provide suggestions for potential enhancements to our series; identify any gaps in our coverage of authors or literary topics, recommending authors or topics for inclusion; analyze the appropriateness of our content and presentation for various user audiences, such as high school students, undergraduates, graduate students, librarians, and educators; and offer feedback on any proposed changes/enhancements to our series. We wish to thank the following advisors for their advice throughout the year.

Jim Aylesworth
1943-

American teacher and author of picture books.

INTRODUCTION

Jim Aylesworth writes stories that are meant to be read aloud. His picture books and early readers are filled with loud sounds, bouncy rhythms, repetitions, and rhymes—"things children like best." As a first-grade teacher, Aylesworth has been in a credible position to know what those "things" are. In an interview with Lois Alter Mark for *Entertainment Weekly* he said, "My students gave me a great education. They made it very clear what works—rhythm, rhyme, repetition, noise, and a certain gross factor . . . Books that go for a sound are the ones that kids will sit for, even on an indoor-recess day when it's raining out and they're wired." Picture books were a part of his daily classroom routine, so he had plenty of opportunities to discover what holds the attention of young children. "I have seen a room full of children sit still and pay attention to a good book when it may be the first time they've been still at the same time all day," he wrote on the *Readin* Website. Aylesworth's hallmark formula has made his books successful in the classroom, and his personal appearances are popular at schools and libraries. As he told Mark, it is easy to judge a book's success: "When they scream for me to read again, I know it's working."

BIOGRAPHICAL INFORMATION

Born in Jacksonville, Florida, Aylesworth's family moved frequently while he was a child. When he was 15, his family settled in Hinsdale, Illinois, where he graduated from high school in 1961, and to which he returned in 1965 after graduating with a B.A. from Miami University in Oxford, Ohio. He worked as a stockbroker for five years, but by 1970 he was dissatisfied with his job and decided he needed to figure out what he really wanted to do. While on this quest, he did some substitute teaching. He spent most of his time in junior high school classes, but one day he was assigned to a second grade classroom. The experience was a turning point for him–he finally knew

what he wanted to do. He began teaching first grade in 1971 while attending Concordia College in River Forest, Illinois, where he earned his graduate degree in elementary education in 1978.

Aylesworth became interested in writing early in his teaching career. Because part of his daily routine included reading to his class at the end of the day, he had soon read hundreds of picture books and decided to try writing one himself. It was a discouraging process—Aylesworth claims he collected a stack of rejection slips six inches high—but his students inspired and encouraged him because of their enjoyment of his stories. With their enthusiasm to urge him on, his first book *Hush Up!* was finally published in 1980, and a steady stream of publications has followed ever since. "Writing children's books," Aylesworth said on the *Readin* Website, "is my way of being the teacher beyond the walls of my classroom for children that I may never know."

Aylesworth worked as a first grade teacher at the Hatch School in Oak Park, Illinois until 1996 when he retired from teaching and moved to Chicago. Since then he has been writing, traveling, and lecturing full time. He is currently an adjunct faculty member at several area colleges serving as a visiting instructor of children's literature. He is also a guest speaker at schools, universities, and libraries all over the United States where he tries to inspire children to read and to write.

MAJOR WORKS

Hush Up!, Aylesworth's first book, is about Talula County's laziest farmer, Jasper Walker, and his farm animals. Jasper is asleep on his rickety porch and, with no one to tell them what to do, the animals all fall asleep too. The peace is broken when a nasty horsefly bites the mule on the nose. The mule's braying wakes the other animals who run around creating a tumult until Jasper finally wakes up and yells, "HUSH UP!" In the ensuing calm, everyone goes back to sleep—except the horsefly. "Younger readers will exult in the madness," said a *Publishers Weekly* reviewer.

Five years in the making and one of Aylesworth's most popular books, *Shenandoah Noah* (1985) is about another lazy man. Noah does not like to work, but when he catches fleas from his dogs, he is forced to build a fire to heat water to wash his clothes. His relatives are amazed by the signs of his activity and send his nephew Johnny up the hill to find out why Noah is working. A critic for *Publishers Weekly* suggested a buildup of silliness: "The giggles will come faster when readers approach the climax of this frolic."

When *Old Black Fly* (1992) was published, it received considerable critical attention with reviewers declaring it would become a classic. Ostensibly an alphabet book, *Old Black Fly* follows a pesky housefly as he does 26 awful things, creating pandemonium as the family he is irritating tries to catch him and leaving a trail of messy disasters behind. Gail C. Ross of *School Library Journal* was enthusiastic. "To be enjoyed at home as a lapbook, to be read aloud with relish at story times, to be chanted again and again and again!" she wrote. *Booklist*'s Margaret A. Bush commented, "The enthusiastic celebration of a universal annoyance will tickle many funny bones."

Several of Aylesworth's books restructure nursery rhymes and traditional stories. One of these particu-

larly well-received by critics is *My Son John* (1994) It is an extension of the "Diddle diddle dumpling, My son John" rhyme that describes a day on the farm for John and his family. At bedtime, John is found in bed with one shoe off and one shoe on. Ilene Cooper of *Booklist* attests to Aylesworth's solid reputation in her review: "Aylesworth, who's always so good with a rhyming beat, introduces a lively cast of characters to clap, march, or jump along with."

"Aylesworth's nimble story keeps the action going, transcending the cautionary tale to deliver an amusing lark," commented the *Publishers Weekly* reviewer of *The Full Belly Bowl* (1999). The story is about a poor old man who lives in the country with only his cat for company. When he saves the life of a "wee, small man," he is gifted with a magic bowl that multiplies anything placed in it. Soon the old man succumbs to greed and forgets to store the bowl upside down. The bowl accidentally multiplies a spider, and the ensuing chaos resulting from multiple remedies creates an overwhelming disaster during which the bowl is broken. In the end, the old man rediscovers contentment with his humble life.

CRITICAL RECEPTION

Aylesworth's books, especially *Old Black Fly*, have been well-received by both critics and children. Many feel that his books provide valuable lessons, for young and old alike, about the importance of courage, dedication and perseverance. His teaching and his books have enabled both large groups and small to include more reading and writing in their lives. He is a popular speaker at colleges, primary schools, and libraries where he delights young children as he reads from his body of work.

AWARDS

Old Black Fly was named an American Library Association Notable Book for Children in 1992 and received the Minnesota Book Award from the Minnesota Center for the Book and the Children's Choice Award from the International Reading Association and Children's book Council, both in 1993.

In 1995 *My Son John* was named a Notable Children's Book by the National Council of Teachers of English.

Aylesworth has also won several awards for merit: Those Who Excel Award from the Illinois State Board of Education in 1975, the Governor's Master Teacher award in 1984, Alumnus of the Year from Concordia University in 1985, and the Reading Magic Award from Parenting Magazine in 1992.

PRINCIPAL WORKS

Hush Up! (picture book) 1980
Tonight's the Night (picture book) 1981
Mary's Mirror (picture book) 1982
Siren in the Night (picture book) 1983
The Bad Dream (picture book) 1985
Shenandoah Noah (picture book) 1985
Two Terrible Frights (picture book) 1987
Hanna's Hog (picture book) 1988
One Crow: A Counting Rhyme (picture book) 1988
Mother Halvorsen's New Cat (picture book) 1989
Mr. McGill Goes to Town (picture book) 1989
The Completed Hickory Dickory Dock (picture book) 1990
Country Crossing (picture book) 1991
The Folks in the Valley: A Pennsylvania Dutch ABC (picture book) 1991
The Cat and the Fiddle and More (picture book) 1992
Old Black Fly (picture book) 1992
The Good Night Kiss (picture book) 1993
My Son John (picture book) 1994
McGraw's Emporium (picture book) 1995
My Sister's Rusty Bike (picture book) 1996
Wake Up, Little Children: A Rise-and-Shine Rhyme (picture book) 1996
Teddy Bear Tears (picture book) 1997
The Gingerbread Man (picture book) 1998
Through the Night (picture book) 1998
Aunt Pitty Patty's Pig (picture book) 1999
The Full Belly Bowl (picture book) 1999
The Burger and the Hot Dog (picture book) 2001
The Tale of Tricky Fox: A New England Trickster Tale (picture book) 2001

TITLE COMMENTARY

📖 *HUSH UP!* (1980)

Publishers Weekly (review date 13 June 1980)

SOURCE: *Publishers Weekly* 217, no. 23 (13 June 1980): 73.

Younger readers will exult in the circular madness [*Hush Up!*] laconically described by Aylesworth and illustrated by [Glen] Rounds's nonpareil scruffy char-acters, Talula County's laziest farmer, Jasper Walker, and his critters. Jasper snoozes on his rickety porch one hot summer day, and the animals also drop off with no one telling them what to do. All is stillness until the area's biggest, nastiest horsefly takes a healthy bite out of the mule's nose. The mule brays loudly and piteously and slams into the barn, alarming the other animals, who race about making noise and, finally, arousing Jasper. Rearing up, he bellows, "HUSH UP!" and then he settles into his nap again while the chastened stock follow suit and all is peaceful except for the buzzing of the horsefly, looking for another target. *(5-8)*

Anne McKeithen-Boes (review date August 1980)

SOURCE: McKeithen-Boes, Anne. *School Library Journal* 26, no. 10 (August 1980): 46.

K-Gr 3—When Jasper Walker [*Hush Up!*], just about the laziest man in Talula County, is napping one hot day, an ornery horsefly bites his mule's nose and sets off a sequence of noise and confusion. It lasts only long enough for Jasper to yell "Hush-up" and set things back to normal. Not much of a story but Glen Rounds' down-home drawings do their dead-level best to rescue the book.

Horn Book Magazine (review date October 1980)

SOURCE: *Horn Book Magazine* 56, no. 5 (October 1980): 510-11.

The artist's sketches [*Hush Up!*] reveal with an authentic sureness the rustic background and characters, particularly Jasper, "just about the laziest man in Talula County." When Jasper succumbs to the heat and falls asleep in his chair, the animals, too, decide to nap—all the creatures except "the biggest, nastiest, meanest horsefly you ever saw." The buzzer bites the mule's nose, thus setting off a chain of instinctive reactions all down the line, from mule to goat, rooster, sow, hound dog, and finally to cat—until they hear Jasper shout, "HUSH UP!" The exaggerated nonsense exudes hillbilly flavor in both story and pictures. The horsefly wears a truly mean expression, and the mule a wonderfully surprised and then a terrified look.

📖 *TONIGHT'S THE NIGHT* (1981)

Publishers Weekly (review date 10 July 1981)

SOURCE: *Publishers Weekly* 220, no. 2 (10 July 1981): 92.

[John C.] Wallner's signature couldn't identify his style more personally. He has filled Aylesworth's new story [*Tonight's the Night*] with vibrant pictures in color and black-and-white, showing Daniel settling into bed and declaring, "Tonight's the night!" He intends to find out how it feels to fall asleep and, while waiting, hears night sounds: father locking the doors, mother's footsteps on the stairs, his sister brushing her teeth, his clock ticking. . . . Daniel hears wonderful sounds in his sleep, as well, and is startled to hear his mother calling that it's time to get up, while he's still waiting. The book is a nice addition to the publisher's Self-Starters (for beginners). But it would pack more punch if the author had kept the secret of what Daniel was on the alert for until the end, instead of giving it away in the beginning. *(4-6)*

Nancy Palmer (essay date December 1981)

SOURCE: Palmer, Nancy. *School Library Journal* 28, no. 4 (December 1981): 73-4.

K-Gr 2— **Tonight's the Night** for Daniel to discover "exactly how it feels to fall asleep." As he lies in bed and listens to sounds both inside and out, Daniel's drift into dreams is chronicled by a series of gradually more surreal ink drawings by John Wallner. Sometimes washed with color, sometimes densely patterned black and white, the square-framed art plays with objects from Daniel's room and from the sounds he hears, combining and transforming them in ways that uncannily reflect that half-sleeping state where the mind cuts loose from ground-bound logic. Jim Aylesworth's story is a refreshing and intriguing change of pace for beginners, who have probably tried to pin down that elusive point of sleep.

MARY'S MIRROR (1982)

Kenneth Marantz (review date November 1982)

SOURCE: Marantz, Kenneth. *School Library Journal* 29, no. 3 (November 1982): 63-4.

Gr 1-2— Once again we get the moral that we should not covet riches [in **Mary's Mirror**], that happiness derives from life's simple pleasures. But somehow this version is unconvincing. Maybe it's the awkward blending of prose, rhymed lines and doggerel (in the form of song). There is a good feeling to the rhythmic listing of her swaps and the parallel, if unrhymed, rundown of what such losses cost her. But instead of a consistent use of poetry, we get some snatches of

prosaic text. The green and sepia illustrations are consistent in their literal depiction of the words, but they are depressing in tone and hardly support the more lighthearted text. The drawings have blurred edges and objects drawn have a smoothly modeled quality, creating solid forms. But with only a few exceptions, there's little attempt to express emotion. The pages are frozen, if well-designed, images. Yet there's considerable psychic trauma implied in the story—an attempt at a massive change in life style. Such passion, even if tacit, needs much more visual explication. And I take exception to a scene of the girl breaking a mirror and leaving it strewn over a path in the final scene, a destructive and irresponsible act.

SIREN IN THE NIGHT (1983)

Nancy Palmer (review date December 1983)

SOURCE: Palmer, Nancy. *School Library Journal* 30, no. 4 (December 1983): 78.

PreS-Gr 2— A haunting yet comforting small story [**Siren in the Night**] of a family taking a "quiet little walk" that is interrupted by a passing fire engine, siren keening, lights flashing. As it roars by, the little boy cries and the dog barks, but they are held by mother and brother, respectively, until the noise disappears in the night and the family continues their quiet walk. The combination of text and art create an atmosphere that is really quite extraordinary. The alternating color and black and white of the almost photo-realistic watercolors, and the simple sentences and sounds of the text form an absolute aura of quiet, punctuated by the soft "clink" of the dog's collar and the "scritch" of shoes on the sidewalk. The intrusion of the flashing red and white machine is deafening—words speed up and get excited, colors blur—then dissipates, as the mother tells the little boy as she hugs him, "Don't be afraid. Firefighters help people." Rarely is mood caught so effectively, and while the fire engine may be the grabber for kids, the whole spell can't help but work upon them.

THE BAD DREAM (1985)

Phyllis K. Kennemer (review date December 1985)

SOURCE: Kennemer, Phyllis K. *School Library Journal* 32, no. 4 (December 1985): 66.

A reassuring story [**The Bad Dream**] about the transitory nature of nightmares, this book features a young boy who dreams he is being chased by a bad dog and awakens when he falls out of bed. Both mother and father appear in his room to comfort him and assure him that dreams are not real. Soft, gray-toned illustrations bordered in a dark blue night scene of trees, stars and the moon contribute to the dream-like quality. The strangeness of dreams is portrayed well with rapid, unexpected changes of circumstances. The sense of running hard but getting nowhere is especially effective. A good choice for reading aloud with young children.

SHENANDOAH NOAH (1985)

Publishers Weekly (review date 26 July 1985)

SOURCE: *Publishers Weekly* 228, no. 4 (26 July 1985): 166.

Aylesworth's tale [**Shenandoah Noah**] is not quite so tall as those involving the scruffy, bucolic, rugged individuals who are unmistakably the creations of [Glen] Rounds and heroes of his sky-high inventions. In this exuberant epic, the illustrator's hand is seen in drawings sparked by a golden tone, depicting an extraordinary day for Shenandoah Noah. "Work is something Noah doesn't care for." He likes to sit with his hounds and doze on his hill, while his kin labor at farming, down in the valley. But Noah has to bestir himself, going through all the onerous tasks to build a fire to wash his clothes and himself when he catches fleas from his dogs. Smoke from the fire amazes his folk and they send Noah's nephew Johnny up the hill to find out why the old codger has broken his lazy habits. The giggles will come faster when readers approach the climax of this frolic. *(5-8)*

Sharron McElmeel (review date November 1985)

SOURCE: McElmeel, Sharron. *School Library Journal* 32, no. 3 (November 1985): 66.

PreS-Gr 3— [Glen] Rounds' line drawings brushed in biscuit brown are rustic and emphasize the subtle humor of Aylesworth's well-told tall tale [**Shenandoah Noah**]. Everybody knew that work was something Shenandoah Noah didn't care for, so when his kin in the valley saw smoke from Noah's place, his nephew Johnny was obligated to check on things. And that led to the humorous finale which put a hole in Noah's roof that he still hasn't fixed because fixing the roof "means work, and everybody knows that work is something Noah just doesn't care for." A tale

comfortably stretched to the brink of believability, with illustrations that bring the humor to a full tickle. Children will enjoy the sad-faced hounds, the long johns drying on the bush, and they will giggle out loud when they realize *why* Noah hid under the bear-skin rug. A book to delight.

TWO TERRIBLE FRIGHTS (1987)

Mary Lou Budd (review date February 1988)

SOURCE: Budd, Mary Lou. *School Library Journal* 34, no. 6 (February 1988): 57.

PreS-Gr 1— A little girl—upstairs—and a little mouse—downstairs—are getting ready for bed [in **Two Terrible Frights**]. Both want a bedtime snack, and although afraid to go downstairs/upstairs to the kitchen by themselves, they manage to reach the room—at the same moment (of course). For an instant they stare at one another and then run from the room. Both are comforted with the motherly perception that one was probably more scared than the other. They are tucked into bed and, falling asleep at about the same moment to dream of—each other. Illustrations are done in softly-hued watercolors, with facial expressions that are evocative of the story's moment; and whimsical detailing is uncluttered. Art and text are in total complement, neither one overshadowing the other. A slight, very readable text moves the story smoothly from its beginning, through crisis, to its completely satisfying ending.

HANNA'S HOG (1988)

Publishers Weekly (review date 15 January 1988)

SOURCE: *Publishers Weekly* 233, no. 2 (15 January 1988): 95.

Hanna is a backwoodswoman, pleased with her chickens and her hog [in **Hanna's Hog**]; none of them ever give her any trouble. Every now and then, a chicken disappears, but, while Hanna suspects her neighbor Kenny has stolen it, she can never prove anything. Then one day her hog is missing, and Hanna confronts Kenny. He says a bear took it, but Hanna is on to him. She waits until dark and plays a trick on Kenny to make him believe that a bear really has been around; after scaring him silly, Hanna and her hog head home. Aylesworth's story is really a joke that goes on a bit too long—after all, why does Hanna put up with chicken theft and not hogstealin'? But [Glen] Rounds's pictures give the story its punch; his crotchety black lines are scratched around surprising colors—like the mustard yellow of the hog and the olive green of an old slop bucket. *Ages 5-8.*

John Peters (review date September 1988)

SOURCE: Peters, John. *School Library Journal* 35, no. 1 (September 1988): 154.

Gr 1-3— The author and illustrator of *Shenandoah Noah* (1985) team up for another backwoods knee-slapper [*Hanna's Hog*]. When Hanna Brodie's prized hog is missing, she suspects her shifty neighbor Kenny Jackson. Rather than admit his guilt, he tells her that a bear has been sighted in the area. However, she finds hog tracks around his barn, so she comes back that night, waits until he goes into the outhouse, and attacks with growls and a garden rake. Hanna gets her hog back, and Kenny is so struck with fear that ever after he carries a shotgun when nature calls. As usual, [Glen] Rounds' scribbly, fluent illustrations capture the characters—Hanna's no-nonsense stride and ferocious scowl, Kenny's nervousness, and even the hog's porcine cheer—perfectly.

📖 *ONE CROW: A COUNTING RHYME* (1988)

Karen Litton (review date December 1988)

SOURCE: Litton, Karen. *School Library Journal* 35, no. 4 (December 1988): 79.

PreS-Gr 1— Simple four-line counting rhymes [*One Crow: A Counting Rhyme*] from one to ten (zero's there, too, but without a verse) take readers on a morning-to-night barnyard tour twice, once for a sunny summer day and once for a cold, snowy winter day. The first two lines of each quatrain focus on the animals representing the given number, while the second two comment on some aspect of nature in the setting. The pattern is worked out comfortably, and the verses are pleasant enough, . . . The clear colors, clean line, and open composition of the illustrations convey a cheerful mood that's in keeping with the text. Uncluttered as the pictures are, they offer plenty of rural detail for young eyes to take in. The

real weight of interpreting the contrast between the seasons falls to the pictures, and they contribute significantly to the book's calm charm.

Amy Cohn (review date 29 January 1989)

SOURCE: Cohn, Amy. *New York Times Book Review* (29 January 1989): 38.

One Crow: A Counting Rhyme, written by Jim Aylesworth and illustrated by Ruth Young, takes children to the familiar world of the farm, replete with puppies and kittens, cows and horses. Using a simple, alternating rhyme sequence, Mr. Aylesworth introduces readers and counters to a different farm animal and then tells something about the farm itself: "Three puppies romp / and wag little tails. / Summer breeze billows / the wash like sails." Ms. Young's illustration depicts exactly what the verse describes, and an oversized, brightly colored digit—in this case, a 3—indicates the number of objects to be counted. Although neither art nor text extends one's understanding of life on a farm or provides enough interest for repeated readings, the simple design of each page, the straightforward rhythm of the verse and the familiarity of the animals and the scenes make this book one a young counter or beginning reader might enjoy.

📖 *MOTHER HALVORSEN'S NEW CAT* (1989)

Karen K. Radtke (review date December 1989)

SOURCE: Radtke, Karen K. *School Library Journal* 35, no. 16 (December 1989): 72.

PreS-K— Mother Halverson's beloved cat has died [*Mother Halverson's New Cat*] and she isn't hardhearted, simply practical, when she sends her husband to the barn for another good mouser. After returning with one cat that is too crabby, another that's too flabby, and one too blabby, the only cat left in the barn is a quiet, shy tabby. Mother Halverson names her Abby, and declares that she is the perfect mouser and, oh yes, the perfect pet. The text has a folksy cadence which begs to be read aloud. The simple, repetitive storyline will engage young preschoolers, while the understated humor will be appreciated by slightly older listeners. The watercolor illustrations, with their solid yet humorous figures, are a perfect complement to the text. Sure to be a hit in story hours or family sharing.

📖 *MR. McGILL GOES TO TOWN* (1989)

Patricia Pearl (review date December 1989)

SOURCE: Pearl, Patricia. *School Library Journal* 35, no. 16 (December 1989): 72.

K-Gr 2— Five men—a miller, a farmer, a mason, a wheelwright, and a farrier—find that if they help one another with their respective tasks, they can all get to town before the sun goes down and have some fun [*Mr. McGill Goes to Town*]. The text is cumulative, with ample use of repetition and rhyming, so that it reads aloud well, although "this wheel's really broke" seems a poor choice of grammar for a beginning reader. The plot is only mildly interesting, but the moral and material value of helping one another for mutual benefit is clearly presented. The five heroes are depicted as sturdy men in a variety of outfits from the miller's peasantlike belted tunic, cap, and high boots to the mason's coonskin cap and red suspenders. The blocky, cartoon-style illustrations done in warm crayon-textured colors are lively, amusing, and suit the laborers well. The picture layout is nicely varied, with full pages, double-page spreads, and vignettes both opening into white space and firmly enclosed in the background setting. The typography is well spaced and crisp, and the vocabulary simple but entertaining.

📖 *THE COMPLETED HICKORY DICKORY DOCK* (1990)

Publishers Weekly (review date 14 September 1990)

SOURCE: *Publishers Weekly* 237, no. 37 (14 September 1990): 124.

This extended version of the familiar nursery rhyme [*The Completed Hickory Dickory Dock*] successfully combines simple counting concepts, the numbers one through 12 and a gentle introduction to telling time. Laced with phonetic harmonies, the additional verses have a nonsensical, bouncing quality that offer a fun-filled challenge for little ones to master. "Honeybee, bunny bee, boo. / The mouse ran into a shoe. / The clock struck three, / He scratched a flea. / Honeybee, bunny bee, boo." The endearingly chubby mouse and his family are humorously portrayed in [Eileen] Christelow's colorful, frantic cartoons. The story's vitality is suitably slowed toward the book's end, as the exhausted mouse drifts off to sleep: "The clock struck twelve, / Now dream some yourselves." *Ages 4-7.*

Jane Saliers (review date February 1991)

SOURCE: Saliers, Jane. *School Library Journal* 37, no. 2 (February 1991): 66.

PreS-K— The title [*The Completed Hickory Dickory Dock*] may sound more like a children's literature thesis than a nursery rhyme, but the content is pure fun. The book begins with the traditional Mother Goose rhyme. As the hours continue to strike, this cut-up of a mouse nibbles cheese and pie, courts a girl, and plays tricks on the cat, ending a busy day with a book and prayers. Following the structure of the original, rhymes roll off the tongue with such sillies as "icicle, bicycle, bert" and "splashery, dashery, dears." Some verses have more image unity than others, but all are entertaining. Large, freewheeling ink and watercolor illustrations express energetic activity. Even the background seems active as walls curve and the grandfather clock bends to be seen from the mousehold. Warm oranges, tans, and yellows are mixed with blues, greens, and violet; and the color washes seem to move as fast as the mice, who romp through full-page illustrations or poke tails and ears out of smaller frames. Most illustrations are from a mouse's-eye view, some with wild-eyed closeups of the pursuing cat. What Mother Goose began, Aylesworth and [Eileen] Christelow have completed in an appealing book that begs to be read aloud.

📖 *COUNTRY CROSSING* (1991)

Publishers Weekly (review date 21 December 1990)

SOURCE: *Publishers Weekly* 237, no. 51 (21 December 1990): 55.

It is a quiet country road, slumbering in the softness of summer moonlight. The peacefulness of the blue night is soon broken by the sputtering of a 1920s-vintage car as it rolls to a stop at a railroad crossing [in *Country Crossing*]. And then, everything happens at once. The crickets' singing and the owl's hooting are abruptly overpowered by the clanging of the crossing bell, and a far-off whistle picks up volume as a train roars closer. The speeding wheels churn up leaves, sparks fly and smoke billows into the sky. A man and boy get out of the auto to enjoy the spectacle of the train cars hurtling by. The reader is first lulled by the tranquility, then jarred awake, then, just as suddenly, put back into [Ted] Rand's dreamy country nightscape, as the old car bumps over the tracks and fades away. Rand's nostalgic paintings—rendered primarily in blues and yellows—feature trees dramatically silhouetted against inky skies and bursts of color for the crossing signal and railroad cars. *Ages 3-8.*

Rachel Fox (review date March 1991)

SOURCE: Fox, Rachel. *School Library Journal* 37, no. 3 (March 1991): 166.

PreS-Gr 2— Country Crossing re-creates the peaceful night sounds of the country as an old motor car "putt putts" its way down a dirt road and comes to a stop at a railroad crossing just as the bell begins to ring and the sound of an approaching train is heard in the distance. The car's passengers—an old man and a young boy—watch as the train noisily passes by. Serenity once again returns to the country as the train disappears and the motor car continues on its way. Aylesworth is able to make the sounds in his text come alive. Readers will actually hear the soft chirping of the crickets and feel the energy and excitement brought about by the loud "chooachooing" of the oncoming train. [Ted] Rand has successfully interpreted the text with his beautiful illustrations. Done in sumi brush and chalk, these drawings work hand in hand with Aylesworth's writing. The soft yellow moon reflecting its color on the car and on a nearby puddle evoke a feeling of warmth while the bright red circles of the crossing light and hard yellow stream of the train's headlight reflect the urgency and importance of the train's job. Together, author and illustrator have made the simple act of a train traveling through the night seem almost poetic.

Mary M. Burns (review date July-August 1991)

SOURCE: Burns, Mary M. *Horn Book Magazine* 67, no. 4 (July-August 1991): 443-44.

Times past are evoked in a combination of onomatopoeic text and richly hued illustrations, re-creating the sound and sight of a powerful freight train passing through a country crossing on a summer's night [in *Country Crossing*]. A boy and his father arrive at the site in an elderly two-seater Ford. As they reach the tracks, clanging bells and flashing red lights warn them that the train is approaching. Using type that increases and then decreases in size as the train appears, roars past, and then fades into the distance, the narrative catches a moment of high drama in an ordinary event. The book begs to be read aloud; indeed, with the current emphasis on using children's literature as a fundamental component in teaching language arts, it could be effectively orchestrated for audience participation, thus contributing to the development of listening skills as children wait for their cues. Ted Rand's illustrations—emphasizing mass and shape through use of the luminous light cast by a full moon—suggest just the right note of tension. The perspective changes at the climactic moment when the enormous black bulk of the train, preceded by the yellow glow of its headlight slicing through the darkness, rushes into view. The next two double-page spreads focus on details: steel wheels racing along steel tracks, the red lights, the crossing sign. The effect of text and pictures is powerful—as close as one can come to total sensory involvement through the pages of a book.

THE FOLKS IN THE VALLEY: A PENNSYLVANIA DUTCH ABC (1991)

Publishers Weekly (review date 6 January 1992)

SOURCE: *Publishers Weekly* 239, no. 2 (6 January 1992): 64.

The valley depicted here [in *The Folks in the Valley: A Pennsylvania Dutch ABC*] lies deep in verdant Pennsylvania Dutch country; each letter of the alphabet begins a clever couplet that describes some aspect of life in a close-knit rural colony. Aylesworth's mellifluous rhymes introduce crafts such as ironmaking and quilting ("Quilts are stitched at quilting bees"), as well as common farming chores such as chopping firewood and mowing hay. [Stefano] Vitale's debut offers an unusual and welcome illustrative departure—he has rendered his warm hues onto wood panels, allowing the natural grain to give each painting a rich texture. The spreads also feature homey borders filled with traditional motifs. Beginning concept books are rarely as multilayered as this winner, which, in addition to providing clear letter identification, offers a simple social studies lesson and a delightful slice of Americana.

Carolyn K. Jenks (review date January-February 1992)

SOURCE: Jenks, Carolyn K. *Horn Book Magazine* 68, no. 1 (January-February 1992): 54.

A gentle rhythm takes the reader through the alphabet and a full day on a Pennsylvania Dutch farm [in *The Folks in the Valley: A Pennsylvania Dutch ABC*]. "Neighbors help / With summer wheat. / Oak is split / For the winter's heat." Each page is devoted to a letter, boldly drawn in upper- and lower-case; two lines of verse and a bordered scene complete the tidy, symmetrical layout. The naive pictures, containing Pennsylvania Dutch motifs, are done in warm autumn colors edged in black and appear to be painted on panels of grained wood. They are full of the motion and industry of farm life; men and women are working, children are playing, and farm animals and pets are everywhere. An author's note explaining that the Pennsylvania Dutch include the Amish, Mennonites, Moravians, and others concludes this simple, atmospheric alphabet book.

Luann Toth (essay date May 1992)

SOURCE: Toth, Luann. *School Library Journal* 38, no. 5 (May 1992): 96-7.

PreS-Gr 2— A horse-drawn cart ride through the alphabet that provides glimpses of life in the bucolic valley that has been home to the Pennsylvania Dutch for generations [is described in *The Folks in the Valley: A Pennsylvania Dutch ABC*]. Aylesworth's gentle rhyming couplets take readers through one family's day from A for "Alarm clocks ring; / It's almost dawn. The folks in the valley / Stretch and yawn" through their collective rural labors that end in "Z's the sound / Of their well-earned rest; / They sleep in peace. / Their lives are blessed." Each letter features a half-page, stylized scene painted on wood in rich, earthy tones surrounded by elaborate borders adorned with familiar folk-art motifs. The fields, barnyard, orchard, and hearth are shown abuzz with the activities of the farmer and his country neighbors. There is no mention of their religious beliefs or philosophies toward technology and education; but the values they place on hard work, family, and community come through strong and clear. A simple, eye-catching alphabet book that speaks volumes.

Carolyn Phelan (review date 1 May 1992)

SOURCE: Phelan, Carolyn. *Booklist* 88, no. 17 (1 May 1992): 1598.

Ages 3-7. From the alarm clock that wakens this Pennsylvania Dutch family in the morning to the "Z" sound of their peaceful sleep at night, this rhyming alphabet book [*The Folks in the Valley: A Pennsylvania Dutch ABC*] celebrates their way of life as it follows them through the day. Using the rhythm and rhyme pattern familiar to readers of his *One Crow,*

Aylesworth creates a series of simple, satisfying verses illustrated here with wit and naive charm. Created on panels of stained wood, [Stefano] Vitale's primitive paintings often include the woodgrain as a subtle pattern in the sky or landscape. The rounded forms of people and farm animals seem to move to the musical rhythm of the verse. In these rural scenes of home, hearth, barn, field, and pasture, much good work and some diverting play lead to the family's contentment. Warm colors dominate in the artwork, which includes many traditional motifs. Whether used to introduce rural life, Pennsylvania Dutch folkways, or the alphabet, this picture book should be read aloud for the warm glow it kindles in those who share it.

THE CAT AND THE FIDDLE AND MORE (1992)

Publishers Weekly (review date 29 June 1992)

SOURCE: *Publishers Weekly* 239, no. 29 (29 June 1992): 61.

As a tribute to Mother Goose, Aylesworth has taken rhyme writing to new lengths in this zippy picture book [*The Cat and the Fiddle and More*]. The prolific wordsmith has fashioned a collection of "Hey Diddle Diddle" ditties that begin with such phrases as "Hey fetter fetter" or "Hey sunny sunny" followed by an appropriately sportive verse. The satisfyingly silly outing has pans and pots, combs and brushes and socks and boots (among other things) running away with each other. An ideal complement to the rollicking text, [Richard] Hull's grainy, textured pastel paintings—his first for a children's book—are almost frantic with action. Vibrantly hued tables, chairs, brooms and rakes bat their eyelashes as they dance across the crowded, borderless pages. Youngsters will relish the energy here and may—as the final verse suggests—tackle rhymes of their own. *Ages 3-6.*

Julie Corsaro (review date 15 September 1992)

SOURCE: Corsaro, Julie. *Booklist* 89, no. 2 (15 September 1992): 150.

Ages 4-8. The pictures are the puzzle in this wacky compilation [*The Cat & the Fiddle & More*] featuring a dozen variations on "Hey Diddle Diddle." "Hey holler holler! The possum found a dollar . . ." Even if precocious preschoolers are familiar with the critters that populate these nonsense rhymes, they may have trouble identifying first-time illustrator [Richard] Hull's imaginative and distorted renditions of them in similar hues and textures. The bustling settings are more versatile, and include a subway station, a summer camp, a merry-go-round, and a fairy tale castle. While the slightly older crowd may be put off by the Mother Goose connection, they're likely to have better luck with the game element. Teachers may also find this useful for spurring creative writing.

John Peters (review date January 1993)

SOURCE: Peters, John. *School Library Journal* 39, no. 1 (January 1993): 90.

Gr 1-3— As he did in *The Completed Hickory Dickory Dock,* Aylesworth takes a familiar nursery rhyme and expands it [*The Cat and the Fiddle and More*], adding 13 verses to "Hey Diddle Diddle." Since each verse has the same structure and similar phrasing ("The little rabbit [girl, worm, lizard, colt, snake, etc.] laughed / To see such sport . . ."), it grows monotonous when read straight through; at the end, the author invites readers to make up their own variations, but many children may already be weary of the game by that point. [Richard] Hull's full-spread illustrations have a grainy, lithographic look, and are packed with rubbery, stick-limbed figures hurling themselves madly about, their silly gestures and expressions tempting children to linger over each scene long enough to make sense of the chaos.

📖 *OLD BLACK FLY* (1992)

Carolyn Phelan (review date 15 February 1992)

SOURCE: Phelan, Carolyn. *Booklist* 88, no. 12 (15 February 1992): 1106.

Ages 3-7. While the shelves may bulge with alphabet books, there's always room for one more—if it's as much fun as this. Aylesworth's rhyme [*Old Black Fly*] bounces along, describing the 26 awful things Old Black Fly did one day. The rhythm is punctuated every few lines by a family's insistent, futile attempts to shoo the pest away: "He ate on the crust of the *A*pple pie. He bothered the *B*aby and he made her cry. Shoo fly! Shoo fly! Shooo." Another artist might have depicted the fly irritating the inhabitants of the house, but in [Stephen] Gammell's interpretation, mere irritation gives way to frenzy as Old Black Fly

unleashes page after page of household pandemonium. As often as not, the fly appears as a trail of flying spatters amid the color-splashed chaos. A good choice for story time, this could easily be read aloud; however, the storyteller who can *sing* it will surely have the kids joining in on the chorus. A wild, alphabetical romp.

Publishers Weekly (review date 2 March 1992)

SOURCE: *Publishers Weekly* 239, no. 12 (2 March 1992): 64.

Aylesworth and [Stephen] Gammell wing their way through the alphabet on the back of a pesky housefly in this ebullient picture-book romp [*Old Black Fly*]. On a summer day, old black fly "bothered the baby," "coughed on the cookies" and "drove the dog nearly out of his wits," as family members attempt to "Shoo fly! / Shoo fly! Shooo." The persistent pest leaves a messy trail of near disasters until finally meeting up with the wrong end of a swatter. Aylesworth's snappy couplets constitute a waggish presentation of a basic concept. A brightly colored first letter highlights one word on each page that corresponds to the objects and action found in the illustration. Gammell's paintings are exuberant splashes of mayhem—rainbows of splattered hues from which truly memorable characters emerge. His appropriately bug-eyed (and cross-eyed) fly and gap-toothed humans sporting crazy hairdos provide a level of dementia that children will relish. *Ages 4-7.*

Gail C. Ross (review date April 1992)

SOURCE: Ross, Gail C. *School Library Journal* 38, no. 4 (April 1992): 88.

PreS-Gr 3— A pesky fly turns a household inside out in this rollicking tale [*Old Black Fly*]. "He ate on the crust of the *A*pple pie. / He bothered the *B*aby and made her cry. / Shoo fly! Shoo fly! Shooo." This fly is on an alphabetical rampage through the house, leaving destruction in his wake as he flits from the *C*ookie to the *D*og to the *E*ggs to the *F*rosting, and so on to a final, satisfying "Swat!" Aylesworth's funny, rhythmic chant is strong enough to stand alone. Add [Stephen] Gammell's spattery, jumpy illustrations, splashed with color, alive with movement, line, and humor, and what emerges is a book that's sure to become a classic. To be enjoyed at home as a lapbook, to be read aloud with relish at story times, to be chanted again and again and again!

Margaret A. Bush (review date May-June 1992)

SOURCE: Bush, Margaret A. *Horn Book Magazine* 68, no. 3 (May-June 1992): 325-26.

"Old black fly's been / buzzin' around, / And he's had a very / busy bad day." Aylesworth and [Stephen] Gammell create a gleeful, messy mix of all the fly's bad doings [in *Old Black Fly*]. The short couplets of text follow in an alphabetical scheme. "He ate the crust of the Apple pie. / He bothered the Baby and made her cry." Each pair of scenes is punctuated with the familiar refrain, "Shoo fly! Shoo fly! Shooo." Gammell spatters all of his crudely sketched watercolor scenes, creating an energetic chaos sure to invite giggles from many children. The fly refuses to be shooed away, but he comes to a predictably bad end after dozing on the window in the summer heat, making a little *X* with his front feet, buzzing about the yarn in Mama's lap, and finally landing on her table with a "flap flip flap" and a final "Zzzz." Bulging red eyes are the predominant feature of the villainous fly, and other animal and human characters look harassed and disgruntled. The rough-hewn pictures sometimes provide specific details, but they are often abstract and suggestive, which may confuse younger readers. The apple pie, for instance, is a shapeless mass of color, and sometimes the fly is not actually visible. Tidy or squeamish viewers will be repulsed, but the enthusiastic celebration of a universal annoyance will tickle many funny bones.

☐ *THE GOOD NIGHT KISS* (1993)

Carolyn Phelan (review date 1 September 1993)

SOURCE: Phelan, Carolyn. *Booklist* 90, no. 1 (1 September 1993): 66.

Ages 3-6. A frog looks out from the pond and sees a raccoon, who moves on until he sees a deer, who looks up and sees an owl in flight, who sees a farmer, who sees a pickup driver, and so on, until a moth sees a child, who is listening to a bedtime story and receives a good-night kiss [in *The Good Night Kiss*]. Illustrating this appealing text are heavily brush-stroked paintings, night scenes in muted hues dappled with brighter spots of color. Visually, the early pages depicting the natural world and those that come later showing the lonely small-town streets and country roads are more striking than the closing scenes with the child, which seem more awkwardly drawn.

Aylesworth's melodic story, with its strings of prepositional phrases and its elusive sense of connectedness, will mesmerize kids. A quintessential bedtime story.

☐ *MY SON JOHN* (1994)

***Publishers Weekly* (review date 7 March 1994)**

SOURCE: *Publishers Weekly* 241, no. 10 (7 March 1994): 69.

As in his *The Cat & the Fiddle & More,* rhyme-slinger Aylesworth enjoyably extends a traditional verse to picture-book length [in *My Son John*]. An idealized day in a farm setting begins with "Yellow yellow sunup, / My son Ed. / Up he jumps / From out of bed." Chores and lessons follow: "Bonny bonny bridle, / My daughter Rose. / Combs her mare / In old work clothes." After dinner, the original rhyme winds up the festivities, with John in bed, "one shoe off and one shoe on." The illustrations similarly spring from the traditional; [David] Frampton (*Whaling Days*) has extended them, too, using vivid oil paints instead of black ink to print both his woodcuts of 14 busy children and the bouncy verses on facing pages. Life on the farm, with every family member cheerfully pitching in, may not be like this anymore (if it ever was), but the musical rhymes and vibrant colors are great fun. *Ages 4-7.*

Ilene Cooper (review date 1 April 1994)

SOURCE: Cooper, Ilene. *Booklist* 90, no. 15 (1 April 1994): 1457.

Ages 3-6. Aylesworth, who's always so good with a rhyming beat, introduces a lively cast of characters [in *My Son John*] to clap, march, or jump along with. In the tradition of "Diddle Diddle Dumpling, My Son John," Aylesworth offers 14 new verses, for example: Bonny bonny bridal, / My daughter Rose. / Combs her mare / in old work clothes. Hay in hair / and dirt on nose. / Bonny bonny bridal, / My daughter Rose." Most of the rhymes have to do with children doing everyday tasks—schoolwork, gardening, or taking care of pets—or playing, eating, and getting ready for bed. The artwork, full-page color woodcuts that face the text, is an absolute delight. The elongated shapes and interesting perspectives are well suited to Frampton's playful use of color mixing; for instance, the picture of the boy drowning his pancakes in maple syrup is executed in three colors: orange, purple, and tan. A charmer that will be especially fun to read to groups.

Judy Constantinides (review date June 1994)

SOURCE: Constantinides, Judy. *School Library Journal* 41, no. 6 (June 1994): 94.

PreS-Gr 2—From the very first "Yellow, yellow sunup, / My son Ed, / Up he jumps / From out of bed," to the last familiar "Diddle diddle dumpling," this book [*My Son John*] is a feast for the eyes and ears. Aylesworth amplifies the simple nursery classic with a rainbow of rich, descriptive verses on additional names, evoking all of the five senses in the process. The rhymes are enhanced by an exceptional layout using brilliant woodcuts done with brightly colored oils. Each double-page spread features a full-page illustration on the left, with the rhyme facing it. A cast of multicultural children is shown joyfully carrying out various farm chores throughout the day. . . . It will be a hit in story time, and could also serve as a creative writing stimulus to children making up similar rhymes to fit their own names. Beautifully integrated in text and design, this is a book to savor and enjoy again and again.

📖 *MCGRAW'S EMPORIUM* (1995)

Publishers Weekly (review date 6 February 1995)

SOURCE: *Publishers Weekly* 242, no. 6 (6 February 1995): 84.

Whether kids or adults will be the most entertained by this nimble collaboration [*McGraw's Emporium*] is anyone's guess—there is plenty here to amuse everybody. Aylesworth's (*Old Black Fly*) zippy rhyme describes a boy's visit to McGraw's antique shop in search of a gift for an ill friend. He finds a dizzying array of goods, e.g.: "A Franklin stove, a cowboy hat, / A parrot cage, a cricket bat, / A little knife for spreading jam, / A sweater with a monogram, / A mandolin, nine picture frames, / A board for playing checker games, / A bowling ball, a kitchen sink, / A statue of King Tut, I think." Making this emporium a visual treat is [Mavis] Smith's innovative collage art. She juxtaposes watercolors and colored-pencil drawings with photos of hundreds of items (a jacket flap reports that she used 432 maga-

zines and three pairs of scissors). The melange is neatly arranged for convenient browsing. Youngsters will have fun identifying the objects mentioned in the verse, while baby-boomers will chuckle over such cultural artifacts as the album cover from *Saturday Night Fever,* a Pet Rock, a photo of the original *Star Trek* cast, a lava lamp and—of course—two pink flamingo lawn ornaments. Delightful. *Ages 4-7.*

Leda Schubert (review date June 1995)

SOURCE: Schubert, Leda. *School Library Journal* 41, no. 6 (June 1995): 76.

K-Gr 3—A bespectacled young fellow wants to buy a present for a sick friend and chances upon *McGraw's Emporium,* a store brimming with wonderful things. In extended rhyme, Aylesworth catalogs such items as "A Franklin stove, a cowboy hat, / A parrot cage, a cricket bat / A little knife for spreading jam, / A sweater with a monogram . . ." In the end, a sign on the wall leads the hero to a kitten, the perfect gift. The inventive collage-and-cartoon illustrations juxtapose all the objects named as well as some that aren't, but pages are spacious enough to find everything mentioned in the poem. The jacket informs readers that it took 432 magazines and three pairs of scissors to create the art. Adults might enjoy sly references to the recent past, such as a *Sgt. Pepper* album cover and a photo of the original *Star Trek* cast, while children will enjoy identifying everything that's named.

Mary Harris Veeder (review date 1 June 1995)

SOURCE: Veeder, Mary Harris. *Booklist* 91, no. 19-20 (1 June 1995): 1782.

Ages 5-8. McGraw's Emporium, which has a bit of everything, is just the shop for a little boy seeking something for a sick friend. That the gift the boy finally chooses isn't available at McGraw's really won't matter to children, because they'll have had the pleasure of a great flea-market jaunt through all sorts of treasures. Smith gives the shop a surrealistic look by placing photographs of objects against hand-colored backdrops. Aylesworth's rhymes—Khyber Pass and hourglass; swan and Saskatchewan—provide the rest of the fun. They're jaunty but not too fast, giving children plenty of time to browse the intriguing pictures. A book that might lead to imitative projects in the classroom.

📖 *MY SISTER'S RUSTY BIKE* (1996)

Publishers Weekly (review date 19 August 1996)

SOURCE: *Publishers Weekly* 243, no. 34 (19 August 1996): 66-7.

Aylesworth takes readers on a preposterous, rollicking romp as his narrator introduces the eccentric individuals he visits during a cross-country bike ride [in *My Sister's Rusty Bike*]. The breezy verse rolls off the tongue as smoothly as the protagonist's wheels whir: in West Virginia, he drops in on a gal named Dee Dee Lee, who "loves her pink pet sheep. / At night they sleep in bed with her / In one warm, woolly heap." From Massachusetts to California, the traveler discovers residents with uncommonly amusing pets, among them bow tie-wearing pigs who dance jigs, goats who sing country tunes and pampered toads who eat their flies à la mode. Easily matching the lighthearted humor of the text, the gouache art offers a playful spin on American primitivism. [Richard] Hull (previously teamed with Aylesworth for *The Cat & The Fiddle & More*) here employs an unusually rich palette in his stylized renderings of these comical characters. Kids will follow this cyclist happily—over and over again. *Ages 5-8.*

Carol Ann Wilson (review date October 1996)

SOURCE: Wilson, Carol Ann. *School Library Journal* 42, no. 10 (October 1996): 84.

Gr 1-3—A cross-country trip on a rusty bike [described in *My Sister's Rusty Bike*] begins in Massachusetts, where the teenaged narrator discovers Pat McDuff and her purple-furred felines, and ends in California, where Ike O'Day owns a snow white crow that can "speak in rhyme and quote from Edgar Poe." Along his meandering route, the young man meets a variety of unusual inhabitants and their even more peculiar pets. The rhyming text of this tall tale repeats a basic eight-line stanza that establishes location, introduces an eccentric personality, and concludes with a description of his or her fantastical and talented animals. After the first several "stops" en route, however, the repetition becomes tiresome and the occasionally forced rhyme more apparent. The lackluster conclusion leaves readers as flat as a punctured tire. [Richard] Hull's folk-style gouache illustrations capture the homey feel of the text and children will enjoy the animal antics. While the setting appropriately reflects Americana, the people and pets are sometimes too static for the action-packed verse;

expressions can be wooden and are sometimes even fierce. The rather muddy palette dampens exuberance, as well. Although this trip traverses the continent, the cyclist encounters neither racial nor ethnic diversity. Children might be tempted to create their own itinerary and verses to extend the concept—but whether they will pedal along to the final destination is in doubt.

Shelly Townsend-Hudson (review date 15 November 1996)

SOURCE: Townsend-Hudson, Shelly. *Booklist* 93, no. 6 (15 November 1996): 592-93.

Ages 5-8. In this original and offbeat picture book [*My Sister's Rusty Bike*], a boy on a bike tours the back roads of the U.S., visiting such locales as Paradise, West Virginia; Carbon Hill, Alabama; and Toomersville, Colorado. Those are real places on a map, but the citizens introduced aren't ordinary folk. Jojo Jones feeds his pet toads flies à la mode; Benny Finn uses real bears for rugs, which works fine till he whips out the vacuum; Ike O'Day, who lives in California, has a white crow that recites Poe. But it is Edward Lear, not Poe, whose spirit haunts these playful rhymes. The boy's strange encounters with oddballs across the country are well matched by [Richard] Hull's surreal, somewhat murky illustrations, and effective use of refrains and humorous alliteration gives the verse a singsong quality that makes this a rollicking good trip along America's less-traveled roads.

📖 *WAKE UP, LITTLE CHILDREN: A RISE-AND-SHINE RHYME* (1996)

Joy Fleishhacker (review date April 1996)

SOURCE: Fleishhacker, Joy. *School Library Journal* 42, no. 4 (April 1996): 99.

PreS-Gr 2—A rhythmic text [*Wake Up, Little Children*] invites two children to wake up and enjoy their day. The countryside is blooming and filled with mysteries to explore: dew-covered sunflowers wave in the breeze, grassy hills wait for children to "roll them just right," and a babbling brook offers mud for toe-print making. There are wild berries to be picked, trees to be climbed, and minnows to be discovered. The language reads aloud well, offering a variety of appealing activities and pointing out things to observe. In a nice change of pace, the children experience a quiet moment in the woods, sitting still and listening as "sun filters through." The oil and vinyl paint illustrations, framed by a brown paper background, glow with the colors of the earth. Sometimes detailed, depicting the flowers on a quilt or a butterfly's wings, and sometimes pleasingly abstract, the paintings create an appealing panorama of outdoor scenes, each with its own mood and perspective.

TEDDY BEAR TEARS (1997)

Hazel Rochman (review date 1 April 1997)

SOURCE: Rochman, Hazel. *Booklist* 93, no. 15 (1 April 1997): 1336.

Ages 2-5. In a touching, cozy story [*Teddy Bear Tears*], a toddler plays reassuring parent to his four teddy bears, who are scared after the lights go out at bedtime. Of course, kids will recognize that he is reassuring himself. Willie Bear hears a scary noise outside the window; Fuzzy is scared there is something under the bed; Ringo thinks there is a bogeyman in the closet; Little Sam wants a bathroom light on. One by one, the boy encourages them. Each time, he takes the bear with him to show that the fear is groundless. Children will know all the scenarios and will enjoy seeing how his toys help him to be brave. The tender colored-pencil illustrations are wonderfully tactile, showing the nurturing boy in the shadowy dark, scared and safe, as he cuddles up close with his furry toys in bed.

THE GINGERBREAD MAN (1998)

Publishers Weekly (review date 26 January 1998)

SOURCE: *Publishers Weekly* 245, no. 4 (26 January 1998): 90.

The familiar tale [*The Gingerbread Man*] of the cookie that outruns a series of countrified characters until he is outwitted by a fox, finds a fresh makeover in the hands of author Aylesworth (*Old Black Fly*) and illustrator [Barbara] McClintock (*The Fantastic Drawings of Danielle*). McClintock's Victorian-inspired drawings with delicately lined borders impart a feeling of olden times. While standing in an elegant parlor (complete with roaring fire and a cat playing with a ball of yarn), a bespectacled "little old man" and an aproned "little old woman" enthusiastically decide to make a gingerbread man. Spot drawings show readers just how they do it, culminating in

a double-page spread of his great escape from the iron oven as the little old man looks on in horror and the little old woman grabs her head. The dashing, feisty cookie taunts his growing list of pursuers—from the aged husband and wife to the bearded young "butcher with a carving knife," a "black-and-white cow" and a "muddy old sow" (the latter two exquisitely rendered with animal heads atop female bodies)—to the catchy refrain of "No! No! I won't come back! / I'd rather run / Than be your snack!" The lively rhythm of the narrative keeps the beat for the parade of runners and propels readers along with it. By the time the baked boy reaches the handsomely turned-out fox reading under a tree, most readers will be utterly disarmed—and may well wish to come back again and again. *Ages 2-6.*

Hazel Rochman (review date April 1998)

SOURCE: Rochman, Hazel. *Booklist* 94, no. 15 (April 1998): 1323.

Ages 2-5. With a chanting, rhythmic text and vital narrative pictures, this version of the popular folktale [*The Gingerbread Man*] will be a favorite for storytelling with young preschoolers. . . . [Barbara] McClintock's illustrations, in watercolor, sepia ink, and gouache, are traditional in style and setting, reminiscent of some early Mother Goose illustrations. Once upon a time, a cheerful old man and a cheerful old woman in their old-fashioned cozy house decided to make a gingerbread man. A series of pictures shows how they bake him, step by step. Then to their consternation, he pops out of the oven and runs away. Now they are no longer smiling—they are mad. They race after the smiling little gingerbread kid, who shouts, "No! No! I won't come back! I'd rather run than be your snack!" He runs from a butcher, an elegant cow, a muddy old sow—until a sly, bookish fox tricks him and gobbles him up. There is a great scene in which all the pursuers, human and animal, stand fuming and helpless while the fox licks its lips and leaves not even a crumb.

Judith Constantinides (review date April 1998)

SOURCE: Constantinides, Judith. *School Library Journal* 44, no. 4 (April 1998): 113.

PreS-Gr 2— An excellent rendition of an oft-told tale that demonstrates that there is always room for one more *Gingerbread Man* on the shelves. Aylesworth has done a perfect job of shaping the text [in *The*

Gingerbread Man] to read aloud smoothly with good repetitive phrases that ring true, such as the Gingerbread Man's response to his pursuers: "No! No! / I won't come back! / I'd rather run / Than be your snack!" The text is matched beautifully with an excellent layout and [Barbara] McClintock's illustrations. Using watercolors, sepia ink, and gouache, the artist has created pictures with an old-fashioned look to them, which she attributes to the influence of the 19th-century French illustrator, Grandville. They also are somewhat reminiscent of the work of Randolph Caldecott. McClintock's anthropomorphic animals are wonderfully realized, especially the wily fox, and the Gingerbread Man is a saucy fellow dressed in a blue jacket and hat, with hands on hips and a big smile. The book comes complete with a recipe on the back cover. A satisfying version in every way.

Ann A. Flowers (review date July-August 1998)

SOURCE: Flowers, Ann A. *Horn Book Magazine* 74, no. 4 (July-August 1998): 502-03.

(Preschool) This hearty retelling of the well-known tale is distinguished by cheery, lively illustrations. *The Gingerbread Man* himself is particularly toothsome and delectable, with shining raisin eyes and a delightful set of sugar-glaze clothes. (And his irrepressible smile is as gleefully irritating as his taunts.) The cow, the pig, and the fox are remarkably anthropomorphic, with human bodies and animal heads, and the scenery resembles that of the eighteenth-century English artist Thomas Bewick. Energy and vigor run through the story as every figure is shown in action. With even a recipe included, this is altogether an old-fashioned and enjoyable version of a favorite tale.

Meg Wolitzer (review date 18 October 1998)

SOURCE: Wolitzer, Meg. *New York Times Book Review* (18 October 1998): 31.

(All ages) The anthropomorphizing of food has had a long history in children's stories. Occasionally the food in question actually wants to be eaten, and feels hurt when it/he/she is overlooked or rejected by a hungry child, adult or animal. But usually—and this seems to make a lot more sense—the food doesn't want to be eaten but would rather be spared and allowed to live life fully, or at least until spoilage sets in. The age-old tale of *The Gingerbread Man* is of

the latter variety. In Jim Aylesworth and Barbara McClintock's extremely appealing version, a little old man and a little old woman lovingly fashion a cookie and then bake it in the, oven, anticipating the gustatory pleasure that will soon be theirs. But as soon as the oven door is opened, "out popped the Gingerbread Man, and he ran across the floor." And here the excitement begins.

McClintock's spirited, memorable illustrations feature fully clothed animals and are greatly influenced, according to the illustrator's note, by the 19th-century French illustrator Grandville. But McClintock's depiction of the Gingerbread Man himself feels contemporary, providing an interesting counterpoint between the hero of the story and his adversaries. Children will respond to the sassy, boastful facial expressions and exclamations of the Gingerbread Man. (Actually, he bears a resemblance to the Pillsbury Doughboy.) And they will quickly be drawn into the story, familiar though it is, following the sure-footed cookie as he confronts a variety of creatures who wish to gobble him up, including a butcher, a cow, a sow and a fox. As the story proceeds and tensions mount, Aylesworth's words demand to be read aloud in an increasingly feverish, fast-paced manner. As if to emphasize this to readers, the hero's final speech in the story is printed in large type.

As a character, the Gingerbread Man is full of himself and immensely cocksure, and perhaps this is why children hardly ever seem upset at his inevitable "death" at the end of the story. In fact, children seem to understand that all cookies—even those in literature—are meant to be eaten. With this in mind, a recipe for gingerbread cookies appears on the back of the book jacket.

THROUGH THE NIGHT (1998)

***Publishers Weekly* (review date 30 March 1998)**

SOURCE: *Publishers Weekly* 245, no. 13 (30 March 1998): 80-1.

[Pamela] Patrick's (*An Amish Christmas*) dark pastels—and her nighttime cityscapes in particular—have an edginess and mystery that occasionally recall Edward Hopper, but visual appeal alone can't compensate for an inconsequential story line [in *Through the Night*]. Here readers follow the progress of a man—a traveling salesman, perhaps—driving a long distance home to his family as night falls. Peaceful countryside vistas give way to the hustle and bustle of the city, from the distant sparkle of the skyline to streets "frantic with neon light." Finally, the driver (whose thoughts, the reader is told repeatedly, are filled with "his children . . . his wife") pulls into a leafy suburban driveway, there to be greeted by his family. Aylesworth's (*My Sister's Rusty Bike*) languid prose and Patrick's vaguely 1950s setting (the man wears a fedora; the cars are all sweeping curves and heavy chrome bumpers and grilles) are deftly and attractively rendered, but, between the adult narrator's perspective and the lack of a compelling plot, the story lacks resonance. *Ages 3-7.*

Susan Scheps (review date April 1998)

SOURCE: Scheps, Susan. *School Library Journal* 44, no. 4 (April 1998): 91.

PreS—Aylesworth's simple, quiet story [*Through the Night*] is set 50 to 60 years ago. It follows a well-dressed man driving home at dusk through rural and urban landscapes to his own doorstep where his wife and children wait with welcoming arms. Full-page illustrations show a road winding through hilly open country beneath a starry sky, tall factory smokestacks and steel girders, twinkling skyscrapers, curving bridges, and neon-lighted shops. Muted colors are rich and dark, and some of the drawings have the appearance of heavy acrylic paintings, although they are all rendered in pastel. Smooth, creamy paper complements the sophisticated tone of the illustrations. The routine nature and timelessness of the plot and the slight mystery of where the man is heading offer just the sort of appeal that will attract young children.

Hazel Rochman (review date 1 April 1998)

SOURCE: Rochman, Hazel. *Booklist* 94, no. 15 (1 April 1998): 1328-29.

Ages 2-6. Set about 50 years ago, this idyllic scenario [*Through the Night*] will have most appeal for nostalgic adults who want to tell kids about how good it was. Dad drives home through the lonely night, past trucks and other cars on the highway, through the city with its factories and glittering buildings and "frantic" neon lights. Always, he longs for home, and when at last the car "almost knowingly" turns into the quiet, tree-lined street, his small daughter and son, who have been waiting at home with

Mom, rush out to hug him, and they all go in together. In [Pamela] Patrick's warm, realistic pastel illustrations, the cars are from the 1940s; the little girl is angelic in a nightgown of flowers, lace, and bows. Of course, there is a timeless appeal in the story of the child who knows, as she waits safely at home, that her loving parent is on his way and longing to get there.

AUNT PITTY PATTY'S PIG (1999)

***Publishers Weekly* (review date 2 August 1999)**

SOURCE: *Publishers Weekly* 240, no. 31 (2 August 1999): 83.

Fresh from *The Gingerbread Man*, Aylesworth and [Barbara] McClintock offer a similarly energetic, folksy retelling of a sequential tale [*Aunt Pitty Patty's Pig*] about a stubborn pig who refuses to pass through a gate to enter the yard of its new owner. Rendered in brown pencil and watercolors, McClintock's earth-toned art conjures a rural 19th-century setting, replete with charming period particulars. The text's repetition and rhythm virtually command readers to chime in, as the determined heroine, Nelly, tries to enlist the aid of a number of initially uncooperative animals and inanimate objects: "Stick, stick, come hit dog. Dog won't bite Aunt Pitty Patty's piggy. It's gettin' late, and piggy's by the gate sayin', 'No, no, no, I will not go!'" Nelly's resolve pays off in an ending propelled by an amusing chain reaction. McClintock's pictures contain spirited details—e.g., a butcher, complying with Nelly's request that he scare an ox, chases the animal while carrying a picture of a steak; and the title character, persuaded at last to enter the yard, licks his chops hopefully as he stares in through the window at a supper shared by his mistress, her farmer suitor and Nelly. A recipe for corn bread appears, invitingly if irrelevantly, on the back of the book jacket. Narrative and art pull equal weight in this cheerful reworking. *Ages 3-7.*

***Horn Book Magazine* (review date September 1999)**

SOURCE: *Horn Book Magazine* 75, no. 5 (September 1999): 618-19.

(Preschool, Primary) Here's a new recipe for an old favorite [*Aunt Pitty Patty's Pig*]: Take Joseph Jacobs's classic "The Old Woman and Her Pig" as recounted in his *English Folk and Fairy Tales* (Jacobs

cites several predecessors and variants for this cumulative tale; alas, Aylesworth doesn't acknowledge a single one). Subtract the sixpence and at least half the woman's age; name her "Aunt Pitty Patty." Appoint a winsome child, niece Nelly, as chief negotiator. Make the language marginally less challenging (but deprive the pig of its one good excuse for its recalcitrance) by changing the stile where Piggy balks into an open gate. Temper the threatened violence (it's still "fire . . . burn stick"; but has become "butcher . . . scare ox" (rather than "kill") and "rope . . . tie butcher" (not "hang"). Extend the tale by adding a handsome farmer to give Nelly hay for the cow to exchange for milk for the cat so the cat will "chase" the rat, etc.; this farmer then comes home with Nelly to eat the supper pretty Auntie's been cooking while Nelly was questing for help getting piggy through that gate. Meanwhile, plump up the tale with extra words, though not enough to alter the meaning much, or to interfere (well, only a little) with its pell-mell trajectory. Lace well with Barbara McClintock's sweetly old-fashioned pencil and watercolor art, which sets this comic saga of willful disobedience in a bucolic nineteenth-century landscape with sunflowers blooming in Aunt Pitty Patty's garden. Top with McClintock's humorously expressive, delicately characterized cast—especially that stubborn, yet ever-cheerful, pig. Yield: one picture book, a bit sweeter and less assertive in flavor (as suits contemporary palates); still, good nutritional value.

Hazel Rochman (review date 15 September 1999)

SOURCE: Rochman, Hazel. *Booklist* 96, no. 2 (15 September 1999): 258.

Ages 2-5. With the same old-fashioned pastoral setting as in Aylesworth and [Barbara] McClintock's *The Gingerbread Man* (1998), this retelling of an old cumulative folktale [*Aunt Pitty Patty's Pig*] is great for reading aloud and joining in. McClintock's delicately detailed double-page spreads in brown pencil and watercolor set the cozy farce in a Randolph Caldecott-style, bucolic farmyard landscape. Aunt Pitty Patty brings a fine, fat piggy home from market, but the piggy won't go through the gate ("No, no, no, I will not go!"). Aunt Pitty Patty's niece Nelly asks the dog to bite the piggy, but the dog won't. She asks the stick to hit the dog, but the stick won't. And so on—until (surprise!) a cat agrees to help if Nelly gets it some milk, and the cow says she'll give milk, if . . . and then everything goes in reverse in a fast-

paced, satisfying turnabout. The creatures' expressions and body language add to the fun, as stubborn disobedience and antisocial behavior give way to a hilarious community effort, ending when that piggy finally does go through the gate.

Corinne Camarata (review date October 1999)

SOURCE: Camarata, Corinne. *School Library Journal* 45, no. 10 (October 1999): 132.

PreS-Gr 1—Aunt Pitty Patty can't get her piggy to go in the gate [*Aunt Pitty Patty's Pig*], so her young niece Nelly tries to get some assistance. She is turned down first by dog, and then by stick, fire, water, and so on, until cow requests hay in payment, and Farmer Brown decides to trade some for the prospect of a good meal. "And little Nelly took the hay and gave it to the cow," starting the chain reaction that leads to the expected and satisfying conclusion. The fun is in getting there. By the same team that did *The Gingerbread Man* (1998), this nicely paced retelling of the old cumulative tale is done in much the same style and format, although these pencil-and-watercolor illustrations don't leap off the page with quite the same wit and energy. Most of the paintings are soft-edged and grainy, thus underscoring the folksy, turn-of-the-century setting. [Barbara] McClintock depicts a bucolic landscape, animals with personality, and a determined and feisty Nelly. A recipe for "Aunt Pitty Patty's Old-Fashioned Corn Bread" is appended on the dust jacket. A winning read-aloud or storyhour selection.

THE FULL BELLY BOWL (1999)

Rosalyn Pierini (review date October 1999)

SOURCE: Pierini, Rosalyn. *School Library Journal* 45, no. 10 (October 1999): 102.

K-Gr 3—Beautiful design enhances this delightful cautionary tale [*The Full Belly Bowl*]. Told in a folkloric style, it tells of a poor old man living a spartan existence in the forest with only his beloved cat for company. While foraging for wild strawberries one day, the man hears a cry for help. Alarmed, he grabs a stick and runs in the direction of the voice. There he spies a "wee small man" caught in the jaws of a fox. He hurls the stick at the beast and the little fellow drops to the ground, injured. The old man tends the sprite for several days and the two get on famously. Then one morning, the little man is gone, but a few days later a beautiful bowl appears on the doorstep with a note. The full belly bowl is a thank-you gift to be used wisely. Experimentation reveals that it will multiply anything placed within it. This, as the old man learns, is a mixed blessing when a spider alights in the enchanted vessel. Predictably, the old fellow becomes greedy and careless and the bowl is finally broken and useless. He then rediscovers contentment in his humble existence and is grateful for the final companionable gift provided by the magic. Exquisite colored-pencil drawings are distinguished by lovely botanical detail and fine draftsmanship. Thoughtful attention to layout, visual detail, and a well-told tale combine to create a gem of a book.

Stephanie Zvirin (review date 1 November 1999)

SOURCE: Zvirin, Stephanie. *Booklist* 96, no. 5 (1 November 1999): 524.

Ages 5-8. From the dainty pictures on the endpapers—where beautifully colored flora and fauna splash across the background and a cat paws at an unsuspecting mouse—to the equally charming artwork inside, this book [*The Full Belly Bowl*] is a feast for the eyes. There's a real story here, too, written with a folktale feel, humor, and touches of magic and message. An old man who is always hungry lives with his cat at the edge of a forest. One day, as he's out in search of food, he stops a fox from carrying off a tiny man in its mouth. In return for the rescue, the tiny man gives his hero a present: a Full Belly Bowl, with a note explaining that it should be used wisely and always stored upside down. In the days that follow, the old man and his feline companion learn both the bowl's secrets and the wisdom of storing it correctly. [Wendy Anderson] Halperin gives both man and cat lots of character, and her intricate, homey pictures, precisely detailed and painted in soft watercolors, extend the boundaries of the wry text. The delicately layered art, ranging from postage-stamp size to sweeping double spreads, bursts with activity, and the motif on the stunningly decorated bowl, which is repeated in borders and backgrounds, is a ribbon of color that leads children gently on to Aylesworth's sweet, satisfying conclusion. A wonderful book to share and a joy to peruse; this may remind some children of the story about the fisherman's wife.

***Publishers Weekly* (review date 8 November 1999)**

SOURCE: *Publishers Weekly* 246, no. 45 (8 November 1999): 67.

[Wendy Anderson] Halperin's (*Hunting the White Cow*) sprightly, elaborately paneled illustrations set a light-hearted tone for this variation on a classic folktale motif [*The Full Belly Bowl*]. When an old man who lives in a cozy but meager home saves a "wee small man" from a fox and then helps him recuperate, he receives the gift of a "full belly bowl." An accompanying letter explains the rules: "When not in use, store it upside down." At first all is well, as the magic bowl multiplies whatever is placed in it, feeding the old man and his cat in grand style. Then the old man decides to use the bowl to multiply coins, and, excited at the prospect of untold wealth, he forgets the rule. The cottage is overrun first by mice (one crawls into the bowl), then by cats (the man multiplies his own cat to catch the mice)—and in the mayhem, the bowl breaks. Aylesworth's (*Through the Night*) nimble story keeps the action going, transcending cautionary tale to deliver an amusing lark. The softly shaded and meticulously drawn images have a homespun quality that underscores the story's domesticity. Multiple panels unfold the plot in a series of airy, intricate vignettes; their borders are alight with elements that echo each scene, from fruit and flowers to birds, cats and mice. Aylesworth and Halperin make a wonderful team: like the magic bowl, their talents runneth over. *Ages 4-8.*

📖 *THE BURGER AND THE HOT DOG* (2001)

Hazel Rochman (review date 1 October 2001)

SOURCE: Rochman, Hazel. *Booklist* 98, no. 3 (1 October 2001): 320-21.

Ages 5-8. The rhymes are lame in this collection of poems [*The Burger and the Hot Dog*], and some of the jokes will appeal more to adults than kids, but the combination of food and nonsense is irresistible and the words and pictures are loaded with puns. There's an overdressed pizza, an angel cake, and a shy hard-boiled egg that won't come out of her shell, even when she's invited to dance by a friendly French toast guy. [Stephen] Gammell's splashy watercolors wallow in the mess, whether it's a double-page spread of two smelly, lonely cheeses who fall in love, or as in the uproarious title poem, a hot dog insults a burger by calling him "flat," and the soda tells them both to stop it or "I will kick you in the buns!" After that, kids may be ready to take up Aylesworth's challenge on the last page and write their own food farce.

Kirkus Reviews (review date 1 October 2001)

SOURCE: *Kirkus Reviews* 69, no. 19 (1 October 2001): 1418.

Kids who devour poems by [Shel] Silverstein and [Jack] Prelutsky will sink their teeth into this collection of poetry [*The Burger and the Hot Dog*] featuring a banquet of fanciful food characters. There's a teacher named Frankie Fish Stick, pungent cheeses named Woodrow and Wanda, and a couple of eager eggs named Yack and Yimmy (two very "yolly guys," who are—naturally—full of funny "yolks"). Aylesworth (*The Tale of Tricky Fox,* 2001) includes lots of favorite foods in his 23 rhyming poems: pizza, bagels, cake, pickles, even chewing gum. Several poems convey subtle lessons about behavior, as in "Nellie and Bill," the story of a sweet pickle who is a more pleasant friend than her sourpuss dill pickle companion. Some poems are pure dessert, as in "Veggie Soup," the story of a country/western band with Bo Beet on fiddle and Tex Tater on guitar, or the title poem, which has a soda breaking up a fight and threatening to kick the participants in the buns. Creative teachers will find lots of ways to integrate these poems into the classroom, especially to liven up lessons on nutrition and the food pyramid. The final poem, "Up to You," encourages young readers to write their own poems about "food folks." Caldecott Medalist [Stephen] Gammell (*Ride*) has cooked up a batch of humorous, mixed-media illustrations in a loose, washy style, using coffee for the brown tones for additional thematic flavor. *(5-9)*

Publishers Weekly (review date 5 November 2001)

SOURCE: *Publishers Weekly* 248, no. 45 (5 November 2001): 67-8.

Zany food rhymes and humorous portraits of bagels and bananas are the special of the day in this new collaboration [*The Burger and the Hot Dog*] from Aylesworth and [Stephen] Gammell (previously teamed for *Old Black Fly*). The 23 catchy verses feature personality-packed edible stars, dilemmas that turn on the food's trademark characteristics and loads of goofy puns. "'You're pretty!' said an orange / To a lemon who seemed pleased. / 'In fact, my dear, so

pretty, / You're at risk of getting squeezed!'" Gammell's fruits and vegetables resemble the California Raisins (to whom the book is dedicated), with tiny arms and legs and squished-together facial features particularly well-suited for registering surprise. He has even more fun rendering the personal crises of his subjects, painting rowdy cookies who disintegrate when they attack a bagel and gooey sticky cinnamon buns who cannot enjoy even the simplest pleasures of social interaction: "'We can't shake hands!' 'No, never!' / 'Simple hugs just can't be done!' / 'And should we bump together, / Oh, my, no, that's never fun!'" The chunky blocks of text share center stage with the smoothly paced images, enhancing the book's visual punch; brushstroked poem titles seem to drip along with the ketchup and mustard. Youngsters will enjoy finding out what the denizens of your neighborhood diner do after the waitresses turn out the lights and go home for the night. *Ages 5-8.*

Caroline Ward (review date January 2002)

SOURCE: Ward, Caroline. *School Library Journal* 48, no. 1 (January 2002): 116.

Gr 2 Up—An uneven collection of humorous poems [*The Burger and the Hot Dog*] featuring foods such as a lemon so pretty she is in danger of getting squeezed, and a shy hard-boiled egg named Betty who is having difficulty coming out of her shell. Lines like "Two pickles went out dancing: / She a gherkin, he a dill" resound with a cadence reminiscent of Jack Prelutsky, but many others are awkwardly constructed. Take the case of an angel cake in Kansas who calls up her boyfriend, "'Come take me out to dinner,' / Is, in short, just what she said." There is some clever wordplay—the slogan of a band comprised of vegetables is: "The Band with a Beet," but a punch line relying on a reference to wax bananas will go over the heads of the intended audience. The exaggerated heads and distorted bodies give a Mr. Potatohead look to the food caricatures. The colored-pencil, watercolor, and pastel illustrations are effective in depicting various dripping and melting dishes, but the scatter-paint effect lends a frenetic feel to the art. This book may elicit chuckles and inspire some creative-writing efforts,

📖 THE TALE OF TRICKY FOX: A NEW ENGLAND TRICKSTER TALE (2001)

Gillian Engberg (review date 1 February 2001)

SOURCE: Engberg, Gillian. *Booklist* 97, no. 11 (1 February 2001): 1055.

Ages 3-7. In the same format and style as their ***The Gingerbread Man*** (1998) and ***Aunt Pitty Patty's Piggy*** (1999), Aylesworth and [Barbara] McClintock offer another nostalgic folktale that's perfect for read-alouds [***The Tale of Tricky Fox***]. Bored with chickens, Tricky Fox boasts that he can steal a pig. "I'll eat my hat if you do!" says his brother, and the bet is on. Playing on humans' natural curiosity, the clever fox tricks two elderly neighbors into filling his sack with treats, but a third woman, a teacher, outwits Fox by putting a bulldog in his sack. Unaware, Fox returns triumphantly with his bulging sack, and Brother eats his hat, literally, before the ferocious pup leaps out. The folly of the well-dressed, rascally animals and their human counterparts, rendered in McClintock's signature style (reminiscent of fine, nineteenth-century illustrations) inspires giggles. Aylesworth's words, in bouncy rhythms and nursery rhymes, will get kids to cheer along with the story. An infectious choice for fans of the team's previous titles.

Horn Book Magazine (review date March 2001)

SOURCE: *Horn Book Magazine* 77, no. 2 (March 2001): 217-18.

(Primary) Although the kindly teacher reading in her one-room classroom sets her tale [***The Tale of Tricky Fox***] in "woods not so very far away," we are still surprised when she emerges as the hero of the story, outsmarting Tricky Fox. In a concise source note, Aylesworth confesses his longtime affection for this New England "trading" trickster tale, in which Tricky Fox brags to Brother Fox that he can steal a pig. ("I'll eat my hat if you do!" says Brother Fox, recklessly.) Three times the fox, feigning age and fatigue, gains entry to nearby cottages and upgrades the contents of his sack, fooling the human owners of the cottages into exchanging a loaf of bread for a log of wood, a chicken for a loaf of bread, and—almost—the prized pig for a chicken. The kindly teacher, herself the fox's third intended victim, overhears him singing his gleeful, sassy song—"I'm so clever—tee-hee-hee! . . . Human folks ain't smart like me"—and, demonstrating a teacher's greater smarts, puts her pet bulldog into the sack instead of the supposed pig. [Barbara] McClintock's lively line gets the tale's mischief just right—her wily Fox even winks conspiratorially at the reader. Watercolor vignettes of varying size with an irregular beige background enliven this winsome story as Fox capers through the spacious antique white pages, appearing sometimes as often as four times on a page in energetic poses of deception and delight. The expectant faces of the polite children listening to their teacher on the first page gives way to contained glee at the end when they listen to the tongue-in-cheek moral that resident foxes have learned: more respect for humans, no singing sassy songs, and no hat wearing. Aylesworth's spirited telling concludes with his great-grandmother's recipe for Tricky Fox's Eat-Your-Hat Cookies.

Barbara Buckley (review date March 2001)

SOURCE: Buckley, Barbara. *School Library Journal* 47, no. 3 (March 2001): 192.

PreS-Gr 2—As they did in ***The Gingerbread Man*** (1998), Aylesworth and [Barbara] McClintock have teamed up again, this time to create the wiliest of creatures in this version of "The Travels of a Fox" [***The Tale of Tricky Fox***]. Acting on a bet he makes with Brother Fox, Tricky Fox vows to bring home a pig rather than a chicken for supper. He begs his way into homes, carrying a bag. When he goes to sleep, he tells the host to keep an eye on his bag, but not to look inside it. Knowing human nature, he figures that the homeowner will take a peek. During the night, he disposes of the contents of the bag and in the morning claims that something better was stolen. Of course, his hostess is embarrassed that this has happened in her own home and replaces whatever the fox claimed was in his sack. He pulls this con on several unsuspecting women until he meets up with a teacher, who sees through the ruse and puts her ferocious bulldog in his sack. What a surprise both Tricky and Brother Fox get when they open the bag at home. The romping good humor of the story is carried by the old-fashioned illustrations in sepia tones. Their size diversity—from small insets to full-page spread—moves the story to its conclusion. The tale is told by the teacher who finally unmasks the rascal. The expressions on Tricky and his unsuspecting victims are priceless.

Publishers Weekly (review date 12 March 2001)

SOURCE: *Publishers Weekly* 248, no. 11 (12 March 2001): 88-9.

The clever collaborators behind ***The Gingerbread Man*** and ***Aunt Pitty Patty's Piggy*** offer another buoyant retelling in this tale within a tale [***The Tale of Tricky Fox***]. A teacher from yesteryear gathers her students around her to read to them a book—

which keen-eyed kids will recognize as the book in their own hands. It introduces Tricky Fox who brags to his brother that "I'm going to get me a fat pig!" Insisting that a fox could not possible carry such a critter, Brother Fox replies, "I'll eat my hat if you do!" The title character grows positively—and contagiously—gleeful as he tricks one and then another woman, so that it seems he just may accomplish his mission. Yet the next would-be victim of his pranks is a teacher (in fact, the very one seen on the opening page), and "Tricky Fox didn't know that teachers are not so easy to fool as regular humans are." Rendered in watercolor, black ink and gouache, [Barbara] McClintock's endearingly antique pictures add to the merriment, especially when the conniving fox winks at readers, drawing them into his joke. Cleverly paced repetition and an unexpected ending make this droll caper a winning choice. *Ages 3-6.*

FURTHER READING

Bibliographies

Aylesworth Family. "Famous and Accomplished Family Members: Jim Aylesworth." *Aylesworth Family Website*: www.aylesworth.net/
    Entry on website run by the Aylesworth family.

Aylesworth, Jim. "Jim Aylesworth: Books." *Jim Aylesworth's Website*; www.ayles.com/
    Listings on Aylesworth's website.

Scholastic. "Jim Aylesworth's Booklist." *Author Studies Homepage.* Scholastic: www2.scholastic.com/teachers/
    Entry on website.

Biographies

Aylesworth, Jim. "About the Author—Biography." *Jim Aylesworth's Website*: www.ayles.com/
    Biographical sketch on website.

Hinsdale Central High School Foundation. "Hall of Fame." *HCHS Foundation—Hall of Fame 1998 Inductee Jim Aylesworth.* Hinsdale, Ill.: hchsfoundation.org/
    Biographical sketch.

McElmeel, Sharron L. "Jim Aylesworth." *Bookpeople: A First Album,* pp. 25-28. Englewood, Colo.: Teacher Ideas Press, 1990.
    Entry on Aylesworth.

———. "Jim Aylesworth." *100 Most Popular Picture Book Authors and Illustrators,* pp. 32-34. Englewood, Colo.: Libraries Unlimited, Inc., 2000.
    Entry on Aylesworth.

Scholastic. "Jim Aylesworth's Biography." *Author Studies Homepage.* Scholastic: www2.scholastic.com/teachers/
    Biographical sketch.

Additional coverage of Aylesworth's life and career is contained in the following sources published by the Gale Group: *Contemporary Authors,* **Vol. 106;** *Contemporary Authors New Revision Series,* **Vols. 22, 45;** *Literature Resource Center;* *Something about the Author,* **Vols. 38, 89, 139; and** *St. James Guide to Children's Writers,* **Vol. 5.**

Sharon Creech
1945-

(Also wrote under the name Sharon Rigg) American author of young adult novels and picture books.

For more information about Creech and her works, see *Children's Literature Review,* Vol. 42.

INTRODUCTION

"Teens will always be searching for identity and a place to belong. Always. And those themes have resonance for me and are probably ones I will continue to explore in different ways," said Sharon Creech in an interview with Judy Hendershot and Jackie Peck for *Reading Teacher.* Creech draws both characters and settings from her personal life. In the *Reading Teacher* interview she commented, "In every book I've done, the characters are combinations of people [I have known]. I do draw very much from my family," and the countryside depicted in books such as *Walk Two Moons* (1994) and *Chasing Redbird* (1997) are taken directly from childhood memories. "Place is important to me," Creech told Hollis Lowery-Moore in an interview for *Teacher Librarian.* "I strongly believe it shapes people. Where we live affects who we are."

BIOGRAPHICAL INFORMATION

Creech was born in Cleveland, Ohio where she grew up in a big noisy family with relatives who told lots of stories. Creech loved the materials of writing, and hoarded writing paper and pencils when she was young. Throughout grade school and high school she wrote and was an enthusiastic reader, especially of romantic fantasy and folk tales. Her cousins told her that she was part Native American, and Creech loved the idea. In the interview with *Reading Teacher* Creech said, "I thought one of my ancestors was an American Indian. I exaggerated this possibility, and I would tell people that I was full-bloodied Indian. I would read Indian myths. I was convinced that I was an Indian."

The summer Creech turned twelve, her family took car a trip from Ohio to Lewiston, Idaho. She recalled it as a wonderful trip during which the family stopped at a Indian reservation where she bought moccasins, a precious gift. The vast country and various people in it excited her, and she derived inspiration from it in later years when she wrote her Newbery award winning *Walk Two Moons.*

Creech earned her B.A. from Hiram College and her M.A. from George Mason University in Washington, D.C. During graduate school she worked in the Federal Theater Project Archives and wanted to be a playwright. After finishing college she worked as an editorial assistant for the *Congressional Quarterly,* but did not care for the job because it was all facts and politics with no chance for creativity. She married, had two children, and divorced. In need of a job to support her family, she traveled to England in 1979 where she obtained a job teaching literature at the London branch of The American School in Switzerland (TASIS), a boarding school for the children of expatriate Americans, located in suburban Thorpe. She met the assistant headmaster, a fellow American, and married him three years later. Shortly after their marriage, both were transferred to the Swiss branch of the school. Then in 1984, they returned to England where her husband became headmaster of the English branch. In 1994 they came back to the United States where her husband took the position of headmaster of the Pennington School in New Jersey. With her children grown and away in college, she finally had time to write.

After her father's death in 1986, Creech was confronted with what she describes as the "dark wall of mortality," and she began to write her first book, *Absolutely Normal Chaos* (1990), in which she drew much from her own childhood and family. When *Walk Two Moons* won the Newbery Medal in 1995, it brought Creech instant celebrity and established her as an important writer for young adults. Her writing has come in a continuous stream ever since. She told Judy Hendershot and Jackie Peck of *Reading Teacher* "I've always thought there were too *many* ideas and not enough time to sit down and develop them."

Her advice to young people who want to write is, "Read a lot. Read anything you can and everything you want to read. All of that will fall into sort of a well that you will use when you write a story. Then write anything you want to. Write poetry, drama, science fiction, or humor. That way you will find what really interests you."

MAJOR WORKS

Creech's first book, initially published in the U.K., was *Absolutely Normal Chaos* (1990). When she was writing it, she did not think of it as a children's book. It is written in the form of a journal, kept by thirteen-year-old Mary Lou as a summer assignment. It is an eventful summer in which she confronts the issues of illegitimacy, death, family, and classic literature with a fresh eye and humorous viewpoint. *Publishers Weekly*'s critic called it an "affable if formulaic tale . . . Despite the occasionally creaky plot, Mary Lou's bouncy entries are still a lot of fun. Readers will enjoy her wry commentary on *The Odyssey*."

Walk Two Moons was the winner of many awards, among them the Newbery Medal. It recounts two stories in one. Thirteen-year-old Salamanca Tree Hiddle is on a trip to Idaho with her grandparents. While traveling, she tells the story of her friend Phoebe whose mother has left home and has not returned. Phoebe's situation is similar to her own, for Sal's mother has died. The two stories intertwine as the girls come to terms with the loss of their mothers. Naomi Lewis of the *Observer* called *Walk Two Moons* "A really satisfying book—funny, poignant, cunning in the unraveling of its mysteries. No point in cheating by looking at the end: you must meet it when it comes. It's worth the journey." Much loved by both readers and critics, *Walk Two Moons* quickly became a classic of young adult literature.

Harking back to her childhood fantasies about her Native-American roots, Creech set *Chasing Redbird* in rural Kentucky. Thirteen-year-old Zinnia seeks refuge from her large noisy family in the calm and quiet of her aunt and uncle's home. When her aunt dies, her uncle becomes eccentric in his grief, but Zinny finds consolation in clearing a long, winding trail behind the house. While working on the trail, she discovers her family history and encounters an attentive young man at the same time. *The Wanderer* (2000) is the name of the boat on which thirteen-year-old Sophie sets sail with her uncle and two cousins. Their voyage from Connecticut to England is to visit their grandfather, a native of England who has returned home. The book is taken from journal entries written by Sophie and her cousin Cody. Although Sophie tells stories she remembers hearing from her grandfather, Cody reveals that Sophie is adopted and that she has never met her grandfather. As the boat faces a dangerous storm, Sophie begins to remember her painful past and embarks on an unsettling journey of self-discovery. Katie O'Dell of *School Library Journal* praised *The Wanderer* as "a beautifully written and imaginatively constructed novel that speaks to the power of survival and the delicacy of grief."

Although most of Creech's books are written for young adults, she has written some picture books for younger children. *A Fine, Fine School* (2001) is based on her headmaster husband and his enthusiasm for learning. The principle of Tillie's school wants it to be a fine, fine school, so he increases the work load, adding schoolwork on the weekends and holidays and late into the night. He is astonished to discover that the students and teachers are not as thrilled as he is . . . until Tillie points out that she has not improved her tree climbing, and she has been unable to teach her brother to skip or her dog to do tricks. The principle realizes that there are things to be learned outside of school too, and school returns to normal. The critic for *Publishers Weekly* thought the book was not only very funny, but "Given current battles over standardized testing and summer sessions, this timely story about extended schooling touches a nerve with a kindly delivery . . . [It] persuasively argues one side of a volatile issue."

Love That Dog: Learning About Poetry from Miss Stretchberry (2001) is presented as a series of poems: poems by William Carlos Williams, Robert Frost, and Walter Dean Myers chosen by Miss Stretchberry for her class to read, and poems written by her student Jack as his assignments. At first Jack's poems are mostly complaints about having to write poems, but finally, inspired by Myers "Love That Boy," Jack writes a poem about his dog who died. The reader can follow Jack's development as he experiments with form, spontaneity, and presentation. When he at last finds power in his poetry, Jack signs his work and sends it to Myers as a tribute. Jennifer Anstiss of *Journal of Adolescent and Adult Literacy* wrote in her review, "Creech has brilliantly crafted a story with the potential to appeal to young adolescents who may relate to Jack's struggles with issues of identity and validation." A critic for *Publishers Weekly* liked it too: "Creech conveys a life truth: Pain and joy exist side by side. For Jack and for readers, the memory of that dog lives on in his poetry. Readers will love that dog, and this book."

CRITICAL RECEPTION

The success of *Walk Two Moons* brought instant attention to Creech's work, and the attention has not diminished over the years. Praised for her multi-layered stories, smooth and imaginative style, and ability to conjure a sense of place, Creech's characters confront death, grief, separation, and loss as they struggle to survive adolescence. This is not to say her books are without humor; her characters, especially when the voice is theirs, often are amused by the absurdities surrounding them. Many of her books are standard offerings in classrooms as selected reading material, and she continues to garner awards and recognition for the quality of her work.

AWARDS

Walk Two Moons won the Newbery Medal in 1995. It was also named Best Book by the *School Library Journal* in 1994. In 1995 it was named a Notable Children's Book by the American Library Association, received the Children's Book Award in England, and the U. K. Reading Association Award, as well as the Newbery Medal. It was also honored with the W. H. Smith Award in 1996 and the Young Readers Award in 1997.

Chasing Redbird was short listed for the Whitbread Award in 1997.

The Wanderer was named a Newbery Honor Book in 2001 and won the Christopher Award in 2000; *Love That Dog* also won the Christopher Award in 2002.

PRINCIPAL WORKS

Absolutely Normal Chaos (young adult novel) 1990
Walk Two Moons (young adult novel) 1994
Pleasing the Ghost (young adult novel) 1996
Chasing Redbird (young adult novel) 1997
Bloomability (young adult novel) 1998
Fishing in the Air (picture book) 2000
The Wanderer (young adult novel) 2000
A Fine, Fine School (picture book) 2001
Love That Dog: Learning About Poetry from Miss Stretchberry (young adult novel) 2001
Ruby Holler (young adult novel) 2002

AUTHOR COMMENTARY

Sharon Creech, Judy Hendershot, and Jackie Peck (interview date February 1996)

SOURCE: Creech, Sharon, Judy Hendershot, and Jackie Peck. "An Interview with Sharon Creech, 1995 Newbery Medal Winner." *Reading Teacher* 49, no. 5 (February 1996): 380-82.

[*In the following interview, Hendershot and Peck discuss with Creech the inspiration for several of her books.*]

[*Hendershot/Peck*]: **Walk Two Moons** *seems so true to life. Is it autobiographical?*

[Creech]: It is autobiographical in the sense that I drew from little pieces of things that have happened to me. It was inspired in part by a message in a fortune cookie: "Don't judge a man until you've walked two moons in his moccasins." That message sparked earlier memories of when I was a child. I loved moccasins because I thought one of my ancestors was an American Indian. I exaggerated this possibility, and I would tell people that I was full-blooded Indian. I would read Indian myths. I was convinced that I was an Indian.

I also remembered the car trip my family took across the States when I was 12 years old. We drove from Ohio to Lewiston, Idaho, where I had relatives. On that journey I got to pick out my first pair of moccasins as a birthday present.

When I began to write, I was living in England and I was missing the States. I was also missing my grown children who had just gone off to college there. I wrote **Walk Two Moons** from the notion of a parent/child separation, and I decided to do it from the child's point of view. These were the kinds of things rolling around in my mind.

Did you also draw from your personal life for the characters you created in **Walk Two Moons***?*

In every book I've done, the characters are combinations of people. I do draw very much from my family, and so I've speculated that Salamanca and her mother are each very much me and my own daughter combined. The other women in the book now seem to be all the women in my family rolled into a ball, and Gramps has traits of all the men in my family.

The relationship of the grandparents to each other and to Salamanca are particularly striking.

I drew those relationships from those of the men and women in my family, my parents and grandparents, where the men are very loving and gentle, and the women are a little bit sassy, but very devoted. There is a kind of loving sparring about them that I tried to develop. You see those feelings in any good marriage. It's affectionate but not perfect.

The idea to layer a story within a story is a very so-phisticated literary technique. Was it difficult to do?

It was kind of an accident. Part of the way **Walk Two Moons** turned out was the result of the economics of publishing at the time I was writing the book. There was a recession going on in that industry [in the U.S.] and in England and editors were being very selective.

I had written my first children's book *Absolutely Normal Chaos* earlier. Then when I submitted the first version of **Walk Two Moons,** my editor liked it, but she didn't know if there was a place for it. She suggested that I expand it. I didn't really want to ex-pand that story; I'd done all I could with it. I decided to develop a new character out of it—one with a wild imagination, sort of like mine. I wrote the story of Phoebe and her mother going away, kind of a re-versal of my children going away to school.

By the time I had the second story done, I had ac-quired a new editor who suggested I expand this one as well. I was ready to toss it into the trash—and then I got the message in the fortune cookie.

I had been thinking about doing a story about a girl going on a trip across the States, so I began the Sal story. Then I touched back on the other stories for kind of a counterpoint. So in a way each story bounced off the others until they became one.

Do you have an audience in mind for all your writ-ing?

No. In fact I rarely do. When a story begins to take shape in my mind, I'm usually very certain of the age of the main character. If it's a 13-year-old girl, I try to write exactly from the consciousness of a 13-year-old girl. If it's a 9-year-old boy, then I try to be in the mind of a 9-year-old boy. If I'm faithful to that, then I know that the story will work.

When I wrote *Absolutely Normal Chaos* I didn't know it was a children's book. I'd written two adult novels prior to that, but in that book the girl just hap-pened to be younger. My agent said it might appeal to a children's market. **Walk Two Moons,** more than anything that I've written, seems to cross the barriers of age. When I do a signing there are 10-year-old children lined up with 80-year-old grandmothers and 40-year-old parents. There are men and there are women. Adults are buying the book for themselves and some for their grandchildren. It is interesting what all these readers have found in the book.

In England it has won several awards voted on by children. I am astonished that British children have found it as worthy as a committee of adults, such as the Newbery committee, found it. Somehow I seem to have tapped into imagery and symbolism that adults are picking up on and responding to. The chil-dren are responding on yet a different level even though they may not be able to analyze what it is they're responding to.

I certainly didn't intend to write a book that appealed on that many levels but I'm very glad—very proud—that I did.

Absolutely Normal Chaos *is a prequel to* **Walk Two Moons,** *written in a journal form about a student who is learning to write and use dialogue. Did you envision it then as a possible teaching tool?*

Journals were just on my mind. I teach high school juniors and seniors in England, and my students were learning how to keep a journal. Dialogue is a hard concept to teach, yet if students of writing just look at examples of good dialogue they mimic it and pick it up quickly. Some of the things I've done with this book are to have students use different scenes and make them into original plays to act out. They love to dramatize, and they love it that they can take dia-logue from the book and act it out. They get the idea how to put into writing the way people talk and in-terrupt each other.

Are you teaching now?

I'm on a leave of absence in order to fulfill a two-book contract. However, since the Newbery I've found that I have a lot of obligations in the coming year; so I'm extending my leave to 2 years. I love teaching and would not like to be away from it for too long.

Obviously, winning the Newbery Medal has changed your life.

At least temporarily. I still don't know how I feel about it. It's like someone has given me this beauti-ful suit of Armani clothes. Normally I would not wear them. They look nice and everyone admires them, but I'm a little uncomfortable in them. I like to wear them for brief periods of time and then change back to my blue jeans.

Part of it is scary. It's hard to know how something affects you. Anything you say is weighed more heavily than it ought to be. But then there are so many freedoms this opens up.

Are there other books besides **Absolutely Normal Chaos** *forthcoming?*

There are two. One is called *The Good Carpet Ghost* [published as *Pleasing the Ghost*]—a funny story for a slightly younger age—7-to-9-year-olds. The one I was finishing when I got the call about the Newbery is titled *Chasing Redbird*. It's more in the vein of *Walk Two Moons* in that it's about a country girl on a quest of sorts.

Ideas are always there. I'm puzzled when people ask if I'm terrified by the prospect of a block or if I might not know what to write about. I've always thought that there were too *many* ideas and not enough time to sit down and develop them.

That's some of the frustration that I am feeling now. I know I will be writing speeches for the coming year and that takes almost as long as book writing. There are revisions for *Chasing Redbird* due this fall. Usually that's when I start a new book—I'm sort of on that school schedule. But this year I know I'm not going to be able to begin writing until spring.

Can you tell us why you are a writer?

I don't know if I have an answer to that. When I was young, I loved books, although I couldn't tell you the titles of books I've read. It was more the *experience* of reading that was so memorable—to be able to be all those different people. I could be a boy, I could be a girl. I could be an Indian or a Greek warrior. Eventually, I thought it had to be the greatest thing in the world to be able to make up all those things.

Were you influenced by teachers?

I had some really good teachers who praised me when I needed praise, encouraged me when I needed encouragement, and helped me to recognize that I could use words. They gave me self confidence about using words. From that I just knew that I wanted to write books.

Yet you seem to have waited to begin your writing life.

For a long time I had other priorities—young children and a full-time job. Then my father had a stroke, and he lost the power to speak and to understand words. It was such a horror not to be able to communicate with someone that you loved. Within a month of his death, I started my first book, and I haven't stopped writing since. Partly, it was the connection that I couldn't keep saying "I'm *going* to write" and an obligation I felt to use all the words my father couldn't use.

What does Sharon Creech tell children about writing?

Read a lot. Read anything you can and everything you want to read. All of that will fall into sort of a well that you will use when you write a story. Then write anything you want to. Write poetry, drama, science fiction, or humor. That way you will find what really interests you.

Sharon Creech and Hollis Lowery-Moore (interview date April 2001)

SOURCE: Creech, Sharon, and Hollis Lowery-Moore. "Creating People Who Are Quirky and Kind." *Teacher Librarian* 28, no. 4 (April 2001): 54-6.

[*In the following interview, Lowery-Moore and Creech examine the author's approach to writing.*]

Sharon Creech, winner of the Newbery Award for *Walk Two Moons,* uses her family and her experiences to craft her stories of teens searching for self and place. Sharon's characters are slightly eccentric, always interesting, and usually exploring new places and ideas. Storytelling is a tool that advances the plot in most of Creech's books and adds depth to the characters. She also uses humor to explore difficult family dynamics in all her stories and the pain of loss and the uncertainty of new places and experiences never become unbearable.

[*Lowery-Moore*]: *You have said that some of your characters and story ideas are based on family members and experiences. Can you tell us about family members that spawned characters?*

[Creech]: Usually I am not aware that I am drawing on family when I am writing. It is only after a book is done that I sometimes see some of the sources. For example, it was after *Walk Two Moons* was published that I recognized that Gram contained pieces of my mother, grandmother and sister (goodness spiced with a little sass), and that Salamanca seemed to contain bits of my daughter and of me (lyrical, stubborn, outdoor-loving). In *Absolutely Normal Chaos,* I drew more consciously from my family, particularly my three brothers. I even (shamelessly) used their real first names. But once they arrived in the story, they ceased being my real brothers and took on their own quirky (and fictional) characteristics.

I attended a conference when you talked about Salamanca in **Walk Two Moons** *and you made the comment, "I didn't know where Sal was taking me." I have heard other authors talk about listening to their characters or being so involved with their characters that they got lost or took wrong turns when driving. How do your characters lead you?*

Once I have the characters' voices, they take off. I know that some people scoff at this, but it is true with me. It feels as if I am only listening and following. I am recording what I see and hear in my mind. It is definitely an altered state! The conscious mind enters during the revision stages, and it is then that I think logically and critically about the story. When I am in the midst of writing a book, the book consumes me in off-hours, too. I am apt to put the telephone handset in the refrigerator, my keys in the microwave, etc., while I am still listening to the characters ramble on in my head.

Several of your books are used for class study in English/Language Arts classrooms. Since you have taught English, which of your books would you choose to study with a class and what instructional activities might you do with the book?

It is such a different thing, being a writer, as opposed to being a teacher, and it is now difficult for me to switch gears. If I had to switch gears, though, it would be far easier to teach someone else's book than my own. I am not sure I could teach one of my own, and I have so much trouble choosing which one to offer.

I've heard from so many gifted teachers who have used my books in such interesting ways, and I've heard from so many students who will never forget these books because of the discussions and activities that their teachers offered, and hearing these responses touches me and reminds me of the value of extended activities. **Walk Two Moons** seems to be the one most frequently taught. It begs to be read aloud. Teachers have extended the book by charting the geographical journey, illustrating the proverbs, dramatizing scenes, etc. One of the upcoming ones, **Love That Dog,** follows a boy through a year of resisting poetry, and because it is both funny and serious and short, I think it would make a great in-classroom book.

Most of your reviewers refer to your unique ability to create a "sense of place" in your stories. What contributes to this strength in your writing and stories?

I first have to see the character and the place in my head, before I even begin the story, but once I have character and place, off we go! I am there in that place with that character, and I am seeing what he or she sees.

Place is important to me. I strongly believe it shapes people. Where we live affects who we are, much as our families and friends and teachers shape who we are. I once heard an educator say, young people need and deserve beauty, and I believe this profoundly. We old(er) people need it, too. Perhaps that is why I choose beautiful settings, ones in which I'd like to spend long hours, and ones in which I think young readers would like to spend their time.

Some people ask me why I don't write darker stories about troubling issues. Well, there is enough darkness and troubling issues all around us, and there are enough skilled writers writing about them. I have so little time, and for now, I prefer to spend it with people who are quirky and kind, and in places that are breathtakingly beautiful.

Several of your novels have a parallel story or second point of view that allows the reader to see characters and situations in different ways. What is your intent in using these devices in your novels?

I'm not sure it is a conscious intent. It is more, perhaps, a need to look at other perspectives, to flush out more complex aspects of a story. Also, often, the main story is a serious one, and the parallel one is humorous. This comes out of who I am. I cannot dwell too long in the serious before lightening the mood with humor.

Your characters often have unusual names. How do you arrive at these names?

The first long story I wrote in college received much praise, but also this note: Your characters names are so boring. I have tried not to make that mistake again.

I love names, especially unusual ones, and I am intrigued by the way names suggest personalities. The name almost always comes first and then suggests not only character traits but also plot points. I found Salamanca's name on a map of New York. It sounded Native American, so most of that part of her background came from her name. Mrs. Cadaver just popped into my head, but later it suggested dead body associations. Mrs. Partridge also just popped into my head, and suggested (because a partridge is a bird) someone a bit flighty.

When you read and write with young adults in school visits, what kinds of things do they want to know about your work?

They always want to know where my ideas come from, and I say that I never really know for sure, although I can usually offer pieces of inspiration which got the story going. So many ideas come in the middle of writing—words generate more words, thoughts generate more thoughts. I think it is important for students to know that they don't have to know the story before they begin. Start with a person or place that intrigues you and then see where it leads. Have fun! Not everything needs to be a finished, perfect piece.

Students also want to know how long it takes to write a book, and they are somewhat aghast when I say that although I might be able to dash off a first draft in three months, it takes from one to three years to polish the story. The revision process is crucial; going over and over and over a piece until it is as polished as I can make it. It seems to help students to know that it takes time for a story to come into its own, although too often in school students don't have the benefit of that time.

Your stories explore the issues of teens searching for identity and a place to belong. This has been a primary task of adolescence since the term was invented. Do you feel that 21st century teens will face issues that adolescents in the past did not have to deal with? If so, which of these challenges are you likely to explore in stories?

First, I think that teens will always be searching for identity and a place to belong. Always. And those themes have resonance for me and are probably ones I will continue to explore in different ways. And yes, I think that 21st century teens will face issues that adolescents in the past did not have to deal with—already they are facing them—but it is impossible for me to speculate which I might explore, since I don't

begin with issues, but rather with character. What is more interesting to me is how current teens are like teens from the past, and what is it that we humans all have in common?

Your audiences are glad to have you living in the U.S. once again. Do you think your move will have impact on your writing, especially the "sense of place" referred to in an earlier question?

Interesting, this question, because the first book published since I returned to the U.S. was based in Europe (**Bloomability**), and the most recent novel, **The Wanderer,** has my characters sailing back to Europe. I was so disoriented when I returned to the States! Sometimes it is easier to write about a place when you are far away from it. Maybe future books will combine elements of the States and of Europe? Or maybe I will move back and forth across the ocean in different books? I don't know. The two most recently completed novels, **Ruby Holler** and **Love That Dog** feel very American, but I am itching to explore a little English village.

Sharon Creech and Jason Britton (interview date 16 July 2001)

SOURCE: Creech, Sharon, and Jason Britton. "Everyday Journeys." *Publishers Weekly* 248, no. 29 (16 July 2001): 153.

[*In the following interview, Britton describes Creech's working environment and the author's experiences of writing several of her books, especially* Love That Dog.]

Sharon Creech opens the front door of her three-story, neo-Georgian, red-brick home and welcomes [*Publishers Weekly*] with a smile. She is dressed casually, in jeans and a dusty-pink cotton shirt. And she is wearing moccasins. Those familiar with Creech's **Walk Two Moons,** which received the 1995 Newbery Medal, know that the book's protagonist also wears moccasins; Salamanca Tree Hiddle's guiding mantra, in fact, is "Don't judge a man until you've walked two moons in his moccasins," In reality, this message came to the author in a fortune cookie, and it changed the course of the book—which in turn changed the course of Creech's life.

The first floor of the house, which is owned by the school in central New Jersey where her husband is the headmaster, has a more formal feel than the couple's living quarters, which are on the second and third floors. Creech explains that the house has just been cleaned in preparation for a faculty picnic to mark the end of the school year. She leads the way to her office: up the stairs and down a hall hung with photos of family and friends, letters from readers and bulletin boards layered with sketches and dummies for her picture books. At the end of the hall is a bright, sunny office. Gifts from friends, family and readers are scattered around the room; many are moons.

Creech uses a gray iMac computer; there is a fax machine, a phone and filing cabinets. Her bookshelves are divided into adult and children's; on the former are the likes of Carol Shields, Anne Tyler, Lorrie Moore and a number of Southern women writers, and the children's side includes David Almond, Kimberly Willis Holt, Richard Peck, Laurie Halse Anderson, Louise Rennison and, fittingly, Walter Dean Myers. "There's this new connection that Walter and I have," she says, referring to her new novel, *Love That Dog,* "so I'd really like to go back and read all of his stuff." It is hard to narrow down her list of favorite children's authors, she says, and it's always growing. "Until I received the Newbery, I didn't know this whole realm of amazing books existed," she admits. "I tend to like novels that are like mine: contemporary, realistic fiction with funny and serious intertwined. I like to read what I like to write."

Throughout Creech's body of work there is, a sense of journey, of travel and self-discovery. She says that travel has always been important to her, starting when she was young and continuing through her life. In fact, when she was 13, her family took a road trip that Creech later re-created in *Walk Two Moons.* "And I also love the way that each book—any book—is its own journey," she says. "You open it, and off you go. You are changed in some way, large or small, by having traveled with those characters."

This idea extends to her writing process as well: "When I begin writing a book, I have no idea who I will meet along the way, nor what they will see or hear or do. I usually have little idea where we are all going together." She describes the experiences of the characters in her two latest books as "everyday journeys."

Creech will spend the summer at her cottage in upstate New York, where she and her husband, Lyle, will relax, enjoy family and get ready for what promises to be a busy fall. Her seventh novel and her second picture book, *A Fine, Fine School,* illustrated by Harry Bliss, will be published by HarperCollins/ Joanna Cotler Books next month. Plus, the author is anxiously awaiting the birth of her first grandchild in October. Though Creech will tour for the two books, the October appearances are somewhat tentative at this point, depending on when her daughter goes into labor. "I do not want to miss this!" she says with determination.

THE WRITING LIFE

Creech was raised in South Euclid, a suburb of Cleveland, and then went to Hiram College in Ohio. She married and had two children, a girl and a boy, and the family relocated to Washington, D.C. There, Creech worked part time as an editorial assistant at the Congressional Quarterly (a position she found less than stimulating) while attending George Mason University for a master's degree in English and writing. It was in grad school, Creech says, that she discovered one needs to read in order to write well. After grad school, Creech says, she wanted to teach but realized she wasn't qualified, since she hadn't majored in education. However, she could teach in private schools that didn't have the same certification requirements.

A friend was working at the Tassis School outside of London, and told Creech about an open position for an English teacher. Newly divorced with two young children, Creech decided to take the job—a move she attributes not to bravery but to naivete. "I had no idea how hard it would be, in so many respects," she says. But her children attended the school free of charge and got to travel all over the world as part of the curriculum, "We had amazing opportunities, so it didn't matter so much that we had no money," she says. "One reason I took the job was that I could give the kids something that I couldn't have given them if I'd stayed in the States." She stayed in England until 1998, when she and Lyle (who were married in England in 1982) moved back to the States.

An ideal day for the author (which she admits doesn't always happen) has her in the office by about 8:30 in the morning. She reads and answers e-mail for an hour and then gets on with writing, which will last until about 12:30, and then it's time for lunch, a walk and maybe a nap. She spends the rest of the afternoon writing, until dinner, and then writes again after that. Some days, though, are given over to other obligations, like activities at her husband's school or bookstore appearances or school visits.

And then there's the matter of fan mail. Creech says that some weeks she can spend an entire day on mail; she reads and personally answers each letter she gets.

"People say I should have an assistant do that," she says, "but it's something I don't think I'd be comfortable handing over to someone else. I want to read the letters." With all the admirers Creech has, though, this is no small task. "I figured out one time how long it takes. It's something like nine minutes to read a letter, write a note, and address and stamp the envelope," she says.

Love That Dog, written in free verse, in a way brings Creech back to the beginning of her career as a writer. She started out writing poetry and had it published in journals from 1979 to 1985, before she turned to novels. "I always thought I'd be a poet if I were to be a writer, but then got into fiction," she says. "But I always wanted to go back and do something in that realm for children. And yet I didn't want to do a collection of poetry for children—there's not much poetry for children that I like; it's either too silly or too serious, so I didn't really set out to write this book as poetry."

The book's main character, Jack, and his story just emerged one day, she says. "I didn't know it was going to come out in the form it came out, but I was so excited when it did. It was the most fun book I have ever written, and it came out fully formed."

But the fact that the book is in some ways a tribute to Walter Dean Myers initially gave Creech some pause, and she put the manuscript in a drawer for several months. Though it took some convincing from Cotler, Creech eventually, reluctantly, sent her the manuscript. "Joanna called within 24 hours of my sending it to her and said, 'Love that book!'"

Myers's poem "Love That Boy" had been a favorite of Creech's since she first read it on a card given to her by a friend while she was living in England. The first stanza of the poem (which she thought was the whole thing) had been on her bulletin board for months before she wrote the book, and it remains there today.

At the moment, Creech says, her plan is to write one picture book for every four novels. The manuscript for *A Fine, Fine School* was done a couple of years ago, but Creech and Cotler were waiting for the right illustrator. "We knew it had to be someone who is funny and could draw funny pictures," Creech says. When Harry Bliss, a New Yorker cartoonist, came along, they both felt he was the one. The story, about an overzealous principal, is absolutely based on her husband, Creech says. "We would see Harry's sketches for the book and about fall off our chairs laughing," she recalls. "He really nailed it." . . .

Since meeting Cotler, six more books have come out: *Absolutely Normal Chaos* (1995), *Pleasing the Ghost* (1996), *Chasing Redbird* (1997), *Bloomability* (1998), *The Wanderer* (2000, for which Creech received a Newbery Honor) and her first picture book, *Fishing in the Air* (2000). "What happens with the Newbery," she says, "is a golden door opens. It creates an audience for you, because everyone hears that the book exists and it's gotten this sort of seal of approval." . . .

[A]bout a week after the Newbery announcement, she says, and she was "shattered for a year" with all of the attention. "I did nothing but answer the phone for six months," she gasps, "and people would call and ask if I could do IRA, ALA, BEA, and I would think, What are you talking about? What do those things mean? I had no clue. I had a cheat sheet for months."

Luckily, when the announcement came, Creech had almost finished writing her next book, *Chasing Redbird,* so she had time to write her Newbery acceptance speech, which alone took her about three months.

The phone rings and it is the headmaster. He has invited us to have lunch with him in the school's cafeteria. We walk on freshly mown lawn past a pond and fountain in the backyard, through a sporting field, past more red-brick buildings and find him waiting outside for us. All of the students have gone home for the summer, and the place feels on the verge of relaxing; the kitchen staff has scaled back the menu to cold cuts and salads, ice cream and cookies. Lyle's enthusiasm for his wife's success is evident; he says he, too, can't quite believe all that has happened in the past few years. Indeed, he has been along on the ride as well, attending a number of those once-mysterious conferences with his wife.

Over lunch Creech shares a bit about what she is working on now, a novel about a feisty Italian grandmother named Granny Torrelli and her daughter. "I think I'm moving to my mother's Italian side of the family now, for inspiration," she says. "The book seems to be about their relationship and the subtle effects they have on each other." Her next novel, *Ruby Holler,* about an eccentric older couple that meets up with a pair of twins, will be out next spring.

With apologies for the school lunch, Creech bids *PW* farewell and is off to a meeting about tomorrow's picnic, and after that she will get on the phone with Cotler for a three-hour editing session. Juggling comes easy to her, it seems. It is all just part of the journey.

Sharon Creech and *School Library Journal* (interview date September 2001)

SOURCE: Creech, Sharon, and *School Library Journal.* "Q & A: Sharon Creech." *School Library Journal* (September 2001): 21-6.

[*In the following interview, Creech discusses writing* Love That Dog.]

Sharon Creech's latest novel, ***Love That Dog*** 2001), tells the story of a young schoolboy named Jack, who gradually comes to love poetry, especially a poem called "Love That Boy" by Walter Dean Myers. We spoke with Creech, a Newbery Medalist, while she was on vacation in New York State.

[School Library Journal]: *Why did you decide to use Walter Dean Myers, an actual, living children's book writer, as a fictional character in* **Love That Dog***?*

[Creech]: Do you know K. T. Horning [a librarian at the Cooperative Children's Book Center]? . . . She has been an incredible source of inspiration for me in many different ways. . . . She sent me a card about three or four years ago. . . . On the card was the first stanza of this poem, "Love That Boy" by Walter Dean Myers. . . . You know how when you read certain things, some things will just grab you? This [one] did. There was just so much energy in that poem, the rhythm of the poem, and the love in the poem. So I cut out the poem and tacked it on my bulletin board, where it still is today. It's been there about four years, and I must glance at it probably a dozen times a day, because it's right there at eye level.

One day, when I looked at it about a year ago, I was thinking about that boy in the poem who is so loved. And I started to wonder, what would that boy love? Maybe he would love a pet, maybe a dog, maybe some teacher, and almost instantly . . . I saw this boy in my mind who was Jack. . . . I could see him sitting at his desk. And perhaps because it was a poem that inspired me to think of this, I knew he was going to respond to poetry in some way. And the story just came out very fast, very fluid.

When you finished the story, what most surprised you?

I was surprised, first of all, when Walter Dean Myers himself entered the story. As soon as he entered, I thought, "You know, I don't think I can do this. I don't think you can have a living person as a character in a story" [she laughs]—think of the legal impli-

cations. So I put the story away for several months. And my editor [Joanna Cotler] kept asking me, "What are you working on? And I said, "Well, I did this story, but there are a few reasons why I think I just can't send it to you." Finally, she convinced me to send it to her . . . and she instantly loved this story. She said, "Sharon, this is incredible." And I said, "But what about Walter Dean Myers in there?" I tried to get him out. I tried to put a fictional author in, but it left this big hole in the story, because [Walter Dean Myers's] poem is pivotal. It has to be that poem. [Walter Dean Myers] is the poet [Jack] would want to write to. That's the poet he would want to meet.

I also felt that I didn't want to use a fictional writer. I wanted to show how these real, living writers, . . . who are writing books today, are affecting kids. So [my editor] said, "Let's just send this to Walter and see what he thinks." And I said, "Good, because if he has any reservations whatsoever, we have no story and I'm putting it away." . . . So [Joanna] sent it to Walter—I had only met him once—and he read the book. . . . I think he was very, very shy about being the hero in this book, because he's—as I've since learned—a very shy and humble man. And yet he could easily see why his presence was needed in that book, why aesthetically it was important. He gave his blessing; he said, "Fine, go ahead." If he hadn't said that, there would be no book.

GENERAL COMMENTARY

Lyle D. Rigg (essay date July-August 1995)

SOURCE: Rigg, Lyle D. "Sharon Creech." *Horn Book Magazine* (July-August 1995): 426-29.

[*In the following essay, written by Creech's husband after she won the Newbery Medal for* Walk Two Moons, *Rigg shares recollections of Creech's writing career.*]

When Sharon and I met sixteen years ago, we were both transplanted Ohioans who had found our ways to Thorpe, Surrey, England. Sharon came to England via Washington, D.C., and I came via Boston and Brazil. I think it was a combination of our Buckeye roots and ice cubes that drew us together. We met on our first day in England, when Sharon borrowed some ice—that rare commodity in Europe—from me. Three years later, we celebrated our wedding with a party on a riverboat floating down the Thames.

If Sharon were not such a skilled writer, we probably would never have met. The headmaster of TASIS England American School who hired me as his assistant headmaster also hired Sharon in the same year to teach English and to write for school publications.

Before receiving an offer of employment, however, Sharon had to convince the headmaster that she, a single parent with two young children, could handle the considerable demands of teaching in an international day/boarding school in the suburbs of London. Although I have never read Sharon's letter to that headmaster, I have heard that it was a masterpiece of persuasion and was instrumental in her being hired.

As a teacher of American and British literature to American and international teenagers, Sharon has shared her love both of literature and of writing. She'd open up Chaucer's world in *The Canterbury Tales* and then head off to Canterbury with her students so that they could make the pilgrimage themselves. She'd offer *Hamlet,* and then off they would all go to Stratford-upon-Avon. Sharon would be the first to admit that *all* TASIS teachers do this and that this is what she loves about the school. "Get them out into the world," Sharon says, echoing the school's founder.

Not surprisingly (and just as the headmaster had warned), the demands of motherhood and a full-time teaching position left Sharon with little time for herself—let alone for her writing. Even less time was available after Sharon and I were married, and we moved to Switzerland, where I assumed the post of headmaster of The American School in Switzerland. Because of Sharon's support, hard work, many talents, and endless diplomacy, I have now "survived" thirteen years as a headmaster in Switzerland and England.

It is difficult to pinpoint exactly when it was that Sharon started to do less writing for the school and more for her own pleasure. She'd studied and written fiction and poetry in college and graduate school, but it wasn't until soon after our "chickabiddies," Rob and Karin, graduated from high school, and shortly after Sharon's father died, that she began to pour her energies into her own work.

I remember her writing poetry—lots of it—with such titles as "Strip Tease," "Victor, Victorious," "Sun on the Bottom," and "A Man on the Road." Much of her poetry shows the same combination of humor and poignancy that is also characteristic of her prose. I like this stanza, for instance, from "The Sun on the Bottom":

In first grade he brought home paintings
black paintings
with the sun on the bottom
and the tree upside down at the top.
"He's disturbed," the teacher said.
"Oh," my neighbor said, "maybe
there wasn't any yellow paint left
and maybe it's upside down."

One day in 1988, a phone call came "out of the blue," notifying Sharon that her poem "Cleansing" had been awarded the Billee Murray Denny Poetry Award (sponsored by Lincoln College in Illinois) for that year. I think that this recognition of Sharon's creative talents was a turning point for her.

Meanwhile—somehow—in the midst of teaching, attending and hosting social events, keeping a household functioning, and allowing me to transfer the frustrations of many of my days to her, Sharon had also completed her first two novels, *The Recital* and *Absolutely Normal Chaos* (her first children's book). Shortly thereafter, she also wrote *Nickel Malley* and a play, *The Centre of the Universe.* Soon after securing an agent in London, she placed all of her books with British publishers, and her play was performed off-off-Broadway in a festival of new plays.

Sharon wouldn't like for me to suggest that this was all as easy as it might sound. She'd also spent two years writing an eight-hundred-page manuscript which sits on her closet shelf, and she received her fair share of rejections along the way. But the next book was *Walk Two Moons,* and as soon as I read it, I knew it was special.

In the midst of all the excitement generated by the Newbery Medal, I have to confess that I also have a few regrets. I regret that I wasn't with Sharon when the phone call from the Newbery Committee came "out of the blue." I had just started a two-week trip to the States to interview prospective teachers for our school. I also regret that this added recognition of Sharon's talents as a writer probably means that she will not be able to return to the classroom on a regular basis. Our students will be losing a first-rate teacher.

There are also some things that I do not regret. I do not regret having some students now refer to me as "Mr. Creech" (Creech is Sharon's maiden name), and I do not regret attending functions where I am introduced as *just* the writer's husband. Sharon has certainly attended her share of functions where she has been referred to as *just* the headmaster's wife. I also do not regret attending events where Sharon has to give the after-dinner speech.

If I were asked to name the things that Sharon probably considers the "smoothbeautiful folds" in her world, I would have to list our children, all her Creech family (even if and when they create "absolutely normal chaos"), reading, trees, summers at our cottage on Chautauqua Lake, theater, sunshine, bookstores, canoeing, naps, fish sandwiches at Grace's Restaurant in Mayville, New York, and, of course, her writing.

Although the writing of *Walk Two Moons* has already made a remarkable difference in our lives, as far as I'm concerned the most important piece of writing that Sharon has ever produced is the letter that she wrote to the headmaster back in 1979 convincing him to offer her a job in England.

Sharon's a wonderful "gooseberry." I'm fortunate that she has added "huzza, huzza" to my vocabulary and to my life.

Let me end with an anecdote from this past February. As I've mentioned, I was in the States when Sharon received the Newbery news, and I was still there a week later, on Valentine's Day. This always happens. I'm *always* in the U.S. by myself on Valentine's Day. But a few weeks earlier, I'd bought Sharon's present and hidden it in my sock drawer. On February 14th, I called her and told her where to look. When she opened it, she cried like a baby (or so she tells me). Here's what I had chosen (*before* the Newbery news): a miniature enamelled egg, with the phases of the moon depicted on it, and around the top were these words—"May all your dreams come true."

Andrea Sachs (essay date 27 August 2001)

SOURCE: Sachs, Andrea. "A Writer Who's 13 at Heart: Sharon Creech Deals with Serious Themes in a Way that Delights Her Young Readers." *Time* 158, no. 8 (27 August 2001): F17.

[*In the following essay, Sachs analyzes some serious themes in several of Creech's books for children.*]

Sharon Creech has long been exquisitely attuned to the comings and goings of the junior set. But when she returned to the U.S. in 1998, after 18 years in Europe, the children's author was caught flatfooted. The life of the American child, she discovered, had lurched into a higher gear during her absence. "There were all these frazzled parents who spent their lives in car pools, getting their kids to ballet lessons and gymnastics," recalls Creech. "And I was thinking,

Goodness, don't the kids ever get time just to climb a tree or lie in the grass? There doesn't seem to be that kind of time for kids anymore."

That sentiment permeates *A Fine, Fine School,* her slyly subversive new book for children four to eight years old. A second new work has also just been published: *Love That Dog,* an innovative novel in free verse for kids ages 8 to 12. Creech has been dazzling critics since 1995, when *Walk Two Moons,* her first children's book to be published in the U.S., won the prestigious Newbery Medal, the Academy Award of children's books. "To win the Newbery Medal on your first book is an astounding feat," says Diane Roback, the children's editor at *Publishers Weekly.* "She is one of these writers whose subsequent books have very much lived up to the accolades she got on her first book."

Creech manages to write about serious themes in a way that engages kids and is never heavy-handed. *A Fine, Fine School* revolves around a principal who loves his work so much that he decides to keep his school open longer and longer, until the students are attending classes on weekends and holidays. It takes Tillie, a little girl, to make the principal come to his senses. "I haven't learned how to climb very high in my tree," she protests. "And I haven't learned how to sit in my tree for a whole hour." Creech's prose is accompanied by the witty illustrations of Harry Bliss, a New Yorker cover artist and cartoonist. On one page, a lunchroom wall is adorned with a sign that implores, WHY NOT STUDY WHILE YOU CHEW?

Love That Dog, for older children, is appealing to adult readers as well. Jack, a reluctant student, resists poetry assignments from his teacher, Miss Stretchberry. "I don't want to because boys don't write poetry," he pouts. But slowly Jack comes to savor poems, through the subtle persuasion of Miss Stretchberry, who is never heard from or described on the page. Through poetry, Jack comes to grips with the death of his beloved yellow dog, Sky: "He was such a funny dog / that dog Sky / that straggly furry smiling dog Sky." The book, deceptively simple and never preachy, is studded with work by acclaimed poets such as Robert Frost, William Carlos Williams and Walter Dean Myers.

Creech, 56, became a children's writer by accident. She grew up in a suburb of Cleveland, Ohio, in a family with four siblings and "a lot of chaos," says Creech. In 1979, newly divorced with two young children and armed with a master's degree in English, she moved to Thorpe, England, to teach literature at a boarding school. It was there that she met and married her present husband, who was the headmaster. Creech set out to become an adult author, but when she submitted **Absolutely Normal Chaos** in 1990 (a story based on her childhood), her agent told her it would be more appropriate as a children's book. To her surprise, a publisher bought the book and asked for another children's book. "I thought I'd better go find out what a children's book was," says Creech.

Winning the Newbery Medal was a dizzying experience, she says. "I was sort of pushed through this very beautiful golden door into this world of children's literature." The Newbery carries no cash award, but money comes rolling in because the medal boosts sales to libraries and schools. Creech was bombarded with phone calls, requests for interviews and invitations to conferences and bookstore events. "Your life is just not your own for the first year afterward," says Creech. Continuing as a teacher was out of the question. "It just consumed me."

Now Creech takes her best-seller status in stride. She lives near Princeton, N.J., with her husband, who is now headmaster of the Pennington School—and was the model for the principal in **A Fine, Fine School.** "He's a very enthusiastic headmaster, in that he's such an advocate for the school and the students and the teachers," says Creech. "He's like a cheerleader for the school. He's just that kind of personality." The two expect to become grandparents for the first time in October.

Creech is not a tortured writer. "I seem to somehow be able to tap into my own 13-year-old self very easily," she says. "If you came up and tapped me on the shoulder when I was in one of my writing trances, I suppose I would maybe talk like a seventh-grader." It's a talent that delights her ever increasing following.

Stephenie Yearwood (essay date spring-summer 2002)

SOURCE: Yearwood, Stephenie. "Popular Postmodernism for Young Adult Readers: *Walk Two Moons, Holes,* and *Monster.*" *ALAN Review* 29, no. 3 (spring-summer 2002): 50-3.

[*In the following essay, Yearwood traces the evolution of Young Adult literature into postmodernism using Creech's* Walk Two Moons, *Louis Sachar's* Holes, *and Walter Dean Myers'* Monster *as examples.*]

One of the ongoing debates in children's and young adult literature recently has been over the issue of whether, and how, and to what extent the literature, broadly defined, is becoming "postmodern." In *The Pleasures of Children's Literature,* Perry Nodelman (1996) describes children's literature as being (among other qualities) simple, action-oriented, and didactic (190). Swedish critic Maria Nikolajeva argues, in *Children's Literature Comes of Age: Toward a New Aesthetic* (1996) argues, to the contrary, stating that children's literature (which, for her, includes YA literature) was showing more and more postmodern qualities. She holds that although "genre" books still dominate the field, more and more "'auteur' books, literary, sophisticated, and complex" have been appearing (207). In 1998, Nikolajeva replied specifically to Nodelman by arguing that "an ever-growing segment of contemporary children's literature is transgressing its own boundaries, coming closer to mainstream literature, and exhibiting the most prominent features of postmodernism, such as genre eclecticism, disintegration of traditional narrative structures, polyphony, intersubjectivity and metafiction" (Nikolajeva, "Exit" 222). As I examine these arguments from the point of view of 2002, it seems to me that if we focus exclusively on young adult literature, we will find that one part of the larger world of "children's literature" has now fully embraced the postmodern mode. To put it a bit differently, whereas the distinctively postmodern YA works have, until recently, been "fringe" or "auteur" books, beloved of critics, they have not been popular favorites. Now they are.

Three recent YA books that are very popular provide examples of works that fearlessly use postmodernist ideas and techniques: Sharon Creech's **Walk Two Moons,** Louis Sachar's *Holes,* and Walter Dean Myers' *Monster.* The first two are well-known Newbery Award winners of 1995 and 1998 respectively, and the third is a 1999 winner of the ALA Michael Printz Award, the Coretta Scott King Award, and a finalist for the National Book Award. Sales figures for these books indicate that they clearly are mainstream reading. Their literary qualities move them out of the historical tradition of simplicity and didactic morality which Nodelman describes, and into the mode which Nikolajeva defines as postmodern. What's more, there are many others like them. The tide has turned, and the turn of this century also marks a turning point for YA literature.

Nikolajeva's definition of postmodernism is comprehensive and functional; however, I will refine and focus it somewhat in order to clarify the essential qualities of these three novels and to highlight some of the striking similarities between them. First, I borrow Brian McHale's proposition in *Postmodernist Fiction* (1987) that, whereas the central question in modernist fiction is epistemological, postmodernist fiction is focused on ontological questions (9). Essential questions of being, McHale says, expand to include other ontological queries: "What world is this? What is to be done in it? Which of my selves is to do it?" (11). From Linda Hutcheon, I borrow the "important postmodern concept of the 'presence of the past'." Hutcheon explains the postmodernist use of, and obsession with, history as being "not a nostalgic return" but "a critical revisiting, an ironic dialogue" (4). Finally, from the Bakhtinian tradition I take the idea of dialogics or intertextuality as central to postmodern fiction—the notion that texts or narratives set up dialogues with other texts, either other previously-written literary texts or other stories, creating new stories in the interstices and frictions and contradictions of various other stories. These three YA novels are all marked by an ontologically-impelled querying of the past within a densely intertextual narrative structure. To various degrees, they all center around gaps (vacancies, missing pieces, unknowns, uncertainties, or holes) and the questions (often unanswered questions) generated by those missing pieces. All are centrally concerned with history (either personal or political), what it is, understanding it, remaking it, and the uncertain relationship between past and present. Finally, all of them foreground issues of intertextuality or internarrativity. They create realms of intertextual reference where multiple stories affect/reflect/interact as the past is questioned, prodded, retold, recovered, or remade. Interestingly, this postmodern "recipe" for YA literature turns out to be extraordinarily well-suited to raising and exploring some of the oldest themes of the genre: identity, self-fashioning, and self-knowledge.

Walk Two Moons

Creech's story is marked strongly from the outset by its missing piece: Salamanca Tree Hiddle's mother. It quickly becomes obvious that the mystery in the novel is more than the epistemological issue of figuring out what happened to her. As we collect Sal's clues, we come to realize that even though we don't know yet what happened to Sal's mother, our narrator Sal surely must know. But in her present state of being, she cannot face what she knows. Sal's ontological essence, her very being, is in question as she pieces together for us and for herself a picture of the past and a self which can accept that picture. We are confused, and so is Sal. Although Sal's narration of

Phoebe's story engages us, and the rambunctious grandparents add a wonderful dimension to the tale, the central story here is Sal's—she gropes to answer her ontological question of how she can continue existence in a world where her mother is dead.

Creech's narrative technique highlights the uncertain and quirky relationship between past and present through the story. The entire story of Phoebe is told by Sal to her grandparents as they travel west to see her mother. The earlier story of Sal's life with her mother and father before she met Phoebe is recounted in an even more fragmented and allusive way as events in Phoebe's tale trigger memories in Sal. It is as though the deep turmoil of that earlier history causes it to break through, push up and intrude into Phoebe's tale. Sal's own history/mystery (and that of her mother) is lost to her conscious recollection and only reassembled as it is reexperienced vicariously through Phoebe, then as that story is retold to her grandparents. Sal knows but does not know this history, and she and Phoebe both try out alternative historical hypotheses about their missing mothers. Has Phoebe's mother been kidnapped by the lunatic? Is she in Paris? Hidden in a well? Murdered by Mrs. Cadaver? Is Sal's mother alive and well and waiting for Sal in Idaho? Is she alive but disabled? Is she coming home? Is she dead? Sal's past is reconsidered, remade and retold in multiple layers here; and it can emerge fully only when she has successfully constructed a new identity for herself—an identity which can face the history.

Finally, this story is made of stories, by stories, and in between stories. Sal tells us initially that, "The story of Phoebe was like the plaster wall in our old house in Bybanks, Kentucky" (3). That wall is the one where her father chipped and chipped away at the plaster to find an old brick fireplace underneath. Sal is aware that "beneath Phoebe's story was another one. Mine" (3). But the internarrative connections in the story are even more complex than that. Other threads of embedded narrative serve as reflecting surfaces in which Sal reads her own, or a difference from her own. There is the mini-tale of Ben's mother in a mental hospital, a woman who reminds Sal strongly of her own mother (370). There is the Blackfoot myth of Napi who created men and women; it reminds her that "People die" (150). The story of Mrs. Cadaver, whose husband was killed and mother blinded in the same car accident, makes Sal think, "It was as though I was walking in her moccasins. That's how much my heart was beating and my own hands sweating" (220). And the enigmatic "messages" which appear on slips of paper at Phoebe's front door work their way into her very being. "All those messages had invaded my brain and affected the way I looked at things" (221). In the intertextual spaces and intersections and frictions between these stories, Sal resurrects her past and simultaneously constructs herself as a different being.

HOLES

Louis Sachar's *Holes* uses the elements of this recipe differently. This story is based not on complex narrative technique, but on vacancy and missing pieces, and on a magically realistic reenactment of history which focuses on the intersecting stories of three different sets of characters generations apart. Ontological issues of being and nothingness interplay through this story in a series of negative/positive afterimages. Stanley Yelnats (whose name is a self-reflective palindrome) is at Camp Green Lake (which is not a lake, but a desert where a lake used to be) because some famous sneakers go missing; his chief occupation there is to dig holes, and he attributes it all to something his mythical grandfather *failed* to do. Stanley himself is nearly a missing person. He is given the nonsense nickname "Caveman," as though he were himself a vacancy, and his best friend is nicknamed Zero.

The setting raises other ontological questions such as "What world *are* we in?" Initially, the idea of a juvenile detention camp set in a desert ringed by mountains seems realistic enough, until we learn about the yellow-spotted lizards whose bite is slow and always lethal. Add to that the presence of a masochistic female camp warden who wears "black cowboy boots [. . .] studded with turquoise stones" (66) and who delights in concocting her own nail polish using rattlesnake venom so that "it's only toxic while it's wet" (90), and we have bypassed fantasy altogether and edged out into the surreal.

Finally, the ontological stakes are raised even higher by the magical realism of the plot with its three intertwined stories. Stanley's often-retold family myth is that his great-great-grandfather was perpetually in the wrong place at the wrong time because he stole a pig from a one-legged Gypsy and was cursed (8). But it turns out that other family stories are just as relevant. It seems that after a Madame Zeroni helped this great-great- grandfather, he failed to honor his promise to carry her up a mountain to a place where a stream ran uphill to let her drink from it (28). Another important story is about the next Yelnats generation and his great-grandfather's encounter with

Kissin' Kate Barlow. One hundred and ten years ago, we learn, the kind schoolteacher Kate Barlow of Green Lake (when it really WAS a Green Lake) encountered racism and the murder of her lover and transformed herself into the outlaw Kissin' Kate Barlow. We learn that the lake dried up as punishment for the transgressions of the community. We also learn that Stanley's great-grandfather was robbed by Kissin' Kate, left for dead in the desert, but managed to survive, saying only that he had "found refuge on God's thumb" (93). Another interwoven story is Stanley's own tale of being hit on the head with a pair of stolen sneakers and sent off to reform camp.

These related narratives coalesce into a truly magical and surreal story at the conclusion to *Holes*. Stanley has been trying to help out his fellow inmate Zero by teaching him to read, and after Zero escapes into the desert (with no water) Stanley decides to follow him. They survive by accidentally finding, in the midst of the dry lakebed, the skeleton of the boat in which Kate Barlow and her lover tried to escape, then drinking the 110-year old spiced peaches which were in the boat when it sank. Stanley carries the sick Zero (whose real name we learn is Hector Zeroni) out of the desert and up to the top of a strange-shaped mountain where they find a most unlikely water hole and the field of onions Kate's lover tended. As they escape, Zero explains that he is the one who stole the sneakers Stanley was caught and convicted for stealing. Along the way, Stanley realizes that they are on "God's thumb" where his great-grandfather before him escaped and survived. It becomes clear to all that Stanley has satisfied his great-great-grandfather's debt to the Zeroni family, re-enacted his great-grandfather's survival, and solved the mystery of who stole those sneakers. The runaway surrealism is capped when the two boys return to camp, are cornered by yellow-spotted lizards, find that the lizards don't bite people who have been eating onions for a week, locate the lost treasure of Kissin' Kate, prove their innocence, and expose the camp as a fraud.

In the introduction to *Magical Realism: Theory, History, Community* (1995), Lois Parkinson Zamora and Wendy Faris point out that magical realism "creates space for the interactions of diversity. In magical realist texts, ontological disruption serves the purpose of political and cultural disruption: magic is often given as a cultural corrective, requiring readers to scrutinize accepted realistic conventions" (3). Indeed, that is precisely what happens here as the plot queries whether it takes magical intervention from four generations back to deal with the problems of children growing up in poverty and with an abusive system of "justice." The marvelously mythical tying up of all these intertextual loose ends creates for Stanley what he has never had before, an identity of himself as himself.

MONSTER

Myers' *Monster* is a book of a different flavor—grim, gritty and realistic—without the comic elements or easy resolutions of the others. Yet even in this form we find the postmodern concerns and questions about being, about understanding the past, and about intersecting texts and versions of that past. This story focuses even more than the others on the question of how an identity is made and whether a writer can "rewrite the text," or in other words, shape the past into a coherent story and invent himself along the way.

The central question of this book at first seems more epistemological than ontological, for initially the story focuses on the uncertain, ambiguous, contradictory issue of what Steve Harmon actually DID in connection to the robbery/murder for which he is being tried. The entire story circles and recircles around that question, presenting us contradictory evidence from witnesses, from Steve himself on the stand, and from Steve's notes. The irresolvable epistemological contradictions are heightened into a philosophical perplex by the structural design of the book. The text we read is actually a film script written by Steve Harmon about his trial, framed and accompanied by Steve's notes which appear to be "handwritten," by photographs, and by occasional "handwritten" marginalia commenting on both. Even the contradictory testimony comes to us only through Steve's film script. An unreliable narrator? Yes, and unreliably unreliable, since he reflects his own contradictions, too.

All the same, ultimately the ontological questions predominate; all of this uncertainty as to what we know and what Steve did becomes the means of raising the question of how he can continue to exist, whether he will continue to be at all, and who he is. "When I look into the [mirror] I see a face looking back at me but I don't recognize it. It doesn't look like me" (1). "I think to get used to this I will have to give up what I think is real and take up something else" (3). "They take away your shoelaces and your belt so you can't kill yourself no matter how bad it is" (59). "If I got out after 20 years, I'd be 36. Maybe I wouldn't live that long. Maybe I would kill myself so I wouldn't have to live that long in here" (144).

"[My attorney] thinks I am guilty. I know she thinks I am guilty" (138). "What did I do?" (140). "I knew [Mama] felt that I didn't do anything wrong. It was me who wasn't sure. It was me who lay on the cot wondering if I was fooling myself" (148).

Steve's only answer to this ontological maze is his film, his act of self-fashioning a being and identity. It includes flashbacks to scenes where he meets other participants in the robbery, a fantasy/fear sequence in which he is being put to death, and action from the trial. As with *Holes,* we are confronted with the question of what world we are in. The fact/fiction line is just as blurred as Steve's face in the photo on page 188.

The story steadfastly refuses to resolve either the epistemological or the ontological issues; hence its contradictory and confusing accounts of the past. Through varying accounts, we view and review the scene of the robbery/murder from a different point of view each time. Witness Lorelle Henry testifies she did not see him in the drugstore, and he testifies that he never entered the drugstore that day. But in his notes he writes, "I walked into a drugstore to look for some mints, and then I walked out" (140). And on page 220, we find two photos of Steve which appear to have been taken by a security camera in a store, with the "handwritten" marginalia "What was I doing?" and "What was I thinking." Are these actual evidence in the trial or shots he envisions as part of his film? Steve Harmon re-fashions the past, again blurring the fact/fiction line.

The intertextual interaction in this novel is a significant element in its complex relationship to the past. The graphic layout of the novel provides us layer upon layer of "text," each with its own version of the past. Some of the text is linguistic, some of it graphic: scene descriptions, descriptions of camera shots, dialogue spoken by characters, Steve's notes, photos and marginalia. Differentiated by typestyles and layout, each of these elements interacts with, confounds, comments on, and clarifies the others.

But like the other novels, these postmodernist elements conspire to create a remarkable exploration of that most central young adult issue: identity. Throughout, Steve struggles with how others see him and how he sees himself. Is he the "monster" whom the prosecutor sees? The suspicious and unknown person his father sees? The innocent boy his mother sees? The guilty boy his attorney sees? Or the "good person" he wants to see in himself? He cannot answer;

thus even at the conclusion of the story, five months after he is acquitted, the ontological question is still driving Steve, and he is still filming:

> I have been taking movies of myself. In the movies, I talk and tell the camera who I am, what I think I am about. Sometimes I set the camera up outside and walk up to it from different angles.
>
> Sometimes I set the camera up in front of a mirror and film myself as a reflection. I wear different clothes and try to change my voice[. . .]I want to know who I am. I want to know the road to panic that I took. I want to look at myself a thousand times to look for one true image. When Miss O'Brien looked at me, after we had won the case, what did she see that caused her to turn away? What did she see?

> *(Monster, 281)*

No answers, no easy resolutions, no insight. Just a central ontological question, obsession and uncertainty about the past, and archaeological layering of text upon text.

Certainly there is room for legitimate debate whether this three-part "recipe" of ontological perspective, historical interrogation, and intertextual multilogue is an adequate definition of the atmospheric and omnipresent concept of "postmodernism" in young adult literature. But these elements highlight issues raised in these three novels and in many others which could have been selected: Creech's *The Wanderer,* Pullman's *His Dark Materials* trilogy, Paterson's *Gathering Blue.* I believe that a broader definition of postmodernism would only emphasize further the extent to which the "cultural dominant" has changed (McHale 9). Young adult works in the postmodern mode may not necessarily predominate, but they are now mainstream and readily accepted by readers.

Nor should this be any surprise since one of the common uses of the term "postmodern" is simply as a descriptive term for contemporary culture. Zipes (2001)voices reservations about how distanced criticism of children's and YA literature has become from the realities of the lives of contemporary young readers (Zipes 37). Nevertheless, it seems to me that in this case, the qualities of these three works that make them critically "postmodern" are exactly the qualities which reflect current anxieties, obsessions, and social realities. Sal's tenuous grip on an unbearable reality of loss, Stanley's near evaporation into a bizarre and corrupt juvenile justice system, and Steve Harmon's radical self-fashioning in the face of society's expectations of young black men: these are themes which invite both postmodern literary treatment and popularity with young readers in our postmodern culture.

Works Cited

Creech, Sharon. *Walk Two Moons.* New York: Harper Trophy, 1994.

Hutcheon, Linda. *A Poetics of Postmodernism: History, Theory, Fiction.* New York and London: Routledge, 1988.

Nikolajeva, Maria. *Children's Literature Comes of Age: Toward a New Aesthetic.* New York and London: Garland, 1996.

Nikolajeva, Maria. "Exit Children's Literature?" *The Lion and the Unicorn* 22 (1998): 221-236.

Nodelman, Perry. *The Pleasures of Children's Literature.* White Plains, N.Y.: Longman, 1992.

McHale, Brian. *Postmodernist Fiction.* New York and London: Methuen, 1987.

Pullman, Philip. *The Golden Compass.* New York: Alfred A. Knopf, 1995.

Sachar, Louis. *Holes.* New York: Farrar, Straus and Giroux, 1998.

Zamora, Lois Parkinson and Wendy B. Faris. *Magical Realism: Theory, History, Community.* Durham N.C. and London: Duke University Press, 1995.

Zipes, Jack. "Do You Know What We are Doing to Your Books?" in *Sticks and Stones: the Troublesome Success of Children's Literature from Slovenly Peter to Harry Potter.* New York and London: Routledge, 2001.

TITLE COMMENTARY

ABSOLUTELY NORMAL CHAOS (1990)

Publishers Weekly (review date 14 August 1995)

SOURCE: *Publishers Weekly* 242, no. 33 (14 August 1995): 85.

In what by now must be a subgenre in YA fiction—the novel cast as a journal written for an English assignment—Newbery Medalist Creech (*Walk Two Moons*) spins an affable if formulaic tale about one pivotal summer [in *Absolutely Normal Chaos*]. Narrator Mary Lou, 13, the second of the five Finney children, is quite put out when she has to play maid for her uncommunicative cousin Carl Ray, 17, who comes to stay while he looks for a job. He gets one, to Mary Lou's surprise, at the hardware store owned by their new neighbor Mr. Furtz, who shortly afterward dies of a heart attack. Not only does Carl Ray remain in his new job, but an anonymous benefactor leaves him money—just like in *Great Expectations,* as Mary Lou points out. There the resemblance to Dickens ends: the astute reader will early on figure out the mystery behind Carl Ray's inheritance. Mary Lou is also slow to pick up clues about why her cute classmate Alex is always hanging around. Despite the occasionally creaky plot, Mary Lou's bouncy entries are still a lot of fun. Readers will enjoy her wry commentary on *The Odyssey* (on the school reading list), and girls especially will identify with Mary Lou's disgust at the giddy behavior of boy-crazy best friend Beth Ann and her own giggly rhapsodies on her first romance ("I am sooooo happeeeeee I can hardly stand it!"). *Ages 10-14.*

Frances Bradburn (review date 1 October 1995)

SOURCE: Bradburn, Frances. *Booklist* 92, no. 3 (1 October 1995): 313.

Gr 5-8. Mary Lou Finney is an absolutely normal 13-year-old living in a delightfully normal—albeit rather large—family during an absurdly normal summer of growing up [in *Absolutely Normal Chaos*]. The assignment to keep a journal during this summer vacation allows Mary Lou the privilege of documenting for other absolutely normal middle-graders the roller coaster process of adolescence—the evolution of friendships, the first kiss, even the gradual understanding and appreciation of people different from themselves. Creech's easy style and skill at writing dialogue are evident throughout. Some of the journal entries concerning Mary Lou's interpretation of her summer reading assignment, *The Odyssey,* may be a stretch for many in the targeted age group, but the chaotic adolescent emotions emanating from each entry are real. *Absolutely Normal Chaos* is absolutely normal 13-year-old angst and will probably have a much wider readership than *Walk Two Moons* (1994).

Mary Hedge (review date June 1996)

SOURCE: Hedge, Mary. *Voice of Youth Advocates* 19, no. 2 (June 1996): 94.

This [*Absolutely Normal Chaos*] is Mary Lou Finney's journal from the summer she was thirteen. The first surprise of the summer is that Mary Lou's seventeen-year-old cousin Carl Ray comes from West Virginia to live with her family, which also includes her parents, an older sister and three younger brothers, in Ohio. At first it seems like Carl Ray does nothing but eat; he barely talks and never does any chores. But he finally lands a job in their next door neighbor's hardware store. Then after that neighbor dies, Carl Ray is informed by a lawyer that he has been given some money by an anonymous person. Mary Lou falls in love with Alex, a classmate who gives her her first kiss, and her best friend Beth Ann dates Carl Ray. Mary Lou reads *The Odyssey* which is on a school reading list and learns that Carl Ray knows the book well. After Carl Ray buys a car, Mary Lou is assigned to ride home with him so he can inform his parents of his good fortune. It turns out that Carl Ray had really come to Mary Lou's town to find his real father who was the next door neighbor who died. The book ends with Carl Ray recuperating from a car accident and Mary Lou's decision that he wasn't so bad after all.

The story has everything a young adult wants in a book, suspense, humor, romance and relationships with family and friends. Mary Lou is easy to like and views almost every event in a humorous way. The book is hard to put down because of her fresh and humorous viewpoints and because the reader will try to figure out Carl Ray's actions and parenthood. How Mary Lou deals with death and homesickness and tolerates events beyond her control will benefit readers. The only perturbing thing about the book is the front cover because the identities of the seven kids pictured are not all clear. The book was originally published in 1990 in Great Britain. The author also wrote *Walk Two Moons* which won the 1995 Newbery Medal.

📖 *WALK TWO MOONS* (1994)

Naomi Lewis (review date 24 July 1994)

SOURCE: Lewis, Naomi. "Angst, Adventure and Bad Teen Dreams." *Observer* no. 10580 (24 July 1994): 18.

Walk Two Moons, by Sharon Creech, is a really satisfying book—funny, poignant, cunning in the unravelling of its mysteries. No point in cheating by looking at the end: you must meet it when it comes. It's worth the journey.

Sal (Salamanca), 13, is beset by questions. Why did her mother go? Why did she suddenly stop writing? Why has Dad moved house to this new dull place with—so it seems—such sinister neighbours? Or does that last idea come from manic school-friend Phoebe?

On a week-long 2,000-mile drive to Lewiston, Idaho, (why? you'll know in time) Sal tells them Phoebe's story—but under it is her own. Characters abound: you won't forget, say, the crazy, wonderful schoolmaster who gives them a 15-second exercise: 'Just draw—don't think—your soul'. A super read.

Publishers Weekly (review date 8 December 1997)

SOURCE: *Publishers Weekly* 244, no. 50 (8 December 1997): 29.

Thirteen-year-old Salamanca Tree Hiddle—Sal for short—has had a difficult time ever since her mother walked out on the family a year ago [in **Walk Two Moons**]. Things have been equally tough on her father, who has rented out their Kentucky farm and moved himself and Sal to Euclid, Ohio. But it's not until Sal meets Phoebe Winterbottom, a girl with a tangled family story of her own, that Sal begins to sort out her confused feelings. She then embarks on an enlightening cross-country road trip with her eccentric grandparents to find—and make peace with—her mother. Sal's discoveries about her family and herself and a number of heart-wrenching surprise plot twists will not soon be forgotten by listeners. Creech's tightly woven, multilayered novel offers [Kate] Harper a broad stage on which to perform her characterizations. Shading her voice with equal parts youthful enthusiasm, teenage rebellion and deeply felt sentiment, Harper deftly portrays young protagonists Sal and Phoebe. She seems as much at ease taking on the slow Kentucky drawl and colorful countrified slang ("my gooseberry" and "chickabiddy") of Gramps and Gram Hiddle as the mournful tone of Sal's father. Her assured handling of the text leads listeners through a most satisfying journey. *Ages 9-Up.*

Kristi Beavin (review date May-June 1998)

SOURCE: Beavin, Kristi. *Horn Book Magazine* 74, no. 3 (May-June 1998): 371.

In outline, [**Walk Two Moons**] is the saddest of stories: a child on a quest that is both unrealistic and impossible—to bring home her dead mother and somehow reclaim the life she has lost. But it is also a laugh-out-loud portrait of a pair of eccentric grandparents whom "trouble just naturally followed . . . like a filly trailing behind a mare." As Kate Harper flawlessly narrates every splendid syllable, all of the characters are released from the printed page to enter the living landscape of the listener. Here is Sal: shy, solemn, sad, scornful, full of the exasperation and exultation of living in a thirteen-year-old body. Here is Gramps, raspy and querulous, lost in a world that relies on maps, but wise in the ways of the heart. Here is Gram, her voice grown whispery, but forever rejoicing in the newness of living. If this is not the perfect recording, it's about as close as it gets.

PLEASING THE GHOST (1996)

Publishers Weekly (review date 22 July 1996)

SOURCE: *Publishers Weekly* 243, no. 30 (22 July 1996): 242.

This simultaneously sensitive and ridiculous romp [**Pleasing the Ghost**] by a Newbery-winning author (**Walk Two Moons**) begins as spunky nine-year-old Dennis explains that ghosts keep visiting him in his bedroom—"a constant parade of ghosts, but never the one I really want." Pining for his late father, Dennis instead finds himself host to a motley crew of spirits, in particular his Uncle Arvie. Arvie wants Dennis to help his widow, Aunt Julia, discover the gifts and money he has left hidden for her in his house. Unfortunately, a stroke he suffered before his death prevents him from finding the appropriate vocabulary to convey his meaning. Kids will enjoy deciphering Arvie's speech: "Good carpet, Dinosaur!" translates as "Good morning, Dennis!"; Aunt Julia's oily suitor and Billy, the class bully, are "beany boogers." Dennis's much-missed father—his "pepperoni"—never does appear, but the boy finds common ground and a possible friendship with Billy, also fatherless. Arvie's earnest affection for Julia and Dennis makes him a role model as well as a clown, and Creech's attention to nuances of feeling grounds this light tale in emotional truth. *Ages 8-12.*

Children's Review Book Service (review date September 1996)

SOURCE: *Children's Review Book Service* 25, no. 1 (September 1996): 10-11.

Ages 8-12. Dennis [in **Pleasing the Ghost**] is a pretty normal nine-year-old boy, except that he has been visited by ghosts of departed family and friends. Helping uncle Arvie settle some unfinished business is difficult because Uncle Arvie speaks using unusual words (the result of a stroke). When the adventure ends, Dennis has made his aunt happy, befriended his class bully and held on to his wish that his deceased father would come to him. Black-and-white illustrations accompany each of the 14 chapters. An unusual, fast moving, fun chapter book that children will enjoy.

Michael Cart (review date 1 September 1996)

SOURCE: Cart, Michael. *Booklist* 93, no. 1 (1 September 1996): 125.

Gr 3-6. According to Dennis [in *Pleasing the Ghost*], he's "your ordinary, basic nine-year-old boy." With one exception: he's visited by ghosts, the first one arriving a month after his father's death. Most of them blow in on "a whisper of wind" and are gone as quickly but not Uncle Arvie, who arrives asking for three favors. There's a problem, however: before his death, the man suffered a stroke that scrambled his speech, and Dennis can't always decipher his requests. What, for example, does "Fraggle pin Heartfoot a wig pasta" mean? A further complication: a new boy at school refuses to believe Dennis can see ghosts, yet he is the only other one who can actually see the invisible Uncle Arvie. Newbery medalist Creech has written a slight but engaging story that manages to deal lightheartedly with emotional loss by offering her readers the enduring promise of hope.

Mary Jo Drungil (review date November 1996)

SOURCE: Drungil, Mary Jo. *School Library Journal* 42, no. 11 (November 1996): 104.

Gr 3-5— A disappointing tale [*Pleasing the Ghost*] about a boy led on a treasure hunt by a ghost. Dennis, nine, has received a parade of spectral visitors since his father's death, though none, alas, is the one he wishes to see. Occasionally, the boy recognizes deceased family members, including his late Uncle Arvie, who wishes to pass on messages to his widow, Julia. Because Arvie's speech was garbled in life by a severe stroke, helping him communicate is no easy task for Dennis. Ultimately, however, Arvie leads him to a small fortune, which will ensure Julia's lifelong comfort. In a subplot, Dennis proves to a disbelieving classmate that his ability to see ghosts is real. This story falls short on several fronts. Character development is particularly ineffective. Dennis, for example, is so easily absorbed in Arvie's affairs that it is difficult, if not impossible, to perceive him as a boy grieving for his father. While linguistic problems are caused by strokes, Arvie's nonsense syllables

seem exaggerated to the point of caricature, thus creating an offensive effect. Billy, Dennis's classmate who also lost his father, thinks Dennis is making fun of him with his talk of ghosts, and in retaliation, smashes several windows in his home. In a tale obviously meant to be lighthearted, Billy's anger seems extreme and inappropriate. The ending reflects Dennis's hopes of someday seeing his father's ghost, but by this point, readers may not care enough about him to wonder whether or not it ever happens.

CHASING REDBIRD (1997)

Publishers Weekly (review date 20 January 1997)

SOURCE: *Publishers Weekly* 244, no. 3 (20 January 1997): 403.

Returning to Bybanks, Ky., the setting of her Newbery-winning *Walk Two Moons,* Creech weaves an affecting tale of love and loss [in *Chasing Redbird*]. Zinnia Taylor, the third of seven children, is shaken by her aunt's recent death; although the doctor attributed it to diabetes, the 13-year-old feels sure that a prank she pulled was the real cause. When Zinny discovers a trail at the edge of her parents' farm, she learns of its history as a 20-mile path once trodden by Indians and trappers. She spends weeks clearing weeds and digging up markers; during the course of her solitary endeavors, which are periodically interrupted by Jake Boone's attempts at wooing, Zinny not only learns of her ancestors' hardships but slowly resolves her internal conflicts. Creech's language is as fresh as the natural wonders Zinny encounters in the woods: an older sister has a temper "hotter than a boiled owl"; zinnias, which Zinny plants to commemorate her role in clearing the historic path, "are like bright sentries marching along the trail" This sturdy but sensitive tale is Creech's best yet. *Ages 8-12.*

Ethel L. Heins (review date May-June 1997)

SOURCE: Heins, Ethel L. *Horn Book Magazine* 73, no. 3 (May-June 1997): 316-17.

Setting the story in Bybanks, Kentucky, where *Walk Two Moons* begins and ends, Sharon Creech has written a striking novel [*Chasing Redbird*], notable for its emotional honesty. Thirteen-year-old Zinny is usually submerged into silence, overwhelmed by a large and boisterous family. Moreover, she has always been deeply attached to her quiet, idiosyncratic relatives next door; but now Zinny has only her beloved elderly Uncle Nate, for her cousin Rose, who was exactly Zinny's age, died at the age of four, and redhaired Aunt Jessie—called Redbird by her husband—has suddenly sickened and died, stunning the family. "It was as if we'd all been slapped, hard, by a giant hand swooping down from the sky." Griefstricken, Uncle Nate grows more and more eccentric, hunting for his Redbird all over the countryside. Then Zinny discovers an overgrown trail starting at their family farm and finds it plainly marked on an old map in the local museum. Her fascination with the discovery soon becomes an obsession. She feels compelled to take on the huge job of clearing the debris from the twenty-mile trail; and in the course of her solitary work, she disentangles some of the family's convoluted mysteries. Meanwhile, Jake, a bumptious, good-looking teenager, vehemently—if obliquely—pursues Zinny, who is convinced that his interest really lies in her boy-crazy older sister. With frequent flashbacks, the first-person narration makes clear the complexities of the story and the interrelationships among the characters, while the unsolved puzzles lead the reader on to the revelations at the end. Despite two deaths and the threat of a third one, the story is neither morbid nor depressing, and there is humor throughout, especially when the confusion of events produces a zany comedy of errors. The writing is laced with figurative language and folksy comments that intensify both atmosphere and emotion: "My thoughts were jumping around like peas on a hot shovel" or "I might as well have been a pig in a dog race." In her Newbery Medal acceptance speech the author spoke of her predilection for mystery and for metaphorical journeys; she has worked both into the novel and, in addition, once again bridges the gap between the generations and binds them together.

Reading Teacher (review date September 1998)

SOURCE: *Reading Teacher* 52, no. 1 (September 1998): 65.

Chasing Redbird, by Sharon Creech, is really an unwitting search by 13-year-old Zinny Taylor to find out who she is and why she doesn't feel connected with her large, rambunctious family. The plot begins when Zinny discovers an overgrown mysterious trail near her family's farm in Bybanks, Kentucky. After some research, she decides to clear and restore its entire 20-mile length, a process that will provide her with time to be alone. This straightforward endeavor, however, soon meets with unforeseen complications

to her life and secrets about her family. In the end, all the tangled strands unravel as Zinny discovers answers to questions she didn't even know she had. Although there is a peripheral connection to Creech's earlier Newbery Medal-winning *Walk Two Moons* (1994), this contemporary realistic novel is not a sequel. Like that journey, there are many twists to this one. A map of the trail helps readers to keep locations straight, and short, fast-paced chapters make this a good read-aloud.

Pamela J. Dunston (review date November 1998)

SOURCE: Dunston, Pamela J. *Reading Teacher* 52, no. 3 (November 1998): 276.

Thirteen-year-old Zinny Taylor discovers a mysterious trail of historic significance that begins on her family's farm in Kentucky [in *Chasing Redbird*]. As she works throughout the summer to clear the trail from beginning to end, Zinny embarks on a journey of self-discovery and learns that the mysteries of the trail are connected to long-kept family secrets. Social studies teachers teaching the westward movement can use the book as a springboard for map-reading activities including orienteering by stars and compass. Students can assume roles of pioneers or outdoor enthusiasts to learn important lessons in wilderness survival and emergency medicine.

BLOOMABILITY (1998)

Publishers Weekly (review date 20 July 1998)

SOURCE: *Publishers Weekly* 245, no. 29 (20 July 1998): 220.

A light first-person narrative [*Bloomability*] and some insightful dream flashes (taken from the protagonist's journal) convey an uprooted 13 year-old's coming of age. Domenica Santolina Doone ("it's a mouthful, so most people call me Dinnie"), whose father is always in search of "the right opportunity," has already lived in 12 different cities. With her father on the road, her older brother Crick in jail and her 16-year-old sister, Stella, giving birth, it's little surprise that Dinnie is "kidnapped" by her aunt and uncle and taken from her "little New Mexico hill town" to the American School in Lugano, Switzerland, where the pair work. Tired of always being on the move, Dinnie is determined not to get attached to her newest environment ("I won't adjust! I won't adapt! I won't! I'll rebel!"), but surrounded by other "foreigners"—students from all corners of the world—she finds it easier than she had imagined to make friends. Guthrie, a classmate, helps her see a sense of possibility, or "bloomability," and to grow from her experiences. Creech (*Walk Two Moons*) skims the surface of Dinnie's gradual emergence from her protective "bubble" rather than delving into Dinnie's feelings about the deeper ramifications of her family's unraveling. The author tells rather than shows the poignant moments (e.g., Dinnie has no reaction when her parents forget her on Christmas; her friend Lila's vacillating moods go unexplained), which results in a reportlike view of the school year, rather than insight into the purported change in Dinnie. Some readers wishing to glimpse an adventure abroad may think this is just the ticket; however, fans of the author's previous works will likely miss her more fully realized characters. *Ages 8-12.*

Nancy Bond (review date September-October 1998)

SOURCE: Bond, Nancy. *Horn Book Magazine* 74, no. 5 (September-October 1998): 605-06.

(Intermediate) Thirteen-year-old Domenica Santolina Doone—Dinnie—is used to being a stranger [in *Bloomability*]. She and her family have moved many times, all over the United States, following her father in search of great opportunities. Dinnie is given her own great opportunity, whether she wants it or not, when her aunt and uncle take her to Lugano, Switzerland. Her uncle has been appointed headmaster of the American School and Dinnie is to be a pupil. For her, the year is one of "bloomability" (a word coined by a Japanese fellow student meaning "possibility"). In the beginning, she dreams of herself in a bubble, looking out at the world; gradually, her dreams change as, reluctantly at first, she allows experiences, diverse new friends, and unexpected and challenging ideas to enter through the pores in this bubble, pushing its walls further and further out. Dinnie says, "I'd always felt as if I were in a sort of suspension, waiting to see how things worked, waiting to see who I was and what sort of life I might lead." Creech surrounds her with a lively, sympathetic, often amusing cast of adult and adolescent characters, and Dinnie herself is an appealing narrator. It's Dinnie's own family, still wandering the U.S. while she's in Switzerland, who don't fully come to life. Dinnie's attachment to and homesickness for them is talked about rather than truly felt, and her two aunts, Grace and Tillie, with their repeated postcard messages, become tiresome. Al-

though *Bloomability* itself feels less unified than the author's previous books, at the end Creech links them when she sends Dinnie "home" for the summer to Bybanks, Kentucky, a town already familiar to her readers.

John Peters (review date 15 September 1998)

SOURCE: Peters, John. *Booklist* 95, no. 2 (15 September 1998): 226, 230.

Gr 5-7. As is her wont, Creech sends readers along on a thoughtful young character's life-changing odyssey [*Bloomability*]. Having lived in 13 states in 12 years, Domenica Santolina Doone, Dinnie for short, has been traveling all her life; but it's still a shock when her parents suddenly hand her over to Uncle Max and Aunt Sandy, and she finds herself headed for the American School in Lugano, Switzerland, where Max is headmaster. During a thoroughly broadening year learning to ski and to speak Italian and re-examining preconceptions about herself and other people, Dinnie gradually loses her sense of being insulated from the world. As if fresh, smart characters in a picturesque setting weren't engaging enough, Creech also poses an array of knotty questions, both personal and philosophical—why, for instance, do Dinnie's parents send her away and subsequently become so uncommunicative? Why by school's end is Dinnie eagerly looking forward to rejoining her family (now living in Bybanks, Kentucky, site of *Chasing Redbird* [1997]), facing a tough decision about where to go to school next year. A story to stimulate both head and heart: wise, witty, and worth the money.

Peg Solonika (review date October 1998)

SOURCE: Solonika, Peg. *School Library Journal* 44, no. 10 (October 1998): 132, 135.

Gr 5-8— This honest, hopeful slice of adolescent life [*Bloomability*] successfully explores how Domenica Santolina Doone, known as Dinnie, comes to terms with her past and establishes a secure identity for the future. Creech's skill at character development and subtle, effective use of metaphor shine in this first-person narrative with crisp, appropriately titled chapters. Deliberately, Creech introduces Dinnie as somewhat of a nonentity. Readers don't learn much about the specifics of her family life, only that her older sister and brother tend to get into various kinds of trouble, and that her parents are always looking for a new "opportunity" in some other town. By the second chapter, Dinnie explains that she's been "kidnapped" by her Aunt Sandy and Uncle Max, who take her with them to Switzerland to attend the school where Max is headmaster. In Dinnie's "second life" in Europe, her family continues to neglect her, forgetting even to let her know where they've relocated. Dinnie gradually adjusts to her new environment as she makes friends with other students from around the world: exuberant Guthrie; bitter Lila; and language-mangling Keisuke, who says "bloomable" when he means "possible." Together, these middle schoolers share classes and adventures, and explore ideas and emotions. As she reflects on her friends, her kind aunt and uncle, and her own vivid dreams, the youngster no longer sees herself as "Dinnie the dot in my bubble." Everyone can relate to the hard struggles of life, but, as the heroine comes to realize, the world is still full of "bloomability."

Alice F. Stern (review date February 1999)

SOURCE: Stern, Alice F. *Voice of Youth Advocates* 21, no. 6 (February 1999): 431-32.

Thirteen-year-old Dinnie has spent much of her life moving from place to place as her father chases his dreams. As the novel [*Bloomability*] opens, Dinnie's older sister is pregnant at age sixteen and her brother is in jail. Dinnie's mother, hoping to save Dinnie from a similar fate, arranges to have Dinnie taken off to Switzerland by her aunt and uncle. There Dinnie will attend the international school where her uncle is headmaster and her aunt teaches. This is instant culture shock for Dinnie; she is in a totally unfamiliar setting, surrounded by kids from all around the world. At first she is uncomfortable in her new life, but gradually this changes as she makes friends, learns Italian, and has new experiences such as learning how to ski.

Dinnie is a likeable character and it is easy for readers to put themselves in her place, feeling like a fish out of water both socially and geographically. The novel has some very clever laugh-out-loud moments, like the letters Dinnie gets from her aunts back in the States. Secondary characters come alive, as does the splendid setting. The result is fun, interesting, and engaging. This book will have wide appeal among middle schoolers looking for a coming-of-age story or readers who want a vicarious adventure.

FISHING IN THE AIR (2000)

Kirkus Reviews (review date 1 July 2000)

SOURCE: *Kirkus Reviews* 68, no. 13 (1 July 2000): 957.

A father shows his son how to "catch" something far better than fish in Newbery-winner Creech's (*The Wanderer,*) first picture book [*Fishing in the Air*]. The young narrator recalls an outing—a journey, as his father promises, to a secret place that turns out to be a riverbank where bubbles of breeze, slices of sun, and vivid memories of another boy and another time hover, waiting to be pulled in on the child's hookless fish line. With dancing swirls and dabs of color, bodies arching across spreads as gracefully as dolphins, and images of past and present flowing together, [Chris] Raschka (*Ring! Yo?,*) exuberantly echoes and amplifies the intensity of the shared experience. At the father's suggestions, streetlights become tiny moons; trees in a row transform into soldiers; and recollections of a boyhood home, other fields, and another father swim into view. Creech's prose is rich in flowing rhythms, tinged with sentiment, and no less replete with evocative images than the pictures. "'Oh,' my father said again. / 'Where is that father / and that boy?' / I reeled in my line. / 'Right here,' I said, / and he turned to look at me, / as I cast my line again / so high, so far." A rare episode, with layers of meaning for readers of several generations. *(6-8)*

Publishers Weekly (review date 10 July 2000)

SOURCE: *Publishers Weekly* 247, no. 28 (10 July 2000): 63.

In an inspired pairing, Creech and [Chris] Raschka combine their considerable talents for this poignant exploration of the ties that bind one generation to another [in *Fishing in the Air*]. Creech (*The Wanderer*) sets the stage for a father-son fishing expedition that's about much more than catching supper. As the two start out in the "blue-black" early morning, the father tells his son, "We'll catch the air! We'll catch the breeze!" The father fires his son's fancy, pointing out street lamps like "tiny moons" and trees like "tall green soldiers standing at attention"; Raschka (*Yo! Yes?*) subtly traces their transformation across neat horizontal rows. When the pair reaches the river, the man drops his line into the water at the top left-hand corner of the spread while the boy casts his line into the air from the bottom right-hand corner of the spread. The father then enters a reverie, recounting memories of his childhood home to his son, in a narrative that winds as gracefully and smoothly as the river itself; in a cumulative echo, the son prompts him to fill in more details. Raschka gradually incorporates each new detail in his illustrations until the reverie overtakes the page; the two characters, once upright, now seem to float like Chagall figures across the spreads, or somersault down the sides—always remaining separate yet answering each other visually as much as verbally.

This gradual building up of narrative and illustrative brush strokes erupts in a glorious climax, in which the father expresses his nostalgia for that lost time ("Oh, where is that house? . . . And where are those fields and that river and that father and that boy?"), and the boy and father now reach for each other, the father having caught his son's line (the boy having answered, "Right here"). Creech's narrative is more poetry than prose; her quicksilver description and quietly repetitive phrases serve to deepen the growing connection between father and son, and her images are made for Raschka's brush. Author and artist evoke an idyllic outing between parent and child and demonstrate that while they may return empty-handed, their hearts are full. *Ages 4-8.*

Louise L. Sherman (review date September 2000)

SOURCE: Sherman, Louise L. *School Library Journal* 46, no. 9 (September 2000): 193.

K-Gr 3— A father and son go fishing [in **Fishing in the Air**] to "catch the air" and to "catch the breeze" and readers see some of the many threads that connect the generations in this poetic story. As they drive through the dark city into the bright country morning, the man's words and [Chris] Raschka's pictures lead the boy and readers to see everyday objects differently and to imagine the past. Streetlamps become moons and trees become soldiers. The father describes his boyhood home and explains that his father took him fishing. When the father muses about what happened to the boy he had been and the father he had, his son replies that they are "right here" and readers will feel that it is true and will continue to be true through the generations. As the text builds images, Raschka's exuberant, Chagallesque illustrations seem to float in colorsplashed circles around it on some pages, reinforcing the cyclical theme. Later, they form a figure eight connecting the father and son, and on the final page they form a valentine sur-

rounding and "catching" the pair. While the text and images are evocative and memorable, this book is likely to have more appeal to adults than to concrete-minded youngsters. Fanciful conceits such as catching "a slice of yellow sun" and a "white white cloud" may be more confusing than meaningful to a young audience. Still, it is a moving celebration of a father-and-son relationship.

GraceAnne A. DeCandido (review date 1 November 2000)

SOURCE: DeCandido, GraceAnne A. *Booklist* 97, no. 5 (1 November 2000): 546.

Ages 5-8. A delirious verbal build-up a la "This is the house that Jack built" is matched by the calligraphic exuberance of images inspired by Chagall and Picasso [in **Fishing in the Air**]. A boy and his father go fishing, a journey to a "secret place" to "catch the air . . . and catch the breeze!" When Dad notes that the streetlights look like moons and the trees like green soldiers, they metamorphose in the pictures. As father and son cast their lines, the child asks about the house his father lived in when he was a boy. Then the images pile one upon another: the house with a red roof, the green fields, and the clear river, as the boy casts his line to pull in a sliver of sky, a slice of sun, a bubble of breeze. The illustrations grow as wild and lush as the words, building a memory palace for father and son. Going home, the parent and child truly catch the air, the breeze, and all of the father's memories: "And we caught a father, / and we caught a boy, / who learned to fish." Intimate and imaginative, as one would expect from a talented author and illustrator.

THE WANDERER (2000)

***Publishers Weekly* (review date 6 March 2000)**

SOURCE: *Publishers Weekly* 247, no. 10 (6 March 2000): 111.

Like Creech's **Walk Two Moons** and **Chasing Redbird,** this intimate novel [**The Wanderer**] poetically connects journey with self-discovery. When 13-year-old Sophie learns that her three uncles and two male cousins plan to sail across the Atlantic to visit the uncles' father, Bompie, in England, she begs to go along. Despite her mother's protests and the men's misgivings, Sophie joins the "motley" crew of the

45-foot *The Wanderer* and soon proves herself a worthy sailor. The novel unfolds through travel logs, predominantly penned by Sophie (with intermittent musings from her clownish cousin, Cody) that trace each leg of the eventful voyage; each opens with a handsome woodblock-like print by [David] Diaz (*Smoky Night*). The teens' insightful observations reveal the frailties of both the boat and its six passengers, whose fears and regrets anchor them down. Sophie, who was adopted just three years ago, proves the most complicated and mysterious of all the characters; her ambivalent feelings about the sea ("The sea, the sea, the sea. It rolled and rolled and called to me . . . but some said I was too young and the sea was a dangerous temptress . . .") correlate to a repressed memory of a tragic accident. Stories Sophie tells about Bompie, as well as clever throwaway bits (such as the brothers' given names: Ulysses, Jonah and Moses), temper the novel's more serious undercurrents. Creech once again captures the ebb and flow of a vulnerable teen's emotional life, in this enticing blend of adventure and reflection. *Ages 8-12.*

Katie O'Dell (review date April 2000)

SOURCE: O'Dell, Katie. *School Library Journal* 46, no. 4 (April 2000): 130.

Gr 5-9— Thirteen-year-old Sophie, her two cousins, and her three uncles sail across the Atlantic Ocean to England in a 45-foot sail-boat, fulfilling the men's lifelong dream [in *The Wanderer*]. The trip is also a perfect opportunity to visit the ailing patriarch of the family, Bompie, who recently left the U.S. and returned to his birthplace. Sophie conveys her fascination with the sea in journal entries and retells many of Bompie's stories. Cousin Cody, also 13, keeps his own journal and it is through his entries that readers learn that Sophie's view of things is not always reliable and that she does not always tell the truth. Sophie is actually adopted and has never met Bompie. What happened to her birth parents? Why does she pretend her adopted family is her only family? And why does she pretend to know a man she has never met? These questions will keep readers motivated to discover the answers to the girl's secrets. During the journey, the shipmates endure a dangerous storm that reveals truths about each of them and allows Sophie to face the truth. The first-person immediacy and episodic nature of the narratives allow for piecemeal but intimate revelation of character. The story is exciting, funny, and brimming with life. For each crew member, there is a conscious journey to Bompie across the sea, and an unconscious one of

self-discovery. This is a beautifully written and imaginatively constructed novel that speaks to the power of survival and the delicacy of grief.

Enicia Fisher (review date 25 May 2000)

SOURCE: Fisher, Enicia. "A Brave Girl Sailing Out on the Wild, Blue Sea." *Christian Science Monitor* 92, no. 129 (25 May 2000): 20.

If you haven't started your summer reading list yet, pick up your paper and pen. Better yet, start a captain's log as you set sail on some new literary adventures, launching with *The Wanderer,* by Sharon Creech.

Like her Newbery Medal-winning *Walk Two Moons, The Wanderer* stars a girl who embarks on a courageous journey (literal and metaphorical, of course) and reconciles herself to a mysterious event of the past.

Sophie proudly announces, "I am thirteen, and I am going to sail across the ocean. Although I would like to go alone—alone! alone! flying over the water—I'm not." Instead, she's brave enough to travel for weeks with a mostly inexperienced crew of men and boys (three uncles and two cousins) aboard a 45-foot sailboat bound for England, where her grandfather awaits them.

Like an old seafaring captain, Sophie spins yarns about Bompie to pass the time. Her cousins wonder how she, recently adopted into the family, knows more about their grandfather than they do. But they're even more curious about what happened to her real parents—a story her uncles say only she can tell.

During the first segment of their journey. Sophie's biggest challenge is to secure meaningful work assignments on the boat besides scrubbing or cooking. She quickly convinces the others that she's more than seaworthy by fixing the bilge. And she's the only one brave enough to make repairs at the top of the mast as the boat sways over the surging sea.

The motley crew encounters a dangerously raging and relentless storm that tests everyone's courage. If any had known this force-10 gale was in store, "with winds at 50 miles an hour and waves like walls of water pounding day and night," they surely would have stayed safely on shore.

When Sophie finally recounts the story, of her real parents, her bravery shines as brightly as the daystar after a storm.

Sophie and her cousin narrate the fast-paced novel through alternate journal entries—and it would be great fun to embark on the voyage taking turns reading alternate chapters with a reading mate. The shifts between her poetic and descriptive prose and his more chatty and playful writing give the text a tidal rhythm like the ocean itself.

Sophie writes, "The sea, the sea, the sea. It rolled and rolled and called to me. Come in, it said, come in." This inviting book will encourage the readers on your crew to take an early their into their summer reading.

Susan Spaniol (review date September-October 2000)

SOURCE: Spaniol, Susan. *Book Report* 19, no. 2 (September-October 2000): 58.

Gr 5-7. This story [*The Wanderer*] is another tale-within-a-tale from master storyteller Sharon Creech. This time the "surface" story is a fast-paced adventure, as 13-year-old Sophie is grudgingly allowed to join her three uncles and two cousins for a cross-Atlantic journey on Uncle Dock's 45-foot sailboat, *The Wanderer*. The only female on board, Sophie must constantly prove herself to the skeptical men, as they sail toward England to visit her grandfather, Bompie. Caught in a storm just shy of their destination, the boat is badly damaged by a rogue wave. Although the crew manages to limp to land, the incident triggers Sophie's long-repressed memories of the similar sailing accident that killed both of her parents when she was four years old. This "inner" story of Sophie's past and her journey to the shelter of her loving adoptive family is woven seamlessly into the plot. As in Creech's earlier book **Walk Two Moons** (1994), this tale is as much a journey of the heart as of place. The adventure is told alternately by Sophie and her cousin Cody through entries in their respective journals, and it's illustrated with b & w drawings by Caldecott Award-winning artist David Diaz. Booktalk this one and watch it fly off the shelf. *Highly Recommended.*

Alice F. Stern (review date December 2000)

SOURCE: Stern, Alice F. *Voice of Youth Advocates* 23, no. 5 (December 2000): 346.

Thirteen-year-old Sophie joins three uncles and two male cousins for a sailing trip from New England to the British Isles. Their story [*The Wanderer*] is told through journal entries from both Sophie and her cousin Cody. On the surface, this novel seems to be a story of six people learning to get along in small quarters despite personality differences and a variety of skill levels, but Creech tells another story here as well. By the sixth chapter, when we see Cody's first journal entry, we learn that Sophie was adopted into the family only three years before, even though she talks as if she always has been a member. Sophie's difficulty dealing with the death of her natural parents creates some tension with the other members of the crew. These emotional components of the story are as suspenseful and dramatic as the sea voyage itself.

Both stories are told in an understated style with humor, making this novel rise above other adventure stories or angst-ridden tales of loss and acceptance. It will appeal to readers with many different tastes. Physically, the book also is of the highest quality, with small line drawings by [David] Diaz heading each chapter. *The Wanderer* belongs in every young adult collection.

Jo Goodman (review date May 2001)

SOURCE: Goodman, Jo. *Magpies* 16, no. 2 (May 2001): 38.

The sea, the sea, the sea. It rolled and rolled and called to me. 'Come in', it said, 'come in.'

So begins this beautiful, subtle novel [*The Wanderer*]. Sophie is fascinated by the sea, dreams of it, learns all she can about it, and now, aged thirteen, has persuaded her parents to let her sail from America to England on *The Wanderer* with her three uncles and two cousins. Her mother talks about the latter, she isn't worried about quiet, studious Brian, but warns her that Cody [is] *too charming in a dangerous sort of way*. Not only is the trip full of excitement and danger, it is a trip of self-discovery for all the crew, as all are challenged about their attitude to life as gradually, painfully, truths emerge. The cousins (mothers don't know everything) and uncles are fascinating, complex characters, as well there is a mystery about Sophie's life and it is not clear that she understands it herself—but her feelings about the sea are central to it.

Creech tells the story through two journals, kept by Sophie and Cody, and each of their simple observations carries a wealth of meaning. Illuminating details establish the fully-rounded characters, and every word rings true. This is literature of the highest order, writing of such subtlety and compassion that the reader can only give thanks for a magical experience. And it's even better on a second reading!

📖 *A FINE, FINE SCHOOL* (2001)

Kirkus Reviews (review date 15 June 2001)

SOURCE: *Kirkus Reviews* 69, no. 12 (15 June 2001): 862-63.

School can be peachy, but that doesn't mean time away from school isn't just as valuable, which is the lesson Principal Keene has to learn in this charming story [*A Fine, Fine School*] of a school administrator utterly rapt in his job. Mr. Keene just can't get enough of his fine school with all that fine learning being taught by the fine teachers to the fine students. So he decides to have school on Saturday, then Sunday, then on holidays, then the whole year through: "He was so proud of the students and the teachers, of all the learning they were doing every day." Literally. But the students and teachers aren't so sanguine about the situation, though no one wanted to prick Mr. Keene's balloon. Until Tillie finally tells him that some others are not learning because of all the school, like her dog, who hasn't learned how to sit, or her little brother, who hasn't learned how to swing or skip, because she's never home to teach them. Indeed, she hasn't learned to climb a tree for all the classroom time she's been putting in. Mr. Keene sees the light, beveling his enthusiasm and putting his good intentions into perspective. Creech's text capably moves the story forward, but it has all the humor of a stoat and the repetitions are overmuch. Yet [Harry] Bliss (*Girl of the Shining Mountain*, 1999) comes through not just to save the day, but to make the story memorable, with appealing characters and numerous silly sight gags and verbal asides, like the post-it notes that read "Massive Quiz Saturday" and "Power Nap 2 PM," the photo in the kid's locker from his parents signed "We Miss You Son!" and the TV screen that reads "The Best Cartoons in the World Start in 5 Minutes!!" just as Tillie is shuffling out the door to school on Christmas. Just fine. *(4-8)*

Publishers Weekly (review date 23 July 2001)

SOURCE: *Publishers Weekly* 248, no. 30 (23 July 2001): 75.

Given current battles over standardized testing and summer sessions, this timely story [*A Fine, Fine School*] about extended schooling touches a nerve with a kindly delivery. The tale centers on Mr. Keene, a good-intentioned but zealous principal, and Tillie, a studious girl who spends free time teaching her little brother to skip and climb trees. When strolling the school hallways, Mr. Keene beams, "Aren't these fine students? Aren't these fine teachers? Isn't this a fine, fine school?" He so adores education that he schedules classes for weekends, then holidays, then summers, too. Tillie's low-key home life is transformed. She checks her watch and lugs a giant briefcase off to class, despite her lonely brother's imploring looks. Meanwhile, Mr. Keene exclaims, "How much we will learn!" He doesn't notice the gasps and grimaces of his stressed-out students and teachers. Creech (*Love That Dog*) styles the principal as proud of his scholars and staff, but shows how his drastic measures diminish quality of life. New Yorker cartoonist [Harry] Bliss, in an impressive debut, foregrounds the core drama between Tillie and the principal, yet also develops secondary characters among Tillie's overwhelmed classmates (toting books called *Really Hard Math* and *The Meaning of Life*) and her precocious dog, Beans (calmly enjoying the "Arts and Leisure" section); comic thought balloons, clever book titles and expressive faces contribute to the tale's success. In the end, Tillie politely convinces Mr. Keene that he has been unreasonable. With quiet intensity, Creech and Bliss persuasively argue one side of a volatile issue. *Ages 4-8.*

Ilene Cooper (review date August 2001)

SOURCE: Cooper, Ilene. *Booklist* 97, no. 22 (August 2001): 2116.

Ages 5-8. Mr. Keene, the principal of a fine, fine school, just loves to see his students learning [in *A Fine, Fine School*]. So happy is Mr. Keene, he calls an assembly, proclaims his pride, and gives an order, "Let's have school on Saturdays, too!" Young Tille is less than pleased. On weekends she likes to climb her favorite tree; show her dog, Beans, tricks; and teach brother how to skip. But soon, she's going to school on Sundays, holidays, and during the summer. Finally, Tille's had enough. She marches into Mr. Keene's office and announces that not everyone is learning. Horrified, Mr. Keene demands to know what she means, and Tille explains: Beans isn't learning his tricks, her brother isn't learning to skip, and she's not climbing very well. Mr. Keene gets the picture immediately, and he revokes his order: "Fine, fine, fine," the students and teachers cheer. This book has it all: a fine, fresh idea; a witty text that's fun to read aloud; and, most of all, intelligent, amusing art that provides an extra load of laughs. [Harry] Bliss, an award-winning cartoonist at *The New Yorker,* takes a good idea and flies with it. He captures the initial intensity of the classroom and elevates it to the blissfully absurd, as banners spring up in the cafeteria ("Why not study while you chew?") and the children wear signs on their huge, stuffed backpacks that read, "How's my walking?" The closer one looks, the more laughs there are, and everyone—kids, parents, teachers, even principals—will want to look more than once.

Grace Oliff (review date August 2001)

SOURCE: Oliff, Grace. *School Library Journal* 47, no. 8 (August 2001): 144.

K-Gr 2— Principal Keene is proud of his school [in *A Fine, Fine School*]. "'Oh!' he would say. 'Aren't these fine children? Aren't these fine teachers? Isn't this a fine, fine school?'" He becomes so enamored of the learning he sees taking place that he decides there should be more. First he schedules school on Saturdays, then Sundays, then holidays, and finally throughout the summer. With each addition, readers are told, "The teachers and the students did not want to go to school [on Sundays, holidays, etc.], but no one knew how to tell Mr. Keene that." Finally, young Tillie confronts him and explains that not everyone is learning—there are little brothers who can't skip and dogs that can't sit—and she herself cannot climb her tree. The principal finally realizes that there are certain kinds of learning that take place outside the classroom and the normal schedule is resumed. Creech's telling of this implausible parable is repetitive and not particularly energetic, but [Harry] Bliss's colorful cartoon illustrations take up the slack with their sly humor and meticulous attention to detail. Children are pictured with backpacks labeled "wide load," and plastered with Post-it notes reading "massive test on your birthday" and "power nap at 2 pm." In this day of the over-scheduled and hurried child, this book could be a good impetus for a discussion of the value of stopping to smell the roses.

Childhood Education (review date winter 2001)

SOURCE: *Childhood Education* 78, no. 2 (winter 2001): 110.

Mr. Keene is the principal of a fine, fine school, filled with busy teachers and happy children [in *A Fine, Fine School*]. Since everyone loves learning, Mr. Keene is sure they would be even happier with more opportunities for school. Before long, school is in session on Saturdays, then Sundays, and finally during holidays and summer vacations, too! How could

anything go wrong, when everyone is learning so much? This delightful, amusing picture book is a wonderful tribute to all those principals and teachers who passionately care about their students' learning. At the same time, it serves as a good reminder that the best kinds of life learning often take place outside of the classroom walls. *Ages 4-8.*

LOVE THAT DOG: LEARNING ABOUT POETRY FROM MISS STRETCHBERRY (2001)

Publishers Weekly (review date 18 June 2001)

SOURCE: *Publishers Weekly* 248, no. 25 (18 June 2001): 82.

In last year's *Fishing in the Air,* Creech took a spare, metaphorical approach to a father-son relationship. Here [in *Love That Dog*] she examines the bond between a boy and his dog to create an ideal homage to the power of poetry and those who write it.

The volume itself builds like a poem. Told exclusively through Jack's dated entries in a school journal, the book opens with his resistance to writing verse: "September 13 / I don't want to / be cause boys / don't write poetry. / Girls do." Readers sense the gentle persistence of Jack's teacher, Miss Stretchberry, behind the scenes, from the poems she reads in class and from her coaxing, to which the boy alludes, until he begins to write some poems of his own. One by William Carlos Williams, for instance, inspires Jack's words: "So much depends / upon / a blue car / splattered with mud / speeding down the road." A Robert Frost poem sends Jack into a tale his verse) of how he found his dog, Sky. At first, his poems appear to be discrete works. But when a poem by Walter Dean Myers ("Love That Boy" from *Brown Angels*) unleashes the joy Jack felt with his pet, he be comes even more honest in his poetry. Jack's next work is cathartic: all of his previous verses seemed to be leading up to this *piece de resistance,* an admission of his profound grief over Sky's death. He then can move on from his grief to write a poem ("inspired by Walter Dean Myers") about his joy at having known and loved his dog.

As in any great poem, the real story surfaces between the lines. From Jack's entries, readers learn how unobtrusively his teacher guides him to poems he can collect and emulate, and how patiently she convinces him to share his own work. By exposing Jack and readers to the range of poems that moves

Jack (they appear at the back of the book), Creech conveys a life truth: pain and joy exist side by side. For Jack and for readers, the memory of that dog lives on in his poetry. Readers will love that dog, and this book. *Ages 8-12.*

Lee Bock (review date August 2001)

SOURCE: Bock, Lee. *School Library Journal* 47, no. 8 (August 2001): 177.

Gr 4-8— Jack keeps a journal for his teacher [*Love That Dog*], a charming, spare free-verse monologue that begins: "I don't want to / because boys / don't write poetry. / Girls do." But his curiosity grows quickly as Miss Stretchberry feeds the class a varied menu of intriguing poems starting with William Carlos Williams's "The Red Wheelbarrow," which confuses Jack at first. Gradually, he begins to see connections between his personal experiences and the poetry of William Blake, Robert Frost, and others, and Creech's compellingly simple plot about love and loss begins to emerge. Jack is timid about the first poems he writes, but with the obvious encouragement and prodding of his masterful teacher, he gains the courage to claim them as his own in the classroom displays. When he is introduced to "Love That Boy" by Walter Dean Myers, he makes an exuberant leap of understanding. "MARCH 14 / That was the best best BEST / poem / you read yesterday / by Mr. Walter Dean Myers / the best best BEST / poem / ever. / I am sorry / I took the book home / without asking. / I only got / one spot / on it. / That's why / the page is torn. / I tried to get / the spot / out." All the threads of the story are pulled together in Jack's final poem, "Love That Dog (Inspired by Walter Dean Myers)." Creech has created a poignant, funny picture of a child's encounter with the power of poetry. Readers may have a similar experience because all of the selections mentioned in the story are included at the end. This book is a tiny treasure.

Betty Carter (review date November-December 2001)

SOURCE: Carter, Betty. *Horn Book Magazine* 77, no. 6 (November-December 2001): 743.

(Intermediate) "I don't want to / because boys / don't write poetry. / Girls do." Jack's free-verse journal [*Love That Dog*] charts his evolution from doubt to delight in poetry. His teacher, Miss Stretchberry, introduces him to poetry, serves as an advocate for his writing, and flatters him into believing he's a poet.

Like an art student diligently copying great masters, Creech has Jack borrowing liberally from the works of others ("Blue car, blue car, shining bright / in the darkness of the night: / who could see you speeding by / like a comet in the sky?") and imitating the form ("I guess it does / look like a poem / when you see it / typed up / like that"). Unfortunately, he is no poet, despite the book's attempt to convince us otherwise. Although Jack finds a personal connection to poems, his linguistic banality restricts his expression of that link and limits his voice. His comparisons are more precious than precocious ("I didn't know about / the spell-checking thing / inside the computer. / It is like a miracle / little brain / in there / a little helper brain"), and, while breathless enthusiasm may show how Jack feels, his verse, as is typical of children's writing, fails to extend such personal response to more universal provocations. Still, Jack's gradual appreciation of poetry is both natural and believable, and the sentence parsing required by the book's format will be a refreshing aid to beginning chapter book readers, whose fluency is threatened by word-by-word reading. The format, generous with white space, allows the book to reach the often-required one hundred pages without containing large chunks of text.

Jennifer Anstiss (review date May 2002)

SOURCE: Anstiss, Jennifer. *Journal of Adolescent and Adult Literacy* 45, no. 8 (May 2002): 794.

Love That Dog by Sharon Creech is a refreshing "novel" that examines the roles a teacher, a poetry journal, and a selection of poems play in a year of a young man's life. The text is written in stanza format and chronicles the reflection entries of Jack, an adolescent in room 105, Miss Stretchberry's class, as he completes pieces of poetry in response to poems read in class over the course of a school year. These reflections trace Jack's development as a writer as he begins to use poetry as a vehicle to find his own voice and as he uncovers the power of words.

The book begins with Jack's first entry on September 1st, "I don't want to because boys don't write poetry. Girls do". This entry reflects Jack's thoughts about poetry at the beginning of the year as he starts what is to become a written dialogue between him and Miss Stretchberry. The subtext attempts to disassemble the myth that poetry is only for girls. This deconstruction is slowly revealed as Jack begins to experiment with form and subject material from his own life and as he attempts to integrate the formats and rhythms of poems read in class with his own writing. This experimentation with language eventually opens him up to allowing the teacher to share his poems on the class bulletin board, provided the teacher promises not to put his name on them.

As the school year progresses, so does Jack. His entries expand as he experiments increasingly with form. He begins to take risks, by spontaneously creating poems, and to understand that his "words were poems". He is careful how his poems are typed and presented to the class and begins to put his name on his work, a sign of pride and validation of his voice as he begins to go "public."

As the novel draws to a close Jack reaches out with a letter requesting a class visit from Walter Dean Myers, whose poetry has inspired him to write a "secret" poem about Sky, his dog that recently passed away. Through this act Jack learns that language is not just the domain of a teacher or an adult "who uses big words and knows how to spell and to type". When the poet arrives for a class visit at the end of the year Jack is no longer the young man who believed poetry to be the domain of girls. He signs his thank-you note to Myers "From your number one fan" and encloses the poem about his dog—the ultimate act of a child who has found his voice.

This novel offers wonderful insight to a young man's changing identity as he uses "sanctioned" poems shared by his teacher to scaffold his own experience with the act of poetry writing and as he reflects on the power of language. This journey through prose entices the reader into the private writings and thoughts of a young boy seeking his own voice.

Creech has brilliantly crafted a story with the potential to appeal to young adolescents who may relate to Jack's struggles with issues of identity and validation.

RUBY HOLLER (2002)

Publishers Weekly (review date 4 March 2002)

SOURCE: *Publishers Weekly* 249, no. 9 (4 March 2002): 79.

The characters introduced here [in *Ruby Holler*]—two abandoned children, their villainous guardians and a kindly country couple—might nave stepped out of a Dickens novel, but as Creech (*Love that Dog*) probes beneath their facades, the characters grow more complex than classic archetypes. Florida and

her brother Dallas, raised in an orphanage run by the cold-hearted Trepids, rely on each other rather than grownups for support. They become suspicious when Mr. Trepid informs them that they are going to a place called Ruby Holler to accompany old Mr. and Mrs. Marcy on separate vacations. Florida is to be Mr. Tiller Morey's companion on a canoe trip; Dallas is to help Mrs. Sairy Morey hunt down an elusive bird. Readying for the trips proves to be a journey in itself as the Moreys, Florida and Dallas make discoveries about one another as well as themselves in a soothing rural environment. This poignant story evokes a feeling as welcoming as fresh-baked bread. The slow evolution of the siblings—who are no angels—parallels the gradual building of mutual trust for the Moreys. The novel celebrates the healing effects of love and compassion. Although conflicts emerge, readers will have little doubt that all will end well for the children and the grandparently Moreys. *Ages 8-12.*

Robyn Ryan Vandenbrock (review date April 2002)

SOURCE: Vandenbrock, Robyn Ryan. *School Library Journal* 48, no. 4 (April 2002): 142.

Gr 4-6—Orphaned twins Dallas and Florida have resigned themselves to living within the confines of the Boxton Creek Home for Children [in *Ruby Holler*]. It's a loveless existence. The Trepids, owners and "rule enforcers" of the home, target the brother and sister at every opportunity and all of the prospective adoptive parents have returned them to the orphanage. Eventually the children are sent to act as temporary companions to an eccentric older couple who live in Ruby Holler, and there they find love and acceptance. While the plot is predictable, the story weaves in an interesting mix of mystery, adventure, and humor, along with age-old and modern problems. Creech does a fine job of developing the unique personalities and the sibling relationship, and the children's defense mechanisms (Dallas's dreamy escapism and Florida's aggression) figure prominently in the interplay among the characters. The text is lively and descriptive with an authentic, if somewhat mystical, rural ambience. This entertaining read from a first-rate author will not disappoint Creech's many fans.

Carolyn Phelan (review date 1 April 2002)

SOURCE: Phelan, Carolyn. *Booklist* 98, no. 15 (1 April 2002): 1328.

Gr 4-7. Thirteen-year-old twins Dallas and Florida are continually in trouble for breaking the many rules of the Boxton Creek Home for Children [in *Ruby*

Holler]. When an elderly couple, Tiller and Sairy, invite Dallas and Florida to stay with them in nearby Ruby Holler and travel with them beyond it, the twins are wary. Previous foster placements have been disasters. Tiller and Sairy, however, treat the children like their own, talking with them, teaching them, trusting them, loving them, outwitting them, and even letting them save face. In an unusual approach for a children's book, Tiller and Sairy's points of view are at least as important as those of Dallas and Florida; and how the foursome play off one another is one of the key points of the narrative. There's a larger-than-life feel to this novel that makes the minor characters and subplots feel a bit out of scale—or out of sync—but the main story rests squarely on the four well-drawn characters. A stylized yet solid story from the author of the Newbery-award-winning *Walk Two Moons* (1994).

Joanna Rudge Long (review date May-June 2002)

SOURCE: Long, Joanna Rudge. *Horn Book Magazine* 78, no. 3 (May-June 2002): 327.

(Intermediate, Middle School) Midway along the road between Lemony Snicket's ironical nightmares and the luminous logic of *Tuck Everlasting* lies *Ruby Holler.* Here, too, villains are avaricious and events schematic, designed as much to support the author's ideas as to propel her protagonists' fortunes. Twins Dallas and Florida, thirteen, have been placed by orphanage proprietors Mr. and Mrs. Trepid (who as villains would be right at home in a Dickens or a Dahl novel) in yet another foster home, the first to treat them kindly. Tiller and Sairy, who much resemble the affectionate grandparents in Creech's *Walk Two Moons,* live in idyllic Ruby Holler, where they cook wholesome meals and support themselves with their exquisite wood carvings of forest creatures. In a bracing dose of reality, even this saintly pair's patience is strained by the twins, whose lifetime of abuse has left them both mischievous and lacking normal skills. Still, they are drawn into the old couple's plans for separate life-affirming journeys, each with one twin. Though their well-founded suspicions of an unfriendly world persist, Dallas and Florida begin to blossom in time to help foil the Trepids and to pitch in, sometimes heroically, where help is needed. Brief chapters, swift action, a hint of mystery concerning the twins' origins, generous doses of humor, engagingly quirky characters, and a lively, kid-friendly voice will all recommend this to a wide range of young readers.

FURTHER READING

Criticism

Kirkus Reviews 69, no. 12 (15 June 2001): 862-63. Review of *A Fine, Fine School.*

Additional coverage of Creech's life and career is contained in the following sources published by the Gale Group: *Authors and Artists for Young Adults,* Vol. 21; *Beacham's Guide to Literature for Young Adults,* Vols. 9, 11, 12; *Contemporary Authors,* Vol. 159; *Contemporary Authors New Revision Series,* Vol. 113; *Literature Resource Center; Major Authors and Illustrators for Children and Young Adults,* Ed. 2; *Major Authors and Illustrators for Children and Young Adults Supplement,* Ed. 1; *Something about the Author,* Vols. 94, 139; *St. James Guide to Young Adult Writers;* **and** *Writers for Young Adults Supplement,* Vol. 1.

Gerald Hausman
1945-

(Also published as Gerry Hausman) American folklorist, storyteller, novelist, and poet.

INTRODUCTION

Known as a reteller of Native American and Caribbean folktales, Gerald Hausman has published many books based on folklore, legend, heroic tales, and cultural symbolism. They include collections of trickster tales such as *Coyote Walks on Two Legs* (1995), cultural stories such as *Duppy Talk* (1994), and origin myths such as *How Chipmunk Got Tiny Feet* (1995). He has also written short stories and novels for young adults, such as *Turtle Dream* (1989) and *Wilderness* (1994), utilizing cultural themes, symbols, and legends to create a psychological setting. "I have always felt that mythology uplifts our spirit into the true context of culture," Hausman said on *Romancing the Web,* "As a mythologist, I have sought those stories, personal and cultural, that make us feel a little better about the world that we inhabit."

BIOGRAPHICAL INFORMATION

Hausman was born in Baltimore, Maryland and grew up in New Jersey and Massachusetts. He attended New Mexico Highlands University, receiving a B.A. in 1968. From 1969 to 1972 he taught poetry in Lenox, Massachusetts, but was drawn back to New Mexico where he became an editor with Bookstore Press from 1972 to 1977, the vice-president of Sunstone Press in Santa Fe from 1979 to 1983, and an English teacher at Santa Fe Preparatory School from 1983 to 1987. As a resident of the Southwest for twenty years, he became interested in Native American mythology and symbols, and in 1989 he published his first young adult novel, *Turtle Dream,* utilizing these cultural symbols. His work is often described as lyrical and poetic, and he thinks of himself foremost as a poet. In an interview for *Something about the Author* Hausman remarked, "My prose writing is deeply influenced by poetry because when I first began to write as a child, I always wanted to tell a story using the poetic form."

For many years, Hausman maintained a summer residence in Jamaica, and with his wife Loretta, founded a school for creative writing there. In this setting Hausman's compelling interest in folktales expanded to include the traditional stories and culture of the Caribbean in the scope of his story collections.

In 1970 Hausman began a new career as a storyteller. He participated in the Poets in Schools Program from 1970 to 1976, traveling and visiting schools throughout New England, and served as poet-in-residence at Central Connecticut State College in New Britain in 1973.

In 1994 Hausman and his wife moved to Bokeelia, Florida. He performs as a storyteller at college writers' programs and young author conferences both in the United States and abroad, and has appeared on radio stations throughout the country. He has also served as storyteller in residence for the Navajo radio station KTNN in Window Rock, Arizona.

MAJOR WORKS

Hausman's first young adult book, *Turtle Dream,* is a collection of five contemplative short stories about young Native Americans at a turning point in their lives. Each story depicts a moment when the main character begins to understand profound truths—whether it's determining a calling in life, facing fear and death, or suffering the tensions in the tug-of-war between cultural traditions and the modern world. A reviewer for *Publishers Weekly* called these stories "lyrical, quietly forceful pieces that effectively portray their characters' links to both the physical and spiritual worlds."

Duppy Talk is a collection of ghost stories from the Caribbean, brought from the African tradition on slave ships. The six tales are from Jamaica, with credited sources, about sprites who reward kindness and good character with spiritual and tangible gifts, and sometimes play tricks. Each story opens with a Jamaican proverb, and the final chapter discusses the origins and meanings of the traditions. Janice Del Negro of *Booklist* said that these stories "should have wide appeal across age and gender lines."

Produced in collaboration with science fiction writer Roger Zelazny, *Wilderness* combines two tales about survival in the American wilderness. Based on true stories, these fictionalized accounts take place in the 1800s. Renowned hunter Jack Colter, who assisted Lewis and Clark, races for his life from the ritualistic torture of pursuing Blackfeet warriors, by running barefoot 150 miles over the mountains and plains until he reaches a safe haven. Hugh Glass, mauled by a bear and left by his companions to die, drags, crawls, and walks 100 miles to get help, urged on by his desire for revenge against those who left him. Hausman and Zelazny use internal monologues to depict characters' emotions, combined with dreamscapes that include Native American symbols. Critics suggested that *Wilderness* is a good history lesson for a sophisticated reader.

Doctor Moledinky's Castle (1995) is somewhat of a departure for Hausman, but was exceptionally well received as both funny and sentimental. It depicts twelve-year-old year old Andy's memoirs of the summer of 1957. His adventures include night-time visits to the town's two oddballs, Doctor Moledinky, who lives in a castle (with a moat), and Mrs. Henshaw who lives next door to him. John Sigwald, critic for *School Library Journal,* had this comment: "Andy's wonder heightens the adventure for young readers who may realize that Berkeley Bend—even with a millionaire and a witch or two—might not really be all that different from their own hometowns."

A subcategory of Hausman's publications is that of animal mythology. One of the most highly regarded of these is *Dogs of Myth* (1999), written in collaboration with his wife, Loretta. It is a collection of thirteen myths about dogs, drawn from international sources. The tales include a creation myth from Africa and stories of trickster dogs from Japanese, Eskimo, and Native American traditions. Some of the stories are mystical and some are tall tales, and each story is provided with historic and cultural context. A reviewer for *Publishers Weekly* called this book "sheer bliss for dog lovers." The Hausmans published a similar collection about cats, *Cats of Myth,* in 2000.

CRITICAL RECEPTION

Hausman has acquired a solid reputation as a folklorist and storyteller. Although his early attempts to retell myths were faulted by critics for romanticism and misrepresentation, his later publications have drawn praise for being both historically valuable and entertaining. Overall, the unique subjects Hausman expounds have been well received by critics, who appreciate the introspective nature of stories and fables which are not widely known. Critics have met his retellings of animals myths with much enthusiasm, considering them a valuable addition to his interesting body of work.

AWARDS

Hausman has been honored for many of his books. *Turtle Dream* was a Great Books Foundation Selection; *Duppy Talk* was given the Aesop Accolade Award by the Children's Section of the American Folklore Society in 1995; *Wilderness* was named Book for the Teen Age by the New York City Public Library in 1995; *Doctor Moledinky's Castle* made the *School Library Journal* Sleepers List of 100 Books Too Good to Miss; *Doctor Bird* (1998) was named a Notable Social Studies Trade Book for Young People in 1999; *Dogs of Myth* received the Society of Illustrators Choice Award, was named to the American Booksellers Kids' Pick of the List, and chosen as a Scholastic Book Club Selection, all in 1999; *Tom Cringle: Battle on the High Seas* (2000) and *Cats of Myth* were both named Bank Street College of Education Best Book of 2000; and *The Jacob Ladder* (2001) was named a New York Public Library Book for the Teenage and a Notable Social Studies Trade Book.

In addition, Hausman received the Union College Poetry Prize in 1965 for *Quebec Poems* and sponsored the Gerald Hausman Scholarship Awarded to two Native American high school students at Santa Fe Preparatory School in 1985.

PRINCIPAL WORKS

Runners (poetry) 1984

Turtle Dream (short stories) 1989

Turtle Island Alphabet: A Lexicon of Native American Symbols and Culture (essays) 1992

Gift of the Gila Monster: Navajo Ceremonial Tales (folktales) 1993

Tunkashila: From the Birth of Turtle Island to the Blood of Wounded Knee (folktales) 1993

Duppy Talk: West Indian Tales of Mystery and Magic (ghost stories) 1994

Turtle Island ABC: A Gathering of Native American Symbols (picture book) 1994

Wilderness [with Roger Zelazny] (fiction) 1994

Coyote Walks on Two Legs: A Book of Navajo Myths and Legends (folktales) 1995

Doctor Moledinky's Castle: A Homespun Tale (fiction) 1995

How Chipmunk Got Tiny Feet: Native American Origin Stories (folktales) 1995

African-American Alphabet: A Celebration of African-American and West Indian Culture, Custom, Myth, and Symbol [with Kevin Rodriques] (essays) 1996

Eagle Boy: A Traditional Navajo Legend (folktale) 1996

Night Flight (fiction) 1996

The Kebra Negast: The Book of Rastafarian Wisdom and Faith from Ethiopia and Jamaica [editor] (philosophy) 1997

Doctor Bird: Three Lookin' Up Tales from Jamaica (folktales) 1998

The Mythology of Cats: Feline Legend and Lore Through the Ages [with Loretta Hausman] (folktales) 1998

The Story of Blue Elk (folktale) 1998

The Coyote Bead (fiction) 1999

Dogs of Myth: Tales from Around the World [with Loretta Hausman] (folktales) 1999

Cats of Myth: Tales from Around the World [with Loretta Hausman] (folktales) 2000

Tom Cringle: Battle on the High Seas (fiction) 2000

The Jacob Ladder [with Uton Hinds] (autobiography) 2001

The Metaphysical Cat: Tales of Cats and Their Humans (folktales) 2001

Tom Cringle: The Pirate and the Patriot (fiction) 2001

The Boy from Nine Miles: The Early Life of Bob Marley [with Cedella Marley] (biography) 2002

The Mythology of Horses (folktales) 2002

Castaways: Stories of Survival (juvenile fiction) 2003

AUTHOR COMMENTARY

Gerald Hausman (essay date 1996)

SOURCE: Hausman, Gerald. "A Special Message from Gerald Hausman."www.romanceweb.com/ (1996).

[In the following essay, Hausman explains the importance of mythology in his own life.]

I have always felt that mythology uplifts our spirit into the true context of culture. As a mythologist, I have sought those stories, personal and cultural, that make us feel a little better about the world that we inhabit. N. Scott Momaday, the great Kiowa poet and novelist, remarked in the introduction of my book **Turtle Island Alphabet** that "the keepers of the oral tradition had a deeper belief in language than have most of us in general. Language was the repository of their well-being, their past and their posterity, the irresistable current of their daily lives."

If you truly understand this concept—that words are sacred—that within the timbre of words carried upon the human tongue, we can hear the drumbeat of history, the story of humankind, then you may realize that the work of the storyteller is also like carrying water in the desert. Each of us must help carry the water jar, if we are each to drink from it. Stories, then, are not decorations or mere entertainments, for they may contain the survival of a people, the essence of what it means to be alive and to stay alive on this earth.

In the Navajo world the word *hozhoni* means harmony. But that is only the literal translation, for *hozhoni* means many different things; it is a word that is not readily turned into English. This is because the word harmony, in Navajo, does not just suggest that one's life is in order. Rather, it implies that everything—the entire loom of life—is not apart, and that Man is not apart within it; and that, particularly, the person experiencing the moment of *hozhoni* is blessed, and thus, is thankful. In such a time of benediction, all things are possible. And it is then that we are said to be walking in beauty; and to see that other forms of life are doing the same.

To put all of this into mythological terms, to explain *hozhoni* at its highest level, there is the Navajo myth of "The Turquoise Horse." I first heard this tale when I was in my twenties and now, thirty years later, I am still awed by its beauty and its insistence on the shared loveliness of life. My old friend Jay DeGroat, the son of a Navajo medicine man, told me that the symbol of the horse was, for the Navajo people, an image of liberation. Once, when he felt that he lacked a sense of Navajo self-esteem and *hozhoni* had departed from his life, he retraced his boyhood steps to the top of Rainy Butte where he had once as a child participated in the Corn Praying Ceremony. There, now fully grown and not knowing what to expect, he met the Turquoise Horse. As he put it, "The horse galloped out of the sun in a golden cloud of pollen and came down out of the sky to meet me. I felt the great horse's power and I knew that this was the gift of the Sun Father. As I looked at the horse it thundered across the mesa and went right through me. It entered my body without hurting me, and went on across the mesa and onto the empty air where it disappeared. I was honored by a living myth, my spirit touched by the presence of *hozhoni*. It has remained with me since that time."

TITLE COMMENTARY

📖 *RUNNERS* (1984)

Publishers Weekly (review date 13 April 1984)

SOURCE: *Publishers Weekly* 225, no. 15 (13 April 1984): 58.

The unifying theme of this volume of poems [*Runners*] is running—setting out in different directions, experiencing different places. Accordingly, the book is divided into four sections marking four cardinal

points. Hausman's work is spare and suggesting, evoking mood through images in the natural world. We are taken to New England's White Mountains, the Deep South and the Rio Grande Gorge. There is particular emphasis on the dry, open landscape of the Southwest, where Hausman lives, and his work is influenced both in style and tone by native American songs. Although Hausman sometimes introduces other people and human relations, these poems tend to be thin and fail to resonate like his strong, clear, elemental poems "Aspens," "Ravens" and "Wood for Winter." Hausman is the author of two previous books of poems, two books for young readers and a mystery novel.

📖 *TURTLE DREAM* (1989)

Publishers Weekly (review date 8 December 1989)

SOURCE: *Publishers Weekly* 236, no. 23 (8 December 1989): 56.

Each of the five stories in this collection [*Turtle Dream*] depicts a young Native American at a moment of epiphany, when profound truths are glimpsed. Lisa, a 12-year-old Navajo, has a vivid dream of a turquoise horse; how she chooses to share her dream reveals her calling as a poet. Sam, half Havasupai, returns to his people's canyon after years away and confronts a paralyzing childhood fear. Beth makes her peace with the afterlife, embracing and even rejoicing in change. Contemplative rather than strongly active, these are lyrical, quietly forceful pieces that effectively portray their characters' links to both the physical and spiritual worlds. Readers are invited to probe such mysteries as visions and ghosts and are also given insight into the tensions between the ways of "the people" and the demands of the modern world. *Ages 12-Up.*

📖 *TURTLE ISLAND ALPHABET: A LEXICON OF NATIVE AMERICAN SYMBOLS AND CULTURE* (1992)

Margaret Tice (review date November 1992)

SOURCE: Tice, Margaret. *School Library Journal* 38, no. 11 (November 1992): 137.

Gr 9-Up—Because of its misleading title [*Turtle Island Alphabet*], this collection of essays might be pegged as a reference book by unsuspecting librarians. Rather, it is an affirmation of an ecologically sane way of life that has been largely lost to our modern age. Hausman has taken a list of symbols important to Native American cultures—such as beads, the eagle, and the totem—and written his thoughts and feelings about those topics and what he has learned about Native American life, past and present, mentioning many different tribes. More of a "spirit" of a dictionary than a tightly organized, dry reference book, *Turtle Island Alphabet* is quite readable and contains many bits and pieces of information, poetry, and stories.

THE GIFT OF THE GILA MONSTER: NAVAJO CEREMONIAL TALES (1993)

Publishers Weekly (review date 11 January 1993)

SOURCE: *Publishers Weekly* 240, no. 2 (11 January 1993): 57.

Hausman (*Meditations with the Navajo*) once again turns his storytelling to the Navajo people, this time [in *The Gift of the Gila Monster*] focusing on their principal "Ways"—ritual pathways whose ancient legends are used to heal, give moral instruction and attain inner harmony, or "walking in beauty." Only a few tales survive today; some of the best known are related here. Part of the Navajo creation myth involving four successive worlds, they all help define and order the Navajo's world and accomplish some sort of transformation. Readers will recognize many familiar characters and themes, such as Mother Earth and the trickster Coyote. The Blessingway includes the story of a man who out-tricks Coyote and a tale of resurrection. The Evil-Chasing Way tells of the encounters of Elder Brother and Younger Brother with the powerful Great Snake. Hausman's decision to retell the tales rather than to record them (as an ethnographer might) proves flawed. While the collection highlights the richness of Navajo spirituality, the voice here is ultimately Hausman's. Hillerman provides a brief but interesting foreword on Navajo theology; Mariah Fox's line drawings of sand paintings add atmosphere.

Donna Seaman (review date 15 February 1993)

SOURCE: Seaman, Donna. *Booklist* 89, no. 12 (15 February 1993): 1014-015.

YA. Hausman has explicated native American symbols and concepts in a host of earlier works, including *Turtle Island Alphabet*. This useful and radiant

little paperback [*The Gift of the Gila Monster*] explains and translates the Navajo cycle of myths and attendant rituals, which are called "Ways." These narrative songs and ceremonies functioned as either rites of healing or vehicles for teachings that inspire harmony both between tribe members and with nature. These events include singing, or chanting, the creation of sand paintings, and the "doctoring" performed by the medicine man. Many, including the Blessingway, celebrate life passages such as birth and reaching adulthood and feature stories about the tribe's origin and place in the cosmos. Only a small fraction of the hundreds of Navajo stories and songs once extant have survived; 11 are interpreted here, accompanied by full descriptions of the characters involved and their symbolic meaning. Hausman's lucid retelling of these vivid morality tales gives us a glimpse into the essence of the Navajo spirit and an understanding of the role these myths play in contemporary Navajo life.

TUNKASHILA: FROM THE BIRTH OF TURTLE ISLAND TO THE BLOOD OF WOUNDED KNEE (1993)

Publishers Weekly (review date 2 August 1993)

SOURCE: *Publishers Weekly* 240, no. 31 (2 August 1993): 60.

Nearly 70 tales from such diverse tribes as Creek, Navajo, Roanoke, Hopi, Lakota and Seminole are loosely strung together into a single epic in this disappointing effort by this popularizer of Indian culture [*Tunkashila*]. While not Native American himself, Hausman (*Turtle Island Alphabet*) traces his interest to the '30s when his mother, then an anthropology student, collected some of the tales used here. The bulk of them, however, Hausman culled from oral and more familiar published sources. Taken individually, some of the stories are well told. Particularly effective is "The Story of the Second Animal Council," in which beasts decide how to combat human encroachment, and "The Story of the White Deer Named Virginia Dare," an account from the Indian perspective of the first white child born in North America. The biggest flaw is at the very heart of Hausman's enterprise: his decision to synthesize myths from different traditions into a putatively linear narrative with little indication of each story's original context. Though the volume purports to give readers the history of North America through the eyes of its original inhabitants, it only provides a stereotyped, romanticized image.

Pat Monaghan (review date 15 September 1993)

SOURCE: Monaghan, Pat. *Booklist* 90, no. 2 (15 September 1993): 118.

YA. Imagine a rock with the passionate wisdom of Joseph Campbell, the encyclopedic learning of Sir James George Frazer, and the eloquence of William Butler Yeats. That rock would be the narrator of this book [*Tunkashila*], which combines tales from many Native American traditions to create a sweeping vision of life on this continent from the dawn of time to the visions of Black Elk. It reads like a complex novel rather than a collection of folktales. It also reads like it should be sung aloud, so strong is the oral nature of Hausman's writing. A splendid addition to any collection of Native Americana.

Edward Hower (review date 21 November 1993)

SOURCE: Hower, Edward. *New York Times Book Review* (21 November 1993): 26.

Once upon a time, according to a Native American legend, our continent was a tiny dab of mud on the back of a great turtle. How it became the home to mountains and rivers, animals and people, is the subject of Gerald Hausman's collection of tales that he calls *Tunkashila*—a word that means "grandfather" in Lakota. All the creations of nature, the author tells us, have divine antecedents, whose spirits will still guide us if we only know how to listen.

Mr. Hausman, who has written a dozen books (including *The Sun Horse* and *Turtle Island Alphabet*) on Indian culture, collected these tales over the past several decades from Native American friends of many tribes (he himself is part Iroquois) and from the notebooks of his mother, who was a student of anthropology in the 1930's.

One quality that differentiates *Tunkashila* from the many other compilations of Indian lore in print is the arrangement of tales in sequence, from the earliest eons of the cosmos to recent times. "Hundreds of tribal myths," Mr. Hausman explains, "are woven together, along with characters who are common to all tribes: the trickster, the chief, the warrior, the shaman and the lover." The interconnectedness of its stories allows the book to be read like a novel, a narrative about the history of the earth viewed from a non-Western, phantasmagorical perspective.

. . . . .

The deities that preceded the first people were awe-inspiring but by no means perfect. They had to learn much of their wisdom while combating the chaotic forces that roamed the newly fashioned earth. The Sun Father contended with creatures like Water Monster, "a witch, a slick and sodden hag whose skin was well-oiled with slime," and Cactus Giant, who had "hair of many-needled nastiness" and eyes that "had no pupils; only white orbs buried in fatty layers of dark green corpselike skin."

The gods and goddesses, like those of many mythologies, were, a lusty race. Sun Father's decision to people the earth arose when he first saw Earth Mother leaning over naked to wash her hair in the ocean. "Throwing a blue blanket on his turquoise horse, he rode down out of the clouds, with a sunbeam for a bridle and a rainbow for reins"—and had his way with her in a rollicking, erotic tussle that shook the universe.

For a time after their creation, people and animals lived together as one race, undifferentiated and interdependent. In one story, a spotted frog warns Listener, an Indian version of Noah, to build a raft in order to rescue his people from a great flood. The hero is then helped by a mosquito that changes into a beautiful woman who becomes his wife.

In another tale, a boy climbs a sacred mountain peak to steal a baby eagle from its nest. Its mother flings him into the abyss below, but when his brother returns the eaglet to its parents, they reward him with a glorious vision of the sky kingdom and the knowledge of medicinal herbs to give to his people.

A character named Bear Guardian marries a man and gives birth to an owl that, trying to mingle with humans, is humiliated at a dance and takes revenge by eating one of the human babies. Thus begins the era when people and animals are first separated, and with it the legend that the owl is the harbinger of doom.

As people evolved, the earth enjoyed periods of harmony, when the stories of their grandfathers guided them, and periods of warfare, from which very different tales of adventure, cruelty and heroism resulted. Stories were told to describe the coming of the foreigners. In one, Virginia Dare, the first child of English parents born on the continent, turns into a magical white doe that can be killed only with a silver arrowhead. The last war between the invaders and the people of Turtle Island ended at Wounded Knee, S.D. in 1890; afterwards, tales of military heroism became mere memories.

No two stories in this book are alike, though some characters—like the marvelous trickster figure, Shapeshifter—appear several times. Gerald Hausman's writing is richly lyrical; his language creates a swirling, lustrous world in which his characters come triumphantly to life.

Occasionally, however, he attempts to illuminate the meanings of the stories in the same lyrical style with which he tells them; this results in some vague, unsatisfying explanations. He provides a glossary of key characters, but one wishes he had included more information about the people whose stories he has told.

None of these problems take away from the pleasure of reading the tales themselves. Gerald Hausman's *Tunkashila* is an eloquent tribute to the first great storytellers of America.

DUPPY TALK: WEST INDIAN TALES OF MYSTERY AND MAGIC (1994)

Susan Scheps (review date January 1995)

SOURCE: Scheps, Susan. *School Library Journal* 41, no. 1 (January 1995): 118.

Gr 4-Up— Duppy (ghost) tales are a part of the African tradition, brought to the West Indies by tribal storytellers who came on slave ships. Hausman retells six tales [in *Duppy Talk*] that he learned in Jamaica, crediting his sources in a note after each one. Unlike those malicious ghosts of Western European and North American folklore, these spirits reward kindness and good character with gifts both tangible and spiritual (although they are not above an occasional good-humored trick or two). In one story, a bus driver delivers two little girls wearing nightgowns to a mountaintop house that he later learns has been gone for many years. His reward: the temperamental starter on his bus is fixed forever! In another selection, a man yearning for good luck reaps a bountiful reward after promising a dying cousin that he will care for his daughter. The language has a Jamaican ring, the notes are informative, and an 11-page glossary explains unfamiliar terms. This is one of the very few collections of West Indian folklore available for children . . . A worthy addition.

Janice Del Negro (review date 15 January 1995)

SOURCE: Del Negro, Janice. *Booklist* 91, no. 10 (15 January 1995): 918.

Gr 4-8. Gathered from storytellers on the north coast of Jamaica, these six tales [*Duppy Talk*] are built on legends brought from Africa to the Caribbean. Famil-

iar motifs are shaped by local lore and history. The stories are linked by a storyteller's voice, which provides unobtrusive background and context. Although all the tales have supernatural or mystical elements. "Chick Chick" is the scariest. It's a truly skin-crawling account of a woman's physical and psychological duel with a vengeful *duppy* (a restless soul believed to haunt the living) sent by an evil obeah man. Each tale opens with a Jamaican proverb, and a final chapter ("The Proverbs of Duppy Talk") discusses each saying's origin and meaning. The volume is attractively designed, with heavy, glossy pages, a generous amount of white space, and crisp black-and white chapter illustrations. There is also a strong glossary. The stories will be easy to booktalk and should have wide appeal across age and gender lines.

TURTLE ISLAND ABC: A GATHERING OF NATIVE AMERICAN SYMBOLS (1994)

Publishers Weekly (review date 9 May 1994)

SOURCE: *Publishers Weekly* 241, no. 19 (9 May 1994): 71.

[*Turtle Island ABC*] is not so much a collection of "Native American symbols" as a smattering of watered-down motifs from Native American cultures, this ABC adds up to not much. A lot of the information here seems empty: Hausman writes, for example, that W is for Wolf, the wanderer who was sent to find the "secret of the dawn" and came back without it, a meaningless anecdote unless told in the Native way, as a palatable offering of a life lesson. An introduction purports to add authority to the selection of words, but the book belies it. For instance, X is said to stand for "the Crossing Place"—a curious and confusing blend of sounds and letters. The "symbols," heavily weighted to the Plains and Southwest cultures, occasionally neglect to indicate origin (as in R is for Round, the shape of the lodge The People live in; this might be a reference to the Navajo hogan, although readers have earlier been shown the boxlike pueblos). Soft-edged, occasionally blurred illustrations in a palette of Southwestern colors are not particularly apt, and the lack of Native design elements results in a very Anglo-looking book. *All Ages.*

Lisa Mitten (review date July 1994)

SOURCE: Mitten, Lisa. *School Library Journal* 40, no. 7 (July 1994): 94

K-Gr 2—This alphabet book [*Turtle Island ABC*], compiled by the author of a number of collections of myths and stories from Indian traditions for adults, serves as a vehicle to present some key elements of Native American philosophies to children. One letter is featured per page on a full-color background in shades of red, purple, orange, or brown. The letter C is illustrated by corn, H by a hummingbird, B by a buffalo, etc., but the images are overwhelmed by the overbearing background palettes. Each entity speaks to readers in its own voice, explaining what it is and what function it fulfills in Native American life. This works well, and the text flows like poetry, conveying feelings much more than information. Everything is attributed to "The People," but only occasionally are the various items linked to their cultural homes. Although never made clear, the focus is on the South-western tribes, reflecting the author's association with them. Some symbols are common throughout the Americas, such as R for round or D for drum, but some are not particularly Native American (L for light and N for name), while others (K for kachina) have a unique tribal connection that is ignored. There is a slight New Age flavor to the book. Illustrations that lack sharpness and specificity mar this well-intentioned effort.

📖 *WILDERNESS* (1994)

Sister Avila (review date 1 February 1994)

SOURCE: Avila, Sister. *Library Journal* 119, no 2 (1 February 1994): 114.

Hausman, an authority on Native American culture and history as well as the terrain, wildlife, and beauties of the wilderness, and [Roger] Zelazny, an sf writer noted for his creative imagination, make ideal partners to produce this tale [*Wilderness*] about the survival of two supermen in the wild. In 1808, the famous hunter Jack Colter races for his life, pursued by Blackfoot warriors. For 150 miles he runs barefoot over mountains and plains, enduring incredible hardships. Hugh Glass, mauled by a bear and left for dead in 1823, drags, crawls, and finally walks from Grand Valley to the Missouri, a better man than when he started. A surprise ending will delight readers of this remarkable novel.

Wes Lukowsky (review date 15 February 1994)

SOURCE: Lukowsky, Wes. *Booklist* 90, no. 12 (15 February 1994): 1062.

YA. Alternating between two equally remarkable survival stories, award-winning science fiction writer [Roger] Zelazny and Native American studies expert

Hausman stitch together a narrative tribute [*Wilderness*] to both the American wilderness itself and the adventurous spirit of those who triumphed over it. In 1808, John Colter, who helped Lewis and Clark blaze a trail through the West, finds himself in a tight spot. As a form of ritual torture, a band of Blackfeet strip him to a loincloth and give him a modest head start before pursuing. Fifteen years later, trapper Hugh Glass is badly mauled by a bear and left for dead beside an open grave. He survives and crawls to the nearest settlement. Though parallel, these tales have their differences. Colter survived his ordeal because he wanted to avoid torture. Glass was driven by revenge. Readers may find the Colter tale more intriguing. He was engaged in a battle of wits with his pursuers, while Glass was at odds only with the elements and his own sanity. Taken together, the two both provide a memorable sense of the hardships that were a very real part of the settling of America.

Claudia Moore (review date July 1994)

SOURCE: Moore, Claudia. *School Library Journal* 40, no. 7 (July 1994): 129.

YA—Alternating chapters present fictionalized accounts of two true-life survival stories from the early days of the American West [in *Wilderness*]. In 1808, John Colter was pursued for 150 miles by Indians. In 1823, Hugh Glass managed to crawl, limp, etc. for 100 miles for help after being mauled by a bear and left for dead beside his potential grave. The opening pages are sure to lure readers inside as they are plunged immediately into the action. Later chapters show each man's introspective nature as he reminisces about friends and events in his life. Conversations exist only in these memories. Descriptions of nature and survival techniques abound. There are even a few comical moments. Animal tracks conclude most chapters and will pique YAs' curiosity. A brief concluding historical note provides information about what is known of the men following their adventures. Two gripping tales of courage, determination, and endurance.

Judith Beavers (review date January-February 1995)

SOURCE: Beavers, Judith. *The Book Report* 13, no. 4 (January-February 1995): 50.

Gr 10-Adult. Based on the lives and the legends of mountain men John Colter and Hugh Glass, this novel [*Wilderness*] alternates chapters focusing on one event in each of their lives. Captured by Black-foot warriors in 1808, Colter is given the opportunity to run for his life or face torture at the hands of his captors. When three of the fastest catch up to him, he feigns madness and dives into a river. Colter stays under water by breathing the air in a sunken log and later hides in a beaver lodge. After numerous encounters with his pursuers, he finally escapes them in Colter's Hell (Yellowstone) and heads across the grasslands to a fort. The Hugh Glass story tells of his attack by a grizzly in 1823. He is left to die by his comrades who are afraid of a war party of Arikaras. Driven by his anger at his companions' desertion, Glass begins his legendary 100-mile crawl to safety. The authors tie the two stories together in a St. Louis tavern in 1812 when the young Hugh Glass meets the old John Colter. At times, the novel is full of action, but the authors also use both interior monologue to reveal the characters' emotions and flashbacks to fill in the details of their earlier lives. At times the characters' journeys become dreamscapes laced with Native American symbols and flights of poetic fantasy. Such techniques make this novel a choice for the sophisticated reader. It will fit in well with American literature and history courses. Added bonus: the novel may inspire readers to find out more about Colter's experiences on the Lewis and Clark Expedition.

COYOTE WALKS ON TWO LEGS: A BOOK OF NAVAJO MYTHS AND LEGENDS (1995)

Lauren Peterson (review date 1 April 1995)

SOURCE: Peterson, Lauren. *Booklist* 91, no. 15 (1 April 1995): 1421.

Ages 6-9. In these five short tales [*Coyote Walks on Two Legs*] based on Navajo myths, Coyote becomes a victim of his own greed and vanity and often causes considerable trouble for those around him. In one story, Coyote steals the water-monster babies, causing the Great Flood and forcing all the Animal People to run up the mountains to escape. In another, Coyote's envy of the spotted coats of the fawns leads him to try to get a spotted coat of his own. The book has much to recommend it: children will adore the antics of a foolish but lovable trickster; and [Floyd] Cooper's realistic illustrations are very pleasing, beautifully rendered in the rich, warm tones of the desert. However, teachers interested in using this in conjunction with a unit on Native Americans will find it best suited to story time, as there aren't enough specifics included about the culture itself.

Beth Tegart (review date August 1995)

SOURCE: Tegart, Beth. *School Library Journal* 41, no. 8 (August 1995): 122.

Gr 2-4—In this fine collection [*Coyote Walks on Two Legs*], a master storyteller relates five traditional tales. In these selections, told in lyrical, free-flowing prose, readers see Coyote as a trickster, a fool, as well as a hero. These are not the silly Coyote stories of Gerald McDermott but rather more serious legends, such as "The Great Flood," "The Guardian of the Corn," and others. Coyote, here, is both everyman and himself, an animal and human prototype. [Floyd] Cooper's fittingly muted, sepia and gold-toned watercolor illustrations have a dreamlike quality. The animals are rendered in a naturalistic, but soft-focused style and are particularly expressive. A well done but additional purchase.

DOCTOR MOLEDINKY'S CASTLE: A HOMESPUN TALE (1995)

John Sigwald (review date October 1995)

SOURCE: Sigwald, John. *School Library Journal* 41, no. 10 (October 1995): 133.

Hausman's "Hometown Tale" [*Doctor Moledinky's Castle*] is a storytelling delight. Andy, 12, is setting down the events of the strange summer of 1957 while it is still fresh in his mind. That particular summer is memorable for several reasons. A girl holds his hand at a chicken beheading, and then runs away with the head; and he and his best friend, Pauly, get a job feeding the animals in Doctor Moledinky's Animal Museum, a daily show that could be as entertaining for the bloodthirsty crowd as it is sporting for the hungry, cage-crazed gators and groundhogs. He and Pauly pay nighttime visits to Berkeley Bend's two weirdest denizens, Doctor Moledinky at his castle (with a moat) and Mrs. Henshaw, who lives in an unfinished shack in the shadow of the castle. These absorbing vignettes are loosely tied together by people and place. Each chapter has its own personality, and Hausman careens from humor to melodrama to melancholy, occasionally even to nostalgia. Each incident is faithfully filtered through an adolescent's eyes and Andy's wonder heightens the adventure for young readers, who may realize that Berkeley Bend—even with a millionaire and a witch or two—might not really be all that different from their own hometowns. This is a summer with more than one "steamy moat-drooling night," one full of unlikely connections.

Janice Del Negro (review date 1 December 1995)

SOURCE: Del Negro, Janice. *Booklist* 92, no. 7 (1 December 1995): 618.

Gr 7-12. In first-person stories that speak directly to readers, Andy tells about his twelfth summer and his somewhat bizarre hometown [in **Doctor Moledinky's Castle**]. In "Bobby the Streak and Joey the Jolt," Andy and his friend Pauly discover a local fleet-footed hood's secret for running like the wind—Bryl-cream and a D.A. ("Duck's Ass") hairstyle. In another episode, the two friends venture into Italian Town, where they confront Joey the Jolt Delmonico, another local bad boy. The narrative voice sometimes lapses into self-conscious philosophizing, and the use of the phrase "two-fisted, bad-sided greaseball" in one story is unnecessarily derogatory. But the language is engaging, often poetic, and frequently humorous as Andy delves into the lives of a town full of eccentrics and tries to make sense of everybody's story.

☐ *HOW CHIPMUNK GOT TINY FEET: NATIVE AMERICAN ORIGIN STORIES* (1995)

Publishers Weekly (review date 29 May 1995)

SOURCE: *Publishers Weekly* 242, no, 22 (29 May 1995): 84.

Hausman's (**Turtle Island ABC**) retelling of seven Navajo, Koasati Creek and Tsimshian tales [**How Chipmunk Got Tiny Feet**] is a standout in an increasingly crowded genre. His tone is casual and unpretentious, his rhythm and pacing impeccable. Because the stories all feature animals that in each tribe "are thought of as people," they offer many subtle lessons about human behavior. In "How Horse Got Fast," slow-footed Horse kindly waits for a poky caterpillar to cross his path. The caterpillar, who then changes into a butterfly, rewards Horse with swiftness rivaling his own. Most stories include a visit by beneficent Mother Earth, who rights wrongs and fosters harmony. Using her customary linoleum block prints painted with watercolors, [Ashley] Wolff (*A Year of Beasts; A Year of Birds*) strikingly combines detailed Native American borders with her almost classical, storybook-style illustrations—a fitting blend, given the book's artfully achieved relevance to two very different cultures. *Ages 4-8.*

Janice Del Negro (review date 1 September 1995)

SOURCE: Del Negro, Janice. *Booklist* 92, no. 1 (1 September 1995): 68.

Gr 3-5, Younger for Reading Aloud. Seven animal origin tales from the Navajo, Koasati Creek, and Tsimshian traditions are succinctly retold in this nicely designed picture book [**How Chipmunk Got Tiny Feet**]. In vigorous retellings with action-oriented plots, Hausman explains "How Coyote Got Yellow Eyes," "How Horse Got Fast," and other mysteries of nature. With their culturally evocative borders, [Ashley] Wolff's illustrations (linoleum block prints painted with watercolors) enliven the tales. The large type, generous white space, and attractive artwork will make the collection an easy sell to transitional readers wanting something to read alone and to parents and teachers seeking a read-aloud that is not too intimidating. No specific sources are given.

Ellen Fader (review date September-October 1995)

SOURCE: Fader, Ellen. *Horn Book Magazine* 71, no. 4 (September-October 1995): 613.

(Younger) Storyteller and scholar Hausman retells seven animal origin stories [in **How Chipmunk Got Tiny Feet**] that he collected from the traditions of the Navajo, Koasati Creek, and Tsimshian. The stories explain such common aspects of nature as why possums have long, skinny tails, why crickets chirp, and why skunks have big bushy tails and are perceived as bashful. Children will relish the magic in "How Horse Got Fast," in which a plodding horse's kindness to a caterpillar-turned-butterfly results in the horse being able to run like the wind. The same story also divulges why horse tracks resemble the two wings of a butterfly. Other tales relate how bat learned to fly, why lizards are flat, and how coyote gained his yellow eyes. In each story, Mother Earth makes an appearance. Although her outer trappings change with the season and setting, her kindly ways never vary: she is the perennial peacemaker and problem solver. Hausman's brief introduction reminds readers that the reason each of the stories has the same message—that we must all learn to live together—is that the tales are told to teach Native children about the ways of the world. The retellings, with their elements of humor, mystery, conflict, and just resolution, are eminently satisfying. [Ashley] Wolff's linoleum block prints, which are enhanced with watercolor, add considerable interest to the tales. She creates three unique borders inspired by the three cultures represented; since the colors are similar from one to the next, the designs serve to tie the tales together.

AFRICAN-AMERICAN ALPHABET: A CELEBRATION OF AFRICAN-AMERICAN AND WEST INDIAN CULTURE, CUSTOM, MYTH, AND SYMBOL (1996)

Brad Hooper (review date 15 February 1996)

SOURCE: Hooper, Brad. *Booklist* 92, no. 12 (15 February 1996): 985.

YA. In A-to-Z format [*African-American Alphabet*], one entry for each letter of the alphabet, and each entry several pages long, the authors use key words to launch themselves on wide ranging discussions of major traditions found in the common-linked cultures of Africa, black America, and the Caribbean. Entries range from "Amistad," the name of a slave ship involved in an important legal case in which captives intended for slavery were set free, to "Zion," a concept that was "for the African-American slave, a dream, a rhythm, a way of life where there was no suffering." In addition to a full commentary in each entry on the specific topic at hand and its relevance to black history and legends, the authors supply accompanying illustrations and lyrics of spirituals, poems, quotes from personal recollections, and other excerpted material to give additional dimension to their presentations. Not simply a book to have fun with, but also one to learn from.

EAGLE BOY: A TRADITIONAL NAVAJO LEGEND (1996)

Publishers Weekly (review date 18 December 1995)

SOURCE: *Publishers Weekly* 242, no. 51 (18 December 1995): 54.

Serene, ethereal pastels underscore the dreamlike nature of this traditional Navajo legend [*Eagle Boy*], seamlessly retold by Hausman. Carried away by Father Eagle to the "country of clouds at the top of the sky," a Native American boy has an encounter with trickster Coyote, receives a new name and is finally returned to his family with the help of a pair of bumblebees and a sacred feather. Readers won't be surprised that, after such an adventure, the boy grows up to become a great medicine man. [Barry and Cara] Moser père et fille, who previously teamed up with Hausman for **Turtle Island ABC,** provide this tale with an eye-catching backdrop, saturated with the rich colors of a Southwest sunset and slightly blurred, as if softly obscured by the mists of time. *Ages 5-9.*

Patricia Lothrop Green (review date February 1996)

SOURCE: Green, Patricia Lothrop. *School Library Journal* 42, no. 2 (February 1996): 94-5.

K-Gr 3—A boy "who dreamed of eagles" [*Eagle Boy*] is caught up by Father Eagle, fed sacred cornmeal, wrapped in the sacred robes, and carried (along with a rock crystal and a sheep's horn to breathe through) to the top of the sky. There the Eagle Chief welcomes him to his "great white cloud house," but tells him not to go out alone. Tempted by Coyote, the boy disobeys and is turned into a coyote himself. Eagle Chief not only returns him to human form, but also gives him a new name of power, Eagle Boy, and sends him safely back to his hogan and family. Although the true significance of this story (the learning of the Eagle Way) is culturally specific to the Navajo, and its morality is alien (the boy is not punished for his disobedience but profits from it), the magic of flying with the godlike birds may still engage readers in the adventure. Almost every page is bordered with blue at the top; a layer of white cloud and tones of yellow and terra cotta in the middle; and vermilion at the foot of the page. It is this red rock-and-sky color scheme that speaks of Navajo land, rather than details of design or costume. A few closeups of the boy and the eagle, and an imaginative bird's-eye view of a hogan, are effective; the other soft, undetailed images are not striking or memorable.

Carolyn Phelan (review date 1 February 1996)

SOURCE: Phelan, Carolyn. *Booklist* 92, no. 11 (1 February 1996): 934.

Ages 5-8. In this Navajo legend [*Eagle Boy*], a boy who dreams of eagles is taken up to the cloud house, where the Eagle Chief tells him he will be happy as long as he does not open the door while the chief is gone. Duped by Coyote the trickster, the boy disobeys the Eagle Chief's instruction and becomes a coyote himself. The Eagle Chief returns the boy to human form and sends him back home, where he grows up to be a great medicine man. Hausman retells the story with simplicity and dignity, but like a dream, it seems distant and has some unexplained elements. The background of each doublepage spread features subtle shades of glowing colors, generally with at least one character beautifully defined in light and shadows. Teachers may find this an effective book to read aloud.

□ *NIGHT FLIGHT* (1996)

Hazel Rochman (review date 1 March 1996)

SOURCE: Rochman, Hazel. *Booklist* 92, no. 13 (1 March 1996): 1174.

Gr. 5-8. Jeff's cool friend Max is anti-Semitic: What would he do if he knew Jeff was half-Jewish? In this first-person narrative, [*Night Flight*] based on a real event in the author's childhood, 12-year-old Jeff Hausman confronts his identity. Max blames the Jews for poisoning the dogs in his lakeside community, and reluctantly, Jeff is drawn into Max's plans for revenge. To his shame, Jeff is haunted by a secret, a nightmare he can't forget, involving a time when Max shot a burlap bag full of live kittens, and Jeff stood by passively. The plot creaks with contrived parallels and heavy metaphors, including a patched-on episode about burned books and a Gypsy librarian-poet who spells out wise messages. The history will confuse kids: the story is set in the 1950s; Jeff's father left Hungary long before World War II; Max's father, however, was a Nazi. Still, Hausman writes with poetry and immediacy about coming to America ("We left farms and family and turned our faces to the faceless sea") and about the moral conflict of a boy who finally finds the courage to identify with his Jewish father and know himself.

Ann W. Moore (review date April 1996)

SOURCE: Moore, Ann W. *School Library Journal* 42, no. 4 (April 1996): 134.

Gr 5-8—In 1957, 12-year-old Jeff and his best friend, Max, have a falling out when their dogs are poisoned, and Max blames local Jews [in *Night Flight*]. Jeff, unknown to Max, is half-Jewish; Max's father, Jeff discovers, was a Nazi. Over the summer, Jeff struggles with mixed feelings toward his friend and confusion about his own identity. By the book's end, he has established a self-image that he feels comfortable with and that even Max admires. *Night Flight* is a potentially intriguing story that goes sadly awry. The two boys are so diametrically opposed that their friendship is implausible (this is compounded by their curious ignorance of one another's families). Hausman's writing is overwrought with excessive description, introspection, and symbolism. He is preachy and relies on stereotypes (Max and his father are the ultimate Nazis, while the Jewish community is so idealized that it becomes comical). There are unexplained gaps in the story line, as well as historically

inaccurate language. Finally, the book is too contrived; people, places, memories, and experiences are tidily assembled to help Jeff mature. *Night Flight* just doesn't take off.

Robert L. Otte (review date September-October 1996)

SOURCE: Otte, Robert L. *The Book Report* 15, no. 2 (September-October 1996): 38.

Gr 6-8. During the summer of 1957, Jeff and his friend Max play look-out in the crow's nest Jeff's grandfather built [in *Night Flight*]. Then the two boys' dogs are poisoned along with other dogs in the neighborhood. Max, a bigot, immediately suspects a Jewish neighbor, not knowing that Jeff is half-Jewish. Jeff then must choose between betraying his heritage and following Max or being loyal to his family and losing his friend. This well-written page-turner combines the mystery of uncovering the culprits and the difficult dilemma of choosing between friendship and honesty. Hausman says the book is based on an actual event in his life. Middle-school readers may find the story is relevant to theirs.

□ *THE KEBRA NEGAST: THE BOOK OF RASTAFARIAN WISDOM AND FAITH FROM ETHIOPIA AND JAMAICA* (1997)

Mike Tribby (review date 1 October 1997)

SOURCE: Tribby, Mike. *Booklist* 94, no. 3 (1 October 1997): 284-85.

Not as trendy as it once was, Rastafarianism still has committed adherents, and they may be more interested in its underpinnings than just in its use of ganja as a sacrament. Hausman's new edition [*The Kebra Negast*] of the Ethiopian compilation of lore that posits that Jesus was black is for such persons. Hausman's preface and the melodic verses of the text, written in rustic, awed tones and full of the lilt of roots Reggae lyrics, take aim at true believers. The text's narrative rambles at times, but not badly for a holy book. To brusquely reduce it to its main thrust, the Kebra Negast supports the claims to black presence in biblical lore through the lineage of King Solomon's Ethiopian children. Hausman augments the main text with a little compendium of parallel quotations from the Bible and the most famous Rastafarian—certainly to "Waspafarians"—the late Bob Marley. Inspirational, informational, melodious stuff.

L. Kriz (review date 1 October 1997)

SOURCE: Kriz, L. *Library Journal* 122, no. 16 (1 October 1997): 88.

Folklorist and author Hausman has combined ten years of informal study in Jamaica, the 1922 version of "The Queen of Sheba and Her Only Son Menyelek" (translated by E.A. Wallis Budge), the Koran, the King James Bible, and the words of reggae great Bob Marley into a new version of the *Kebra Negast* ("the glory of the Kings"). This "lost bible," the core of Rastafarian wisdom and faith, has survived through oral tradition in many Caribbean nations, even though it has been banned because of its African glory themes. Hausman effectively puts the *Kebra Negast* into the words of the Rastafarian community, presenting the core—that "we must learn to live by the laws of compassion rather than judgment"—through anecdotes from the author's travels in the Rasta community. A recommended introduction to the *Kebra Negast.*

📖 DOCTOR BIRD: THREE LOOKIN' UP TALES FROM JAMAICA (1998)

Publishers Weekly (review date 11 May 1998)

SOURCE: *Publishers Weekly* 245, no. 19 (11 May 1998): 67-8.

The Doctor Bird [in *Doctor Bird*] is a rainbow-winged, streamer-tailed hummingbird that lives only in Jamaica—and is that West Indian island's beloved national bird. Here, in a trio of wordy folktales, a top-hatted Doctor Bird uses magical powers plus his own wisdom to teach other creatures important lessons. Working in her characteristic combination of black gesso and rich gouaches, [Ashley] Wolff (previously paired with Hausman for *How Chipmunk Got Tiny Feet*) features lush foliage and exotic lizards and monkeys in dark outline and deep, crepuscular colors. One page might vividly illustrate a scene from the story (e.g., Doctor Bird teaches Mongoose not to steal by subjecting her house to an onslaught of disturbances, ending in a snowstorm) while an inset on the facing page amplifies details (Mongoose pours her delicious hibiscus tea to sweeten up Doctor Bird). Each tale ends with the tag: "And if this story isn't true, let the keeper of heaven's door say so now." Yet the messages are muddy. Mongoose, for example, reverts to "the way she always was, is, and forever will be"; the only difference is that she now returns what she "borrows" whenever it snows. While the folksy rhythms of the sentences and occasional vernacular words add charm and authenticity ("he was going to hoo-doo all the people at the Guango party"), the text ambles and characterization is weak. Overall, the writing is not the equal of the intriguing, lively art. *Ages 5-Up.*

John Peters (review date 1 June 1998)

SOURCE: Peters, John. *Booklist* 94, no. 19-20 (1 June 1998): 1754.

Gr 3-5. In this trio of animal stories [*Doctor Bird*] gathered from Jamaica's north coast, the wise and lovely streamer-tailed hummingbird, found only on the island, sets straying animals back on the right path: a dimwitted owl who tries to crash a party in Doctor Bird's clothes and almost loses his tail feathers; a homeless mouse who unexpectedly finds food and refuge in the trees; and a light-pawed mongoose who resists Doctor Bird's magic but is at last persuaded to give up her "borrowing" ways—temporarily, at least. The text is printed in a heavy typeface that stands up well to Wolff's bold lines and strongly defined forms. With a top hat to complement his long, streaming tail and rainbow-hued wings, Doctor Bird cuts an elegant figure as he hovers amid tropical vegetation and similarly clad wildlife. Rather than write in dialect, Hausman lightly evokes oral cadences with a few scattered words or turns of phrase, and he names his sources (people, not books) in an appended note. Young readers and listeners will be drawn to Doctor Bird by his good cheer and his good advice alike.

Marilyn Iarusso (review date September 1998)

SOURCE: Iarusso, Marilyn. *School Library Journal* 44, no. 9 (September 1998): 191-92.

Gr 1-3—Three stories about a popular Jamaican folktale character. *Doctor Bird,* a beautiful hummingbird, displays optimism, wit, the ability to work magic, and a penchant for using rhymes and riddles to teach lessons as he tries to reform a thieving mongoose, encourages and comforts a homeless mouse, and shows an owl that it's important to be yourself. The tales have easy-to-follow action and morals that children will appreciate. A traditional ending is used for all three: "And if this story isn't true, let the keeper of heaven's door say so now." The inclusion of unfamiliar creatures such as Mr. Pocket Parrot, Miss Banana Quit, and Uncle Galliwasp, and references to vegetation, games, and other local practices provide regional flavor. The handsome full- and double-page paintings are done with black gesso and gouache. Because many of the animals wear hats and other bits of clothing, the illustrations are more cartoonlike than some of [Ashley] Wolff's other work, but they are charming and beautifully composed, with sprightly animals and lush images of the landscape and the seashore. The storytellers from whom the tales are drawn are named, but no details are given on individual stories. A great book for sharing, particularly for those who have roots in the Caribbean.

THE MYTHOLOGY OF CATS: FELINE LEGEND AND LORE THROUGH THE AGES (1998)

Florence Scarinci (review date July 1998)

SOURCE: Scarinci, Florence. *Library Journal* 123, no. 12 (July 1998): 121.

It is common knowledge that cats have been the familiars of witches and that they possess nine lives. But how many people know that Buddha and Muhammad had beloved feline companions or that throughout the ages cats have been regarded in a positive manner as healers, caretakers, spirit guides, harbingers of good luck, martyrs, and deities who confer fertility on the fields? The Hausmans, authors of *The Mythology of Dogs* (1997) and other books on mythology, spent two decades researching the lore of cats. The result [*The Mythology of Cats*] is an entertaining compilation of legends from ancient Egypt, Greece, Rome, and Asia; folktales from medieval Europe; and literary references from modern poetry and fiction. Each tale concludes with a description of a specific breed that seems to typify the legend. An extensive bibliography is included. . . . [T]his book is recommended for public libraries with large folklore or pet collections.

Barbara Jacobs (review date August 1998)

SOURCE: Jacobs, Barbara. *Booklist* 94, no. 22 (August 1998): 1943.

There is an invisible danger attached to the Hausmans' paean to cats [in *The Mythology of Cats*]. It is extremely difficult to sift throuqh the 30 different personalities and almost as many breeds before succumbing to temptation and bringing home a mewing kitten. Other than that, the book is an ailurophile's delight, with literary excerpts and legends to remember. The Cheshire cat (aka British shorthair) evokes *Alice in Wonderland* memories, while good-luck cats—as exemplified by the Burmese, Chartreux, and Korat—effectively destroy myths of devil affiliations. After a while, the prose occasionally lapses into a sing-song rhythm; all in all, though, a reference for party chatterers, a browser for idle leisure time, and an homage to feline companion animals. *YA.*

THE STORY OF BLUE ELK (1998)

Ilene Cooper (review date 15 May 1998)

SOURCE: Cooper, Ilene. *Booklist* 94, no. 18 (15 May 1998): 1628.

Ages 5-9. A baby of the Pueblo people is born destined not to utter a word [in *The Story of Blue Elk*]. However, he is blessed by the visit of an elk on his birthday. The boy, named Blue Elk, grows up to establish a friendship with his elk, and when the elk dies, its antlers are planted in the ground and become one with a cedar tree. This wood and horn union yields a flute that becomes the boy's voice and allows him to "speak" musically to the woman he loves. Hausman says in the author's note that there are many versions of the Blue Elk story; this one employs elements from two fellow storytellers. The watercolor-and-colored-pencil artwork is bold and very effective when depicting settings, though less so when it comes to people, who sometimes appear stiff. Libraries looking for legends of the Pueblo Indians will find this a useful version.

Judith Gloyer (review date August 1998)

SOURCE: Gloyer, Judith. *School Library Journal* 44, no. 8 (August 1998): 150-51.

Gr 2-5—The appearance of an elk that casts a blue shadow in a pueblo village marks the birth of a boy who is unable to speak [in *The Story of Blue Elk*]. Several years later, he falls in love with a girl but is unable to tell her. He encounters the great elk, his "name giver," again and they share idyllic times together. When the animal dies, a cedar tree grows where his antlers lay. Years later, Blue Elk creates a flute from the wood. With it he is able to enchant animals and people and eventually win the girl he loved as a youth. Hausman deftly weaves together several versions of this tale, which he describes in an author's note. With beautiful, vivid language, he conveys the interconnectedness between Native Americans and the natural world and the gifts each gives. [Kristina] Rodanas's realistic paintings, done in oil-based colored pencil on watercolor wash, show respect for the individuals and the setting. A lyrical tale from a gifted and experienced storyteller.

📖 THE COYOTE BEAD (1999)

Darcy Schild (review date January 2000)

SOURCE: Schild, Darcy. *School Library Journal* 46, no. 1 (January 2000): 132.

Gr 7-Up—In the 1860s, the American army was attempting to place the Navajo people on a reservation more than 300 miles from their homeland, where many of them died, or were killed outright. The Ute fought them, or helped the white soldiers. It is during this turbulent period that this story [*The Coyote Bead*] begins. When Tobachischin's parents are killed by soldiers and Utes in Canyon del Muerto, AZ, the wounded boy makes his way up the steep walls to his grandfather's hogan. This elder, knowledgeable in the ways of healing and spirits, helps the boy recover physically, then begin a spiritual and literal journey to safety. As the story progresses, reality merges more and more with the mystical aspects of life. In the beginning, signs are read from animals, and wounds are healed with cures from nature and chants. By the climax, battle is being fought against the wind, the rain, phantom horses in the air, and a creature capable of changing into various human and animal shapes. The characters accept the power of magic as a part of everyday life, and so they easily take readers with them as the tale grows in complexity and depth. Youngsters willing to suspend disbelief and follow this journey will become caught up in a culture and a tale that whirls them through an unexpected landscape. A unique and intriguing historical novel.

📖 DOGS OF MYTH: TALES FROM AROUND THE WORLD (1999)

Michael Cart (review date 1 November 1999)

SOURCE: Cart, Michael. *Booklist* 96, no. 5 (1 November 1999): 520.

Gr 3-5. In this picture book for older readers [*Dogs of Myth*] with illustrations by Barry Moser, the Hausmans offer a baker's dozen retellings of dog stories

they've culled from far-flung sources. There's a creation myth from Africa about a basenji who steals fire for the first man and loses his bark in the bargain. From the mythology of the British Isles comes the tale of an enchanted bloodhound only two inches tall. There are trickster dogs from Japanese, Eskimo, and Native American traditions, enchanted dogs, super dogs, and even a few shaggy dogs. The 13 stories, from as many different cultures, are grouped in six categories, with each story followed by an afterword that provides historical context and commentary. Six of the stories are recycled from the Hausmans' earlier book *The Mythology of Dogs* (1997), and all of the tales are a bit flat. But the book is so elegantly designed, and Moser's paintings of dogs are so irresistible, that most readers probably won't care.

Publishers Weekly (review date 8 November 1999)

SOURCE: *Publishers Weekly* 246, no. 45 (8 November 1999): 68.

[Barry] Moser's (*My Dog Rosie*) luminous watercolors light up this anthology [*Dogs of Myth*] of 13 rarely told folktales that pay homage to canines. Grouped by type ("The Trickster Dog," "The Guardian Dog," and so on), the stories span a wide range of cultures and breeds. From Celtic faery lore, for instance, there's an enchanted bloodhound; from the Eskimos, a husky whose absentmindedness has cosmic consequences; and from ancient China, a devoted sharpei who wins the hand of the emperor's daughter. An instructive afterword follows each selection, explaining its origins as well as providing additional facts about the featured dog. The Hausmans' (*The Mythology of Dogs*) storytelling flows in an unbroken, lyrical stream, right from the poetic introduction ("Step softly now into that fresh dawn, when a man went out for a walk in the light, and found Dog"). Moser's portraits could serve as nature studies, and whether he is depicting a massive rottweiler clenching Thor's hammer in his jaws, a sleek saluki or the soulful eyes of a curly-coated retriever, his watercolors are rooted in realism and lovingly evoked. This book is sheer bliss for dog lovers. *Ages 7-Up.*

Cheri Estes (review date March 2000)

SOURCE: Estes, Cheri. *School Library Journal* 46, no. 3 (March 2000): 254.

Gr 2-6—An engaging collection of 13 tales from around the world [*Dogs of Myth*]. The well-written stories are grouped into six categories: "The Creation

Dog," "The Trickster Dog," "The Enchanted Dog," "The Guardian Dog," "The Super Dog," and "The Treasure Dog." These divisions give a nice continuity to the tales and provide a sampling of world cultures and myths. Canines are as varied as an Akita in Japan, a Norse rottweiler, a wolfhound in Wales, and a bichon frise in France. Notes on each story offer background and related information; source notes are included at the end. [Barry] Moser's illustrations are gorgeously rendered in his trademark watercolor style, but they are decorative and don't add anything to the understanding or energy of the selections. The overall design of the book is attractive, with excellent page layout and choices of typefaces and colors. Purchase where dog stories are popular or where readers might be looking for multicultural tales outside the norm.

CATS OF MYTH: TALES FROM AROUND THE WORLD (2000)

Publishers Weekly (review date 20 November 2000)

SOURCE: *Publishers Weekly* 247, no. 47 (20 November 2000): 70.

A companion to their *Dogs of Myth: Tales from Around the World,* Gerald and Loretta Hausman's oversize *Cats of Myth: Tales from Around the World* gathers nine stories from traditions as far-flung as Bahamian, Japanese Zen, East Indian and German-Swiss, with the everyday cat viewed as a mystic, trickster, guardian and more. Paired with watercolors by Leslie Baker, these sumptuously told, exotic stories (and their informative afterwords) should grab lovers of folktales as well as feline fanciers. *Ages 6-Up.*

Nancy Call (review date December 2000)

SOURCE: Call, Nancy. *School Library Journal* 46, no. 12 (December 2000): 133.

Gr 3-5—East Indian, Japanese, Jamaican, German, Czech, Egyptian, and other traditions were tapped to provide fodder for this thoughtful look [*Cats of Myth*] at the many roles in which cats are cast in traditional mythology—creator, trickster, goddess, monster, and guardian. [Leslie] Baker's lively full- and double-page watercolor illustrations enhance the 10 tales, bringing out the innocent, humorous, or regal qualities of the feline in question. An afterword follows

each smoothly written selection, providing additional facts about an individual breed or elucidating cultural references. Entertaining whether read alone or aloud, this attractive volume is a good companion to the Hausmans' *Dogs of Myth,* presented in the same format with Barry Moser's illustrations.

Ilene Cooper (review date 15 December 2000)

SOURCE: Cooper, Ilene. *Booklist* 97, no. 8 (15 December 2000): 813.

Gr 3-6, Younger for Reading Aloud. This handsome, oversize book [*Cats of Myth*] is not just a treat for cat lovers but also for readers who enjoy a good folktale. The authors offer nine stories about cats, dividing them into categories such as the trickster cat, the guardian cat, the goddess cat. The tales come from many places and times: ancient Egypt, Southeast Asia, Europe, and Polynesia. From India comes a story about how the cat became domesticated—at the expense of its friend the tiger. A Japanese Aen tale describes a martial arts confrontation between an old temple cat and a rat. Leslie Baker's enchanting watercolor art using layered washes appears throughout the stories, and each tale begins with a Barry Moser-like portrait of the cat protagonist. Giving the book extra heft are the notes and sources that discuss both the tales and the cats featured in them. A worthy purchase.

TOM CRINGLE: BATTLE ON THE HIGH SEAS (2000)

William McLoughlin (review date November 2000)

SOURCE: McLoughlin, William. *School Library Journal* 46, no. 11 (November 2000): 154.

Gr 4-8—A 13-year-old English boy offers a firstperson account of eight adventurous months at sea during the War of 1812 [*Tom Cringle: Battle on the High Seas*]. Tom's coming-of-age story begins with his appointment as a midshipman on the *Bream,* a guard vessel ordered to protect Britain's Caribbean colonies against prowling ships, many of which have been commandeered by pirates. Admired for his "eagle's eye" that can spot enemy ships miles away, Tom quickly becomes the chief lookout and the captain's favorite. When a violent storm destroys the ship, only the boy, his dog, and two other crew members survive. Eventually the group is taken aboard the *Blackbird,* a pirate ship commanded by Obediah Glasgow, a haughty Scottish freeman who accepts their gold buttons as payment for safe passage to a British naval station. Tom is simultaneously fascinated and frightened by the scurrilous Obediah, and the two forge a strange, unlikely friendship. The first third of this novel is fast-paced and entertaining, brimming with colorful descriptions of life aboard the *Bream,* where Tom experiences drudgery, disease, thrilling naval battles, and the death of a companion. After the vessel is destroyed, however, the plot begins to flounder, moving erratically through a disjointed series of events and settings that do little to sustain readers' interest. Hausman writes with flourish and can fill five pages with the description of a sword fight's acrobatics, but doesn't flesh out his characters or plot with the same detail or fervor.

Carolyn Phelan (review date 1 November 2000)

SOURCE: Phelan, Carolyn. *Booklist* 97, no. 5 (1 November 2000): 526.

Gr 6-8. This fictional diary [***Tom Cringle: Battle on the High Seas***] chronicles seven months in the life of Tom Cringle, an English lad who decides to go to sea in 1812. Most of the action takes place in the Caribbean during two improbably eventful months that are fraught with peril: battles at sea, the deaths of friends and shipmates, an earthquake, a shipwreck, a mutiny, a sword fight, and a drowning. The many period details and the constant waves of incidents seem to impede character and story development rather than moving them forward. Based on two nineteenth-century accounts of youths serving on ships in the Caribbean, this novel will appeal most to readers whose liking for fictional historical diaries springs from a true fascination with history and an affinity for action stories. For larger collections.

📖 *THE JACOB LADDER* (2001)

Ellen Vevier (review date April 2001)

SOURCE: Vevier, Ellen. *School Library Journal* 47, no. 4 (April 2001): 140.

Gr 4-7—An autobiographical slice of Jamaican village life in the 1960s [***The Jacob Ladder***], based on co-author [Uton] Hinds's boyhood experiences. Tall T watches his father, who has a weakness for alcohol and bone dice, pick up his suitcase and leave the family one day to go live next door in the home of the *obeah* (voodoo woman) and her flirtatious daughter. When Tall T's mother gathers the children to tell them, "Brothers and sisters stick together. They don't wash away like gully water," the theme and tone for this excellent book are established. Tall T is given the honor of marching with his father and the other Jonkonnu men on Christmas Day, yet his father ignores him. Lacking the money for proper school clothes, the boy escapes to the library, where he is befriended and tutored by a librarian. The book ends with Tall T making a literal and symbolic climb up the "Jacob Ladder" used by the banana workers to ascend from the boats in the sea, where he reaches a new level of understanding about love, family, human frailty, and his own resources. The characters are complex and real people; there are no good guys/bad guys here—not even the boy's father, whose behavior Tall T ultimately is able to put in perspective. Readers will be quickly drawn in by the protagonist's honest and questioning preadolescent voice. A compelling and vibrant book that will give young readers a real look into the Jamaica behind the postcard and cruise-ship images.

Hazel Rochman (review date 1 May 2001)

SOURCE: Rochman, Hazel. *Booklist* 97, no. 17 (1 May 2001): 1678.

Gr 5-8. Based on the childhood of Jamaican coauthor, Uton Hinds, [***The Jacob Ladder***] is a harsh story of poverty and betrayal. It's also about family love and faith. When his charismatic father, Brother John, abandons the family and moves in with the woman next door, Tall T (Uton) can't afford clothes for school, but the librarian teaches him to read fluently and the boy helps his mother keep the family going. Then at Christmas, Brother John offers Tall T the chance to be part of the exciting traditional Jonkonnu musical procession. He's thrilled; should he trust his dad? There's a contrived metaphor connecting Jacob's ladder in the Bible with the steep scary cliff that Tall T climbs to find his manhood, but the story's strength is in the boy's immediate first-person, present-tense account of the village, place and people, music, magic, and food. What's most moving is Tall T's relationship with his father. Brother John's a village leader, even though he's an adulterer and a compulsive gambler. He's a scary stranger, but his son loves him.

THE METAPHYSICAL CAT: TALES OF CATS AND THEIR HUMANS (2001)

School Library Journal (review date February 2002)

SOURCE: School Library Journal 48, no. 2 (February 2002): 157.

Adult/High School—[The Metaphysical Cat is a] cornucopia of myth, history, feline literary references, and firsthand observations by unabashed animal lovers. The book's sweetness is balanced with facts that could be used by teens doing a project on cats or animal behavior. In spite of any of the monikers that cats have carried through the centuries (all explained by the authors), readers will simply call them special after picking up this title. The feline's place in our society, households, and psyche is thoroughly explored and dotted with drawings, resulting in a cat fancier's pleasure.

TOM CRINGLE: THE PIRATE AND THE PATRIOT (2001)

Roger Leslie (review date 15 September 2001)

SOURCE: Leslie, Roger. Booklist 98, no. 2 (15 September 2001): 222.

Gr 4-8. Hausman's lively sequel to Tom Cringle: Battle on the High Seas (2000) [Tom Cringle: The Pirate and the Patriot] has the good-natured but trouble-bound 14-year-old helping sail the Kraaken. Tumbles, fumbles, and constant bumbles make for slap-stick mayhem as the crew discovers a menagerie of wildlife on board the ship and encounters threats of slave and pirate ships. With his loyal canine, Sneezer, and a cast of menacing foes and admirable cohorts, Tom falters his way into ever-greater heroics, and shares a few insights about the evils of slave trading along the way. With a lighthearted tone and tongue-in-cheek bravado, Hausman clearly has fun with his readers, always making sure they're in on the jokes. His epistolary format and Treasure Island-like dialogue will appeal to young readers, as will [Tad] Hills' rough-and-ready illustrations. Hausman doesn't hint at another Tom Cringle adventure, but he has certainly left room for the possibility.

Patricia B. McGee (review date October 2001)

SOURCE: McGee, Patricia B. School Library Journal 47, no. 10 (October 2001): 160.

Gr 5-8—The War of 1812 is raging in this action-packed sequel to Tom Cringle: Battle on the High Seas (2000) [Tom Cringle: The Pirate and the Patriot]. Fourteen-year-old Tom, now promoted to first lieutenant in the Royal Navy, is serving on the brig Kraaken, assigned to patrol the waters between Jamaica and Cuba and to capture American privateers and slave smugglers. While at sea, the crew encounters violent weather, loses the cabin boy to a shark attack, and captures a pirate ship with a cargo of stolen slaves. When its escort brig attacks the Kraaken, Tom and his men board it and set fire to the powder magazine, causing the vessel to explode and sink. Tom, barely recovered from his battle wounds, is then given the task of returning the slaves to Cinnamon Hill plantation. He is torn by this difficult assignment; in his heart he believes that slavery is wrong. On the overland trek through the Jamaican jungle, he and his men endure a series of violent attacks from American pirates led by his nemesis. In a rousing climax, Tom captures the pirate Jenkins and his ship. Unfortunately, the issue of returning the slaves to servitude is dealt with in a facile manner. Captain Smythe conscripts them into the British Navy, a dubious fate since Royal Navy life at this time was brutal. Although marred by the failure to explore this moral issue, the lively plotting, picturesque language, and colorful setting make this an exciting tale.

THE BOY FROM NINE MILES: THE EARLY LIFE OF BOB MARLEY (2002)

Tim Wadham (review date August 2002)

SOURCE: Wadham, Tim. School Library Journal 48, no. 8 (August 2002): 178.

Gr 3-4—[The Boy from Nine Miles is a] brief account of the musician's childhood in Jamaica, cowritten by his daughter [Cedella Marley]. The two chapters cover the first five years of Marley's life with his mother and grandparents in Nine Miles, and a year he spent in Kingston. The book is full of conversations and descriptions of the young boy's thoughts and feelings as the father he has never known arrives and takes him to be educated in the city, and the writing is at times amateurish. An afterword sketches Marley's career. Framed full- and double-page illustrations in vibrant colors appear throughout. Unfortunately, they fall short of the folk quality to which they clearly aspire. While some young readers may be interested in Marley's life and music, the narrow focus of this book limits its appeal and usefulness.

📖 *CASTAWAYS: STORIES OF SURVIVAL* (2003)

Publishers Weekly (review date 9 June 2003)

SOURCE: *Publishers Weekly* 250, no. 23 (9 June 2003): 54.

Gerald Hausman explores an array of situations across various centuries (many inspired by true stories) when men—and one woman—survive seafaring tragedies in a half dozen tales—*Castaways: Stories of Survival*. A Spanish traveler is the sole survivor of a shipwreck off the coast of Peru in 1540 and finds himself on a desolate island; a man aboard a Portuguese schooner in 1752 meets an old man on an island filled with beasts; and the haunting tale of Henry Roi describes an inhabitant of the island of Bequia in the Grenadines in the late 1940s who "cheated death."

Vicki Reutter (review date June 2003)

SOURCE: Reutter, Vicki. *School Library Journal* 49, no. 6 (June 2003): 161.

Gr 5-9 These six stories [in *Castaways: Stories of Survival*] were inspired by tales of real people who survived shipwrecks. In 1540, Peter Serrano, a Spanish traveler, was marooned on a barren island near Peru and survived by eating sea turtles and using their shells for shade and shelter. In the 1940s, 15-year-old Henri Roi's swimming prowess made him a legend. In the water with shipmates after their boat capsizes, Henri says, "We gonna make it. I not gonna let you drown. I got the Great Maker in my heart and King Neptune in my bones; I can swim forever. This sea, this angry sea, is nothing to me." The teen's story is told in colorful language and with the dramatic flair of a storyteller. Ghosts and mythical creatures appear throughout the stories, especially in **"The Beasts of Philip Ashton,"** in which the castaway succumbs to madness trying to ward off the night beasts and day beasts. A story about Logan Welsh and a ghostly encounter with the Pinta is loosely based on the real adventures of Joshua Slocum. While some stories are stronger than others, this collection would make a good read-aloud for middle grades.

FURTHER READING

Bibliography

Hausman, Gerald. *Gerald Hausman Papers*. Thomas J. Dodd Research Center, University of Connecticut Libraries: www.lib.uconn.edu/DoddCenter/ (January 1998).
  Collection of Hausman's papers and publications.

Biographies

Hausman, Gerald. "Biography." *Gerald Hausman's Website*: www.geraldhausman.com/
  Biographical sketch.

Hausman, Gerald. "Gerald Hausman's Biography." *Romancing the Web*: www.romanceweb.com/ (1997).
  Biographical entry.

Julie Lawson
1947-

Canadian author of books for children and young adults.

INTRODUCTION

An appreciation for the outdoors and an interest in lyrical storytelling are defining features of Julie Lawson's books for children and young adults. Many of her titles, including *Cougar Cove* (1996) and *Goldstone* (1998) are set in the wilderness of Lawson's native British Columbia, while major works like *The Dragon's Pearl* (1992), and *Emma and the Silk Train* (1997) take place in China, whose culture and traditions the author greatly admires. Lawson's body of work is additionally notable for its broad range of themes. For instance, the picture book *Midnight in the Mountains* (1998) is a gentle, poetic account of a girl's first night in a cabin in the mountains, while the young adult adventure novel *Danger Game* (1996; published in Canada as *Fires Burning,* 1995) introduces Beth, a teenage sexual abuse victim, who participates in a frightening game of risk.

BIOGRAPHICAL INFORMATION

Born in British Columbia, Canada, in 1944 to Charles and Jean (Anderson) Goodwin, Lawson was raised in Victoria, but spent her summers at her family's cabin on the Sooke Basin, a sheltered inlet on the southwest tip of Vancouver Island. Lawson earned her B.A. from the University of Victoria in 1970 and taught in France for a year before returning to British Columbia where she worked as a school teacher. In 1991, Lawson realized that her full-time job was not allowing her enough time to become the writer she longed to be. "I still kept saying, I'll be an author when I get older," she recalled. "Well, I got older and older, and finally I said to myself, stop thinking about it and do it!" Lawson took a six-month leave of absence and began work on her first book, *The Sand Sifter* (1990). In the next five years, she would publish six more picture books and two novels. Lawson's inspiration comes from her love of folklore and history, as well her explorations of other cultures and

her own scenic home on Vancouver Island, where she lives in a house in the woods that she and her husband built. In addition to writing, Lawson gives workshops and lectures to school children and library groups.

MAJOR WORKS

Lawson's many works for children and young adults are remarkable for their vivid western Canadian landscapes. In addition, two of her best-loved novels, *The Dragon's Pearl* and *Emma and the Silk Train,* are shaped by her love of Chinese culture. On a trip to China, Lawson grew fascinated with elements of the country's traditional imagery, including the Chinese dragon. "I'd always thought they were ferocious fire-breathing monsters," she explained. "But in China I discovered Oriental dragons are benevolent, good-natured creatures that don't breath fire; they breath clouds and make the rain." Lawson put her new knowledge to work in *The Dragon's Pearl,* in which Xiao Sheng discovers a pearl that will bring prosperity to his mother's drought-parched land. To protect his prize from thieves, the boy swallows the pearl, only to find his body experience a bizarre transformation into a dragon. In keeping with the beneficient dragon of Chinese mythology, Xiao Sheng's new shape lets him breathe clouds into the sky and brings rain to the land and hope to his family. "Despite its few artistic imperfections, the book as a whole is a lovely package of writing and visuals that will be enjoyed as read-aloud, cultural lesson, and folk fantasy," wrote *School Library Journal*'s Susan Scheps.

Based on the actual derailment of a silker train along the Fraser River in 1927, the picture book *Emma and the Silk Train* tells the story of a train carrying bolts of silk which derails and loses its beautiful cargo in a nearby river. Emma spends weeks combing the water for fabric, but when she finally finds grabs hold of a length of bright red silk she is swept away by the current and washes up on a small island. Using the material as a flag, she catches the eye of a silker crew. Before long, she is safely home, and her mother sews her a dress from her hard-won treasure.

The novel trilogy that begins with *Goldstone* unfolds in early twentieth century British Columbia. Twelve-year-old Karin considers herself a modern Canadian girl and is embarrassed by her mother's traditional Swedish ways. However, when her mother is killed in a landslide, Karin is shocked out of her rebellion. Now she must wrestle with her guilt and the strange implications of her mother's pendant, which gives its wearers dreams of the future. When Karin dreams of another landslide, she wonders whether she'll be able to warn those at risk in time. In her review of *Goldstone, Booklist*'s Shelle Rosenfeld commended Lawson's "descriptions of the avalanches and their physical and emotional impact on survivors and landscape." *Turns on a Dime* (1999) moves the action of the story forward two generations to a setting in 1950's Victoria, British Columbia. The goldstone has been passed down to Jo (a descendent of Karin), an impetuous 11-year-old who is more interested in telling stories than swooning over boys with her friends. Critic Maureen Garvie considers *Turns on a Dime* less rich in historical detail than *Goldstone,* but notes that Lawson effectively conveys the experience of life a generation ago, even as contemporary "readers will have little trouble understanding Jo's dilemmas." In the final installment of the trilogy, *The*

Ghost of Avalanche Mountain (2000), the gemstone once again changes hands. Jo, now a mystery writer, gives her niece Ashley Gillespie the powerful gem. Wearing the goldstone, Ashley begins to experience ominous dreams of the future. The story concludes with an avalanche and the appearance of a boy who comes to return the gem's magic to the mountain where it was fashioned.

Lawson's twentieth book, *Destination Gold!* (2001), weaves together maps, historical fiction and nonfiction to document the experiences of three young people against the action-packed backdrop of the Klondike gold rush. *Quill and Quire*'s Jessica Higgs notes, "Lawson's uncomplicated text makes this chapter of Canadian history accessible, but also conveys emotion and insight. As well as engaging young adult readers in the personal trials of the three lead characters, this book will leave them with a healthy respect for those who accepted the Klondike's challenge." In *The Klondike Cat* (2002), Noah disobeys his father by bringing along his cat, Shadow, on a move to the Klondike during the gold rush. After father and son make the long, arduous journey, which includes the disappearance of Shadow, the pair reach their destination only to learn that the gold claims are either staked already or too expensive. Shadow's reappearance at the end of the story, however, comes as a symbol of coming success. One *Kirkus* reviewer commended the book's "realistic touch," calling it "a believable slice of robust American pioneer history."

A departure from Lawson's more involved narratives, *Midnight in the Mountains* is the quiet, lyrical story of a young girl's first evening in a cabin in the mountains. Repetition of such phrases as "It's quiet in the mountains. So quiet I hear the cold" evoke a meditative mood, and images like the beating of an owl's wing and the making of snow angels stir up memories of the past. "This is a book for young and old," writes Joanne Findon of *Quill and Quire,* "but particularly for those who love mountains, midnight and snow." Another picture book, *Bear on the Train* (1999) uses a similar gentle, rhythmic style to tells the story of a bear who spends a winter secretly hibernating aboard a moving train.

In the young adult title *Danger Game* three cousins meet for a vacation on Vancouver Island's southern coast, each one haunted by a secret. During a treacherous outing to a remote cave, the teenage characters only narrowly escape death. Lawson's narration frequently switches point-of-view, building tension and giving the story the sense that "the teenagers must somehow compete for the role of protagonist," wrote one *Kirkus Reviewer,* who characterized the novel as "expertly told."

CRITICAL RECEPTION

Critics have praised Lawson's accurate portrayal of her striking British Columbia settings and her expert handling of elements of Chinese culture. Ronald Jobe of *School Library Journal* called the author's lyrical style and representation of natural scenes in novels like *Midnight in the Mountains* "evidence of her love of the sounds of the language and her consummate storytelling ability." Others agree that Lawson has a sympathetic ear for the cares and troubles of her young characters and regard the three books of the renowned Goldstone series as strong enough to stand alone as complete works. Critics, however, have noted some flaws in Lawson's titles. Some feel action-packed titles like *Danger Game* rely on an oversimplification of character, yet even these reviewers tend to conclude that what small imperfections exist in Lawson's stories, they are easily glossed over by her absorbing narration.

AWARDS

In 1993 Lawson was named to the Ruth Schwartz Book Award shortlist and the Canadian Library Association Book of the Year Award shortlist. She also received the National Parenting Publications Award for Folklore in that year. All three awards were for *The Dragon's Pearl.* For *White Jade Tiger* (1993), she received the Shelia A. Egoff Children's Prize (1994), was placed on the Silver Birch Award shortlist and the Canadian Library Association Book of the Year Award shortlist. The book was also named a Canadian Library Association Honour Book. In 1996, *Whatever You Do, Don't Go Near That Canoe!* (1996) was runner-up for the Governor-General's Award for Illustrations. She was the winner of the CNIB's Tiny Torgi Award, was an International Youth Library White Ravens Notable, and received the Amelia Frances Howard-Gibbon Award for the same title in 1997. She also received the Ontario Silver Birch Award, Regional Winner and Finalist, for *Cougar Cove* that year. She was placed on the American Library Association Best Books for Young Adults list and Manitoba Young Readers' Choice Award shortlist, in 1996 and 1998, for *Danger Game (Fires Burning).* In 1998, *Goldstone* was also named to the CNIB Torgi "Talking Books" Award shortlist and re-ceived the Ontario Silver Birch Award, Regional Winner and Finalist. *Emma and the Silk Train* was named to the B. C. Book Prize Honour Books, was a Junior Library Guild Selection and winner of the Sheila A. Egoff Award, Shortlist, in 1998, and received the I. R. A. Teachers' Choice in 1999. Also in 1999, Lawson was named to the National Chapter of Canada IODE Violet Downey Book Award shortlist for *Turns on a Dime,* and was placed on the Amelia Frances Howard-Gibbon Award, shortlist, for *Midnight in the Mountains. Destination Gold!* received much acclaim, including: Best Children's Books of the Year from Bank Street College of Education, New York, Books for the Teen Age List from the New York Public Library, and the Rocky Mountain Book Award shortlist in 2002. Her other numerous awards include being placed on the Canadian Library Association Book of the Year Award shortlist and Hackmatack Award shortlist, for *A Ribbon of Shining Steel* (2002); being named a B. C. Book Prize Honour Book for *The Klondike Cat*; being named to the Red Cedar Award shortlist and receiving the Silver Birch Award, Regional Winner and Finalist for *The Ghost of Avalanche Mountain.*

PRINCIPAL WORKS

My Grandfather Loved the Stars (picture book) 1990
The Sand Sifter (picture book) 1990
The Dragon's Pearl (picture book) 1992
A Morning to Polish and Keep (picture book) 1992
White Jade Tiger (picture book) 1993
Cougar Cove (juvenilia) 1996
Danger Game (young adult) 1996; published in Canada as *Fires Burning,* 1995
Whatever You Do, Don't Go Near That Canoe! (picture book) 1996
Emma and the Silk Train (picture book) 1997
Goldstone (juvenilia) 1998
Midnight in the Mountains (picture book) 1998
Bear on the Train (picture book) 1999
In Like a Lion (picture book) 1999
Turns on a Dime (juvenilia) 1999
The Ghost of Avalanche Mountain (juvenilia) 2000
Destination Gold! (juvenilia) 2001
Emily: Across the James Bay Bridge (juvenilia) 2001
Emily 2: Disaster at the Bridge (juvenilia) 2002
The Klondike Cat (picture book) 2002
A Ribbon of Shining Steel: The Railway Diary of Kate Cameron (juvenilia) 2002
Arizona Charlie and the Klondike Kid (picture book) 2003

TITLE COMMENTARY

📖 *A MORNING TO POLISH AND KEEP* (1992)

Sarah Ellis (review date May 1992)

SOURCE: Ellis, Sarah. *Quill and Quire* 58, no. 5 (May 1992): 32.

(Ages 4+) Out on an early morning fishing trip with her family, young Amy is reeling in the big one when passing killer whales distract her. She loses it all—rod, hook, line, sinker, and salmon, too. The day is saved when Amy's brother miraculously hooks the same fish and retrieves the gear.

A Morning to Polish and Keep has the flavour of a family story, with a shared love of fishing and its rituals, equipment, and delicious specialized vocabulary ("hoochie-koochies" and "Tom Mack spoons"); an understated portrayal of family dynamics (Amy's sulk is the genuine article); and the elegiac feel of a happy time remembered.

[Sheena] Lott's illustrations are handsome watercolours that capture the changing light of dawn and the ever-changing surface of the sea. The leisurely introduction and conclusion that frame the fish tale celebrate things maritime and contain some beautifully-observed moments. When dawn breaks the father checks his watch and announces, "Right on schedule." The narrative bogs down slightly at the few points where Lawson's style becomes a bit precious. But the story, strong and genuine at the centre, keeps the whole thing buoyant.

📖 *THE DRAGON'S PEARL* (1992)

Publishers Weekly (review date 22 March 1993)

SOURCE: *Publishers Weekly* 240, no. 12 (22 March 1993): 79.

Dragon fans will hail the arrival of a cloud-breathing, rainmaking dragon of Chinese folklore [*The Dragon's Pearl*], who provides a captivating (and benevolent) alternative to the European fire-breathing variety. Despite a severe drought, Xiao Sheng discovers a pearl that bestows good fortune upon his mother's land. When thieves attempt to steal the gem, the panicked boy swallows it, unleashing an "intense heat" that "seared through him, as if he had swallowed a ball of fire" and transforming him into a dragon. Far from being a curse, Xiao Sheng's new incarnation empowers him to breathe clouds into the sky, bringing rain and prosperity to all. In a polished display of verbiage, Lawson invests her colorful text with passion and drama, inspiring a fresh appreciation of the mythological beast. (Though occasionally the story's disparate elements threaten to become diffused, their focus unclear.) An absorbing explanation of Chinese dragon lore following the tale elucidates their revered status as water-gods. [Paul] Morin's (*The Orphan Boy*) arresting collage illustrations incorporate scraps of painted burlap, stalks of grain, coins and pearls into lustrous oil paintings, enhancing the singular appeal of this impressive collaboration. *Ages 5-9.*

Hazel Rochman (review date 15 April 1993)

SOURCE: Rochman, Hazel. *Booklist* 89, no. 16 (15 April 1993): 1513.

Ages 4-8. The beneficent dragon of Chinese mythology is the power in this tale of transformation [*The Dragon's Pearl*]. Xiao Sheng is a boy who works hard all day and loves to sing. In a time of shriveling drought, he finds a magic pearl that brings food and riches to him and his mother. When robbers try to steal the pearl, Xiao Sheng swallows it, and it's as if he'd swallowed fire. He's changed into a powerful dragon that brings the rain from the skies and carves out the great river as his home. Astonishing in their variety, [Paul] Morin's glowing, textured illustrations, which show a subtle use of collage and light and shadow, dramatize the story's sense of shifting reality and glorious change. Perhaps the most beautiful picture is of a delicate dragonfly hovering over the water, an indication to the grieving mother that her son is everywhere in the world around her. Things are not what they seem. "Today may not be the same as yesterday."

Susan Scheps (review date July 1993)

SOURCE: Scheps, Susan. *School Library Journal* 39, no. 7 (July 1993): 62, 67.

Gr 2-5— [*The Dragon's Pearl* is a] well-crafted story with many folkloric qualities that successfully presents Chinese tradition and culture in a manner that is both enlightening and entertaining. The tale is of a poor but optimistic boy who cuts and sells grass for fuel or fodder in order to buy food for himself and his mother. When a drought ruins the land, killing the livestock and leaving the people poor and hungry, Xiao Sheng discovers a magic pearl that keeps his mother's food jars and money box full. She returns her neighbors' earlier kindness by sharing her wealth with them, while the pearl changes the boy's life and the fortune of the village in a most dramatic way. Lawson has appended a page of notes about Chinese dragons (water-gods) that sheds light on the unusual aspects of the story. Many of [Paul] Morin's oil paintings on canvas show clothing, foliage, and grass that are carefully textured with sawdust and fibers. His skillful portraits are an indication of his great artistic talent. However, several panoramas—two of them featuring an ochre/yellow heat-parched land—lack the depth that gives similar scenes in Morin's exquisitely rendered book, *The Orphan Boy* (1991), a photographic quality. Xiao Sheng seems flat and unrealistic as well. Collages of painted fiber and realia (coin, fishhook, pearl) adorn white pages of text, with the whole encased in a neat, geometric border on fiber background. Despite its few artistic imperfections, the book as a whole is a lovely package of writing and visuals that will be enjoyed as read-aloud, cultural lesson, and folk fantasy.

📖 *COUGAR COVE* (1996)

Maureen Garvie (review date May 1996)

SOURCE: Garvie, Maureen. *Quill and Quire* 62, no. 5 (May 1996): 34.

(Ages 8-11) It can seem like a tragedy when you're 11 and something you've looked forward to for ages doesn't live up to your dreams. Samantha's first visit to Vancouver Island starts out as a bad trip: as she writes sadly in her journal, "I made a mistake." She gets carsick and seasick and lost in the woods. Robyn and Alex, her twin cousins who were so much fun on their visit to Toronto, have become lanky, superior 14-year-olds who tease her relentlessly. Sam is tormented for being young, short, gullible, and a city child, and for dropping Robyn's fishing pole overboard. But Sam (Sam-bone, as Robyn calls her) displays a practical, resourceful side, spending her time alone, exploring and reading nature guides to learn the names of the West Coast flora and fauna. After all, her cousins have threatened, "there'll be a test." As far as Sam's concerned, it's a test of endurance that started back in the airport.

Cougar Cove is the second foray into fiction by West Coast writer Julie Lawson, already well established in the picture book field. This new book mixes family adventure with lots of wildlife lore, and the attractive drawings by David Powell place the young characters against a backdrop of wilderness and sea. But Sam's mean-spirited treatment by her cousins, though it generates enough sitcom plot to carry us along until more serious threats arise, is overdrawn. By comparison, the greater dramas, such as getting lost in the bush or stumbling on a dangerous wild animal, feel abbreviated and underdrawn. The cougar seems less important as an animal than as a plot device, a symbol of a higher order of significance that transcends petty, quotidian bickerings—a wolf, whale or unicorn would have worked as well.

Elisabeth Palmer Abarbanel (review date September 1996)

SOURCE: Abarbanel, Elisabeth Palmer. *School Library Journal* 42, no. 9 (September 1996): 204.

Gr 4-6— [In *Cougar Cove,*] Sam, a city girl from Toronto, expects to have a wonderful time when she visits family on Vancouver Island, but she is sadly disappointed. Her 14-year-old twin cousins tease her endlessly, and nickname her Gullible. She labels them The Horribles. Eventually, she decides to spend most of her time alone, watching the fawns and butterflies and rowing in the bay. As she admires the wilderness, she sees a cougar and her two kittens nearby. After her sighting, which nobody believes, she becomes caught up in learning all she can about these creatures. When she and the twins come across another cougar, she knows just how to frighten it away. The Horribles find new respect for Sam, and all three of them become interested in the fate of the large cats on the island. This adventure story is both humorous and touching. While some readers might find Sam's extreme gullibility hard to believe, her self-reliance and independent nature are qualities one can't help but admire. With short chapters and a lot of dialogue, this is a quick read for those who have an interest in the natural world—others may find the many details of the flora and fauna a bit slow.

📖 *DANGER GAME* (1996)

Kirkus Reviews (review date 1 February 1996)

SOURCE: *Kirkus Reviews* 64 (1 February 1996): 229.

Tragedy narrowly misses three troubled teenagers as they help one another in a melodramatic tale [*Danger Game*] from the author of *Dragon's Pearl* (1993).

The three meet at a vacation spot on Vancouver Island's southern coast: Beth, feeling betrayed because Diggon, longtime friend and her first boyfriend, has not kept in touch; Diggon, terrorized and full of self-loathing after watching schoolmates beat a passerby, possibly to death; and Chelsea, Beth's cousin, a pyromaniac who has been driven by sexual abuse to fold herself up inside like the origami cranes she creates. The three begin to share their secrets on an outing to a remote cove; caught by changing weather, they barely make it back to Beth's house alive, where Chelsea learns that her abuser and her mother are now married. Only Beth's intervention prevents her fiery suicide.

Lawson switches between points of view, so that readers always know more than the characters; it effectively builds tension, although it also gives the story a crowded feel—as if the teenagers must somehow compete for the role of protagonist. The adult cast is a realistic mixture of helpers and villains and the plot's resolution is conventional (Diggon goes home to face the music; Chelsea's would-be stepfather faces trial) but not contrived. Expertly told. *(11-15)*

Lucinda Lockwood (review date April 1996)

SOURCE: Lockwood, Lucinda. *School Library Journal* 42, no. 4 (April 1996): 154, 157.

Gr 8 Up— This novel's southwest British Columbia location and summer vacation setting lend themselves well to a teenage adventure. It takes a long time, however, for the adventure to get underway. The beautiful protagonist, 16-year-old Chelsea, is guarding a deep secret. She is torn between her divorced parents, and she has a deep dislike for her mother's fiancé, Simon. She demonstrates that she is unhappy by setting small fires. The troubled teen is shipped off to live with her father, until he is seriously injured in an accident. Then she is sent to live with her aunt and uncle at their summer cabin on Vancouver Island. When she gets together with her cousins and their friend Diggon, the four young people play a daring game to test their mettle. Under Chelsea's influence, the game becomes especially dangerous. Eventually, she realizes that she must face the truth and help herself. Readers will not be surprised to learn that Simon has been sexually abusing her for years. The incredible plot twists and the leaps between diverse locations are the weakest elements of *The Danger Game.* The characters, however, are interesting, and the setting is unique enough to keep YAs reading. The plot seems to lurch from incident to incident, eventually coming together as a fishnet, rather than as a seamless cloth.

Publishers Weekly (review date 13 April 1996)

SOURCE: *Publishers Weekly* 243, no. 16 (13 April 1996): 69-70.

Using recurring images of fire and water, Lawson (*Water Jade Tiger*) spins a psychological yarn [*Danger Game*] about the inner torment of a teen who has been sexually abused. Most people, including the protagonist's exmodel mother, view 16-year-old Chelsea as a thoughtless vandal, but readers soon learn that her fascination with flames is connected to deep-seated anger and fear. Chelsea keeps her these emotions hidden—until she moves in with her cousin Beth's family, on a Canadian island, and meets a runaway named Diggon who is hiding a few dark secrets of his own. During a dangerous game of truth or dare, Chelsea opens her heart to Diggon, but, ironically, it is practical-minded Beth who eventually comes to the rescue. Packed with a number of life-threatening episodes, this novel may sweep readers into its momentum, leading them to overlook contrivances in plot and black-and-white characterizations of both cousins' parents. Ultimately, this book offers an intriguing mixture of ordinary and sublime elements; fragments of ancient myths, unselfconsciously woven into the text, add depth and color. *Ages 12-Up.*

Horn Book Guide (review date fall 1996)

SOURCE: *Horn Book Guide* 7, no. 2 (fall 1996): 302.

Spending the summer with her cousins [in *Danger Game*], sixteen-year-old Chelsea turns what starts as a game into a frightening way to hide from her past. She sets a fire that endangers her cousin and finally reveals the childhood abuse that drives her to pyromania. The relationship between the cousins is particularly believable in a novel filled with dramatic moments.

Jennifer Fakott (review date October 1996)

SOURCE: Fakott, Jennifer. *Voice of Youth Advocates* 19, no. 4 (October 1996): 211.

When Chelsea's emotionally distant mother can no longer stand her daughter's accusing silences, she sends her to live with her gentle, photographer father in Hawaii [in **Danger Game**]. Chelsea, thinking that perhaps she can finally be happy now that she has escaped her mother and her mother's slimy boyfriend, Simon, begins to unfold and let her emotions open up. She is entranced by an erupting volcano, and the image of the goddess Pele, whom she thinks she sees. But Chelsea is shipped off to Canada, to live with her Uncle and distant cousins she has never met. Chelsea once again folds up her emotions like the origami cranes she makes and only starts to emerge when her cousins, Beth and Field, take her to Deadman's Island to meet Diggon, a runaway friend. There they start the Danger Game—a game of dares and risks that Chelsea soon makes even more dangerous by playing with fire. Finally, it is only Beth who is strong enough to stand up for her beliefs and to discover the secret of sexual abuse that has been keeping Chelsea folded, inaccessible—and dangerous.

Lawson has written a sensitive book about abuse, and the emotional distancing and destructive coping strategies it can produce. Beth, criticized by the other youths, as being prudish and immature, proves to have the strongest values and beliefs. Beth is able to put aside her jealousy of the beautiful, enigmatic Chelsea, and extend the hand of friendship and of trust. From her example, Diggon, fleeing the consequences of a crime he took part in, and Chelsea, careless of physical pain and danger, are able to face their separate truths.

Lawson's narrative style is slightly uneven, however, and the book feels overextended. One has the impression that Lawson is trying to tie in too many disparate themes and symbols-Hawaiian mythology, Japanese paper folding-which create more confusion than unity. Nevertheless, teens will relate to issues of peer pressure surrounding the Danger Game, and find in Beth an unlikely but positive role model, which may give them the courage to speak out against a hazardous situation. Good for mature middle grade readers through senior high school, given the range of the characters' ages.

WHATEVER YOU DO, DON'T GO NEAR THAT CANOE! (1996)

Maureen Garvie (review date October 1996)

SOURCE: Garvie, Maureen. *Quill and Quire* 62, no. 10 (October 1996): 46.

(Ages 3-7) Warned not to touch Captain McKee's canoe [in **Whatever You Do, Don't Go Near That Canoe!**], no matter what, two children and a toy kanga-

roo hijack it and head out to sea in the fading light. They have an extraordinary adventure with five dozen piratical seafaring knaves, return home more by good luck than good management, and get off without a scolding. The further admonition not ever to touch the captain's "twin-engined sleigh" they also take as a challenge rather than a prohibition. At least, thinks the scandalized adult, the rascals were wearing life jackets in the canoe. Will they remember to pack parachutes in the Twin Otter?

Kids will probably recognize this as the fantasy it is, a variant on the classic theme of defying adult authority and learning and growing through the consequences. Lawson's sing-song rhymes and Zimmermann's superb watercolours, a dreamlike mix of real and surreal, signal to the attentive child that this is, after all, a story.

Young listeners will squirm with delicious terror at the two kids entering forbidden zones; good readers will enjoy twisting tongues around pirate threats to "reel 'em and keel 'em" and "splinter their giddles and twickle their toes." Soon enough all comes clear: when the pirates shout "Flame grill the dogs!" they mean a weenie roast, and they're tickled pink at an excuse to break out the marshmallows. Captain McKee is equally delighted to find the miscreants have brought back treasure, even if the gold is chocolate centred.

Evidently Lawson and Zimmermann, seasoned producers of books for children, and neither of them strangers to a paddle, feel confident that their book won't start a rash of pre-pubescent boat thefts. But call me old-fashioned, call me an over-protective '90s parent: Peter Rabbit got his comeuppance at the hands of Mr. McGregor, the elephant's child ended up with a long nose, and when a couple of wet-behind-the-ears little landlubbers make off in a canoe without permission, *somebody* should suffer.

EMMA AND THE SILK TRAIN (1997)

Annette Goldsmith (review date July 1997)

SOURCE: Goldsmith, Annette. *Quill and Quire* 63, no. 7 (July 1997): 50.

(Ages 4-9) Julie Lawson is a fine storyteller, and her latest picture book, based on the September 21, 1927 derailment of a silk train along the Fraser River, is another winner. Emma, the daughter of the station-

master, knows her trains. The silk trains ("silkers") are her favourites because they carry such a rare Chinese cargo, travel at fantastic speeds, and make other trains wait. When a silker ends up in the river, the railroad offers a reward for the lost bales, so the whole town goes fishing for silk. Emma gets carried away, continuing to hunt for the silk long after everyone else has stopped. Finally she finds a brilliant redgold length in the river, but is carried away (this time literally) by the current as she clutches her prize. She manages to crawl onto a tiny island, and ties the silk to the trees, fashioning a banner that catches the light of a passing silker. The train doesn't stop—silkers never do—but it slows down long enough at the station to let Emma's father know where she is.

Artist Paul Mombourquette, a newcomer to children's books, does justice to Lawson's exciting story. His dramatic, mostly double-page spreads combine the loose look of watercolour with the richness of acrylic. His work reminds me somewhat of Geoff Butler's paintings in *The Killick* and Les Tait's for *The White Stone in the Castle Wall*. Like them, Mombourquette employs a painterly style and a strong palette, and creates characters who are at one with their setting. (My British Columbia-born spouse assures me that the landscape is right, though he wonders whether the small rowboat that rescues Emma would be able to resist the Fraser River's current.) Mombourquette certainly captures the terror of being swept away: he depicts this scene from above, with Emma (a vulnerable purple dot) attached to the silk (a larger scarlet swirl) in an immense churning blue river.

Lawson has explored both Chinese culture and British Columbia (sometimes together) in her books; *Emma and the Silk Train* seems a natural extension of these interests. She credits the staff of C.P. Archives and the Revelstoke Railway Museum, so has clearly done her research. The story concludes with a historical note. Pair *Emma* with *Shortcut,* by Donald Crews, for another train adventure with *frissons* and a happy ending.

Publishers Weekly (review date 7 September 1998)

SOURCE: *Publishers Weekly* 245, no. 36 (7 September 1998): 94.

After a train carrying bolts of precious silk derails [in *Emma And The Silk Train*], a girl, obsessed with longing for a silk blouse, spends weeks combining the nearby river for fabric. She finally finds a length of bright red silk, but the fast current strands her on a small island, where she despairs of being rescued. Eventually her family finds her, and her mother makes her a silk dress. The episode is inspired by the 1927 derailment of a silk train in British Columbia, known as the Million-Dollar Wreck. Lawson (*Cougar Cove*) sews up her tale with a fascinating historical note about the speedy silk trains (silk was insured by the hour). Debut illustrator [Paul] Mombourquette builds careful, historically accurate paintings from dense, visible brush strokes. The artwork is somber in palette, as if it were perpetually overcast; even the swath of red silk is more dusky than brilliant. Whether finding a bolt of fabric counts as high adventure for contemporary readers remains to be seen, but the sheer contrast between the powerful rushing trains and their luxurious cargo takes hold of the imagination. *Ages 4-9.*

Ronald Jobe (review date October 1998)

SOURCE: Jobe, Ronald. *School Library Journal* 44, no. 10 (October 1998): 105.

K-Gr 3—A young girl living alongside the railroad tracks is fascinated by the speed of the "silkers." Her station-master father explains that these trains carry silk from the Orient and must quickly get to New York with the cargo. Based on a true incident in 1927, this story [*Emma and the Silk Train*] tells of one such train that doesn't make it and its bundles of cloth are dumped into the Fraser River in British Columbia. Emma helps the local folks try to find the fabric because she is determined to get a piece to make a dress. As she reaches to grab the wonderful piece of red silk floating in the river, she is swept away by the current and becomes trapped on a small rocky island. There, she uses the material as a flag to attract the attention of another "silker" crew. Soft, impressionistic paints evoke the ruggedness of the canyon setting, the subtle warmth of autumn colors, and the beckoning contrast of the red silk caught in the turbulent river torrents. [Paul] Mombourquette has created a memorable feeling of another time, place, and community, a moment when all are one with the river and the passing trains. Readers get a sense that the illustrator is a steam train buff, as the detail of the trains and railroad life is quite remarkable. The gentle softness of Lawson's lyrical style gives evidence of her love of the sounds of the language and her consummate storytelling ability. Contrasting sentence lengths and the clever use of repetition insist that the story be shared and read aloud.

GraceAnne A. DeCandido (review date 1 November 1998)

SOURCE: DeCandido, GraceAnne A. *Booklist* 95, no. 5 (1 November 1998): 504.

Ages 6-10. Sometimes a nugget of history can be polished into a shining story , . . . and that is certainly true here [with *Emma and the Silk Train*]. The silkers, trains that carried raw silk and finished cloth from West Coast ports to the East, set speed records in the 1920s. Emma, whose father runs a train station, loves to see the silkers fly through British Columbia. When a silk train is derailed and its precious cargo lost in the river, Emma joins those trying to retrieve the bales for a reward, but secretly she longs for some silk of her own. Even after weeks go by, Emma continues to search. When a red-gold skein catches her eye farther downriver than she should have been, she plunges in after it and finds herself and the silk stuck on a small island. Emma uses the silk as a rescue banner and is astonished to learn, when safe with her family, that she had been spotted by a silk train that slowed down long enough to tell Pa where she was. [Paul] Mombourquette's paintings have a lively, impressionistic surface of broken brush strokes, making the colors and forms of silk, water, landscape, and clothing shimmer. Paintings range from double-page spreads to small vignettes, and the text sometimes floats on the images and sometimes has its own space on the page. A fine adventure that combines the romance of trains with the sweet swoop of Emma's new birthday dress. Lawson bases her story on the actual derailment of a silker along the Fraser River in 1927.

☐☐ *GOLDSTONE* (1998)

Maureen Garvie (review date January 1998)

SOURCE: Garvie, Maureen. *Quill and Quire* 64, no. 1 (January 1998): 38.

(Ages 12+) Born in Canada to Swedish immigrant parents in the early 20th century, 12-year-old Karin sees herself as a modern Canadian girl. Her father speaks English: why does her mother cling to her language and old-country ways? Karin is shocked out of her adolescent intolerance by her mother's sudden tragic death in a mountain avalanche. Her body is never recovered, although Karin does find the goldstone pendant her mother wore: she always took it off at night because she said it brought her frighten-ing dreams of the future. When Karin herself wears the goldstone, she finds that foreknowledge carries with it a heavy responsibility.

The pendant with its prophetic powers lends an element of fantasy to this historical fiction. *Goldstone*'s roots are in the stories of prolific British Columbia writer Julie Lawson's own maternal grandparents, the real-life models for Karin's father and his second wife. While Karin and many of the book's other characters are invented, Lawson vividly recreates the railway town of Donald, a community where lives are shaped by the weather and the CPR. She conveys deep admiration for the heroism of earlier generations working in cold, dangerous conditions far outside our experience. She handles the devastating loss of a much-loved parent sensitively and convincingly, and though there is a breezy sitcom glibness to much of the younger characters' dialogue, the psychology rings true. The book is briskly paced and suspenseful; we are aware that terrible things may happen, for the real world that Lawson evokes offers no guarantees of a happy ending.

Lawson intends *Goldstone* as the first book of a trilogy, and while it feels complete, there are plenty of promising threads to be spun out, such as Karin's relationship with her loyal friend Stuart.

Lucinda Lockwood (review date May 1998)

SOURCE: Lockwood, Lucinda. *School Library Journal* 44, no. 5 (May 1998): 146.

Gr 5-8—Lawson beautifully re-creates life in 1910 British Columbia through the eyes of the 13-year-old daughter of Swedish immigrants [in *Goldstone*]. Karin lives in the soon-to-become-defunct town of Donald, high in the mountains. It is a railroad town, and an average annual snowfall in excess of 30 feet makes life exciting, as well as treacherous for the men who toil on the railroad. Woven into the historical details of the early 20th-century mountain community are the usual travails of early adolescence. For example, Karin initially rejects her parents' old-country lifestyle and values, only to embrace them after the tragic death of her mother in an avalanche. She also experiences the first stirrings of romantic love with the son of an innkeeper. A goldstone pendant belonging to Karin's mother plays an important role throughout the narrative. Anyone who wears it to sleep dreams of future events; thus it provides an effective foreshadowing tool. The second devastating avalanche in which many members of Karin's father's crew are lost convinces him to leave his job with the railroad. Lawson has narrowed the time between two tragic historical incidents for this novel, but it does not suffer as a result. There are wonderful touches, such as a close call with a grizzly bear while on a mountain picnic and a description of the traditional Swedish *Luciadagen* celebration on December 13.

Shelle Rosenfeld (review date July 1998)

SOURCE: Rosenfeld, Shelle. *Booklist* 94, no. 21 (July 1998): 1882.

Gr. 5-7. In turn-of-the-century British Columbia, 12-year-old Karin enjoys being a "modern" Canadian girl and can't understand why her mother won't let go of her old-fashioned Swedish ways, which Karin finds so embarrassing [in **Goldstone**]. But suddenly her mother is gone, the victim of a devastating landslide, and Karin must come to terms with her guilt and regrets about their relationship. Complicating matters is her mother's pendant, which seems to give its wearer dreams of the future—with frightening accuracy. And when Karin dreams of another landslide, she wonders if she'll be able to warn her father and the railroad crew in time. Based on actual events, this historical novel makes for a quick, suspenseful, and entertaining read. The extensively researched details of pioneer life in a newly settled territory add authenticity; characters and their relationships and dialogue are realistic. Particularly effective are the descriptions of the avalanches and their physical and emotional impact on survivors and landscape. With the recent onslaught of natural disasters, this novel, presented as the first in a trilogy, has a timely relevance.

📖 *MIDNIGHT IN THE MOUNTAINS* (1998)

Joanne Findon (review date December 1998)

SOURCE: Findon, Joanne. *Quill and Quire* 64, no. 12 (December 1998): 35.

(ages 4-8) A young girl sits by the fire [in **Midnight In The Mountains**]. This is her first night in the mountain cabin, and although her parents and her brother are asleep, she is excited and wakeful. As the fire burns to embers she listens to the sounds of the winter night: the rustle of owl's wings, the muffled chatter of a frozen stream, the far-off howls of

wolves. As she listens, she also remembers the daytime fun of making snow angels and dogsledding on the lake, and looks forward to the next day's skiing adventure. Past and future weave in and out of the present as the girl listens and gazes out at the snowy, moonlit mountains.

This is a beautiful book. The language is simple yet lyrical, perfectly conveying the meditative mood of the story. Lawson deftly repeats the line "It's quiet in the mountains" with variations throughout. In the first half of the book, pages with two lines of text (such as "It's quiet in the mountains. So quiet, I hear the cold") alternate with descriptions of daytime activities. Words and ideas are also repeated and echoed from page to page; for instance, the beating wings of the owl at night call to mind the wings of the snow angels made by day. The result is a rhythmic text that carries the reader along, linking each page verbally with the next.

Sheena Lott's stunning watercolour illustrations match the impressionistic mood of the text. Alternating between night and daytime scenes, they capture both the joyful sunlit world and the quiet mystery of the night. Her snowy owl with his bright, startled eyes is particularly fine. This is a book for young and old, but particularly for those who love mountains, midnight, and snow.

Linda Ludke (review date January 1999)

SOURCE: Ludke, Linda. *School Library Journal* 45, no. 1 (January 1999): 97.

K-Gr 3—A young girl is spending her first night in the mountains and is too excited to sleep [in **Midnight in the Mountains**]. She sits by a window and listens to the night sounds that conjure up images of events earlier in the day: the brush of an owl's wings reminds her of making snow angels, the "rush of a fast-moving stream" triggers memories of sliding on a frozen creek. Lawson plays with language and the effect is often an elegant blending of the senses: "It's quiet in the mountains. So quiet, I hear the cold." The short, gentle refrains are perfectly balanced by full-page watercolor glimpses into the tranquil winter evening. The dreamy blues and purples of the serene night pictures contrast pleasingly with the active daylight scenes where both text and illustrations brim with energy. This book beautifully captures a child's sense of wonder and would make a lovely addition to a seasonal story-time.

Horn Book Guide (review date spring 1999)

SOURCE: *Horn Book Guide* 10 (spring 1999): 35.

Illustrated by Sheena Lott. Too excited to sleep on her first night in the mountains [in *Midnight in the Mountains*], a girl thinks about the quiet magic of the cold, snowy landscape. Watercolors depict the family's snowy adventures hiking, skiing, and playing an icicle xylophone. The overly lyrical text is written in the first person but does not come close to the thought or speech patterns of a young girl.

IN LIKE A LION (1999)

Hadley Dyer (review date January 1999)

SOURCE: Dyer, Hadley. *Quill and Quire* 64, no. 1 (January 1999): 43.

(Ages 5-9) Although it's recounted by a fictional character, *In Like a Lion* is based on the true story of a cougar that strolled into the Empress Hotel in Victoria, B.C., the night of March 3, 1992. The fictional narrator of Julie Lawson's latest picture book is the daughter of a conservation officer called to help with the search after the animal is first spotted. Her father eventually succeeds in capturing the elusive mountain cat, but the real star of this story is the cougar itself. Hidden throughout the watercolour illustrations, it's an apparition lurking in the bushes.

As in her first picture book, *Secret Dawn,* purple, green, and blue are Yolaine Lefebvre's colours of choice. The wash of colour adds depth to the pictures, illuminating the evening shadows and reflecting the eerie, yet enchanting, nature of the story. Even when the cougar is totally visible, it retains its ghost-like qualities.

Lawson keeps the text simple, her phrasing short and breathless. An audible hush falls at the end of every sentence: "They didn't know there was a cougar in town. And I didn't tell them." The climax of the book is not when the conservation officer carries the tranquillized cougar out of the hotel, but when his daughter runs her fingers through its silky fur.

BEAR ON THE TRAIN (1999)

Hazel Rochman (review date 15 October 1999)

SOURCE: Rochman, Hazel. *Booklist* 96, no. 4 (15 October 1999): 455.

Ages 3-7. One fall day Bear smells grain, and he follows the smell down the mountain onto the hopper of a train [in *Bear on the Train*]. Nobody sees him but Jeffrey, who watches the train leave the prairie for the East and return many times for more grain, with Bear hibernating comfortably through weeks of snow and cold, until he wakes up in the spring and lumbers away up the mountainside. It's a bit hard to accept that no one would find the bear all winter, but kids will enjoy the secret adventure story with its rollicking train rhythms and dramatic brown-shaded oil paintings, which move from close-ups of the great bear to sweeping landscapes of the powerful train roaring down the canyon and thundering through the woods. And the only figures we see are Jeffrey and Bear.

Christina Dorr (review date November 1999)

SOURCE: Dorr, Christina. *School Library Journal* 45, no. 11 (November 1999): 122.

K-Gr 3—In the fall, a bear smells grain, climbs onto a train, eats his fill, and stays to ride [in *Bear on the Train*]. Jeffrey, a boy about 10, is the only one who sees him, and he tries to coax Bear off each time the train passes by: "Hey, Bear! Get off the train! / You'll freeze when it snows and get wet when it rains! / You'll be scared in the tunnels; you'll be all alone! / Your friends will be worried; they'll want you back home! / So, Bear! Get off the train!" Bear ignores the boy's entreaties, and spends the winter sleeping and riding, undiscovered. He finally awakes "to the succulent taste of spring" and an astonished-looking Jeffrey watches him leave the train. Lawson's spare prose is filled with imagery, rhyme, rhythm, repetition, alliteration, consonance, and assonance. This style is reminiscent of the author's *Midnight in the Mountains* (1998). [Brian] Deines's rich oil paintings, done in earth tones on canvas, are executed in a realistic style. They are attractively textured, which is especially appropriate for Bear's fur and the surrounding foliage. Occasionally, however, the paintings are a bit too dark to see Bear easily. This story is best shared as a read-aloud to appreciate fully the language and captivating illustrations.

TURNS ON A DIME (1999)

Maureen Garvie (review date November 1998)

SOURCE: Garvie, Maureen. *Quill and Quire* 64, no. 11 (November 1998): 47.

(Ages 10+) In the first book in Julie Lawson's *Goldstone* trilogy, a goldstone pendant sustained a motherless girl growing up in a mining town. In this

book—the trilogy's second—the setting moves to Victoria and time advances two generations. Its central character is Jo, not quite 12, intense, competitive, imaginative. At school she has a reputation as someone who doesn't let truth stand in the way of a good story. In an era—the 1950s—that rewards herd behaviour, someone like Jo has a tough time. But her parents and even her pesky little brother are loving and forbearing. She also has a wonderful extended family: grandparents who provide a rich Swedish legacy that includes language, customs, and spicy meatballs.

When Jo's older best friend suddenly seems much more interested in boys and Elvis Presley, Jo is lucky to find a new soulmate, an English boy newly arrived in Canada. Their friendship allows Lawson to explore the need for acceptance and boy-girl relationships.

Into all this comes a bombshell that shatters Jo's world. Here the cover notes are justifiably discreet: when Jo learns she is adopted (I'm revealing this only because booksellers and librarians should know it), it comes as a shock to the reader as well. As Jo responds by rejecting the familial love she so badly needs, adrift from everything that has anchored her, she too finds the goldstone pendant.

Lawson's new book can be enjoyed independently from its prequel, although that means missing the pleasure of re-meeting old friends. While not as rich historically as *Goldstone, Turns on a Dime* does a good job of conveying a time of a generation ago; and although some things have changed in 40 years (Elvis is dead, the Spice Girls live) Lawson's readers will have little trouble understanding Jo's dilemmas.

Gerry Larson (review date June 1999)

SOURCE: Larson, Gerry. *School Library Journal* 45, no. 6 (June 1999): 134.

Gr 5-8—In this sequel to *Goldstone* [*Turns on a Dime*], set in British Columbia, a family heirloom is passed from one generation to the next. Jo, 11, feels out of sync. Her classmates are swooning over Elvis and boys, and her beloved baby-sitter, Mack, is absorbed in romance. Jo finds solace in friendship with a new boy in her neighborhood whose humor, interests, and anxieties seem to match hers until peer pressure threatens to pull them apart. Jo's world turns upside down when she learns that Mack is pregnant, and then Mack tells Jo that she is adopted. In shock

and anger, Jo rejects her friend and her devoted parents and flees in distress to her grandparents. They comfort her with their own stories of harsh family realities and tragedies and encourage her to treasure the relationships that have brought her happiness. From her deceased aunt, Jo inherits the goldstone pendant that links her to her adopted family and the past. Numerous references to the 1950s add to the setting and give a historical framework to the story. The solid characterization, well-paced plot, and Jo's journey of discovery will appeal to readers. Jo is markedly naive and impetuous in keeping with the conservative but changing tenor of the times. While the mystique of the goldstone pendant continues from the first novel, *Turns on a Dime* can stand alone as a complete, satisfying coming-of-age story.

THE GHOST OF AVALANCHE MOUNTAIN (2000)

Teresa Toten (review date April 2000)

SOURCE: Toten, Teresa. *Quill and Quire* 66, no. 4 (April 2000): 51.

(Ages 9-12) *The Ghost of Avalanche Mountain* is the final book in Vancouver Island writer Julie Lawson's Goldstone trilogy. The stories span several generations, each propelled by a mystical gem and its effects on the people who wear it.

We enter this story early in the 20th century and deep in the recesses of Mount Revelstoke, British Columbia. Young Jonathan Silver (the ghost) and his grandfather eke out an isolated existence by fashioning exquisite goldstones. When a goldstone that has been rendered magic by lightning is lost, Jonathan makes a fateful promise to his grandfather to return it no matter what happens or how long it takes. The language in the Jonathan chapters is particularly evocative and sure.

We enter the present through 12-year-old Ashley Gillespie, who has been given the goldstone by Aunt Jo (a character readers met in the second book, *Turns On A Dime*). By now, we're aware that the goldstone allows the bearer to dream the future, but Ashley's dreams become increasingly unsettling and ominous. Is the gem cursed? Is Ashley's life threatened? Eventually, she encounters the ghost when she's caught in an avalanche.

Lawson neatly intersects past and present, historical fact and clever fiction. She is less sure-footed with her modern characters, who seem curiously bland.

We're with Ashley for more than 200 pages but witness little change or growth. Her interaction with her friends (for example, when she accuses Erica of stealing the goldstone) often feels engineered to serve the plot rather than to reveal more of the heroine. That said, the plot—two people, one out of time, heading on a collision course toward each other—is compelling. *The Ghost of Avalanche Mountain* is a fine conclusion to the Goldstone trilogy and a satisfying read on its own.

Heather Dieffenbach (review date January 2001)

SOURCE: Dieffenbach, Heather. *School Library Journal* 47, no. 1 (January 2001): 132.

Gr 5-9—This title [*The Ghost of Avalanche Mountain*] completes Lawson's trilogy begun in *Goldstone* (1998) and continued in *Turns on a Dime* (1999). When Ashley's famous mystery-writing Aunt Jo sends her the family goldstone necklace for a birthday present, Ashley is thrilled. She is especially intrigued when she discovers that if she sleeps while wearing the heirloom, she dreams of the future. Usually the dreams are vague and trivial, shady faraway images, but one of them is singularly disturbing. It is of a boy with long black hair and worn winter clothes whom she sees not only in her dreams, but disappearing in and out of real life. The tension builds as the dreams grow more frightening. Finally, an avalanche brings her face to face with the boy ghost who has lingered through death and time to recover the goldstone and return its magic to the mountain where it was crafted. While the plot moves quickly and the suspense will hold the most reluctant of readers, the dialogue is forced and awkward, the characters are thinly drawn, and resolutions seem easy and convenient. A lackluster addition to a genre that is already full of superior selections.

Ruth Cox (review date February 2001)

SOURCE: Cox, Ruth. *Voice of Youth Advocates* 23, no. 6 (February 2001): 433.

This final book [*The Ghost of Avalanche Mountain*] in the Goldstone Trilogy brings twelve-year-old Ashley face to face with the ghost of a British Columbia Native boy who has been searching for her over three generations. He is determined to return the goldstone that she wears around her neck to the mountains that his grandfather loved. Since his death one hundred years earlier, Jonathan has learned how to make himself appear real, but he still cannot move the goldstone unless Ashley meets him in the place between life and death. Causing an avalanche that buries Ashley long enough for her to lose consciousness allows Jonathan to make peace with Ashley and fulfill the promise he made to his grandfather. The goldstone remains buried beneath the mountain snows as Ashley safely returns home with an empty heirloom chain about her neck.

Lawson beautifully describes the grandeur of British Columbia through the eyes of Ashley and her friends, whose activities include mountain hiking and skiing. This book's Canadian flavor will not deter the American reader who is intrigued by the magical goldstone or the friends' adventures. Although Lawson refers to characters from her earlier novels *Goldstone* and *Turns on a Dime,* this book stands on its own. The references to Ashley's aunt and great-aunt, the two women who previously wore the stone, and to their encounters with the ghost Jonathan, however, might have readers returning to the library to ask for the first two books in the trilogy.

DESTINATION GOLD! (2001)

Jessica Higgs (review date November 2000)

SOURCE: Higgs, Jessica. *Quill and Quire* 66, no. 11 (November 2000): 40.

(Ages 10-15) Award-winning author Julie Lawson's 20th book [*Destination Gold!*] documents the emotional growth of three young people against the dramatic backdrop of the Klondike gold rush. Sixteen-year-old Ned Turner's adventure begins in Victoria in 1897, when he boards a steamer to the goldfields, hoping to eliminate his late father's debts. Catherine, also 16, frantically travels north, escaping the brutal gambler who won her in a card game. Thirteen-year-old Sarah, Ned's sister, searches for the beloved brother she misses as well as for her own sense of self.

"Befriended" by Montana Jim Daley, Ned quickly realizes his own vulnerability in the face of awful conditions and the unscrupulous actions of seasoned stampeders like Montana. Ned eventually crosses paths with Catherine, whose internal resilience helps her to bear the journey's hardships but prevents her from forming the human relationships she subconsciously craves. When Sarah makes her own trek several months later, she resolves not only to find her brother, but to connect with the withdrawn Catherine who reluctantly joins Sarah's party en route.

Weaving together maps, archival photographs, historical fact, and well-paced fiction, Lawson accurately depicts the physical hardship, the deplorable treatment of animals, and the human greed rife during the gold rush. Her main characters face reality with a believable combination of fear, fallibility, and strength. Lawson's uncomplicated text makes this chapter of Canadian history accessible, but also conveys emotion and insight. As well as engaging young adult readers in the personal trials of the three lead characters, this book will leave them with a healthy respect for those who accepted the Klondike's challenge.

Roger Leslie (review date 15 February 2001)

SOURCE: Leslie, Roger. *Booklist* 97, no. 12 (15 February 2001): 1128.

Gr. 6-12. Voluminous research and interviews with descendants of prospectors during the Klondike gold rush allow Lawson to weave a story [*Destination Gold!*] rich in historical detail. Despite believing he's not much of an adventurer, 16-year-old Ned Turner sets off for Dawson City to find gold and save his widowed mother and younger sister, Sarah, from destitution. Meanwhile, a sullen but determined teen named Catherine tries to escape an abusive past by running away to the Klondike herself. Then Sarah heads north to find her brother, giving readers three separate journeys to follow, which culminate in an exciting climax spurred by the return of Catherine's abuser. Blended together and supported by fitting black-and-white photographs, some correspondence to vary the prose, and maps to establish the setting, the young people's stories will be gold for fans of historical fiction and wilderness adventure.

Betsy Fraser (review date April 2001)

SOURCE: Fraser, Betsy. *Voice of Youth Advocates* 24, no. 1 (April 2001): 44.

It is 1897, and Ned Turner is determined to make his fortune in the gold fields of the Klondike [in *Destination Gold!*]. He sets off, certain that in no time he will send enough money back to his mother and sister in Victoria, British Columbia, to support them. He envisions a quick trip, followed by a period of scooping gold up off the ground he intends to claim. His twelve-year-old sister, Sarah, is not so sure. Sarah is practical, not a dreamer like Ned and their mother. Little does Sarah know that soon she also will be

sent to the Klondike when Ned disappears. Catherine, a sixteen-year-old on the run, heads to the Klondike for reasons of her own. The lives of these three characters become intertwined as they undergo a series of adventures that put all their lives at risk.

Lawson's research in Dawson City in the northern Yukon has helped her to produce a richly textured landscape that shows the excitement and difficulties faced by the hopeful thousands struck by gold fever. Astute readers will foresee Ned's dilemma long before he does, but they will be unsatisfied with the sparse explanation of Catherine's problematic past. Sarah's character surely will captivate readers. This shy, practical, and terrified girl discovers strength of character and resourcefulness she never expected. This story, set amidst one of the most frantic dashes in North American history, is a delightful discovery for readers of historical fiction.

Ashley Larsen (review date July 2001)

SOURCE: Larsen, Ashley. *School Library Journal* 47, no. 7 (July 2001): 110.

Gr 5-8—It's 1897, and 16-year-old Ned Turner is caught up in the excitement over the discovery of gold in the Klondike [in *Destination Gold!*]. Leaving his mother and sister with promises of riches, he sets off from Victoria, British Columbia, for Skagway, with little knowledge of the grueling trip that lies ahead, and with a naïveté that causes him to lose his entire outfit in a card game shortly after his arrival. A gambler wins it back for him, but in return for the favor, Ned has to share his food, supplies, and labor with Montana on the long journey to Dawson City. Also traveling to the Klondike is 16-year-old Catherine, whose father lost her in a card game with Montana. She escaped and sees the gold country as a chance to start over, little knowing that she is headed straight to where Montana waits for revenge. On her way, she meets Ned's younger sister, Sarah, who is searching for her brother. Their three stories gradually come together in a satisfying conclusion. This novel captures the harshness and danger of the gold country, and the optimism and often eventual despair of those who ventured there. The details of gold mining and traveling in the Klondike are well researched and vividly described, with accompanying photographs of the time period scattered throughout the book. The characters are likable, if a little one-dimensional, and Lawson does a good job of switching story lines at critical moments to build suspense and dramatic tension. On the whole, this is an exciting, fast-paced adventure.

Horn Book Guide (review date fall 2001)

SOURCE: Larsen, Ashley. *Horn Book Guide* 12, no. 2 (fall 2001): 310.

In 1897, sixteen-year-old Ned leaves his home in Victoria, British Columbia, in pursuit of Klondike gold [in *Destination Gold!*]. The novel charts his struggles in the north while following Catherine, a teenage girl running away from her past, and Ned's twelve-year-old sister, Sarah, as they, too, make the dangerous trek to the mining town. The plot is full of coincidences, but the characters are appealing and the setting is wonderfully realized.

Ann M. G. Gray (review date September-October 2001)

SOURCE: Gray, Ann M. G. *Book Report* 20, no. 2 (September-October 2001): 63.

Gr 5 & Up. Lawson's tale of adventure [*Destination Gold!*], set in the gold fields of the Klondike in 1897, interweaves the story of 16-year-old Ned Turner with that of his 13-year-old sister, Sarah, and a 16-year-old girl named Catherine. After the death of his father, Ned is forced to abandon his dream of attending college. Upon learning of the money to be made in the gold fields, he decides to head to the Klondike, leaving his mother and sister behind. On the trip he meets up with an unscrupulous gambler named Montana and his cohorts, who teach Ned some hard lessons. Luckily, Ned is later befriended by Frosty Jack and his friends, who help him through the long winter. Meanwhile, Sarah and her mother worry when they don't hear from Ned, and Sarah decides to head north herself, escorted by a local family. On the way she befriends a lonely girl named Catherine, who is heading to the Klondike, alone, to escape a troubled past. This tale of adventure and intrigue paints an exciting picture of what life was like for the thousands of destiny seekers who ventured to the Alaskan gold fields. Scattered throughout the book are actual photographs taken of people traveling to the Klondike; these photos greatly enhance the story. Students reading Lawson's historical fiction will gain valuable insight into this period of North American history. *Recommended*

THE KLONDIKE CAT (2002)

Kirkus Reviews (review date 1 October 2002)

SOURCE: *Kirkus Reviews* 70, no. 19 (1 October 2002): 1474.

There are many ways to make your fortune, as a boy and his father serendipitously find when they relocate to the Klondike wilderness during the gold rush [in *The Klondike Cat*]. Noah disobeys his father's wishes by bringing the family cat, Shadow, on the arduous journey to their new home in gold country. Noah and his Pa must work hard to move the huge bulk of supplies downriver, and Pa condescends to allow Shadow along if she is no trouble, therefore Noah balances his heavy loads with concerns over the beloved kitty. With hard work, courage, and aplomb, the pair reaches their goal in the end only to find the gold claims are either staked already or too expensive. There is no room for sentimentality in the Klondike, and Lawson (*Destination Gold!*) never mentions what has happened to the mother, but she uses other realistic touches such as the kitty disappearing into the ship on the first leg of the trip, creating a believable slice of robust American pioneer history. She trudges her characters up hill, down dale, and over a snow-covered mountain to a hard-flowing river. In the end, Shadow brings them luck and financial reward so the trio can start their new lives together after all. [Paul] Mombourquette's (*Fog Cat*, 1999) illustrations are broad brushed and colorful, evoking the gritty spirit that opened this last frontier. A lengthy historical note includes a synopsis of the actual history of the territory and era addressed in the story. *(5-9)*

Additional coverage of Lawson's life and career is contained in the following sources published by the Gale Group: *Contemporary Authors,* Vol. 196; *Literature Resource Center;* and *Something about the Author,* Vols. 79, 126.

Joan Lingard
1932-

(Full name Joan Amelia Lingard) Scottish novelist, children's writer, and young adult author.

INTRODUCTION

Joan Lingard has written for adults as well as teens and children, but it is her work as a young adult novelist that has gained the most recognition. Her empathetic portraits of young people caught in the midst of prejudice, political turmoil, or simply the throes of growing up have won her international acclaim. She is regarded as an exceptional storyteller whose books are candid and thought-provoking, interesting and accessible.

BIOGRAPHICAL INFORMATION

Lingard was born in Edinburgh, Scotland, in 1932. Lingard and her family moved to Belfast, Northern Ireland, when she was very young. She lived in Belfast until she turned eighteen. She has often said that she began to write when she was very young because she couldn't find enough to read.

When Lingard was fourteen, her mother was diagnosed with breast cancer, and died a year later. Lingard spent the next years traveling, feeling, as she would later note "completely disoriented." Upon her return to Belfast, she took a job as a secondary school teacher in a very poor area of the city. She would continue to teach, even after moving back to Edinburgh the following year.

Soon after moving to Edinburgh, she married and moved to a small village outside the city where she taught and began writing seriously. Her first adult novel, *Liam's Daughter,* was published in 1963, the same year Lingard gave birth to her first child. A few years later, she had a second child. But by 1969, her marriage was on the rocks, and she divorced the following year. After her divorce she moved back to Edinburgh and wrote a book, *The Lord on Our Side* (1970), about the Catholic/Protestant tension in Northern Ireland. One of her friends then suggested that she write a book about that conflict but from the

point of view of young people. Thus, Lingard embarked on the Sadie and Kevin series of books. The Sadie and Kevin series follows a young couple from Belfast, one Catholic and one Protestant, through adolescence and on to marriage. The series comprised five volumes, and was very well received. It established Lingard as a major young adult novelist.

Lingard married again in the mid-1970s, and continued writing for young adults. Another series of books, the Maggie series, was very well-received. Throughout the 1980s Lingard's work was continually praised by critics of books for young adults. In the 1990s Lingard forayed into writing for children, publishing her Flippers series. She continues to reside in Edinburgh.

MAJOR WORKS

Lingard published six adult novels before she embarked upon *The Twelfth Day of July* (1970). It is the first book in her Sadie and Kevin series. In it, Lingard focuses on the Catholic-Protestant strife in Northern Ireland through the actions of several fictitious children caught in the crisis. The result was very successful, and the sequel, *Across the Barricades* (1972), became Lingard's most popular book.

In her Maggie series, Lingard chronicles, the life of a working-class girl who wants to go to university and fulfill her potential. Through sheer determination and careful enterprise, she succeeds, and even establishes a plumbing business for her father. Her career is contrasted with the life of her middle-class boyfriend, a listless sort. This series comprises the books *The Clearance* (1974), *The Resettling* (1975), *The Pilgrimage* (1976), and *The Reunion* (1977).

CRITICAL RECEPTION

A reviewer for *Times Literary Supplement* called *The Twelfth Day of July* "a good and important book" whose story "is told with admirable impartiality and with a realism children will appreciate." "The family backgrounds are as vivid as ever, and . . . the ending is an honest one," noted another *Times Literary Supplement* contributor in a review of *Across the Barricades*. And a *School Library Journal* critic praised *Hostages to Fortune* (1976) for rendering "characters and backgrounds economically and well."

In her Maggie series, Lingard features a "sprightly Glasgow heroine," noted Dunlop, further remarking that "Lingard has stated that she began to write her 'Maggie' quartet as a respite from thinking about [Northern Ireland] and its problems. Certainly this series, which has been televised, is much lighter in tone, although its concerns are perhaps closer to the experience of most young readers. Told with humour and panache in the first person, the series follows the doings of Maggie, a working-class girl who wants to go to university and fulfill her potential."

AWARDS

Lingard has been the recipient of the following awards: Scottish Arts Council bursary, 1969; German Buxtehude Bulle Prize for Children's Literature, 1987, and the MBE for Services to Children's Literature 1998. *The Twelfth Day of July* was awarded the ZDF Preis der Leseratten, West Germany, in 1986, and *Across the Barricades* won the Buxtehüder Bülle—West Germany, in 1987. In 1988, Lingard's *The Guilty Party* was shortlisted for the Federation

of Children's Book Groups award. *After Colette* and *Tom and the Tree House* won the Scottish Arts Council Award in 1994 and 1998, respectively. *Tug of War* was shortlisted for the 1989 Carnegie Medal, received the Federation of Children's Book Group Award and the Sheffield Book Award in 1989, and was runner-up for 1990 Lancashire Children's Book Club of the Year.

PRINCIPAL WORKS

Liam's Daughter (novel) 1963

The Lord on Our Side (novel) 1970

The Twelfth Day of July (young adult novel) 1970

Across the Barricades (young adult novel) 1972

Frying as Usual (young adult novel) 1973

Into Exile (young adult novel) 1973

The Clearance (young adult novel) 1974

A Proper Place (young adult novel) 1975

The Resettling (young adult novel) 1975

Hostages to Fortune (young adult novel) 1976

The Pilgrimage (young adult novel) 1976

The Reunion (young adult novel) 1977

Snake Among the Sunflowers (young adult novel) 1977

The Gooseberry (young adult novel) 1978; also published as *Odd Girl Out,* 1979

The File on Fraulein Berg (young adult novel) 1980

Strangers in the House (young adult novel) 1981

The Winter Visitor (young adult novel) 1983

The Freedom Machine (young adult novel) 1986

The Guilty Party (young adult novel) 1987

Rags and Riches (young adult novel) 1988

Tug of War (young adult novel) 1989

Can You Find Sammy the Hamster? (children's fiction) 1990

Glad Rags (young adult novel) 1990

Between Two Worlds (young adult novel) 1991

Morag and the Lamb (children's fiction) 1991

Hands Off Our School! (children's fiction) 1992

Clever Clive and Loopy Lucy (children's fiction) 1993

Night Fires (young adult novel) 1993

Lizzie's Leaving (young adult novel) 1995

Sulky Suzy and Jittery Jack (children's fiction) 1995

Dark Shadows (young adult novel) 1998

A Secret Place (young adult novel) 1998

Tom and the Treehouse (children's fiction) 1998

The Egg Thieves (children's fiction) 1999

Natasha's Will (young adult novel) 2000

AUTHOR COMMENTARY

Joan Lingard (essay date 1977)

SOURCE: Lingard, Joan. "On Writing Realistically for Teenagers" in *Books for Your Children* 12, no. 4 (1977): 16-7.

[*In the following essay, Lingard discusses the underlying themes of her books.*]

I had published six adult novels before I came to write my first book for children, and I owe my entry into this field of writing to the late Honor Arundel who was a close friend. When she had finished reading my sixth novel **The Lord On Our Side,** which is set in Ulster in the period from the forties to the early sixties, she suggested that I write a book about Belfast for children. At that time, 1969, the current troubles were just beginning to build up. I thought about it and in fact realised that I had a book in my head more or less ready made; the character Josie in my adult novel was transmuted into Sadie, her brother Billy into Tommy, and the incident where their father asks them the sequence "*Who is the good man?*", "*Who is the bad man?*" etc., I retained. I created Kevin, the Catholic boy, as a balance to Sadie and his sister Brede as a counterweight to Tommy. Thus Sadie and Kevin were born and **The Twelfth Day of July** was on its way. It was a book that fell into place for me very easily; I alternated the chapters between the Protestant and Catholic children and I chose the five days leading up to the "Glorious Twelfth" for my time span. This story could have been set during almost any time in the previous fifty years, but almost as soon as I had finished it the situation grew worse in Northern Ireland and I realised that it was all very well for me to preach tolerance and leave the children picnicking on the sands of Bangor having overcome their prejudices towards one another, but what then? What would happen when they went back to their separate areas, to the hardening attitudes of all the people around them, not least their own families? I felt that I had a responsibility to find out, to go further with them, and so I wrote **Across The Barricades,** in which Sadie and Kevin are 16 and 17, have left school and are trying to find their feet in an adult world as well as the troubled streets of Belfast. This meant that I was now writing for teenagers, or young adults, as they are sometimes referred to, which presented no real problem: the subject matter dictated the approach. Sadie and Kevin are essentially simple people, not highly educated, not intellectual, and I have always felt it necessary to write in fairly simple terms about them.

Subsequently, I have written **Into Exile,** in which they marry and go to London; **A Proper Place,** set in Liverpool and Cheshire where they have their first child bringing further complexities to their mixed marriage; and **Hostages To Fortune,** where they are forced to leave their Cheshire cottage and seek a new home across the border in North Wales. I would very much like to write a sixth and final book about them, to round out and consolidate the series. When I started I had no intention of writing more than one book, but I have found it tremendously interesting and rewarding to be able to explore two characters in such breadth and depth, and to follow them through the passage from adolescence to maturity.

As a relief almost, in order to get some respite from thinking about Ulster and its problems, I created Maggie, a 16-year-old Glasgow girl. Her granny and her cottage were the starting point here for in an Inverness-shire glen where I used to spend holidays with my children there lived an old lady in such a cottage which one day was burnt to the ground and all her lifetime's possessions destroyed. I linked this with nineteenth century clearances in the Highlands and called the book **The Clearance**; and at the end, when Maggie returns to Glasgow, she finds that her family has just received notice to go since their tenement is about to be demolished, which means that yet another clearance is to take place. Maggie, I decided, must be a different kind of girl from Sadie who, although spirited and a rebel in her own way, was going to follow the traditional pattern of most girls by marrying and having children. I wanted Maggie to be set on a career—social anthropology—and to have wider ideas of what life might hold, ideas which her family could not understand but tolerated, and to think of marriage as something she might or might not do but not consider as an end in itself, as most of her school friends would. I wanted, too, that she should be more intellectually discerning than Sadie about herself and her emotional reactions to situations and relationships, both within and without her own family. Again, I did not think of writing more than one book, but I got so involved with Maggie that I had the desire to follow her also for a while and to bring her to a point in which she must question more closely various concepts and attitudes, which I did in **The Resettling, The Pilgrimage,** and in the final book of the quartet, **The Reunion,** to be published in the autumn.

Both sets of characters are caught up in social change: Sadie and Kevin because of external events, Maggie because she is being educated beyond the level of her family which will lead her to go out and explore a much wider world than any of them have ever done. I am particularly interested in characters involved in social change, with all its attendant problems and stresses, as well as the pushing out of boundaries and greater awareness it brings to their lives; also in the relationships within families. With Sadie and Kevin and their families the gulf can only get wider because of the political and religious differences; with Maggie and hers the gulf is there, too, but is bridged by genuine affection on the part of them all.

I realise that the themes underlying my books are rather serious but I do always aim to lighten them with humour: I like characters to have a strong sense of humour, to be able to see the amusing side of the blackest situation; and I believe that the most important thing that a writer for any age group—but particularly for children or young adults—must do is to entertain, for unless one can do that and capture the interest of the reader one will achieve nothing.

Stephanie Nettell (essay date March 1988)

SOURCE: Nettell, Stephanie. "An Interview with Joan Lingard" in *British Book News Children's Books* (March 1988): 2–3.

[*In the following essay, Nettell analyzes how Lingard's experiences have affected her writings.*]

'I'm not so naive as to think I can change the world, but I do want my readers to think about issues and not be apathetic. Apathy is a crime: one should never sit back and say, "Let's leave it to *them*—they know more than we do."'

Nevertheless, Joan Lingard is astonished by the label 'issues writer', when she herself sees her themes as springing from people and relationships. Yet it's not entirely surprising: Josie, the spirited young heroine of her last novel, **The Guilty Party,** and the sheer guts with which she faces rigid authoritarianism, triggers memories of the impact of **The Twelfth Day of July** in 1970, when the spunky wee Sadie first defies the tribal laws of Northern Ireland. That was the first of the 'Sadie and Kevin' quintet with which most readers link Lingard's name: even today it and the second in the series, **Across the Barricades,** are bringing her literary and television awards from Germany.

The Guilty Party is a story about the survival of democracy and individual hope: Josie, newly arrived in England from Ireland, joins a peaceful protest against a seaside nuclear power station, landing herself with gallant stubborness in Holloway gaol. 'It's an anti-nuclear book but not, as so many, about *after* the holocaust, apparently saying "This is bound to happen," but trying to say, "It's possible to raise your voice *now* and protest."'

It's a deeply personal book, dedicated to her youngest daughter, Jenny, whose career as a veteran of Greenham Common began at fifteen by being arrested for flyposting a Youth CND jumble sale, and ended at nineteen after eight arrests and a spell in Holloway. One reviewer dared to wonder if the prison scenes were accurate.

'I put on a tape for Jenny and asked her to relive it step by step—that's how I recall my own childhood. My middle daughter, Bridget, camped on the pavement outside the prison, putting up a banner—"Jenny, we love you"—just as the girls do in the novel, so I had her point of view as well. For me it was a dreadful time—you never think of your daughter being locked up!—but she showed tremendous courage for an eighteen year old.

'After Jenny's experiences I felt I had to do something, and founded Scottish Writers Against the Bomb. Scotland has more than its share of nuclear spots, so most of the respected, well-known writers signed the petition we handed to the Secretary of State for Scotland. At first I had thought it must be Jenny's story, not mine, but after Chernobyl I became concerned with a power station about to go on stream outside Edinburgh, and decided that instead of writing letters to the *Scotsman* I really must write a book for young people. But Jenny is by no means Josie: I don't write documentaries—I *create* characters but *use* material.'

And, regardless of the ideological standpoint, she insists it is from characters that inspiration always comes. The wary optimism at the end of **The Guilty Party** seems to promise a sequel, but she is curious only about what happens to Tracey, the desperate little prostitute who shares Josie's cell.

'When you write for young people, you lower your bucket into the well of your own childhood and adolescence. That's my framework, and I realise it more and more the older I get. So Josie has an Irish background, though the setting had to be English because of Jenny and Holloway.' Joan Lingard was born in Edinburgh but grew up in Belfast, from the age of two till eighteen, and it is from those divided Irish streets that she views the world. Her mother came from a working-class background; her English father was brought up, one of eleven, in a Stoke Newington pub ("The Monarch' in Green Lane—I've always wondered if it was still there, and we've just found it!'). He joined the navy at fourteen, and was recalled from the RNVR to spend the war years working in Belfast.

Her grandmother, a wee body of under five feet who ran the pub, had a smallholding in Welwyn, Hertfordshire—in those days quite rural. Joan went there for holidays and it has a strong place in her imagination: 'She surfaced at least partly as Maggie's grandmother, transported to the Highlands in her wraparound floral overall and men's lace-up boots.' That grandmother has a powerful symbolic role in the 'Maggie' quartet, with its conflicting themes of freedom and emotional ties, open hills and Glasgow tenements, of forced clearances and resettlements.

She left school when she was sixteen, bereft by the death of her mother to whom she had been close, and became an untrained teacher in a Belfast slum school—fifty-four six year olds in horrific Dickensian conditions—before moving in defeat to the Ulster Bank. A scholarship to a fee-paying girls' school had given a gloss to her accent and social class; the quaintly relaxed Christian Science upbringing she owed to her mother meant she had been an outsider all her childhood, belonging neither to Northern Ireland nor anywhere else. For a writer, however, it contributed a uniquely balanced position among the religion-haunted *angst* of the Irish-bred. This childhood is beautifully evoked in her 1984 adult novel, *Sisters by Rite,* an exploration of one of her dominant themes, friendship, with Cora the closest of all her characters to herself.

At eighteen she returned to Edinburgh to live with her father. One day, when she was eleven and fed up with their tatty local library, her mother had suggested she write her own book: from that moment she knew that some day, some way, she would be a writer. It was not the kind of family to prompt her into university, and it was almost by accident that she found herself training to be a primary school teacher—'three years of the most stultifying experiences of my life'. From them came her first novel, a diatribe which she eventually burnt—'a hymn of hate not to be foisted on the public!' But it led to another, the first of six adult novels from Hodder & Stoughton.

It was after she had published a novel about Ulster that fellow Edinburgh writer Honor Arundel suggested she write for young people about what was

happening in Belfast. It was 1969. 'I realized I had *The Twelfth Day of July* just waiting to emerge—it's the one novel that has simply popped out. I thought there would be no more, but I *had* to write *Across the Barricades* to find out what happened to Sadie and Kevin.'

Protestant Sadie and Catholic Kevin meet as a result of a prank, but even jokes have tragic results in the ghetto streets of Belfast. Yet the novel is more than a lightened Romeo and Juliet tale: already it shines with those qualities that have made Lingard a favourite with both readers and critics—a blend of tenderness and sharp humour, an open frankness about emotions, an acute sense of social nuances and dialogue (and accents) that speak effortlessly in the mind.

GENERAL COMMENTARY

Audrey Laski (essay date 12 August 1983)

SOURCE: Laski, Audrey. "Place and Chips." *Times Educational Supplement* no. 3052 (12 August 1983): 16.

[*In the following essay, Laski outlines how Lingard's early childhood became essential to the author's own writings.*]

There is a certain kind of soft Celtic voice which regularly confuses me: north of the border or west of the Irish Sea? When I met Joan Lingard recently and heard that delightful sound I was for once perhaps justified in my vagueness; she says of herself, "I am Scottish-Ulster". All her growing up years, from 2 to 18, were spent in Belfast, while most of the rest of her life has been spent in Edinburgh, and all her readers will know how important both those cities are in her fiction.

But perhaps more essential to her writing than the two places themselves has been the nature of the experience of being a stranger in someone else's city, which she clearly felt even at the early age at which she moved to Belfast, perhaps because of the close family networks there: "I didn't have all the myriad relations." It has meant that one of the recurring themes in her work is that of displacement and the attempt to resettle; in the Kevin and Sadie books, the title of the third, *Into Exile* speaks for itself; in the Maggie series, there is the shadow of the Clearances, while in her newest novel, *The Winter Visitor* (published on Monday), the hero's best friend is always being moved on in the interests of his father's work. It is significant that in talking about the breakdown of Nick's attempt to get Joe to stay with him until he has completed his examination course, Joan Lingard says, "he could never have been completely at ease in Nick's house—not his place".

She gained other advantages from her growing season in Belfast. Not only was she a newcomer, she was alien in a more vital sense; her family were Christian Scientists, and she was therefore set outside the simple sectarian antagonism which controls experience in Belfast. This made possible the concerned detachment which makes *The Twelfth Day of July* and *Across the Barricades* so powerful and so controlled. She knows how to value this essential quality; a member of Scottish Writers against the Bomb, she will not write a novel about the nuclear issue because she cares too much.

At the age of 11, she was already writing—her sense of being slightly lonely in Belfast had "bonuses for a writer"—and writing complete stories. However, like most children's writing, they were about exotic places and people; she had not yet realized that her own experience was interesting enough to write about. Her first published novels were for adults; it was Honor Arundel who suggested that she should write specifically for young people, and so, in 1969, the *Twelfth Day of July* came "without effort, as if it had been waiting to come out". She remarks sadly that it is now an historical novel—things are even harder for the Kevins and Sadies of 1983—and with mild astonishment, that its sequel *Across the Barricades,* is a CSE set text. Those books imposed themselves as a series—"I couldn't abandon them at that point"—as did the Maggie books; others, like *The Gooseberry* and the latest novel, are as clearly complete in themselves.

The history of *The Gooseberry* is curious; it was written as a six part television serial, but first the complexities of setting up a production, and then the new possibility of the dramatization of the Maggie books, pushed it further and further away from realization, and she re-thought it as a novel. She is sharply aware of what television cannot do; though quite pleased with the way the Maggie stories worked on the small screen, she is not certain that the essence of the books was caught; because the novels had been told in the first person, they had Maggie's own voice and the development of her thoughts difficult, if not impossible, to capture in dramatization. And the development of Maggie's thoughts matters,

because here, as always, Joan Lingard is writing about "the push through adolescence to maturity"; this counts, and is hard to show from the outside.

For her it is such broad themes that are interesting; "I don't see myself as picking problems." When problems of adolescence appear in her novels it is because they would naturally occur in the lives of her characters, not because she has made an arbitrary decision to write about this or that issue. She is conscious of there still being an enormous amount to explore in such young lives, but she is drawn to the idea of writing for younger children; she published one story for 9 to 12-year-olds, *Frying as Usual,* as early as 1972. That revolved around a chip shop; she remarks that someone has noticed that there is a chip shop in every one of her books—a memory of young days when there wasn't enough money for chips. Whatever she does will be interesting, and it will be positive: "I feel it is quite wrong to be downbeat in children's novels. I don't mean I want to give them tidy solutions—there are none—but hope."

Stuart Marriot (essay date spring 1985)

SOURCE: Marriot, Stuart. "'Me Mum Says It's Bigotry': Children's Responses to *The Twelfth Day of July.*" *Children's Literature in Education* 16, no. 1 (spring 1985): 53-61.

[*In the following essay, Marriot presents research on how some students have responded to Lingard's* The Twelfth Day of July.]

Between February and June 1983 an entire cohort of pupils in their final year of primary schooling in the town of Coleraine in Northern Ireland (293 children from 9 schools) participated in a research project concerning children's voluntary fiction reading. In one part of the study, children were asked to choose a book that they had not read before, from fifteen possible titles, and to read it during the ensuing week. Subsequently, the children were interviewed in order to assess their responses to the novel they had chosen. *The Twelfth Day of July* by Joan Lingard was the most popular choice among all the titles presented to pupils, and was selected by 36 children. In this article some of their reactions to the book are considered.

The Twelfth Day of July is the first of a sequence of five books about the Protestant Jackson family and the Catholic McCoy family in the context of the Northern Ireland "troubles", and specifically in

Belfast. Joan Lingard herself was brought up in the city, but no longer lives in the province. The central characters are Sadie Jackson and Kevin McCoy, who in *The Twelfth Day* are in their early teens, and the book is centred around their childish antagonism, which gradually changes to a mutual respect. In the later books their relationship matures, culminating in marriage, which because of the difficulties involved in Protestant/Catholic relationships, necessitates exile in England.

In *The Twelfth Day,* the Jackson and McCoy families are living in clearly separated areas of Belfast, but physically very close. In the days leading up to the twelfth, Catholic children, including Kevin, paint "Down with King Billy" on a gable-end picture in the Protestant area. The Protestant children, led by Sadie, retaliate, and much of the book consists of the children chasing each other back and forth, capturing each other, getting lost and left behind in the "wrong" area, and so on. Gradually Kevin and Sadie come to respect each other, initially simply as combatants, but at the end of the book there is a serious fight in which Brede, Kevin's sister, who is portrayed as a moderate and sensible girl, gets badly hurt. In spite of fierce family pressure, both Sadie and her younger brother Tommy decide not to take part in the parades on the following day (the twelfth), but instead to spend the day out at the seaside with Kevin.

The Twelfth Day is a book which seems very appropriate for 10- or 11-year-old children in Northern Ireland. The basic themes of family and community conflict are a constant backcloth to the story, but much of the book is light-hearted in tone, and sometimes very funny (Sadie and some other children, cooking chips, set the kitchen on fire). The characters are sharply observed and credible. Sadie, for example, is hasty, bad-tempered, sharp-tongued, rather bigoted, and occasionally violent, yet very human and very likeable. No doubt, too, children would recognise many of the minor characters like Mrs. Mullet and Pat Rafferty from their own experience. The adventures in the book are realistically exciting in ways which upper primary school children could enjoy and appreciate but, at least until the fight at the end of the book, they are distanced from the real horrors of contemporary Northern Ireland by the lightness of the author's style and the constant humour of much of the plot. In this respect *The Twelfth Day* differs from the later books in the series, especially *Across the Barricades,* in which a grim and sombre Belfast with its casual and apparently mindless violence is no place for childish pranks.

Of the children who chose to read the book for us, 21 were boys and 15 girls; 25 came from working-class and 8 from middle-class social backgrounds, respectively (we were unable to determine the social class of the remaining 3 children); 27 were Protestant and 9 Catholic pupils. Strictly speaking, we have no information on the religious affiliation of any of the children we interviewed, and thus should say "pupils at controlled (or maintained) schools." In the context of Northern Ireland, however, it is reasonable to assume that the vast majority of children attend a school which reflects their religious identification. While children of both sexes and both social class and religious backgrounds picked the book, a disproportionately large number (13) of Protestant working-class boys chose it.

Nearly all the readers managed either to finish the book (19) or at least read a substantial part of it (12), in spite of such problems as "I was watching Dracula on Saturday night so I couldn't read it then" (W/P/B).[1] A large majority liked it "very much" (26), and most (5) of the rest "quite liked it." The children's comments on the book as a whole were almost always positive. For example, many children thought that it "was really the best book I've read" (W/P/B); or stated that "I thought the book was really really good" (M/P/B); or just "it was great" (M/C/G). Only one or two children made comments like "It was sort of boring" (W/P/G), although a few more referred to the unfavourable impressions of relations: "My brother thinks it's revolting" (W/P/B).

Although children generally held a high opinion of the book as a whole, some parts of it were particularly popular. Generally, it was the passages of action and adventure that appealed to the children most: the fights and the chases, the painting on the walls, the chip pan fire. The following examples of pupils' answers to the question "what was the best part of the book?" are taken more or less at random from transcripts of interviews:

> I liked when Sadie she sneaked . . . out and she wrote on the table and they caught her I thought it was very good. (W/C/B)

> The night when they went round to paint the walls and things. (M/P/B)

> I thought whenever the Protestants and Catholics came to start fighting I liked that bit it got exciting. (M/P/G)

> They were always squabbling and all and always fighting and then Kevin come in Sadie's house and scared the wits out of her mother and Sadie went in the middle of the night to him with a pen and she wrote all over the table. (W/P/B)

Pl: She was making chips, and she left the pan on the gas and then went out.

I: What happened?

Pl: It went on fire the kitchen went on fire. (W/ P/G)

Most of the children's enthusiasm for the book was based on such criteria: it was a fast and entertaining read, with lots of exciting action set in a realistic yet humorous context, with credible characters. However, some children took a more analytical view; for example, in several interviews the language of the book was contrasted favourably with that of others:

Pl. 1: It was easy . . . I can read other books an' they say all these all like posh words . . . posh words y'know.

Pl. 2: An' these words are like the words we use.

Pl. 1: Slang y'know some o' them.

I: Yes . . . what kind of books are there that talk posh then?

Pl. 2: Och y'know the way them Famous Five ones they're always so posh y'know. (W and M/C/B)

Another group commented on the fact that, unusually in books for children of this age, there are no illustrations except for the picture on the front cover. One boy in particular felt that their absence stimulated his imagination: "You have to sorta use your imagination a bit to see what they're doing." But if pictures were included, "they'll be in your book for you to look at it y'know not for you to look at in your mind" (W/P/ B).

The children's responses were not however, entirely uncritical. Some felt, for example, that real life Mums and Dads would have been much more worried about their children's escapades than they appear to be in the book, and much more direct in response to misdeeds: "My Ma would murder me instead of sending me up to bed" (W/P/G).

Another group of children spotted what was clearly to them a vital flaw:

King Billy doesn't ride a white horse he rode a brown one me Granda told me . . . I went first to my sister and then I went to my Granda and me Granda said it was a brown horse. (W/P/B)

Mention of King Billy and his horse brings us inevitably to consideration of children's responses to what, in the eyes of adults at least, is a central theme of the

book: the relationships of Protestants and Catholics. Most respondents raised such issues in the interviews without prompting, if sometimes only in rather oblique ways. In each case the interviewer encouraged children to talk around the subject as much as they wished, but without attempting to force them to comment if they did not want to do so. Generally, the interviewer's attitude of puzzled incomprehension (such as why Sadie and Tommy decided not to go to the parade) elicited careful explanation and considered opinions.

First, however, it may be worth examining children's reaction to the question, "Who was the most interesting person (or character) in the book?" Most of the responses mentioned Sadie and Kevin, and occasionally Tommy (Sadie's brother), Brede, or others. It was, however, particularly informative to examine the responses of Protestant boys in the sample. Generally, one would expect 10- or 11-year-old boys to identify most strongly with the leading male character in a story, in this case Kevin McCoy. But Kevin is a Catholic. Which would be the most powerful influence on these boys' choice? Would their choice of character be based on religion or gender? In fact, in most cases, identification in terms of religion seemed to predominate; in other words, nearly always Sadie was mentioned first and her character and actions discussed before the boys spoke about Kevin. For example:

I: Which character did you like best in it?

Pl. 1: Er I liked Sadie.

I: Sadie?

Pl. 1: Yes . . . she was tough.

I: Ah you thought she was tough did you?

Pl. 1: She was tough.

Pl. 2: I liked Linda an' Sadie they were alright.

Pl. 1: An' Tommy.

I: Tommy yeah why did you think Sadie was tough in it?

Pl. 1: 'Cos she always fought the boys an' all she didn't care. (both W/P/B)

In this example, then, not only Sadie, but other Protestant children in the book (Linda, Tommy) are mentioned with approval ahead of Kevin. In total ten interviews with one or more of the Protestant boys were held: twelve boys mentioned Sadie with approval first, as in the extract above; in one interview a boy talked about Tommy first; and three boys discussed Kevin first. In contrast, in the interviews involving the four Catholic boys in the sample, Kevin and Brian (Kevin's friend) were discussed first, and it was Sadie who took second place. This is a most unusual pattern of response: in children's reactions to other books used in the study it was very rare indeed to find the kind of cross-gender identification exhibited by the Protestant boys in relation to *The Twelfth Day.*

The second area in which the children's responses were of particular interest was in relation to the ending of the book, where Sadie and Tommy decide not to take part in the parade on the twelfth, but instead to go to the seaside with Kevin. Why, the children were asked, didn't they go to take their place in the parade, the most important event in the year for Protestants? The children's answers were varied, but fell about equally into three categories. The first was apparent incomprehension; for example:

> I think she just couldn't be bothered or somethin'. (W/P/B)

> Pl: They didn't want to walk . . . their Mummy spent a lot o' money on the uniforms an' then they didn't want to go.

> I: Why didn't they want to go?

> Pl: I don't know. (W/P/G)

Other children had clear views on the subject, but not perhaps ones which the author intended to convey:

> Pl: At the end it wasn't very good the way it just sort of . . . they were fighting and then they just sort of chickened out.

> I: Who chickened out?

> Pl: Tommy and Sadie didn't walk on the twelfth I thought that was a bit chicken. (W/P/B)

> They were going to show themselves up at the twelfth if they went to the twelfth they would show themselves up . . . everybody would probably look at them as if as if to say what are them what are they doing here the day and what's the carry-on because of the night before. (M/P/G)

The third variety of response was one which demonstrated understanding of the reasons which, perhaps, Joan Lingard intended the reader to infer:

> (They) didn't want to go they wanted to go and see Brede to see how she was because it was really their fault . . . they went and she was all right so they went to the beach. (W/P/G)

> Well they felt sorry for her. (W/P/B)

For some children, then, Sadie and Tommy's decision was hard to make sense of. Perhaps the connection between the fight and the parade, which is implicit in the story but not spelt out in detail by the writer, was difficult for children of this age to grasp.

Similar problems in dealing with rather abstract ideas were sometimes evident in children's comments on the issue of Protestant/Catholic relationships in general. In order to focus the topic more concretely, the interviewer approached the topic by asking whether the events in the book "could happen in this area." Usually, the children denied that it was possible, claiming that such things only occurred in Belfast or Derry, but they frequently went on to explore the more general questions. For example:

> It happens in Derry in Londonderry in Belfast . . . it shouldn't be Catholics and Protestants it should just be ordinary streets not separated ones. (W/P/B)

Other children tried hard to come to terms with what they clearly saw as complex issues; even in transcript it is perhaps possible with some of the children's comments to get a sense of their struggle with difficult ideas:

> Pl. 1: The part about the Catholics catching Sadie an' taking house I didn't think that I didn't think they would do that there.

> Pl. 2: Nah.

> Pl. 1: 'Cos I think they're decent people. (W/P/B)

> Pl. 1: I thought it was y'know a bit funny the way they didn't go in the parade just 'cos y'know 'cos y'know they were loyalists and you'd think they wouldn't miss the twelfth for anything.

> I: Well why didn't they go on the parade?

> Pl. 1: They just felt y'know sick about Brede y'know normally they would go y'know . . . y'know boys that throw bricks at each other an' they don't care if they hit a person normally.

> I: So you didn't think it was very realistic?

> Pl. 1: Och y'know it was a bit 'cos y'know Sadie she liked oh Brede y'know 'cos o' the day she gave Brede gave her the tea in the house.

> Pl. 2: I didn't think they would go to the beach I didn't think they'd be that friendly.

> Pl. 1: On the twelfth especially.

> I: Yes yes.

> Pl. 1: It was funny . . . y'see when the police came you'd think they'd just run they just y'know stayed there . . . normally if it's Protestants and

Catholics y'know fighting just y'know squirt when they hear the sirens . . . they just stayed. (M and W/C/B)

I: Whose fault was it?

Pl: None of them were in the right.

I: None of them were in the right?

Pl: Because it was their boths faults there were two faults because they shouldn't have started it in the first place anyway and er the Catholic the Kevin and that did it first so I think that um the Kevin and that did it more than what Sadie and that did it because Sadie was only paying them back what they did and I think the both of them weren't doing the right thing. (M/P/B)

To suggest that by the age of 11 or so children are firmly embedded in the cultural traditions of either Protestantism or Catholicism is hardly hot news. It is interesting, however, to see children working at the reconciliation of an "us and them" view of the world with the idea that in many respects "they" are much the same as "us"; many children made comments like the "they're decent people" quoted above, which in a way encapsulates the tension of such a view. In the final quotation also, a Protestant boy tries to come to terms with the fact that the Catholic children "started it" (and therefore according to a common code of children deserved "paying back") with the idea that *both* groups were nevertheless in the wrong.

Although the exploration of such themes was part of children's response to **The Twelfth Day,** as suggested earlier it would be a mistake to expect a sophisticated theoretical analysis of the problems of Northern Ireland from children of this age. Quite often, indeed, the children seemed to find the abstractions involved incomprehensible (or at least difficult to articulate), as with the boy quoted in the title of this article:

Pl: Me Mum she says it's bigotry.

I: Bigotry?

Pl: Yes.

I: What does that mean?

Pl: I don't know (laughs). (W/P/B)

It is clear from the evidence presented in this account that in many respects Northern Ireland children respond to their reading in ways which are common to all children of this age: they like fast moving and realistically exciting stories, and material that is humorous and written in accessible language. As with

all 10- or 11-year-olds, perhaps the more abstract ideas are sometimes difficult to understand. But in relation to at least some of the themes of **The Twelfth Day,** Northern Ireland children's cultural and religious affiliations do seem to act as a filter of their responses in ways which are unique to children born and brought up in a divided community.

Note

1. The following codes were used to identify children participating in the study: W, working class; M, middle class; P, Protestant; C, Catholic; B, boy; G, girl; Pl, pupil; I, interviewer.

References

Lingard, Joan, *The Twelfth Day of July.* London: Hamish Hamilton, 1970. Nashville: Nelson, 1972.

——, *Across the Barricades.* London: Hamish Hamilton, 1972. Nashville: Nelson, 1973.

Celia Catlett Anderson (essay date September 1997)

SOURCE: Anderson, Celia Catlett. "Born to the Troubles: The Northern Ireland Conflict in the Books of Joan Lingard and Catherine Sefton" in *Lion and the Unicorn* 21, no. 3 (September 1997): 387-401.

[*In the following essay, Anderson cites how the conflicts in Northern Ireland have influenced Lingard's books.*]

The battle for the allegiance of young people is a crucial part of the Ulster conflict. From their early years, children in Northern Ireland are exposed to the slogans and ballads and sermons that proclaim the righteousness of the Protestant or the Catholic cause. And they are early aware that this righteousness may turn violent at any street corner. Until recently, the curriculum of religiously segregated schools reinforced these divisions. In counterbalance are both personal and fictional accounts, which have at their center a plea for a resolution to the conflict, a chance for the new generation.

In 1985, the Standing Conference of Youth Organizations in Northern Ireland sponsored the publication of a collection of writings by young people. While some of the pieces emphasize the warmth of family or the beauty of the land, the majority are dark indeed. A teenager in Northern Ireland, Elaine Harbinson, seventeen at the time of a 1984 visit to her home by "The Organization," writes of opening the back door of her house only to be "confronted by a small hand gun and beckoned into the living room" (*Being Young in Northern Ireland* 16). The family, held captive throughout the night, was forced to let The Organization borrow the family's car. After a week filled with police interrogations, the car was found, "but the army blew it up, not taking any chances. It might have been booby-trapped" (18). Harbinson comments, "My mother still bears the scars of that night; she still imagines we are being watched" (18). Among the many other pieces of prose and poetry one of the most moving is a poem entitled "Rainy Sunday" by Gavin Stewart. It reads in part

> The rain cries at my window
> . . . . .
> The mask laughs and the children weep;
> . . . . .
>   rain falls on earth;
> Yet nothing good dare grow here
> For fear of being washed away in tears and blood.
> . . . . .
> A rain of sorrow, a hail of bullets,
> Cannot the sun pierce this blanket of dark?
> I have no memory of its shining.
> Eighteen years it has rained in our hearts.
>
> (*Being Young in Northern Ireland* 21)

"I have no memory of its shining." Between the summer of 1969 when the most recent era of Irish "Troubles" erupted with riots in the Northern Ireland cities of Derry and Belfast and the summer of 1994 when Sinn Fein announced the much heralded IRA ceasefire, a generation of young people in Ulster grew up believing that bombings and reprisal killings were just the way life was. In fact, many of *their* children have grown to consciousness under the same political tensions: grown up in close companionship with armored car patrols, military checkpoints, and the ongoing possibility that the bus they ride, the store where they shop, even the home where they live may be subject to a bombing, a shooting, or an intrusion by terrorists or soldiers. They are the latest victims of a centuries-old struggle between the Protestant British presence in Ireland and the Catholic Celtic population. The ceasefire has itself ceased on occasion, and, although, according to a local source, the tension and violence have not yet returned to pre-1994 levels, a resolution seems ever receding.

Martin Waddell, in an unpublished paper that he presented at a 1989 UNESCO conference in Paris, speaks of the children he has met during school visits throughout Northern Ireland, children who

> go home through street[s] that are marred by a so-called Peaceline, through fields guarded by

watch towers, to houses impoverished by bitterness in some cases, and resignation in so many others.

> These children are the experts in their own predicament, but the problem is that the ideas that form them and the ideas they articulate when confronted by a camera or a journalist or a writer-on-the-make are the ideas imposed on them by their daily lives in their own communities.
>
>   (n.p.)

If there has been an easing of these hardline beliefs among the current generation, teachers and organizers who have worked for the integration of religious groups in schools are due some of the credit.[1] So are those authors who have written thoughtful fictional accounts of the blighting effects that the recurring violence has on those raised under its threat. A focus on the young is frequent even in "Troubles" fiction written for an adult audience,[2] but a number of authors have specifically reached out to a youthful audience.[3] Their aim is, avowedly, to educate the upcoming generation about the physical, emotional, and political waste that sectarian disputes have visited on their land.

Two of the most widely read of these authors for young people are Joan Lingard and Martin Waddell[4] (writing under his pseudonym Catherine Sefton). Lingard's quintet (***The Twelfth Day of July, Across the Barricades, Into Exile, A Proper Place,*** and ***Hostages to Fortune,*** 1970-1976) has been extremely popular and widely used in school systems in Northern Ireland. The five books explore the difficult relationship between Catholic Kevin McCoy and Protestant Sadie Jackson. The Sefton Irish trilogy (*Starry Night, Frankie's Story,* and *The Beat of the Drum,* 1986-1989), linked thematically rather than through a continuing story line, has also had an impact on the school children of the area. In addition, both authors have written several other books that deal less directly with the "Troubles" and covered the topic in their fiction for adults, Lingard in ***The Lord on Our Side*** (1970) and Waddell in *A Little Bit British: Being the Diary of an Ulsterman, August 1969* (1970).

Lingard and Waddell/Sefton share more than just a topic for fiction. Although both are from Protestant backgrounds (she Christian Scientist and he Presbyterian), they assign responsibility for the "Troubles" to both Protestants and Catholics. They each give vivid fictional accounts of the numbing effect of growing up with violence; they each use the sorrows and struggles of their young characters to convey the need for mutual acceptance. They differ, however, in the aspect of the conflict that is central to their novels on the "Troubles." Lingard's series, centering as it does on the problems of a mixed marriage, emphasizes the personal harm that the religious divisions inflict. Waddell/Sefton's Irish trilogy, with its three separate stories, considers the interpenetrating harm to all communities in Northern Ireland.

Both authors strive to paint a clear picture of the political situation in Northern Ireland and to integrate the problems of sectarian conflict with the lives of their characters. For example, the title of Lingard's opening novel *The Twelfth Day of July* refers to the yearly Protestant celebration of the 1690 victory of King William over the Papist-tainted James II at the battle of the Boyne (a river a few miles above Drogheda in County Louth in the current Republic). The Orange Lodges, named for this same William of Orange, hold an annual July parade, featuring flutes and the huge lambeg drums, which have become a symbol of militant Protestantism. Each Protestant neighborhood strives to have the biggest bonfire, on which an effigy of the Pope (or of some contemporary Catholic agitator) is burned. Working-class Protestant areas go all out to decorate their streets with red, white, and blue streamers and to repaint the curbs and the gigantic murals of King Billy, who rides his white horse on the gable ends of many row houses.

This Protestant political artwork figures in the opening of Lingard's *The Twelfth Day of July.* Kevin McCoy, who lives a few blocks away on a Catholic street, plans with a friend "to go into the Prods area and paint 'Down With King Billy' under one of his murals" (19). It happens to be the mural on the Jacksons' house that they deface, and Sadie and her brother Tommy surprise them in the act. Retalitory raids turn serious. Kevin's gentle sister Brede, the voice of peace and reason, is gravely hurt in a gang battle between the two territories. Sadie and Tommy have developed a grudging respect for Kevin and Brede, and the life-threatening injury causes them to reassess the meaning of the July 12th celebration. They forego their chance to march, much to their parents' shocked dismay. Instead they visit the hospital to inquire about Brede's state. Lingard's first book on the "Troubles" ends hopefully with friendship overcoming sectarianism as Kevin, Sadie, and her brother share an outing on a beach in Bangor, a resort town near Belfast.

In Waddell/Sefton's novel *Frankie's Story,* there is an example of the Catholic version of gable painting,

but a less unified neighborhood reaction to it than on Lingard's fictional Protestant street, where support is virtually unanimous. Catholic Frankie's cynical voice informs us that

> "The end gable of the row the Hagens [the street's militant Catholic family] live in is covered in Republican slogans and painted flags. It is their way of showing the world, but it doesn't go down well with most of the neighbours. . . . The Provo [Provisional IRA] supporters don't mind, I suppose, and the others can't do much about it for fear of getting a stone through the window. Anyway, the words are on the wall, and as far as the cops are concerned that makes everybody down here a potential cop-killer, which we're not."

> (2)

In Waddell/Sefton's *The Beat of the Drum,* the title refers to the boom of the lambeg, the rallying sound of the Protestant marching season. IRA crippled, Protestant but tolerant Brian Hanna, hero of the book, informs us that the "demented beating . . . wasn't a heart beat, although it made the blood race. It was the bam-bam-bam of something waiting to burst" (23). Brian understands the psychology behind the bravado of the parades:

> Fear is the stitch that holds the whole thing together. You can sense it, in the beat of the drum.

> (77)

Lingard and Waddell/Sefton also use Protestant and Catholic slogans, street songs, and taunts to create an atmosphere of prevailing prejudice and to allow their young readers to examine the harm bred by this streetlore that is so familiar to them. In the opening pages of Lingard's first book of the series, Sadie Jackson and her brother Tommy are counting down the days to the "Glorious Twelfth!" Their father is good-humoredly catechizing them:

> "Who's the good Man?"

> "King Billy," they choroused. . . .

> "[W]ho's the bad man?"

> "The Pope!" they shrieked. . . .

> They knew all the right answers, for he had taught them well.

> (*Twelfth* 7)

This exchange is, in fact, the genesis of Lingard's book. In 1969 an Orangeman, the husband of a visiting friend, taught it to Lingard's young children:

It was a joke, but underneath the fun the message was serious.

. . . . .

I pondered on how easy it was to brainwash children and how early the prejudice starts.

("Through Seven Years" 21)

Lingard and Waddell are well aware of the cultural conditioning they are contending with in their attempts to reach young people through the art of fiction when the street art of primitive paintings and taunting chants has preceded them. As Waddell put it in his UNESCO speech, these and "the endless heroic pub and street songs of the glories of Our side and Our heroes. These jingles perpetuate evil" (n.p.).

In Lingard's third book, *Into Exile,* when Sadie, reluctantly agrees to a second marriage ceremony before a priest, even as the priest performs it she is distracted by a Belfast street jingle running through her head:

If I'd a penny,
Do you know what I'd do?
I'd buy a rope
And hang the pope
And let King Billy through.

(65)

I quoted this bit of verse during a presentation to the faculty of my university about my research in Northern Ireland, and the next day a colleague e-mailed me the Catholic riposte that her Irish-American husband had known since childhood:

Up the long ladder and down the short rope,
To hell with King Billy and God bless the pope.
If that doesn't do it, we'll tear him in two
And send him to hell with his red, white and blue.

The childish cleverness of this pair of rhymes is both humorous and heartbreaking. Similar street songs and grafitti serve as refrain in many novels about the "Troubles." In *Frankie's Story,* Waddell/Sefton includes some grafitti slogans of radical Catholics: "PROVOS RULE! . . . BRITS OUT . . . SS R.U.C. BASTARDS and TIOCFAIDH ÁR LA—*Our Day Will Come*" (12). Lingard's and Waddell's novels are reasoned responses to such a barrage of angry words.

Joan Lingard wrote ***The Twelfth Day of July*** at a time when Northern Ireland's sectarianism was in a violent stage, but perhaps about to be solved by the presence of supposedly neutral British troops and by promises of greater educational and professional equity. Lingard had intended for the book to stand

alone, but the further escalation of the "Troubles," as well as requests from young readers, prompted her to write more about Kevin and Sadie. In ***Across the Barricades*** the exchanges between Protestant and Catholic neighborhoods have gone beyond teenage high jinks, slogan-trading, and stone throwing. Grim headlines in the newspapers speak of the more deadly violence that has superseded them. This second novel recounts the blossoming of the young couple's love in an atmosphere of terrorism, and the tone is set at the beginning of the book when Kevin and Sadie, meeting by chance, pass "a newspaper billboard, SHOP GUTTED BY BOMB, TWO KILLED, ONE INJURED" (8). Kevin, who now works in a scrapyard, reflects

Scrap in the streets: burnt-out cars and buses and armoured vehicles, torn-up paving stones, barbed-wire coiled up to form barricades. And along the streets went soldiers on patrol with fingers on the triggers of their guns, men and women eyeing them watchfully, suspiciously, and bands of children playing at fighting and sometimes not just playing. Sadie and Kevin were quiet. The subject was too difficult to talk about.

(7)

Northern Ireland, Joan Lingard, and the young characters she created had traveled a dark road since the July 12th that ended the first novel. The three years between brought more riots, the British army, and no solutions. The promise of reconciliation and friendship that Lingard presented symbolically at the end of the first book—the peaceful and happy day on the beach—had not (and has not) been fulfilled. Lingard has a more pessimistic message in ***Across the Barricades.*** She is saying that reasonable people are being and will be driven away by the mindless sectarianism that is destroying the possibility of a decent life in Northern Ireland. The second book ends with the young couple's flight to England.

As the third book, ***Into Exile,*** opens, Kevin and Sadie have escaped the immediate threats to their safety, but the fear that the violence will touch their families back home has followed them across the water. In London, Sadie reads over the shoulder of a fellow commuter:

BOMB EXPLOSION IN BELFAST said the headline, leaping out from the paper to hit her in the eye. FIVE KILLED TEN INJURED. Her heart beat faster, she felt sickness rise from her stomach to her throat. She stood on tiptoe craning her head to read a bit more of the report. It was not in her area, or in Kevin's. It was probably all right. It was strange: in a way she worried more about the bombs and shootings here than she had done in Belfast. There, they had lived with them, accepting them as part of everyday life; here, . . . it seemed fantastic to expect to live with such horror every day.

(21-22)

And yet, Sadie "wanted to go home to Belfast bombs and all" (28). Kevin, at his place of work, reads the same news story and has a similar reaction. When the homesick pair do make up their minds to quit their jobs and take the ferry back, on the next morning

The first item on the news was about Ulster. Two soldiers had been shot in Belfast during the night, one was dead. . . . A bomb had exploded in a public house: two people were injured. . . . And a young girl had been tarred and feathered for going out with British soldiers.

(41)

They realize sadly that they cannot possibly return until that elusive "someday when it's all settled" although "How it could be settled they could not begin to imagine" (*Exile* 44). They increasingly worry about the safety of their families, especially Kevin's who "lived in one of the most troublesome areas in Belfast" (98). The fear is legitimate: Kevin's father is killed in a pub bomb blast; his Uncle Albert loses his legs in the same bombing.

In the last two books of Lingard's quintet, the Ulster violence crosses the water in the form of psychologically damaged relatives who come to visit Kevin and Sadie—or to live with them. Kevin's younger brother Gerald (who had connections with the Provos) is sent over by the desperate mother for straightening out. Kevin cannot reach him with words and knows that a friend's advice to "kick him" is equally futile. "Gerald was almost immune to violence; he had seen too much of it" (*Proper Place* 64). Immune, or so we think, until a gas main explosion shatters Gerald's composure and leaves him dazed, icy, and trembling violently. We learn that not only has he lost his father in the pub bombing, but that when Gerald and a friend once attempted to take a car for a joy ride, "There was a bomb planted in it. Gerald was blown across the street. . . . His friend was blown to bits" (*Proper Place* 79). Sadie, in spite of her speculation that Gerald and his friend might well have planted the bomb, begins to try to understand the boy. Ultimately he does come around. However, in the last book of the quintet, *Hostages to Fortune,* another of Kevin's younger siblings, his sister Clodagh, arrives

at their doorstep. Clodagh proves to be beyond redemption. The theme of exile runs through the last three books.

The Waddell/Sefton books are all set in Northern Ireland and more immediately woven into the life of that country than are Lingard's. Lingard's Kevin and Sadie leave Ulster just when violence is becoming a part of daily life (early 1970s). In Waddell/Sefton's Irish trilogy (1980s) his three protagonists are enmeshed in the religious bigotry of their communities and the violence it begets. The "Troubles" constantly rumble in the background in the first book and crash into the characters' lives in the latter two.

During an interview I had with him in 1994, Waddell said of *Starry Night* that it poses the questions about sectarianism which the other two books deal with more specifically. *Starry Night* is set in Kiltarragh, a fictional town in Northern Ireland which, in its Catholic population's assessment, is "just the wrong side of the border" (5). A quiet rural place, it has its calm marred by British troops and helicopter surveillance. Children nonchalantly bicycle past "the blast hole at Cone Cross, where the soldier lost his leg" (28). The protagonist Kathleen has absorbed the local attitude that the British presence is the entirety of the problem, and believes, "If we can't vote them out, we'll blow them out" (34). She cannot grasp her Belfast friend Ann's broader understanding of the political complexities. When Kathleen accuses Ann (who is also a Catholic) of being "for the Protestants" (34), Ann replies that she is for "ordinary people . . . Not men with big drums running Catholics out of the shipyards, and not Irish heroes in behind the hedge with their bombs, waiting to blow other Irish men to bits" (34).

Kathleen's sister-in-law Carmel is another catalyst for the awareness that leaves Kathleen questioning her own political beliefs. Carmel contends that the Irish "heroes" would be better off working for their ideals than killing or dying for them and that a withdrawal of the British would simply shift the battle against "somebody else that doesn't happen to agree . . . Somebody else with different dreams, that they call ideals" (*Starry Night* 107). Kathleen is left speculating about the origin of her ideals:

Where had I got my dreams from? Maybe the dreams were getting in my way, making me somebody I wasn't. *Maybe the dreams were just a trap.*

(110)

What a deadly trap sectarian "dreams" can be for the victims of those who hold them is demonstrated in the two following books of the trilogy. In the second,

Frankie's Story, Frankie is a Catholic girl who is independent-minded about her culture rather than brainwashed by it, which nearly leads to her death when her family's house is fire-bombed in retaliation for her supposed collaboration with the "enemy"—in this case the police. At the end of the book, Frankie, like Kevin and Sadie, in a solution that has been painfully common in Northern Ireland, escapes in exile to England to live with an aunt, where, at least, "nobody's going to lay down what I should or shouldn't think" (12). The final words of the novel are

> It is funny, being free.
> It takes a bit of getting used to.

> (122)

The words carry a portent they did not have before the 1994 ceasefire and so far failed peace talks. The talks could offer such freedom to the current younger generation of Protestants and Catholics in Northern Ireland—if the generation holding the talks could get used to the thought of compromise.

The final book of the trilogy, *The Beat of the Drum,* is told in the voice of Brian Hanna, a Protestant boy who was permanently crippled as a baby by the IRA bomb that killed his parents. A perfect candidate for the bitterness that the uncle who helps rear him feels, Brian instead develops the tolerant view that his aunt fosters. Brian comes across as the sanest of the three protagonists. Neither the grimness of being confined to a wheelchair for life nor the grimness of the history he is living has destroyed Brian's sense of humor. He comments about one ridiculous aspect of the "Troubles"—the need for the paramilitary forces to police and punish their own sides to enforce loyalty—that "The Provos blow off Catholic kneecaps, and the UDA [Ulster Defence Association] blow off Protestant kneecaps, so everybody has an even chance" (11).

Waddell told me that he tends to discuss *The Beat of the Drum* when his audience is mainly Catholic students and to discuss the other two books when the audience is mainly Protestant. He believes that the crucial lesson is to learn to transcend the us-them syndrome, which he sees as a universal problem, scarcely confined to Northern Ireland.

Waddell/Sefton reiterates throughout the trilogy the harm that each side inflicts on its own as well as on the enemy. Whether he is revealing the narrow-mindedness that dead-ends Kathleen and the Catholic people of Kiltarragh or the equally blinkered vision

of Brian's militantly Protestant uncle or is depicting the gangster techniques that radical Protestants and Catholics use to keep their respective troops in line, Waddell/Sefton conveys to his readers the double-edged nature of sectarian violence. In Frankie's housing estate, for instance, a character named Con McCluskey is, as Frankie Rafferty sarcastically describes him, "a kind of cross between God and Gerry Adams" (*Frankie's Story* 13) and is "the Easter Revolution and the thirty-two county Socialist Republic all wrapped up in one person" (42), but he does not confine himself to terrorist acts against Protestants. McCluskey is behind the shooting of a Catholic cop; he is the prime suspect in the bombing of the Rafferty home. In *The Beat of the Drum* it is the Protestants who are depicted as vengeful against the police. The characters who are Orange Order devotees think that the RUC (Royal Ulster Constabulary) should be in business solely to keep down the "Micks." That the RUC also work to stop Protestant terrorism is unforgiveable. When the police confiscate a stash of Protestant arms, Brian's friend Hicky is killed, very likely by the UDA, for his role as police informer. Between Hicky's disappearance and the discovery of his body, Brian goes through an agony of speculations:

> *Maybe Hicky will just get a beating.*

> *Sometimes they use planks with nails in them. Sometimes they use baseball bats. . . .*

> *They might just break his arms and legs, or take a poke at his kneecaps with a power drill. . . .*

> *Hicky could be dead by now. . . .*

> (98)

Brian blames both the British Security Forces who bribed Hicky to inform and the paramilitary UDA—both of whom are presumably on the Protestant side. At the funeral Brian wonders "how many of the mourners know who killed him" (102). Hicky's body was found in a bloody sack, under which are some "GOD'S WILL FOR ULSTER" (81) leaflets, propaganda written by a Loyalist Protestant minister. "The blood must have trickled out on to them. They were sodden with it" (103).

Although Brian has often wanted to move elsewhere and although he is shaken by his uncle's involvement with terrorist weapons and by the UDA's execution of Hicky, he decides to remain in Northern Ireland. He has developed a feeling of responsibility towards the scarred social terrain of his birthplace. This solution for a fictional Protestant protagonist is not one that Waddell believes is entirely viable for his own Catholic sons (Waddell's wife is Catholic). The problem for his sons is, as Waddell states in his UNESCO speech, "quite simply Catholic teenagers are always a possible target, both for the terrorists of both sides, and the Authorities" (n.p.). He discusses how his keen awareness of the effect of the "Troubles" on his three sons has colored his perspective. Waddell speaks of his "feeling for the reality of their lives and what their lives could be, or could have been had they been born and brought up in a different place at a different time" (UNESCO n.p.). Their childhoods were affected by such events as nearly losing their father to a bomb placed in a church and by the murder of a local policeman. Waddell says of this last that

> The body lay fifty yards from our door for four hours while the police and army searched. . . . [His youngest son] stood at the window and watched—and watched—and watched, while we tried to explain.
>
> I have still not found a way to explain it.
>
> (UNESCO n.p.)

The Waddell/Sefton Irish trilogy is, if not an explanation, at the very least a thorough examination of the problem. Waddell, by the way, early on refused to write problem novels for children and young adults. His sons' reactions were in large part the catalyst for his taking on the "Troubles" as a subject for juvenile fiction.

Religious differences are the constant background in the Waddell/Sefton trilogy. In Lingard's quintet, religion is foregrounded. Kevin and Sadie slowly exorcise the bitterness that their differing faiths can evoke, but religion is a hot spot in their relationship with flare-ups that occasionally burn them. Only late in the final book of the series do they begin to make serious attempts to understand each other's viewpoint. Sadie, left by herself while the others attend Mass on Christmas Eve, falls off a ladder while trying to straighten a treetop ornament and injures herself seriously enough to bring about the loss of her unborn second child. Afterwards, in the hospital, she meditates:

> It had been ridiculous to climb a pair of steps to rescue a fairy, to put her baby at risk. But she knew why she had done it. She had been seething with resentment because Kevin had gone to mass. So many people in the world were seething with resentment over something, boiling over with it, achieving no other end but wastefulness. Kevin's

father dead. His Uncle Albert legless. Thousands of others killed maimed, devastated. What she had done to their child—hers and Kevin's—was no better. She had lost the baby because of those black feelings she had nourished. . . .

> If she was to go on living with Kevin she could not go on hating his religion. It would poison her and their life together. But how did you stop hating?
>
> For a start, by wanting to, she supposed.
>
> (*Hostages* 130-31)

Both Lingard and Waddell/Sefton emphasize this fundamental need to change attitudes in Northern Ireland in order to change the actual circumstances, although neither author is naively optimistic about the means to effect such a change.

The final book of Lingard's quintet leaves the reader with hope for Kevin and Sadie's personal future. They have the prospect of refurbishing a Welsh cottage and living in peace, even if in exile. Lingard does not touch on the future of the country they have left. Speaking of her series in an interview with Stephanie Nettell, the children's book editor of *The Guardian,* Lingard said that she had once planned to bring Kevin and Sadie back to Northern Ireland, "but even after all these years they couldn't return, because nothing had really changed. . . . [T]hey're still in exile, still suspended" (qtd. in Taylor 12). Waddell/Sefton's trilogy challenges young people to question the confining hatred of sectarianism, but he, like Lingard, does not pretend that there are easy answers in sight.

Both authors have given their young audience books that read well as fiction while carrying an important message about the need for reconciliation and tolerance in Northern Ireland, thereby creating a literature that some might label as merely didactic. Lingard has, however, the respect for her audience to craft a series with emotional impact, consistently strong plots, and sequels that develop the psychological complexity of the characters. Similarly, Martin Waddell, using his Catherine Sefton persona creates vivid characters and believable plots into which he interweaves the variety of religious, economic, and political factors that influence the coming of age in Northern Ireland.

Folk art forms have helped keep alive centuries of hatred in Northern Ireland. Whether King Billy or the Irish Republic's tricolor adorns a gable wall, whether the old ballads or newly coined jingles spew taunts at "Taig" or "Prod," whether the Protestant lambeg or Celtic bodhran beat to fire the pulses of followers, a metaphoric form of violence has been part of the education of many generations of Ulster's children. Can the literary art of writers like Joan Lingard and Martin Waddell counterbalance this long folk art tradition? Reasoned thought moves forward and outward; bigotry stands fast in its circle of closed-off argument. A few novels, destined to be read by only a percentage of working-class children, all of whom have grown up with the slogans, the songs, and the political paintings, may seem of slight weight. We can only hope that fictional voices like those of Kevin and Sadie, of Kathleen, Frankie, and Brian impel enough young Northern Irelanders to step out of the truly vicious circle that has trapped their elders for so long.

Notes

1. Education segregated by religion is being challenged. See, for example, *Education Together for a Change: Integrated Education and Community Relations,* edited by Chris Moffat.

2. Among those "Troubles" books written for a general audience some worth pursuing for their vivid accounts of growing up in Northern Ireland are Mary Beckett's *Give Them Stones,* Mary Costello's *Titanic Town,* Briege Duffaud's *A Wreath upon the Dead,* Jennifer Johnston's *Shadows on Our Skin,* Glenn Patterson's *Burning Your Own,* and John Quinn's *Generations of the Moon.*

3. In a paper presented to the annual conference of the Reading Association of Ireland in 1987, Robert Dunbar surveyed the "Troubles" books about Ulster written between the 1880s and the 1980s for a juvenile audience. He makes the point that both the designation the "Troubles" and the reality behind it have a long history in Ireland. In addition to the Lingard and Sefton novels covered in this present essay, he recommended as good background Lingard's *The File on Fraulein Berg* (set in Belfast during World War II) and Sefton's historical ghost stories, *The Back House Ghosts, Emer's Ghost, The Ghost Girl,* and *The Sleepers on the Hill.* I would add to this list the Sefton title *Island of the Strangers.* Dunbar also recommends (and I concur) Peter Carter's *Under Goliath* and Sam McBratney's *Mark Time.* Three "Troubles" books of interest published since Dunbar's presentation are Elspeth Cameron's *In the Shadow of the Gun,* Tom McCaughren's *Rainbows of the Moon,* and John Quinn's *One Fine Day.*

4. For more information on Waddell's many books for children, see Celia Catlett Anderson's "Stories for Everychild: The Books of Martin Waddell/Catherine Sefton."

Works Cited

Anderson, Celia Catlett. "Stories for Everychild: The Books of Martin Waddell/Catherine Sefton." *Teaching and Learning Literature* 6.4 (March/April 1997): 39-48.

Beckett, Mary. *Give Them Stones.* New York: Morrow, 1987.

Being Young in Northern Ireland. Belfast: Information Unit, Standing Conference of Youth Organizations, 1985.

Cameron, Elspeth. *In the Shadow of the Gun.* Dublin: Blackwater, 1994.

Carter, Peter. *Under Goliath.* London: Puffin, 1977.

Costello, Mary. *Titanic Town: Memoirs of a Belfast Girlhood.* London: Mandarin, 1992.

Duffaud, Briege. *A Wreath upon the Dead.* Dublin: Poolbeg, 1993.

Dunbar, Robert. "Children's Fiction and the Ulster 'Troubles'." *Proceedings of the 12th Annual Conference of the Reading Association of Ireland* (September 1987): 73-91.

Harbinson, Elaine. "Visitors." *Being Young in Northern Ireland.* Belfast: Information Unit, Standing Conference of Youth Organizations, 1985: 16-18.

Johnston, Jennifer. *Shadows on Our Skin.* London: Penguin, 1977.

Lingard, Joan. *Across the Barricades.* London: Penguin, 1972.

———. *The File on Frauline Berg.* London: Puffin, 1993; Elsevier/Nelson, Julia MacRae Books, 1980.

———. *Hostages to Fortune.* London: Penguin, 1976.

———. *Into Exile.* London: Penguin, 1973.

———. *The Lord on Our Side.* London: Hodder & Stoughton, 1970.

———. *A Proper Place.* London: Penguin, 1975.

———. "Through Seven Years of Their Lives." *Children's Books in Ireland* (May 1993): 21.

———. *The Twelfth Day of July.* London: Penguin, 1970.

McBratney, Sam. *Mark Time.* London: Abelard, 1976.

McCaughren, Tom. *Rainbows of the Moon.* Dublin: Anvil Books, 1989.

Moffat, Chris, ed. *Education Together for a Change: Integrated Education and Community Relations in Northern Ireland.* Belfast: Fortnight Educational Trust, 1993.

Patterson, Glenn. *Burning Your Own.* London: Minerva, 1993; London: Chatto & Windus, 1988.

Quinn, John. *Generations of the Moon.* Dublin: Poolbeg, 1995.

———. *One Fine Day.* Dublin: Poolbeg, 1996.

Sefton, Catherine (pseudonym of Martin Waddell). *The Back House Ghosts.* London: Faber, 1974; as *The Haunting of Ellen.* New York: Harper, 1975.

———. *The Beat of the Drum.* London: Hamish Hamilton, 1992, 1989.

———. *Emer's Ghost.* London: Hamish Hamilton, 1981.

———. *The Ghost Girl.* London: Hamish Hamilton, 1985.

———. *Island of the Strangers.* London: Mammoth, 1990; Magnet, 1984; Hamilton, 1983; San Diego: Harcourt Brace, 1985.

———. *Frankie's Story.* London: Teens Mandarin, 1992; Hamish Hamilton 1988.

———. *The Sleepers on the Hill.* London: Faber, 1973.

———. *Starry Night.* London: Teens Mandarin, 1994; rpt. from 1990/92; Hamish Hamilton, 1986.

Stewart, Gavin. "Rainy Sunday." *Being Young in Northern Ireland.* Belfast: Information Unit, Standing Conference of Youth Organizations, 1985. 21.

Taylor, Anne. *Joan Lingard: From Belfast to the Baltic.* Linden, Swindon: School Library Association, 1992.

Waddell, Martin. "Children and the War in Northern Ireland." Unpublished speech to the UNESCO Conference, Paris, 1989.

———. Interview with Celia Catlett Anderson. Newcastle, Co. Down, Northern Ireland. September 13, 1994.

———. *A Little Bit British: Being the Diary of an Ulsterman, August 1969.* London: Tom Stacey, 1970.

TITLE COMMENTARY

THE TWELFTH DAY OF JULY (1970)

Anne Thwaite (review date 5 March 1971)

SOURCE: Thwaite, Anne. *New Statesman* 81, no. 2085 (5 March 1971): 312.

The scene of Joan Lingard's *The Twelfth Day of July* is present-day Belfast. If it doesn't show the full horror of the situation, it certainly demonstrates 'the mindless futility of prejudice' through a story as lively and moving as any written for itself alone.

Children's Book Review Service (review date November 1972)

SOURCE: *Children's Book Review Service* 1, no. 3 (November 1972): 19.

Ages 10+. The twelfth of July is a day of general celebration for Northern Ireland's Protestants. There are bonfires and firecrackers, house decorating and parades. Around this date is woven a story [*The Twelfth Day of July*] about two sets of brother and sister from two families, one Protestant and one Catholic. The whole story runs true. The people are very real. Their bigotries and conflicts are understandable and convincing, and the ending, in its violence and ugliness, is very lifelike and believable. This book is not great literature, but it is good storytelling and will be appreciated by children who like family stories, stories about people in other lands, realistic stories about children, and problem stories.

Jean Mercier (review date 4 December 1972)

SOURCE: Mercier, Jean. *Publishers Weekly* 202, no. 23 (4 December 1972): 62.

(11-Up) The Protestants and the Catholics (Prods and Micks) are separated by only one street in this novel [*The Twelfth Day of July*] about Belfast youth. But their ideological differences have created a vast space between them; they hate and fear each other. While the Prod children—led by Sadie and her brother, Tommy—are preparing to celebrate the 12th of July (commemoration of the victory of William of Orange at the Battle of the Boyne), they are hindered by Kevin and his Mick friends. Attacks and retaliations continue till Kevin's gentle sister, Brede, is badly

hurt by a thrown brick. The children recognize the stupidity of their quarreling and become friends. A rather superficial treatment of a continuing and tragic situation but the book is thought-provoking and entertaining.

Anne Wood (review date 20 October 1973)

SOURCE: Wood, Anne. *Spectator* 231 (20 October 1973): R21.

The Twelfth Day Of July, by Joan Lingard, its companion in a recent batch of Puffins. Originally published in 1970 when the Irish Troubles were thought to be at a head, three years later *The Twelfth Day* seems even more relevant. The real story of children in Belfast, their confusions, distortions and hatreds is far more dire and urgent than a children's novel could ever be.

Joan Lingard has made a fine attempt to present the divided loyalties and loves of a group of children in terms that make it possible for other children to begin to understand. She brings out with beautiful precision how violence escalates from an almost childish escapade—paint splashed by Roman Catholic children on Protestant walls; one recalls the rival activities of 'Bonfire Gangs' in collecting wood and junk to make the biggest pile—to kidnapping and potential killing:

"Doors were opening all up the street. They only needed a few insults on either side, a stone or two, and they'd have a riot on their hands . . ."

As an almost documentary account of life in our times *The Twelfth Day of July* is a unique and significant achievement.

Commonweal (review date 23 November 1973)

SOURCE: *Commonweal* 99, no. 8 (23 November 1973): 216.

A timely trilogy [*The Twelfth Day of July, Across the Barricades,* and *Into Exile*] (each independent) about the friendship of a Protestant girl and Catholic boy in embattled Belfast and the violence and prejudice that threatens to separate them. The final volume tells of their difficulties and hopes when they marry.

📖 *ACROSS THE BARRICADES* (1972)

Children's Book Review Service (review date September 1972)

SOURCE: *Children's Book Review Service* 2, no. 4 (September 1972): 114-15.

Sadie Jackson is a Protestant. Kevin McCoy is a Catholic. The setting is Belfast. The ensuing tragedy [in *Across the Barricades*] would seem far-fetched were it not for the news bulletins that each day confront us with some new horror.

Three years have passed since *The Twelfth Day of July.* Suspicion and hostility have remained. Once it is known that Sadie and Kevin have begun to meet again, tongues begin to wag, daubers get to work, and fists start to fly. Before long Mrs. McConkey's shop has been blown up with her in it and Mr. Blake, their old Geography teacher who has committed the crime of befriending them, has been killed by a petrol bomb. All the time the soldiers uneasily roam and the children openly taunt.

The reader can scarcely fail to be both moved and depressed, for the issues depicted are grave illnesses requiring prolonged and far-reaching treatment. It may be more artistically satisfying if Juliet dies beside her Romeo, but few, I hope, will object here to their both fleeing to England. This solution to their problems may seem negative but the possible alternatives have been made all too clear. Recommended.

Joan Murphy (review date September 1972)

SOURCE: Murphy, Joan. *School Librarian* 20, no. 3 (September 1972): 258.

I lived in Belfast until I was twenty-one and now I am about sixty miles north of the city. In between I spent twenty years in places as far apart as Moscow and New York. I feel I have to say this to show that I can, I hope, judge this novel [*Across the Barricades*] impartially and yet with understanding. It is not a great piece of literature, but the author does create place, time and atmosphere with deep feeling. She has a remarkable ear for dialogue, she manages to find the inflections of the different parts of the city with accuracy and also to describe the feelings of helplessness and weariness and the desire for peace of many of the people who simply cannot find a way out. An example of this from p. 149: Mrs Jackson. . . . 'It's funny how you can get used to murders after a bit'. 'You can get used to anything', said Tommy. 'You have to live'.

The novel is a modern *Romeo and Juliet* and as such it can be read; but it really goes to the bare bones of the conflict. Here and there are glimmers of hope. Tommy, for example, refuses to join his father's Orange lodge though he 'is a good Protestant'. I hope many boys and girls of twelve and over in Great Britain will read this book because the author gives a very clear and true picture of life in Belfast not only today but also yesterday and, I fear, tomorrow, and this is a situation which could develop elsewhere with, say, colour or political belief replacing religious conflict.

Zena Sutherland (review date November 1973)

SOURCE: Sutherland, Zena. *Bulletin of the Center for Children's Books* 27, no. 3 (November 1973): 46-7.

6-10. A sequel to ***The Twelfth Day of July*** [***Across the Barricades***] brings Kevin and Sadie together several year after their first hostile encounter when, as Catholic and Protestant children of beleaguered Belfast, they had fought about demonstrating on the anniversary of the Battle of the Boyne. Now they are adolescents, and their first tentatively friendly chance encounter leads to falling in love. Opposition from both families forces them to meet secretly in the home of an understanding former teacher, Mr. Blake. Reprisal against him leads to his death, and Kevin and Sadie decide there is no solution for them but to go to England together. This has more focus than the earlier book, and better construction; like ***The Twelfth Day of July*** it gives a vivid if depressing picture of the trouble in Ireland and of the tragedy of prejudice.

INTO EXILE (1973)

Children's Book Review Service (review date December 1973)

SOURCE: *Children's Book Review Service* 3, no. 6 (December 1973): 178-79.

I approached ***Into Exile*** without any preconceptions, not having read any of Joan Lingard's previous books, and I found it thoroughly convincing. Kevin, aged nineteen, the Catholic, and Sadie, aged seventeen, the Protestant, from Belfast, are married and living in one room in London. Life is lonely and seedy; they dislike their jobs. Just when Kevin gets a good job and starts to make progress, his father is killed by a bomb and he has to go home. He and Sadie have to work out their future within a context of religious bigotry and local danger. Neither of their families will accept them: they begin to doubt each other. The book remains open-ended. Kevin and Sadie still have to find a place where they can live together happily.

The picture of London life is depressingly realistic. Although they take second place in the book, the latest violence in Ulster, always erupting or on the point of erupting, the unthinking, unfeeling hostility of the Orangemen and the Micks, and the way these condition the people who have grown up with them, are clearly and strongly conveyed. A fine achievement, too, to make such an 'ordinary' couple, in search of love and freedom, a fully interesting pair of leading characters.

Zena Sutherland (review date March 1974)

SOURCE: Sutherland, Zena. *Bulletin of the Center for Children's Books* 27, no. 7 (March 1974): 113-14.

7-10. The last of a trilogy of novels dealing with the relationships between Irish and Protestant young people in the atmosphere of today's bitter hostility, this [***Into Exile***] follows ***The Twelfth Day of July*** and ***Across the Barricades,*** in which Protestant Sadie and Catholic Kevin had fought as children, met as adolescents and fallen in love, and decided to flee to England. Here they are newlyweds living in London; they have no friends and little money, and all of the adjustments of marriage and of homesickness are exacerbated by the fact that Kevin and Sadie feel like aliens in England, and that their religious differences cannot be ignored. Called home by his father's death (killed by a bomb), Kevin goes to Ireland and finds his mother insistent that he stay and still unreconciled to his marriage. The solution of the young people's problem is achieved in part by the willingness of each to compromise and in part by the advice of an older man who, although a Catholic, is not as biased as Kevin's family and who sees that the two must go off on their own if the marriage is to survive. A candid exploration of prejudice, the story stands on its own but is more meaningful as a sequel to the earlier books.

FRYING AS USUAL (1973)

Children's Book Review Service (review date December 1975)

SOURCE: *Children's Book Review Service* 3, no. 6 (December 1975): 175.

Recently, Hamish Hamilton seem, in their Reindeer series to be trying to satisfy a current demand for books with an interest age considerably higher than their reading age. This title [***Frying as Usual***] is a typical example. Written by an author who has previous experience of writing for older children, it keeps well within the scope of a Reindeer in terms of vocabulary and length. Joan Lingard always gives the impression of being a down-to-earth person, who nevertheless does not lack imagination and this comes over here. Three children are left to run the family fish and chip shop whilst their Italian mother is visiting relatives and their father is in hospital. Custom drops off, but they eventually succeed in making the shop break even, though not without some difficulty. Characterisation is credible, dialogue is imaginative and realistic and suspense is well-maintained to a good climax. The text is illustrated with typical line drawings. Worth buying for children with a reading age of eight or nine plus, but with an interest age of up to fourteen or fifteen years.

Marcus Crouch (review date April 1986)

SOURCE: Crouch, Marcus. *Junior Bookshelf* 50, no. 2 (April 1986): 79.

I have often thought that the basic ideas of books in the 'Reindeer' and other such series were far too good to be squandered in this way. Joan Lingard thought so too, and she has rewritten her 'Reindeer' of the same title, originally published in 1973, retaining the plot but developing both the characters and their setting. The result is a cheerful, perceptive and always lively novel. When Mr. Francetti, owner of a fish-and-chip shop, falls off the roof and breaks a leg, while his wife is on holiday in Italy, Grandpa comes joyfully out of retirement and the children, even Paula whose mind is more on boys than chips, buckle to in order to keep the business going. Toni is sensible and hard-working, and good at handling tough customers, but it is Rosita who has the imagination, even if her ideas are sometimes embarrassing. It is all right to proclaim: FRANCETTI'S NEVER CLOSES, but when notices which promise 'Continuous Cabaret' appear all over town Toni is seriously worried. But all is well. Rosita's fish-and-chip calypso is a winner.

In its expanded form *Frying as Usual* is still small-scale but nevertheless a jolly and wholly enjoyable story.

Robert Dunbar (review date June 1986)

SOURCE: Dunbar, Robert. *School Librarian* 34, no. 2 (June 1986): 169.

When it first appeared, in 1973 in the Hamish Hamilton 'Reindeer' series, Joan Lingard's *Frying as Usual* came as a diversion from her first two Belfast stories.

This is a new, extended edition, attractively produced and illustrated; but set against her earlier and subsequent books it is a slight piece of work. The values which it endorses—warm-heartedness, initiative, familial strength and loyalty—may be beyond reproach, but for most of the age group for which the book is intended the plot's the thing, and this is extremely disappointing. At its centre are the ex-patriate Francetti family, engaged in running a fish-and-chip business, and threatened with disaster when the father breaks his leg. As Mrs Francetti is visiting relatives abroad, responsibility for running the shop passes to the three children. Most of this burden is willingly, indeed lovingly, assumed by the youngest, whose imaginative endeavours to keep the business flourishing manage eventually to withstand the critical commentary of studious brother, indolent sister and querulous grandfather. The pace is frantic, the responses melodramatic and the tone throughout this well-intentioned story of everyday Italian folk teeters somewhere between that of a comic opera and a *Carry on* film.

📖 *THE CLEARANCE* (1974)

Margery Fisher (review date September 1974)

SOURCE: Fisher, Margery. *Growing Point* 13, no. 3 (September 1974): 2450.

Atmosphere is all-important in **The Clearance.** Here is no time-slip but, rather, an emotional bond between the generations. It is a double bond, in fact—between Maggie from Glasgow and her grandmother, who lives alone in a remote Highland glen, and between Granny McKinley and her own grandmother, another Margaret Ross who was evicted in the Clearances of 1854 and whose story is told (almost in fact recreated) to the city girl. Maggie, for her part, is receptive to the atmosphere of those sad distant times because she is herself in something of a ferment because of James Fraser, a young man on holiday in the glen with his middle-class intellectual family. Class difference, however tactfully concealed, disturbs their relationship, and Maggie has a further anxiety in her grandmother's future, since it is becoming difficult for the old woman to manage on her own. Joan Lingard has shown simply and clearly an interaction of times and people that could touch the thoughts and feelings of young-adult readers very closely.

Vivienne Furlong (review date September 1974)

SOURCE: Furlong, Vivienne. *School Librarian* 22, no. 3 (September 1974): 250, 253.

Maggie has come to spend the summer with her old grandmother who lives alone in a remote Scottish glen where her ancestors have lived since the days of the Scottish clearances [in *The Clearance*]. The Frasers, weekenders from Edinburgh, are the only company available and Maggie strikes up a friendship with their son James. A fire destroys the old cottage and Granny has to be rehoused, which forces Maggie to consider her own history and environment in a different light. On her return to Glasgow she discovers that her home too is part of a clearance scheme, a conclusion which is a little too well rounded.

The story develops at a rather sluggish pace and the characters lack life, so it is difficult to feel real concern for any of them. Maggie is lively enough but her reactions are shallow and the problems she faces are dealt with in a superficial way.

Publishers Weekly (review date 25 November 1974)

SOURCE: *Publishers Weekly* 206, no. 22 (25 November 1974): 46.

(12-Up) The setting of Ms. Lingard's new book [*The Clearance*] is not Ireland this time, as it has been in her previous novels which dealt with the Troubles. Now she takes us to Scotland, to the Glen of Inverness-shire, where in 1854 landlords had forced crofters (peasant farm families) from their homes during the infamous Highland Clearances. Young Maggie McKinley comes from her home in Glasgow to spend the summer with her Granny in the glen. Expecting a boring summer, Maggie brightens when she makes friends with James Fraser who lives across the road with his family. Their idyll is imperiled when Granny, left alone one night, knocks over a lamp and starts a fire. This time, the Clearance is accidental. Though Granny is saved, her cottage burns to the ground and Maggie learns an important lesson. It's a warm, loving story.

Zena Sutherland (review date January 1975)

SOURCE: Sutherland, Zena. *Bulletin of the Center for Children's Books* 28, no. 5 (January 1975): 81.

6-9. Maggie McKinley knew that her father neglected his mother, and she was happy to spend the summer at Granny's cottage in Inverness [in *The Clearance*], but it was a boring time. She loved to hear Granny's tales of the clearances, of the courage of her Granny's granny, but she didn't enjoy being pushed into friendship with the summer visitors—until she got to know James, who was one of them. It was in part due to her being with James that Granny's cottage caught fire, and then Maggie had to cope with getting Granny settled in a new home. Like their ancestor, both Maggie and Granny show their resilience and initiative when forced to change a way of life. The writing style, setting, characters, and dialogue are competent, the structure economical, but the pace of the story is uneven and the shift—in the last eight pages—seems abrupt and it seems also that Maggie's discovery, when she comes home to Glasgow, that the family is being evicted, is a bit contrived to round out the pattern of the clearances.

A PROPER PLACE (1975)

Peter Ackroyd (review date 12 April 1975)

SOURCE: Ackroyd, Peter. *Spectator* 234 (12 April 1975): 444.

A Proper Place is presumably a book for new adults rather than children, since it concerns the struggles of a young married couple, Sadie and Kevin with the unfortunate name of McCoy, to make a new life among the tenements of Liverpool. They have left behind the even more grimy reality of Belfast in order to live here, but the children of violence are never far behind. Kevin's brother, Gerald, travels from Ireland to stay with them and this rattled and battle-scarred youth refuses to settle down. And Sadie's mother, a Belfast matron of the Protestant school, pays a flying visit in order to confirm her prejudices: anti-Catholic, anti-black and anti-happiness. But it seems that no children's story can afford to stay in the flat world of social reality for very long, and Joan Lingard exports her characters out of the city and into the dull country. Kevin becomes a farm labourer, Gerald works with horses, Sadie buys a puppy—and the baby, Brendan, is doing very nicely too. The hard grind gives way to rural and doggy pursuits, experience bows to innocence, discord to concord. This is a world in which everything turns out for the best.

I do not know if that is a tone which the children's writers' pressure groups impose upon all their members, or whether it comes naturally to those who prefer anodynes to the real thing. But I have an uneasy feeling that children are supposed to identify with these one dimensional characters; of course I have no idea whether they enjoy or appreciate them. In the writing designed for them, everything is spelled out as simply and as self-consciously as possible, the prose veers toward the *faux-naif,* the plots are generally of the flimsiest kind and the characterisation barely credible. If you wanted to kill an adult with boredom, this would be the handiest weapon—and children can be just as discriminating and just as easily bored as adults. I imagine that there are a great many children laughing up their sleeves at happy endings and cardboard villains.

Joan Murphy (review date September 1975)

SOURCE: Murphy, Joan. *School Librarian* 23, no. 3 (September 1975): 248.

Sadie and Kevin have returned to England [in *A Proper Place*]. They are living in Liverpool when the book opens. Sadie's mother, the personification of Protestant Belfast, comes to stay. There is a wonderfully evocative description of her as Sadie meets her off the boat. Mother and Kevin have never met and though they avoid open conflict the visit is not a roaring success. Mrs Jackson takes a very poor view of their home and is horrified when the priest calls about the baby Brendan's christening and she has to be in the same room as him. English readers may find this hard to understand but it is a typical reaction of a woman from the Shankhill Road. Later Kevin's brother comes to stay and finally they move from the narrow Liverpudlian street to a farm where Kevin gets a job, and we leave Sadie adjusting to this totally new environment strong in the belief that she will cope with it just as she has all her other problems.

Sadie is an established and very popular heroine with teenage girls. Though few can comprehend her background many can identify with her in her fight to break her family's narrow tradition. There is something totally honest about her which appeals to readers of all ages. I think that the secret of Joan Lingard's success is that she is writing about a very poignant situation which she fully understands. She never tries to elaborate or explain, the characters do this for her by their natural reactions. Perhaps after reading these books some English girls will understand a little of the agony that has been the lot of their contemporaries across the water.

Cynthia Adams (review date September 1975)

SOURCE: Adams, Cynthia. *School Library Journal* 22, no. 1 (September 1975): 122.

Gr 7 Up—Having fled Belfast in *Into Exile* (1973) young marrieds Sadie and Kevin McCoy, an Irish Protestant-Catholic duo, try to establish themselves in a poverty-ridden section of Liverpool [in *A Proper Place*]. Realistic conflicts arise because of religious differences, Sadie's mother's visit, Kevin's brother's taking up residence in the McCoy's two rooms, their best friends moving to a suburb in Manchester. Wanting a better existence for themselves and their infant son, Kevin seeks employment as a farmhand on a large estate near Chester, and the McCoys find what they consider their "proper place" in the country. Lingard concentrates on the ups and downs of a mixed marriage, country life versus city life, finding happiness in work that one enjoys, and overcoming poverty through determination and hard work. Dialogue and action are slow moving, but the descriptions and characterization (with the exception of Kevin) are good.

Children's Book Review Service (review date October 1975)

SOURCE: *Children's Book Review Service* 4, no. 2 (October 1975): 17.

Ages 12+. Kevin and Sadie McCoy, youthful, city-bred parents from Northern Ireland, start a new life in rural England [in *A Proper Place*]. In-laws on opposite sides of the religious battles, a struggle to feed themselves and to help his family, and a rebel brother-in-law should provide tension and suspense but are disappointingly quiet. We know and enjoy Sadie, but her hardship is talked about rather than shown. Although dialogue has keen flavor, the story seems lacking in thematic point.

Jean Mercier (review date 8 December 1975)

SOURCE: Mercier, Jean. *Publishers Weekly* 208, no. 23 (8 December 1975): 50.

Readers of the three previous novels about the young Belfast couple, Sadie and Kevin, will welcome Ms. Lingard's further adventures of the exiles [in *A Proper Place*]. Protestant Sadie and Catholic Kevin learn that even if love doesn't conquer all, it certainly helps. The two are living in Liverpool when

Mrs. Jackson, Sadie's mother, arrives. With her complaints about how her daughter could have done better than to marry a "Mick," Mrs. Jackson is a burden rather than a welcome visitor. The woman even suggests that Sadie come back home and bring "her" baby, Brendan. It's a relief when Mrs. Jackson goes back to Belfast, but further troubles pile up to try the loyalties of the young family. Among their problems is that Kevin's bitter brother Gerald shows up, hot on the heels of their departing guest, and gives every sign of staying forever. The story is convincing and expertly handled. *(12-Up)*

Zena Sutherland (review date March 1976)

SOURCE: Sutherland, Zena. *Bulletin of the Center for Children's Books* 29, no. 7 (March 1976): 113.

6-10. Like the preceding books in this well-written sequence of stories about a young Irish couple, *A Proper Place* gives American readers a vivid picture of the depth of religious prejudice existing in Ireland today. Kevin is Catholic, Sadie is not; there has been no way to sustain their marriage but leaving home. Here they are parents, living in a Liverpool slum; while the story takes them to a new life on a Cheshire farm, with a difficult adjustment for the gregarious Sadie, it is just as interesting for the problems it poses about familial acceptance of the marriage when the couple are visited first by Sadie's bigoted mother and then by Kevin's surly younger brother.

📖 *THE RESETTLING* (1975)

Pamela D. Pollack (review date January 1976)

SOURCE: Pollack, Pamela D. *School Library Journal* 22, no. 5 (January 1976): 54.

Gr 6-9—Setting up stolid Dad as a self-employed plumber and engineering a move from the Glasgow highrise that's turned acrophobic Mum into a pill-popping zombie, Maggie McKinley plays Little Miss Fix-It to her bumbling blue-collar family [in *The Resettling*]. The girl is such a go-getter that the conflict between taking charge of her clinging clan and going her own way surfaces only in a fudged showdown—there's no hard feelings when Maggie inevitably takes college over bailing out the plumbing business. Sequel to *The Clearance* (1974), *The Resettling* settles for a skin-deep treatment of cutting family ties.

A. R. Williams (review date February 1976)

SOURCE: Williams, A. R. *Junior Bookshelf* 40, no. 1 (February 1976): 49.

Miss Lingard [in *The Resettling*] begins with a situation all too common today and perhaps not yet sufficiently explored by writers of her calibre: a fairly old-fashioned family translated from a "homely" terraced house to the kind of flat provided for the rehousing of families in areas now falling to the bulldozer. Perturbed by the growing melancholia of her mother in this Glaswegian fortress, Maggie employs her own kind of bull-dozing to persuade her father and uncle to start a family plumbing business which eventually accomplishes its objects but, through an ironic paradox, comes near to wrecking the freedom of Maggie's future which has become so full of promise. The main thread is interwoven with strands of class distinction, romance, scholarship and humanity. The plot line is not entirely predictable but cause and effect are coherently related and what might be called critical path technique in literary guise is effectively employed.

Children's Book Review Service (review date April 1976)

SOURCE: *Children's Book Review Service* 4, no. 9 (April 1976): 54.

Ages 11+. When Maggie of Glasgow goes to help her Ma move, she ends up starting her father in the plumbing business. The focus of this extremely well-written novel [*The Resettling*] is on Maggie's conflict between obligation to self and her future and obligation to her family's needs. Young love, professional training, and the urge to achieve are all here. The style has verve and excitement as Maggie herself involves the reader in examining her own similar obligations.

Publishers Weekly (review date 31 May 1976)

SOURCE: *Publishers Weekly* 209, no. 22 (31 May 1976): 198.

A sequel to *The Clearance* [*The Resettling*] finds Maggie McKinley back with her family in Glasgow as she tries to juggle school work, visits to her true love in Edinburgh and difficult family problems. The McKinleys have trouble adjusting to life in a highrise; Ms. McKinley is terrified of the elevators and has a breakdown when she's stuck between floors one day. Taking hold, Maggie persuades her father to go into business for himself, in a shop with a cozy flat attached. He does, but this venture means Maggie has to help out. Her lover, James, resents the time she spends in her father's shop and they break up; her academic career is also in danger. Ms. Lingard has once again created an absorbing story, based solidly on well-realized characterizations. Young readers should be happy to follow her attractive heroine through her vicissitudes and smile at the satisfactory solutions to her problems. (12-up)

Books for Keeps (review date July 1987)

SOURCE: *Books for Keeps* no. 45 (July 1987): 19.

I *like* Joan Lingard. I've never yet used one of her books without success and she's that rare thing—a writer who really appeals to a wide ability range. These two books [*The Clearance* and *The Resettling*] form the first half of a quartet of stories about 16-year-old Maggie McKinley, Glasgow dweller through and through. Or so she thinks—until she is dispatched by her family to spend the summer with her grandmother in a remote Scottish glen.

She meets the Fraser family and forms a mutual attachment with their son, James, grows to love the glen and to feel part of it, and finds herself having to take responsibility for her grandmother and for her family's emotional and financial problems.

The books are entertaining, realistic and accessible to almost all third and fourth-year readers. They would be particularly useful with the notorious 'bottom set' third years, dealing successfully with such issues as family life, teenage love and the burdens and pleasures of elderly relatives.

📖 *HOSTAGES TO FORTUNE* (1976)

Publishers Weekly (review date 17 January 1977)

SOURCE: *Publishers Weekly* 211, no. 3 (17 January 1977): 84.

The fifth novel [*Hostages to Fortune*] about Protestant Sadie and her Catholic husband, Kevin, is another of Lingard's moving and witty works. With their baby Brendan, the exiles from Belfast face another crisis when the owner of the farm in England where Kevin works dies. They have to move on, once more; this time, they are taken in by friends in Wales.

Beginning to save for a place of their own, they anticipate better times and settle in to await the birth of their second child. Then Kevin's 15-year-old runaway sister, Clodagh, turns up. She's wholly amoral and will be remanded to an institution if Kevin won't take her in. His loyalty to family gives him no choice. Sadie's resentment of the girl and of Kevin's devotion to his religion leads to a crisis when he goes to mass on Christmas Eve and leaves her alone. The book is a fine, realistic account of people battered by political and personal forces. *(12-up)*

Junior Bookshelf (review date April 1977)

SOURCE: *Junior Bookshelf* 41, no. 2 (April 1977): 117.

At this rate, Kevin and Sadie bid [in *Hostages to Fortune*] fair to rival the famous American Elsie Dinsmore (whose series ended at *Christmas with Grandma Elsie!*). After so many difficulties overcome—their Catholic-Protestant backgrounds, the horrors of life in Belfast—it seemed that they had reached a happy ending with young Brendan in their tied cottage on a Cheshire farm. But no'? The farmer dies, and Sadie's belief that something will turn up takes several hard knocks before at last they settle in Wales, (which appeals to them as less predictable than England) and achieve a tumbledown cottage of their own which they will restore. The problem of Kevin's family becomes overwhelming in this book, with their responsibility for runaway delinquent Clodagh, the ever possessive mother in Ireland, and even Uncle Albert, who arrives in his wheelchair to stay at the end of the book. Sadie's mother, also, descends on them to create further difficulties, and the young couple have no chance to develop their own home life. Their religious difficulties at last come into the open when Sadie's baby is stillborn as a result of them, and they face the situation instead of continuing to gloss it over. All laudably absorbing and relevant to today, for those who have followed the McCoys' adventures so far. The style is so naturally Belfast in grammar and idiom that one can hear the accents.

Children's Book Review Service (review date May 1977)

SOURCE: *Children's Book Review Service* 5, no. 10 (May 1977): 100.

Ages 12-14. Kevin and Sadie are young Irish who prefer a struggle for existence in England to the bombings, family interference, and intolerance of their mixed marriage they would find in Northern Ireland. This quiet, realistic narrative [*Hostages to Fortune*] about one eventful year in their lives might gain a small readership among some teens, but it is not really intended for a juvenile audience.

Peggy Sullivan (review date September 1977)

SOURCE: Sullivan, Peggy. *School Library Journal* 24, no. 1 (September 1977): 146.

Gr 7 Up— The fifth book [*Hostages to Fortune*] in the chronicle of quiet, steady Kevin and volatile Sadie McCoy depicts characters and background economically and well. The plot has more than its share of soap-operatic elements (to name only a few, Sadie has a stillborn child, a chance acquaintance offers them a home and work, Kevin's younger sister who is staying with them is convicted of shoplifting). However, the story of this young Irish couple in a small Welsh village coping with the demands put upon them by relatives as well as with their own struggles as parents could be just the thing for young teens (and adults) looking to read a mild, gentle romance.

THE PILGRIMAGE (1976)

Margery Fisher (review date September 1976)

SOURCE: Fisher, Margery. *Growing Point* 15, no. 3 (September 1976): 2941-942.

Joan Lingard's low-keyed, almost matter-of-fact style imparts a wry humour to the changing relationships in *The Pilgrimage*. Her earlier stories of Maggie McKinley and James Fraser have already suggested to readers that this is a love affair unlikely to develop very far and in the new book Maggie, impatient and independent as always, admits finally to herself and to the rather lethargic James that she is not ready to accept a settled future. The two young people set off hopefully enough on a bicycling holiday, a pilgrimage in effect, since Maggie is determined to visit Greenyards and the scene of Maggie Ross's eviction so often described by her grandmother. James, patient but petulant, finds himself pushed into the background not only by Maggie's preoccupation with the past but also because she is a good deal more willing than he is to join up with the two young Canadians met on the way, one of whom has come over to Scotland on a similar search for family history. There is a rueful reality in this unvarnished, unsensational se-

quence of events and feelings, in which I miss the intensity of Joan Lingard's novels of Northern Ireland but enjoy her sidelong, shrewd domestic insights.

Kirkus Reviews (review date 1 October 1976)

SOURCE: *Kirkus Reviews* 44, no. 19 (1 October 1976): 1101.

Indomitable Maggie McKinley of *The Clearance* (1974) and *The Resettling* (1976) is forced to break stride [in *The Pilgrimage*] when her middle-class boyfriend James presses for an early marriage, her attraction to a Canadian student she meets on a bicycling tour causes her to doubt her own commitment, and the continuing family financial crisis drives her out of school and into work at a bookbinding factory. Maggie's energetic tackling of every new experience and her conviction that "I could do with two or three lives all running at the same time. One doesn't give you enough scope" makes her congenial, invigorating company. But as Lingard herself seems to be settling in for a long acquaintance, this installment is more episodic and less conclusive than previous ones. For those who know Maggie as an old friend and will be pleased to see her persevere. *11-14.*

Deborah Robinson (review date February 1977)

SOURCE: Robinson, Deborah. *School Library Journal* 23, no. 6 (February 1977): 72.

Gr 6-9—Maggie McKinley and her boyfriend, James Fraser—protagonists of the author's *The Resettling* (1976)—are shocked when his teenage sister decides to get married because she is pregnant [in *The Pilgrimage*]. This situation becomes the impetus for Maggie to decide whether to marry James or to pursue her dream of becoming a social anthropologist. During a "pilgrimage," a bike trip from Invernessshire, Scotland to the home of Maggie's great great grandmother, Maggie, inspired by the courage of her relative, chooses a career over a husband. Although the characters are contemporary Scots, American readers will readily relate to their feelings and conflicts and Maggie is a heroine who has great determination and a sense of humor.

David Churchill (review date March 1977)

SOURCE: Churchill, David. *School Librarian* 25, no. 1 (March 1977): 62.

A youth-hostelling and cycling holiday in the Scottish Highlands gives Maggie, sixth-form schoolgirl, an opportunity to visit the valley from which her great-great-grandmother was evicted in the tragic Clearances [in *The Pilgrimage*]. She has saved up for the holiday, together with her boy-friend, and both look forward to the freedom it offers. The pregnancy and hasty marriage of a friend awake in Maggie a search for her own feelings for James, and about marriage in general. His intolerance and his emotional demands, particularly when she is friendly towards two Canadian boys they meet, push her towards self-discovery as the book develops. This is a deeply satisfying and at all times entertaining book which must be recommended with much enthusiasm. It is good to have met Maggie.

Zena Sutherland (review date April 1977)

SOURCE: Sutherland, Zena. *Bulletin of the Center for Children's Books* 30, no. 8 (April 1977): 129.

6-9. Third in a series of stories [*The Pilgrimage*] about doughty Maggie McKinley, a Glaswegian lass who has been enthralled by the stories her Granny tells about the family's Highland background. Here Maggie and her boyfriend James go off to bike and hike in the north country; James is less interested than Maggie in local history, and he's jealous when a Canadian hiker, Phil, shares Maggie's enthusiasm. In fact, Maggie finds that she responds more to Phil's one kiss than all the protestations of love and pressure for an early marriage from James. Maggie really wants to go to college, but her family feels they need her help—so Maggie gets a job. As always, Lingard treats issues that concern young people—independence, life goals, peer relationships—and, as always, she is realistic in maintaining the credibility of events as they are proscribed by social and financial pressures. The characters and dialogue are convincing, the writing style competently restrained.

◫ *THE REUNION* (1977)

Barbara Richardson (review date May 1978)

SOURCE: Richardson, Barbara. *School Library Journal* 24, no. 9 (May 1978): 77.

Gr 7 Up—The fourth of Lingard's Maggie books [*The Reunion*] moves swiftly from Scotland to Canada as the 18-year-old heroine readies herself for a career in social anthropology. The summer in Toronto gives Maggie the opportunity to once again see Phil Ross, the handsome geology student she met at home the previous year. Unfortunately, Phil has taken up with another girl in the meantime, making for an uncomfortable situation. As the summer progresses, however, the personal relationships, as well as Maggie's employment problems, slowly work themselves out. Although sprinkled with clichés, the writing style matches Maggie's bubbly personality, and characters and plot will appeal to younger teens with a romantic bent.

Children's Book Review Service (review date June 1978)

SOURCE: *Children's Book Review Service* 6, no. 11 (June 1978): 109.

Ages 13-16. This fourth title [*The Reunion*] in a series of books about Scottish teenager Maggie McKinley tells of her eighteenth summer, when she leaves home for the first time and travels to Ottawa for work as a mother's helper. Things don't happen as planned, either with the job (she quits) or with the young man who arranged her visit (on her arrival she finds him involved with another girl), but by the story's end, they are in each other's arms. This is basically a mild, old-fashioned romance, but Maggie has pluck and a growing sense of self-reliance. There will be many young girls who will enjoy identifying with her.

Elisabeth Sykes (review date June 1978)

SOURCE: Sykes, Elisabeth. *School Librarian* 26, no. 2 (June 1978): 161-62.

This [*The Reunion*], the third book about Maggie McKinley, describes her trip to Toronto to work as an au pair in order to earn some extra money for her university course. Waiting for her in Toronto, she hopes, is Phil Ross, a Canadian student whom she met in Scotland the previous summer. However, Maggie finds it is not so easy to pick up her relationship with Phil and her au pair job turns out to be rather too eventful and as a result she finds herself alone and unemployed in a strange city.

Joan Lingard portrays Maggie's ups and downs in this strange new life with sympathy and understanding and many teenage girls will be able to sympathise with Maggie's hopes and fears. We are also given a taste of several different Canadian lifestyles, none of which, Maggie realises, is for her. A sensitively handled and well written sequel to the earlier novels.

Mary Laska Cannella (review date January 1979)

SOURCE: Cannella, Mary Laska. *Best Sellers* 38, no. 10 (January 1979): 331.

This is Joan Lingard's fourth novel [*The Reunion*] in a series about Maggie McKinley, a Scottish teenager. Maggie is vacationing in Canada, hoping to have a romantic reunion with a young man she met the year before in Scotland. At first, Maggie's infatuation is unrequited, but, as the summer wears on, things change. Along the way, we hear of Maggie's ups and downs, mostly downs, as a live-in babysitter to two different families in Toronto. As an added bonus, there is a travelogue of Toronto and the Canadian wilderness. The travelogue, however, has the air of a stale geography lesson.

The book may appeal to adolescents who are dreaming of their first romantic encounter. The young teenagers who fantasize about what it would be like to be eighteen may find that this is the book for them. This reviewer, though, found Miss Lingard's prose to be rather leaden and her characters wooden. The book is too easy to put down; its character fail to arouse the proper empathy or sympathy.

There are two errors that the editor should have caught: the dust jacket refers to the heroine as Maggie McKenzie (spelled at different points as McKenzie and then MacKenzie). In the text of the book, her name is Maggie McKinley. Secondly, and minor at that, the jacket calls this book the third in the Maggie series; actually it is the fourth. This reviewer is not looking for the fifth. (Ages 12 and up)

Patricia Cocker (review date August 1979)

SOURCE: Cocker, Patricia. *In Review* 13 (August 1979): 36.

Maggie arrives in Toronto from Scotland one rainy summer day, only to discover that things are not as she had anticipated. The previous summer she had met Phil, a Canadian student, on a cycling holiday in Scotland. Although Phil has found her a job as a mother's helper, as promised, he is otherwise occupied. Maggie must come to terms with herself and the situation in which she finds herself: the first time away from her home and family; the death of her grandmother shortly before her departure from Scotland; job which proves to be somewhat less than ideal; and her relationships with Mike, Phil and Lois. This she does in a believable manner although it seems a bit far-fetched at times.

In her fourth and final book about Maggie McKinley [*The Reunion*], Lingard writes in a manner that will no doubt appeal to teenagers. Her language tends to be theirs. We learn about Maggie through what she says and does, but more importantly we learn about her through what she thinks—of the present and of incidents in the past. Maggie is a very introspective young woman.

Young teens will quite possibly be drawn to Maggie and her problems; they will identify with her to a certain extent. *The Reunion* should help fill the Canadian gap in the field of young adult fiction.

SNAKE AMONG THE SUNFLOWERS (1977)

Margery Fisher (review date July 1977)

SOURCE: Fisher, Margery. *Growing Point* 16, no. 2 (July 1977): 3145.

The dilution of adult emotion in *Snake Among the Sunflowers* is not only the result of telling the story from the point of view of the young—in this case Claudine, Paul and Sophie Grant, on holiday with their French grandparents. The reactions of fifteen-year-old Claudine and Paul, who is a year younger, seem curiously immature for the 'seventies when they find, by overhearing, guessing and boldly questioning, that their attractive aunt from Paris and the German Professor at the house with the sunflowers were once in love and parted because of the ferociously active opposition of her father, a resistance fighter in World War II. One can accept Sophie easily enough as the *enfant terrible* whose prying is largely responsible for a partly happy resolution of old sorrow, but the older boy and girl display the kind of innocence better suited to pony stories and so there is no chance to see, through them, any real substance in the renewed love between Nicole and Otto Brander. Joan Lingard is always good to read, with her sharpness in matters of social behaviour, background and day-to-day event, but this book remains, all the same, another diagram, not likely to impress permanently readers of twelve or so and certainly without the depth which older readers ought to expect.

Kirkus Reviews (review date 1 October 1977)

SOURCE: *Kirkus Reviews* 45, no. 19 (1 October 1977): 1054.

Three (more) children spend their summer stumbling over an old mystery and hatching plots, but what passes the time for them is strictly tedious to readers [in *Snake Among the Sunflowers*]. Observing tense family reactions to the news of tenants returning to a vacant house, Claudine, Paul, and Sophie can't get any straight answers so they check out old newspaper files at the library; before you can say *crime passionnel,* they dig up the wartime story of their French grandfather's prison sentence for shooting his neighbor Otto Brander, a German and his daughter Nicole's amour. The children and their new friend, the German's son, arrange a surprise reunion between Brander, a widower, and visiting Aunt Nicole, and a few days later secret wedding plans are revealed. Perhaps they've all been out in the Lot-et-Garonne sun too long for the plot twists are ludicrous (Grandpère, raging again, has a heart attack) and the adults have the insight of sausages. And the title's too marginal to explain. *11-12.*

Caroline S. Parr (review date November 1977)

SOURCE: Parr, Caroline S. *School Library Journal* 24, no. 3 (November 1977): 59.

Gr 5-7—Lingard has departed from her usual Irish and Scotch locales for this average romantic mystery [*Snake Among the Sunflowers*] set in southern France. Sophie, Paul and Claudine visit their mother's birthplace in Lotet-Garonne each year and always speculate about the "Sunflower House," a deserted farmhouse nearby. One summer, a German art professor and his teenage son Christian move in, and the children's curiosity is aroused when Grand-père prohibits them from seeing Christian. When their Aunt Nicole comes to visit from Paris, the children finally learn that she and the professor had been engaged 20 years before, but that Grand-pére, a French Resistance fighter, had opposed his daughter's marriage to a German. The children arrange for Nicole and Professor Brander to meet, their love is rekindled, and they decide to marry against the wishes of Grand-pére who inadvertently learns of the plan and has a heart attack when he angrily confronts the pair. The novel with its appealing element of old family secrets is competently written, but the setting is never sharply defined and none of the characters stand out.

***Children's Book Review Service* (review date January 1978)**

SOURCE: *Children's Book Review Service* 6, no. 5 (January 1978): 49.

Ages 11+. Every year the children spend the summer in their mother's home village in France [in *Snake Among the Sunflowers*]. They think of the empty house with the sunflowers as their own, after having played in its garden so often. But this year the house is occupied by a young German boy and his father. When the children try to find out more about the house and its owners, the villagers will say nothing. Then their grandfather forbids them to speak to the boy. In the end, some secrets are laid bare, but others have to be kept from grandpere. A story to inspire thought—and admiration—for its fine delineation of locale and characters.

THE GOOSEBERRY (1978); ALSO PUBLISHED AS ODD GIRL OUT (1979)

Anne Thwaite (review date 1 December 1978)

SOURCE: Thwaite, Anne. *Times Literary Supplement* no. 4000 (1 December 1978): 1394.

Joan Lingard is still probably best known for her Belfast books. but *The Gooseberry,* like many of her recent stories, is set in Scotland. The Gooseberry is Ellen Ferguson, a determined, resourceful girl who, five foot eleven at fourteen, often finds herself on the edge of other people's romances. The crucial romance is her own mother's. Ellen's attempts to prevent her mother's remarriage and their removal to the suburbs are both funny and painful. Joan Lingard is always worth reading.

***Junior Bookshelf* (review date February 1979)**

SOURCE: *Junior Bookshelf* 43, no. 1 (February 1979): 55-6.

What better way for a sensitive child to grow up than beside a river—even if the river is the Water of Leith, mud-brown and enriched with old boots and other rubbish [in *The Gooseberry*]? Ellen belongs to Edinburgh, to a decaying tenement which she shares with her faded-pretty mother. Ellen is neither faded nor pretty. She is five foot eleven with hair coarse 'like a pot scourer' and 'the colour of burnt carrots'. Ellen does not enjoy her role as perpetual gooseberry to her sexy girl-friend, but otherwise she loves her life. Her mother dreams of a bungalow in the outer suburbs.

Mother's dream comes true, for Herbert, recently freed from a life of servitude to a formidable mother, proposes and is accepted. With the marriage Ellen's own carefree life threatens to disintegrate. Above all she will lose the piano which she loves—and which her mother for good reason hates—and which links her with her lost father. She finds some kind of solution through Nicolas, an elderly Czech pianist who needs a home-help. Ellen needs sympathy and practical help with her playing, so the arrangement promises well. With a girl like Ellen nothing is easy, however, and there is much anguish before she exorcizes the ghost of her father—he is not dead, by the way—and finds a career and a boy-friend.

This is an enjoyable 'read'. If it is not more, this is due to some failure in the central character who, while amusing and sympathetic, is not quite as big and idiosyncratic as the author would like and the plot demands. It might have helped if Edinburgh, rather than Ellen, had been the hero, but there is some ambivalence in the author's approach to her theme. The book demands total identification with the heroine, but this reader at least found no difficulty in maintaining a detached attitude. Enjoyable, certainly, but not the smash hit it ought to be.

Margery Fisher (review date March 1979)

SOURCE: Fisher, Margery. *Growing Point* 17, no. 6 (March 1979): 3486.

Conscious of her unusual height, which contrasts alarmingly with the miniature charms of her best friend Isadora, Ellie accepts her role as confidant all the more readily because of the secret fantasies she pursues about her supposedly dead father [in *The Gooseberry*]. When her mother decides to marry middle-aged Herbert and move from the city to a suburban bungalow, the girl has to face the truth about herself and about the past. There is humour here besides a shrewd assessment of the romantic proclivities of a girl in the early 'teens, and the Edinburgh setting is skilfully used to give life to a group of strongly identified individuals.

Caroline Parr (review date May 1979)

SOURCE: Parr, Caroline. *School Library Journal* 25, no. 9 (May 1979): 64.

Gr 5-8—Ellie lives with her mother in the slums of Edinburgh and idolizes her dead father. She feels like the *Odd Girl Out* because of her height and her friend Isadora, who is always involved with one boy or another. When her mother remarries (to dull, quiet Herbert with a bungalow in the suburbs), Ellie feels even more left out and runs away. When Ellie is

found a few days later, her mother confesses that the child's father did not die but ran off with another woman. The combination of this revelation and Herbert's sympathetic understanding of his stepdaughter's feelings result in her finally coming to terms with her new parent and her life. Lingard's characters tend to be too straightforward and pragmatic for Ellie's identity crisis to seem quite believable, but the likable, spunky heroine and her feelings of being out of step will appeal to young teenagers.

Dorothy Nimmo (review date June 1979)

SOURCE: Nimmo, Dorothy. *School Librarian* 27, no. 2 (June 1979): 161.

When Joan Lingard is not dealing with Ulster one feels a certain loss of dramatic tension. This story [*The Gooseberry*] is set in Edinburgh where red-haired Ellie, nearly six feet tall, lives in a flat with her mother and fantasises about her father, who was a pianist. She takes secret piano lessons from a blind Czech, builds castles in the air to house his nephew who may come to England, and resents her mother's engagement to suburban Herbert who can't eat salami and lives in a bungalow. She runs away but is recovered and reconciles herself to a reality which includes Davie next door, the revelation that her father is not dead but absconded to Australia, and Herbert, who is not all bad since he turns out his mother's china cabinet to make room for her piano. It is a perfectly adequate book, readable, moral and sensible, but not challenging.

***Children's Book Review Service* (review date July 1979)**

SOURCE: *Children's Book Review Service* 7, no. 13 (July 1979): 128.

Ages 12+. Contrasted with her best friend Isadora [in *Odd Girl Out*], blond-haired and dating a dozen boys, Ellie—who is 5'11" and further burdened with frizzy red hair and a healthy appetite—feels like the "odd girl out." Yet she is comfortable in the noisy, crowded Edinburgh neighborhood where she and her mother live. Ellie feels her already confusing life coming apart when her mother remarries and they go to live in a suburban house that is both depressing and oppressive to Ellie. She escapes into romantic fantasy and fierce idolization of her father. Gradually, with the help of friends, she confronts the truth about her father, and learns to accept and adjust. Ms. Lingard writes as sympathetically and skillfully as ever, clearly evoking Ellie and her predicament, but this lacks the vitality and impact of some of her other stories. Nevertheless, it is an appealing and affecting story.

Zena Sutherland (review date October 1979)

SOURCE: Sutherland, Zena. *Bulletin of the Center for Children's Books* 33, no. 2 (October 1979): 32.

Set in Edinburgh, [*Odd Girl Out* is] a contemporary story of adolescent rebellion and adjustment is distinctive for its depth in characterization and its smooth yet vigorous writing style, particularly in the felicitously natural dialogue. Fourteen, awkward, and almost a six-footer, Ellen's only friends are Davie and Isadora, neighbors in the tenement neighborhood where she feels at home and from which her mother yearns to escape. Escape comes in the form of a prissy suitor; Ellen detests him because she has to live in his cluttered bungalow on the other side of town, and because she idolizes the father who had died when she was three. She knows her mother hadn't been happy with her first husband; Ellen's father had been a negligent and profligate musician. Mum doesn't even like Ellen's interest in music, and resents the fact that an old man for whom Ellen does chores is giving her piano lessons. Ellen, sulky and rebellious at home, takes refuge in daydreams about the old man's nephew, a Parisian, dreams that end when the young man's visit is cancelled. She runs away, is found, and learns from her mother that her father isn't dead but had deserted them and is remarried and living abroad with his new family. Brought down to earth, Ellen compromises with reality and sees for the first time that her maligned stepfather is really a kindly and generous man. A fine and flowing book.

📖 *THE FILE ON FRAULEIN BERG* (1980)

Margery Fisher (review date May 1980)

SOURCE: Fisher, Margery. *Growing Point* 19, no. 1 (May 1980): 3702.

1944 again, this time in Belfast, where for three schoolgirls war means deprivation rather than danger, muddle rather than misery [in *The File on Fraulein Berg*]. When Fraulein Berg arrives to teach German at their school, Kate and her friends Sally and Harriet, avid readers of junior thrillers, decide she must

be a spy slipped over the border. Surveillance is difficult but absorbing, and it is not till twenty years later that a chance meeting shows Kate, who tells the story, just how foolish and cruel their actions must have seemed to the refugee. The author focuses on the war years as they really might have seemed to a trio of lively, prejudiced girls. Enlivened by humour and sharp in social definition, her novel should make young readers think as well as smile.

Jack Forman (review date May 1980)

SOURCE: Forman, Jack. *School Library Journal* 26, no. 9 (May 1980): 77.

Gr 6-8—An historically instructive but inconsequential story [*The File on Fraulein Berg*] about three 13-year-old girls in 1944 Northern Ireland and their attempts to expose the supposed spying activities of their new German teacher, Fraulein Berg. They snoop around her house, trail her around Belfast, break up her budding romance with the only male teacher at school, and implicate her in a customs fracas after a trip to Dublin. Fraulein Berg finally leaves and the girls find out later—much to their guilty embarrassment—that she was not only not a German spy but a Jewish refugee who lost much of her family in the Holocaust. Adolescent insensitivity is matter-of-factly portrayed, and an interesting picture of Irish Protestant-Catholic political, social, and religious conflicts in World War II is presented here. But the plot is slow and never leads to much, and the "surprise" of Fraulein Berg's real identity falls flat because readers really don't get to know much about the teacher, except that she was "persecuted" by the three girls.

Paul Heins (review date August 1980)

SOURCE: Heins, Paul. *Horn Book Magazine* 56, no. 4 (August 1980): 414-15.

In 1944 when North Ireland, unlike Eire, was subjected to wartime conditions, three Belfast girls became suspicious at the arrival of Fraulein Berg, who was to teach German at their school [in *The File on Fraulein Berg*]. Kathleen Carson, whose widowed mother was a dressmaker; Sally MacCabe, whose father was a butcher making the most of the black market; and Harriet Linton, whose father was a successful lawyer, were all sure that the new teacher was a spy. They began to observe and follow her doings outside of school and even to keep a somewhat amateurish dossier on her activities. The story is told in retrospect after twenty years by Kathleen, who realizes that she and her friends had persecuted the unfortunate woman; not until the epilogue, however, does the reader learn that Fraulein Berg was Jewish. The narrative, which also underlines Protestant prejudice against the Catholics, never becomes doctrinaire or didactic; for Kathleen and her friends pursue their private activities in a social milieu, and the author deftly and humorously articulates the differences that make the schoolgirls, the teachers, and the parents recognizable individuals.

Ann G. Hay (review date autumn 1980)

SOURCE: Hay, Ann G. *British Book News Children's Supplement* (autumn 1980): 26.

The first book [*The File on Fraulein Berg*] to be produced by the new firm of Julia MacRae indicates that this publisher has no mean ability. Joan Lingard gets them off to a flying start. She has put aside her modern saga of Sadie and Kevin and returned to Belfast in the last war to tell of the lives of three schoolgirls who are convinced that their German teacher is a spy. They decide to follow the woman and document her every move. Little details of wartime life are lovingly related—queuing, sweet-rationing, broken biscuits being cheaper—and on one occasion the girls go to Dublin on a shopping spree and are astonished to find the luxuries available in a neutral country, though they have problems returning across the border. The girls are well contrasted and the plot is strong enough to hold our interest. Eventually, they begin to tire of the pursuit and feel that it is becoming a persecution, so it tails off, as it would do in real life, when they find other interests. When we discover in a postscript the truth about Fraulein Berg the rug is jerked from under us as it was from under the girls, and we share in their feelings of guilt. A very strong novel for girls from eleven up.

Journal of Reading (review date March 1981)

SOURCE: *Journal of Reading* 24, no. 6 (March 1981): 549.

During recent years, several fine pieces of literature set during World War II have been published for young adults. *The File on Fraulein Berg* by Joan Lingard and *Autumn Street* by Lois Lowry are two novels that now can be added to this collection. In *The File on Fraulein Berg,* which takes place in

Belfast, Ireland, the war is more of a nuisance than a threat. Three of the four main characters are teenage girls, bored with both the inconveniences of war and life in general. When Fraulein Berg, "a real live German," arrives to teach in their school, she becomes the antidote for their boredom. Almost immediately the three brand her a spy and set about searching for evidence by following her home, setting up watches outside her apartment and generally misconstruing everything they see. The climax occurs when, through a witless act committed by one of the girls, all three and Fraulein Berg are detained and searched at the border as they are returning from Dublin. Shortly thereafter the Fraulein leaves her teaching post, and the girls are left with their guilt as they realize the consequences of their childish actions.

Books for Keeps (review date November 1993)

SOURCE: *Books for Keeps* 4, no. 83 (November 1993): 13.

Three school friends in wartime Belfast [in *The File on Fraulein Berg*], convinced that their new German teacher is a spy, embark on a campaign of tracking the suspect, finding sinister overtones in everything she does. Few readers will be surprised to find that they're quite wrong, regretting their victimisation when they discover she's an escaped Jew whose family has died in concentration camps, though the 'awful truth' does not have the impact it deserves. Contrasts between the three girls and their families enliven the story.

STRANGERS IN THE HOUSE (1981)

Brian Patten (review date 19 December 1981)

SOURCE: Patten, Brian. *Spectator* 247, no. 8006 (19 December 1981): 33-4.

Joan Lingard writes about the chaotic emotions of children and young teenagers whose private worlds are invaded by adult problems. Without moralising, she shows how, outside their own company, children have no authority and how it is to the authority of adults that they are expected to bend, and by it that their emotions are suppressed.

Her latest novel, *Strangers in the House,* explores the uncomfortable relationship between a newly acquainted step-brother and sister, and the boy's early resentment of his step-father: here is a man who will not only quash the boy's hope that his mother will be reunited with his real father, but who, it seems to him, is intent on stealing his mother from him as well.

Robin Barlow (review date March 1982)

SOURCE: Barlow, Robin. *School Librarian* 30, no. 1 (March 1982): 55.

Joan Lingard laboriously charts [in *Strangers in the House*] the process of readjustment of fourteen-year-old Calum and his six-year-old sister Betsy when their mother remarries a widower with a thirteen-year-old daughter of his own. The story is one of unrelieved gloom. Poor Calum has the worst of it: he moves into the new family home and has to sleep in a cupboard; his bike is stolen; his one true friend, his dog, is run over by a bus; he loses his girlfriend; and his step-sister detests him. The rest of the family do not fare much better. His mother has to work her fingers to the bone to support the family; his step-father is a reformed alcoholic; his sister goes missing for the night when she is left in his charge; his real father's new wife does a bunk; and his step-sister breaks her ankle, which mends in time for her to run away from home.

Children's Book Review Service (review date July 1983)

SOURCE: *Children's Book Review Service* 11, no. 13 (July 1983): 139.

Ages 12+. Because his mother has remarried, fourteen-year-old Calum [in *Strangers in the House*] and his younger sister have to leave their seaport home and move to a cramped apartment in Edinburg along with his new thirteen-year-old stepsister, Stella. The two teenagers try their best to avoid one another, but when Stella runs away, it is Calum who finds her. Together they realize it is up to them to work out their problems and make this new family work. A perceptive novel about a relevant problem.

Kate M. Flanagan (review date August 1983)

SOURCE: Flanagan, Kate M. *Horn Book Magazine* 59, no. 4 (August 1983): 455.

The situation is not new [in *Strangers in the House*]: one family moving in with another after a remarriage and everybody struggling with the subsequent problems. But the author takes familiar ingredients and creates—by means of well-defined characters and an eye for the details of daily household life—a perceptive account of two sets of people learning to get along with each other. Fourteen-year-old Calum MacLeod was dead set against his mother's marrying Tom Cunningham—a man she barely knew—and the boy resented moving from their seaside home to Edinburgh. And thirteen-year-old Stella Cunningham could not fathom why her widowed father would want to take on a wife and two children. Although Calum's six-year-old sister settled right into their new life, the two teenagers were at loggerheads from the start, and their relationship did not improve when Calum became close to Stella's best girl friend. Conflicts among the family members were exacerbated by cramped living quarters, and the first six months after the wedding were trying for both the MacLeods and the Cunninghams. The author brings her characters through various domestic crises to the point where everybody—particularly Calum and Stella—reaches a level of understanding that bodes well for the whole family. And such is her skill that the reader genuinely cares.

Kathleen W. Craver (review date August 1983)

SOURCE: Craver, Kathleen W. *School Library Journal* 29, no. 10 (August 1983): 78.

Gr 7 Up—Teenage readers should easily identify with the adjustment problems of the main characters in this contemporary story [*Strangers in the House*] of divorce and remarriage. Crammed into a small Edinburgh flat are the newly arrived MacLeods: Willa, her teenaged son Calum, 6-year-old Betsy and their dog; and the Cunninghams: Tom and 13-year-old Stella. Calum is hoping to be invited to live with his father's new family; Stella watches the fissures widen in the marriage in the hope that the MacLeods will soon depart. Both adolescents suffer from misfortunes which force them to reconcile their dreams with reality. When the invitation to join his father finally arrives, Tom realizes that he would rather remain with his mother and sister in Edinburgh. This decision and the loss of her best friend to Calum lead Stella to run away. Calum stubbornly follows her trail, finds her, and, in doing so, initiates the first step in fashioning a bridge between the two families. *Strangers in the House* realistically portrays the feelings, reactions and expectations of teenagers caught in the first stages of a remarriage situation. It does not provide the proverbial happy ending, but it offers positive signs for the future. Lingard has written an excellent addition to the genre of divorce-remarriage fiction.

Barbara Stiber (review date October 1983)

SOURCE: Stiber, Barbara. *Voice of Youth Advocates* 6, no. 4 (October 1983): 204.

When his mother remarries [in *Strangers in the House*], 14-year-old Calum and his sister Betsy must not only adjust to a new stepfather but also to a new home which includes a sullen stepsister named Stella. Calum's readjustment is hampered by the breakup of his father's second marriage. The beginnings of acceptance and adjustment begin to occur when Stella runs away from home and Calum finds her hidden in the family cottage. Lingard does have her fans and they will enjoy this latest work. The book will be difficult to sell to readers who have trouble reading. The setting in Scotland will also hinder some readers. Larger collections with Lingard fans should purchase, all others should consider passing this one up.

THE WINTER VISITOR (1983)

Margery Fisher (review date September 1983)

SOURCE: Fisher, Margery. *Growing Point* 22, no. 3 (September 1983): 4131-135.

Adolescent perceptions and uncertainties are demonstrated in *The Winter Visitor* with Joan Lingard's special combination of good sense and warm commitment. When Nick's mother takes a lodger into their Edinburgh house he is surprised because this is usually only a summer practice and a little suspicious about Ed Black's Irish background. But with his father working in Kuwait, there is a room empty and, besides, Nick finds the lodger a pleasant man to talk to, and it is some time before the boy and his older sister Andrea notice that their mother seems unnecessarily friendly with him. Family relationships are already strained because of Andrea's unsuitable attachment to the much older Italian Guido, and Nick's discovery of an old photograph, together with his grandmother's tales of their Irish forebears as Orangemen, points to alarming conclusions. Sectarian and political differences lie behind a friendship renewed from the past which threatens the stability of the family. Joan Lingard explores the situation and resolves it, keeping the point of view of the boy in the forefront but taking due measure of the other characters caught in a dilemma very much of our times.

A. R. Williams (review date December 1983)

SOURCE: Williams, A. R. *Junior Bookshelf* 47, no. 6 (December 1983): 260-61.

The winter visitor [in *The Winter Visitor*] to a seaside boarding house is a mysterious person who seems to have some sort of connection with Nick Murray's mother, which, in the absence of Nick's father, is a worrying matter for the boy and his sister, though the girl is too occupied with her Italian boy friend to take a great deal of notice of what is happening at home. Joan Lingard's main concern is with the problems of a boy growing up in this unsettled environment in which other people seem too involved in their private affairs to give him the undivided attention and companionship he has come to take for granted. The background of school, hobbies or other interests, and experiments in social life are sympathetically drawn and even the menace of the stranger is transformed into friendship of a kind with a little amateur detective work thrown in. The outcome, possibly, is a picture of the resilience of children and young adults which enables them to survive the squalls of adolescence so long as some help is at hand.

Cecilia Gordon (review date March 1984)

SOURCE: Gordon, Cecilia. *School Librarian* 32, no. 1 (March 1984): 69.

This story [*The Winter Visitor*], set on the Scottish coast in the middle of winter, explores the effect of the arrival of a new lodger from Northern Ireland at the home of teenager Nick Murray. Winter lodgers are rare and Nick soon senses that there is something mysterious about Ed Black. He discovers that Ed has known Mrs Murray in the past, and this worries him because his father is away working in the Persian Gulf.

Joan Lingard writes in her usual plain, simple style and once again reveals the depth of her understanding of adolescent doubts and preoccupations. The adults are far from being mere background figures and are shown to have their fears and difficult decisions too. These have a strong influence on the young people and help them to develop in understanding. What happened in troubled Belfast long ago is alive in the minds even of those unborn at the time, as is the sinister antagonism between Catholic and Protestant. The story unfolds amidst a clear picture of everyday incidents: family life, school life, fraught relationships and sudden emergencies. Joan Lingard knows all about contemporary issues and how to handle them deftly. She can also bring a character vividly to life in a very few words.

A book that will be read by sensitive teenagers with pleasure and recognition.

📖 *THE FREEDOM MACHINE* (1986)

Adele Geras (review date 5 December 1986)

SOURCE: Geras, Adele. *New Statesman* 112, no. 2906 (5 December 1986): 29.

Sometimes it is their *physical* absence which is the mainspring of the story; their spirit pervades the narrative. In Joan Lingard's *The Freedom Machine* Mungo's Dad is in gaol for embezzlement. Mungo, a very grown-up ten-year-old, rather than stay with vinegary Aunt Janet during his mother's sojourn in hospital, takes to the high road on Gulliver, his bicycle, which was a present from his father. Through Mungo's first-person narrative we come to know his Dad very well, and to understand the endearing fecklessness that has led him to prison. It's an absorbing and entertaining book.

Spectator (review date 13 December 1986)

SOURCE: *Spectator* 257 (13 December 1986): 4131.

For slightly older children and in a more sombre mood Joan Lingard's latest novel *The Freedom Machine* belongs to the new school of social realism. Mungo's father is in prison, his mother in hospital, his life in a mess. His only reliable friend is his bicycle, Gulliver, his freedom machine, on which he tries to escape from all his problems. There are echoes of Victorian children's stories, for Mungo finds sanctuary with what is virtually the Old Squire and his grand daughter, but it is a perceptive picture of a loner looking at life through 11-year-old eyes.

Sandra Hann (review date May 1987)

SOURCE: Hann, Sandra. *School Librarian* 35, no. 2 (May 1987): 155.

The Freedom Machine is written with Joan Lingard's customary persuasive lucidity. The reader's curiosity is aroused on the first page—and gradually is revealed the tangled confusion of reasons why ten-year-old Mungo McKinnon decides to leave his Edinburgh home and run away on his bicycle—his freedom machine. The apparent reason is to avoid spending a month with his aunt while his mother is in hospital. However, that is only a small part of it. Mungo is escaping to freedom on the move. It is important that he can continue to leave things behind when they threaten to control him rather than the other way around. Edinburgh represents a prison in more ways than one.

There is a happy ending, rather a contrived one, but the book's readers could be younger than twelve. This is what makes me worry about a scene in the novel which shows Mungo accepting a car ride and food from a woman who picks him up in a fairground. The worry is increased just because Joan Lingard is a writer of such quality. For example, her description of Mungo releasing trapped birds from an attic filled with the skeletons and decomposing bodies of others, made my scalp prickle.

The jacket design serves the book badly. It is brown and black and hardly likely to make a young reader reach out eagerly for it.

Books for Keeps (review date July 1988)

SOURCE: *Books for Keeps* no. 51 (July 1988): 9-10.

If you can believe Mungo's rather pally relationship with his bike [in *The Freedom Machine*], Gulliver, this is a satisfying enough read. Boy and bike make a break for freedom when it looks as though a stay with the vitriolic Aunt Janet is in the offing. They finally hole up in an abandoned mansion with a dubious history, where everything turns out as well as expected and they even see a ghost.

Joan Lingard adds a deeper dimension with the imprisoned father to produce a story worth stocking for older junior/lower secondary readers.

📖 *THE GUILTY PARTY* (1987)

M. Hobbs (review date October 1987)

SOURCE: Hobbs, M. *Junior Bookshelf* 51, no. 5 (October 1987): 237.

Joan Lingard is good at examining unpopular but important attitudes, historical and modern, to war and violence. The opening of a nuclear reactor [in *The*

Guilty Party] nearby is dividing the seaside town to which Josie and her mother have come to stay with strait-laced relatives. Her father has been killed in Northern Ireland, and she has already been arrested once for taking part in a peaceful anti-nuclear demonstration in London, so that when she is caught bill-sticking for a march against the reactor, the police sergeant expects her to be a troublemaker and does his best, on this and other occasions, to provoke her.

The townspeople are very well drawn: the hidden and the overt sympathisers with the young peoples' stance, the selfish, concerned only that their comfortable circumstances remain safeguarded, the nuclear scientist whose son Rod is Josie's particular friend, and her mother, who is galvanised into action by Josie's attitude after her long period of inert mourning. The ups and downs of Josie's friendship with Rod, their mutual attraction despite their great division over the nuclear question, the lessons that both have to learn—self-control for her and flexibility in opinion for him—are convincingly and sympathetically portrayed. The latter part of the book, Josie's week in Holloway Prison, is in a sense a digression—an impressionistic and on the whole believable outline of the frustrations and hatefulness of life in a women's prison today. Most of the representative types are (lightly) touched on, including her prostitute cell-mate, who breaks under the life. Josie is expiating a teenage burden of guilt, about living up to her father's memory—he died because he tried to run a mixed-religion youth group in Belfast—about not conforming to her aunt and uncle's suburban standards, about her mother having no home. She is also curious to experience prison life. She realises that, unpleasant as the week is, compared to the others she is merely playing at it, but from it she finds her choice of future career, the law. The least convincing part, because the least factual or detailed, is inevitably Josie's speech after the march, on the perils of nuclear warfare, but the thought-provoking plot and characters succeed in gripping the reader.

Caroline Heaton (review date December 1987)

SOURCE: Heaton, Caroline. *British Book News Children's Books* (December 1987): 31.

14+ The Guilty Party explores the issue of nuclear power through the story of a young teenage activist, Josie. When she and her mother leave Belfast after her father's death, they find refuge with relatives in a sleepy coastal town. But the presence of a nuclear

power station rouses all Josie's fighting spirit, and life soon becomes anything but sleepy as she campaigns with friends for the station's closure. Her fierce dedication to this cause rapidly brings her into conflict with the authorities and strains even her closest relationships. Eventually, she accepts a prison sentence for non-payment of fines rather than compromise her principles, and the book concludes with the prospect of a public enquiry into the power station.

Josie is an attractive character and the story is supplied with convincing detail on the difficulties and stresses of campaigning in an area where local jobs depend on the nuclear industry. The ostrich-like reactions of Josie's small-minded uncle and aunt also ring true to life, as does the hesitation of Josie's quieter boyfriend who cannot match her conviction. However, I found *The Guilty Party* a rather pedestrian read and had a sense of a compressed story, in which conflicts are resolved too rapidly for real drama to be sustained. But the book does have the great merit of emphasizing the individual's power to effect change.

Rosemary Stones (review date January 1988)

SOURCE: Stones, Rosemary. *Books* no. 10 (January 1988): 11.

Joan Lingard's *The Guilty Party* is a punchier offering with spirited teenage Josie demonstrating outside a nuclear power station and then refusing to pay her fine. Holloway does not sound fun. The nature of moral choice, political action and the response of the state are themes expertly woven into this story of one anti-nuclear teenager and her friends.

Anne Everall (review date February 1988)

SOURCE: Everall, Anne. *School Librarian* 36, no. 1 (February 1988): 30.

After her father's death, Josie and her mother come to England to stay with relatives [in *The Guilty Party*]. Josie discovers that a nuclear power reactor has been built nearby and, in the light of Chernobyl, she and her friends decide to act. This brings her into conflict with relatives, her boyfriend, and the police. She is arrested at a peace march and finds herself faced with a difficult choice: she can pay the fine and keep the peace at home, or do what she feels is right and go to prison. In the end she goes to prison for fourteen days and the experience teaches her a great deal about herself. An interesting novel raising the issues of nuclear power and the rights of young people to stand up for their beliefs in the face of adult opposition. It is good to see a novel where the major characters are girls and women, sensitively and maturely drawn, and the central female character is a strong, decisive leader. Some of the situations, for example the confrontation with the police and the prison system, are a little bland and therefore less than convincing, and the ending is too neat. A book worth reading, however, which could be used to stimulate discussion.

RAGS AND RICHES (1988)

Marcus Crouch (review date December 1988)

SOURCE: Crouch, Marcus. *Junior Bookshelf* 52, no. 6 (December 1988): 307.

What an engaging writer Joan Lingard is. Her plots may not be very original, her characters not specially subtle, but the warmth of her personality pervades her books and makes them most persuasively readable.

Rags and Riches shows her at her most characteristic. The scene is (of course) Edinburgh, the time more or less today. Samantha and Sebastian (Sam and Seb), who tell the story in alternate chapters, live with their lovely hare-brained mother in one of the less fashionable streets of the city, opposite mother's second-hand clothes shop. Father (Torquil—the family go in for exotic names) lives elsewhere, and turns up when he wants something. When the family are broke, which is often, they turn to Granny, not 'one of those grandmothers who sits and knits in the chimney corner'. This Granny works in the supermarket and has the practical sense the family sadly lack. Various things happen: Seb falls in love out of his social and financial class, mother gets involved with a con-man, Granny succumbs, for once, to holiday madness, 'Giddy Aunt' Clementina leaves her husband and moves in with them.

This is an episodic novel, and none the worse for that. After all there are distinguished precedents, notably E. Nesbit, with whom Joan Lingard has other things in common. A thin thread of continuity holds the story together, but it is not technical story-making

that makes this writer notable. There is a soundly consistent viewpoint throughout, strengthened rather than weakened by the shared narrative. Sam and Seb quietly correct one another's versions as the action proceeds. The character-drawing stays safely on the right side of caricature. The writing is always lively, fresh and colloquial, with an occasional felicitous phrase or image. Sam, buying ice-cream for the Flowers of the Field (Clementina's daughters Daisy, Buttercup and Clover), walks home 'with the three of them clinging to me like trailing vines'. The reader comes to relish these people even if he cannot altogether believe in them. The book is above all good fun with none of the concern for 'serious' issues of Ms Lingard's recent books.

Carol Hill (review date May 1989)

SOURCE: Hill, Carol. *School Librarian* 37, no. 2 (May 1989): 75.

A book by Joan Lingard gives the reader expectations of enjoyment and, although her latest novel [*Rags and Riches*] is very different from her last one, the reader will not be disappointed.

Samantha and Sebastian, known as Sam and Seb, are brother and sister and they relate their story in alternate chapters. They live in Edinburgh with their liberated mother who runs a secondhand clothes shop in a basement across the street. Their father is a drifter and is rarely on the scene to help the family through their many crises. It is their grandmother, with her many words of wisdom, who guides the children and their mother along the difficult path of family life. There is an abundance of characters within the story and each one is worth meeting. There are the children's friends, Morag and Hari, and Granny's friend, Eta. They all have their own amusing characteristics. The children's aunt, Clementina, lands herself and her three children, collectively known as The Flowers because they are named Daisy, Buttercup and Clover, on the family thus adding to the general confusion and chaos.

Whatever the state of their own families, young people usually enjoy a story about family life and this one, with its keen sense of fun and colourful narrative, will certainly amuse and titillate. Anyone fortunate enough to be asked by a young reader, 'What shall I read?' should certainly consider handing them this first-class book.

Books for Keeps (review date September 1993)

SOURCE: *Books for Keeps* 4, no. 82 (September 1993): 19.

This is an unusual, spirited and moving story [*Rags and Riches*]. Sam and Seb's mother runs a second-hand clothes shop at the 'wrong' end of Edinburgh, whilst their feckless father flits in and out of their lives. Money's very tight and they all have their emotional problems, too: Seb falls for the upper-class, moneyed Viola; mad-cap auntie flees from her husband and descends with her unruly children; Mum and Dad tentatively try to mend their marriage; even Granny falls in—and out—of love with a dominant butcher. Eve Karpf's narration conveys the vitality of this warm, very real family.

📖 *TUG OF WAR* (1989)

Margery Fisher (review date November 1989)

SOURCE: Fisher, Margery. *Growing Point* 28, no. 4 (November 1989): 5233-234.

This is the best kind of fiction about the past, relating to broad political and national issues but establishing its own individual and absolute authenticity through dialogue that reveals character as well as explaining events and description that satisfies the reader's inner eye for place and circumstance. Joan Lingard's gift for particularisation has never been better than it is in *Tug of War,* the story of two families, neighbours in a Latvian town, who in the terrible, confused Europe of 1944 become homeless, stateless refugees. Lukas Petersons, a university professor of liberal views, is on a proscribed list in Russia and as the Soviet forces advance into Latvia he and his wife and two children set out with their neighbours for Germany, where one friend in Leipzig may be able to help them to some kind of future. During appalling journeys—by cart, on foot, in crowded trains—the people become real to us through their reactions to events over which they have no control. For small Tomas the worst moment comes when his beloved one-eyed bear Bruno is lost (and is found later by happy coincidence); old Granny Janson's continual complaints are excused because of her determination to survive; the fourteen-year-old twins Astra and Hugo are the central figures through whom four years or so of chaos in the West are brilliantly recreated. Early in their travels Hugo is separated from the rest of the group; lying hurt by the railway track, almost blind when his spectacles are torn off and trampled, he is rescued by a German signalman and becomes almost a substitute for his dead son. The story follows separately Hugo's life in Hamburg in what becomes the British Zone and the fortunes of the rest of the Petersons and the Jansons who move through Poland to Leipzig, only to find their friend's house in ruins and the family dead. The twins long to be re-united but none of the available channels of information can help to locate Hugo and when the two do meet several years later the young man has a difficult decision to make. Betrothed to the daughter of his benefactors, he wants to stay with her but is desperate also to renew the bond with his family, who are now off to a new life in Toronto, free of post-war social hostilities but bitterly regretting the loss of their homeland, swallowed up in the Soviet Union.

The open ending of the book is as sturdily realistic and personalised as its absorbing whole. Nobody could fail to be moved by the unsentimental accounts of the indignities war inflicted on these hard-working citizens—the compulsory stripping and delousing in the refugee camp (where modest Astra envies her friend Mara the partial privacy of long hair), the anxieties concealed by the parents from their children as long as possible, the sight of unburied bodies and devastated streets, the bombing of refugees on open roads. Here is an example of the strong, unassuming, selective prose that carries the tale along. Hugo has just been saved from almost certain death from exposure:

> *"Surfacing from time to time into consciousness, Hugo became aware, little by little, of his surroundings and of the people who tended him. Everything and everyone he saw was blurred, with fuzzy edges, as if ringed with light. He came to recognise first the inside of the cupboard-like place in which he lay; it was lined with planks of yellowish-brown wood and encompassed him on three sides. He stared for long spells at the wood, trying to fathom the flecks in it, trying to identify them. Were they knots? Words slipped from the edge of his mind. Mists still swirled in his head, clouding it."*

Books about the second World War proliferate. This one deals with the relatively unfamiliar fortunes of the Baltic States and is worth noting for this reason alone, but the virtues of strong story-telling, recognizable characters, emotional balance and extreme actuality make it a notable novel in its own right.

Times Educational Supplement (review date 17 November 1989)

SOURCE: *Times Educational Supplement* no. 3829 (17 November 1989): 30.

Recent news items from the Soviet Baltic republics lend a helpful topicality to Joan Lingard's story [*Tug of War*]. Readers might otherwise have had no idea where Latvia was, or any comprehension of its people's tragic situation at the end of the Second World War. Astra and Hugo are 14-year-old twins. Their family has to abandon its home as the occupying Germans fall back before the Russian advance. Thus the viewpoint is novel for western children. In this saga of incessant hardship and misery the ordinary Germans seem relatively sympathetic and Germany the safest place to make for. The Russians, represented only by an ominous growl of gunfire beyond the horizon, are the bogey. The western allies are too remote to impinge upon the situation. Only at the end do Canada and the United States figure as lands of promise, yet pose the heartrending dilemma that forms the climax of the book.

The central situation is the separation of the twins. The family is swept along in the flood of fugitives, zigzagging across a devastated landscape, for ever scrambling desperately into over-crowded trains with unpredictable destinations. In one such flurry the short-sighted Hugo has his glasses crushed underfoot. He misses the train and loses his family. Each is finally forced to assume the death of the other.

This powerful book is written with impressive empathy, understandable since the writer's husband was a displaced person from Latvia who reached Canada in 1948. Doubtless helped by his memories, she has been able to crowd this long story with vividly authentic—and agonizing—details of the hunger and cold, the horror and aching grief. Some may say, "too much, too long, intolerable". But many young readers, sensitive and imaginative but also tough, should find this a book they will never forget.

D. A. Young (review date December 1989)

SOURCE: Young, D. A. *Junior Bookshelf* 53, no. 6 (December 1989): 297.

It is 1944 in Latvia [in *Tug of War*]. The twins Astra and Hugo are preparing to leave home before the Russians return. Four years previously the Russians

had occupied their country for a year until driven out by the Germans. But now the tide had turned. The Allies and Russia were pushing the German forces back into the heartland of the Reich and the years of wandering for displaced persons started.

So the Petersens joined the refugees. Sometimes they travelled by slow-moving trains, once by sea and often on foot in the company of other stumbling, cart-pulling lost souls. Hugo and Astra are parted but meet again just as the family is about to sail for Canada. Hugo has been befriended by the kindly Schneiders for three years and has become deeply attached to their daughter Bettina. He decides to go to Canada for a year or two and then return to his sweetheart and his medical training in Hamburg.

Joan Lingard has painted a brilliant and crowded canvas of the turmoil and hardship endured by so many following five years of conflict. She brings out the tenacity with which people will cling to standards of decency and find reasons for rejoicing in the greyest of times. She has drawn upon the experiences of her husband who, himself, left Latvia in 1944 and was on the refugee trail until he and his family arrived in Canada in 1948.

It might be that her other successful novels are but curtain-raisers to the story she has always wanted to tell and in its telling a debt of honour has been repaid. Readers of all ages should be grateful for the chance to share in the heart-lifting account of human strengths in those dark times.

Horn Book Guide (review date January-June 1990)

SOURCE: *Horn Book Guide* 1, no. 2 (January-June 1990): 249.

In 1944, a Latvian family flees from the approaching Russians, but twins Hugo and Astra are separated at a crowded railroad station [in *Tug of War*]. Five years later, as the family is about to leave for Canada, a chance meeting reunites them, and Hugo must choose between staying with his fiancee and the family that saved his life or accompanying his own family. A vivid, compelling story.

Alison Hurst (review date February 1990)

SOURCE: Hurst, Alison. *School Librarian* 38, no. 1 (February 1990): 29.

There is always a compelling 'readability' about Joan Lingard's novels and *Tug of War* is a highly satisfying read. The story is based on the experiences of the author's husband's family. The Petersons are forced to leave their home in Latvia, one of the Baltic states, during the closing stages of the Second World War. They are escaping from the Russians and are aiming to reach the home of a friend in Leipzig, Germany. Their gruelling journey is convincingly described—the most agonising moment being when Hugo, the fourteen-year-old son and twin brother of Astra, gets separated from the rest of the Petersons at a Polish railway station. The fortunes of Hugo and the rest of his family are then related independently. Will they ever meet again?

Reading this book one is made acutely aware of the desperate insecurity, humiliation and suffering of refugees, as well as the sheer pointlessness and waste of war. A book to be savoured, and surely a must for every secondary school library.

Ellen Fader (review date September 1990)

SOURCE: Fader, Ellen. *Horn Book Magazine* 66, no. 5 (September 1990): 606.

Illustrated with a map. The year 1944 finds the Peterson family fleeing Latvia as the Russians approach [in *Tug of War*]. At a crowded, chaotic railroad station where they hope to get a train for Germany, Hugo is separated from his fourteen-year-old twin sister. His precious glasses are knocked from his face; as he bends to retrieve them, he receives a severe head wound and consequently boards the wrong train. Abandoned by the other passengers when he is unable to hike from the train to a refugee camp, he is discovered and nursed back to health by a signalman, Herr Schneider, and his family. Well-plotted, alternating chapters tell the story of Hugo and his family's separate lives; Hugo, believing his family has died in a bombing in Leipzig, settles into school and life with his kind adopted German family, while the Petersons barely survive in a series of refugee camps. When the twins chance to meet as the Petersons are about to embark on the final leg of their journey to Canada, Hugo is faced with the tremendously difficult choice of staying with his fiancée and the Schneiders or accompanying his newly rediscovered family. Lingard's novel—based on her husband's family's experiences as Latvian refugees in 1944—is immediate and emotionally poignant. The combination of vivid, compelling images, relentless pacing, and strongly realized characters makes this story one readers won't soon forget.

Marlene M. Kuhl (review date October 1990)

SOURCE: Kuhl, Marlene M. *Voice of Youth Advocates* 13, no. 4 (October 1990): 219.

In 1944, the Peterson family—mother, father, 14 year old twins Hugo and Astra, and eight year old Tomas—flee their native Latvia rather than live under Russian rule [in *Tug of War*]. Their destination is Germany, where they have been promised refuge by a friend. In a crowded train station, Hugo is separated from the other family members, who assume he has boarded another car. They will not be reunited for four years! What happens during those years is movingly related. The thwarted plans of asylum in Germany, the horror of refugee camps, and the pain of a family torn apart by events beyond their control are intertwined with acts of human kindness, and an undying sense of hope and determination that enables the human spirit to survive. The characters take second place to the plot's action which quickly engages the reader's interest and makes this a page turner. Excellent booktalk material.

CAN YOU FIND SAMMY THE HAMSTER? (1990)

Margery Fisher (review date July 1990)

SOURCE: Fisher, Margery. *Growing Point* 29, no. 2 (July 1990): 5378.

Ultra-simple words and soft water-colour pictures conduct a very young child through rooms pleasantly furnished with recognisable objects [in *Can You Find Sammy the Hamster?*]. As the missing animal is sought an alert viewer will see that each scene contains something that *could* be a hamster—a mouse-slipper under the bed, the end of a brown scarf dangling from a cupboard door, a brown animal sponge in the bath and so on. The small puzzles culminate in the reappearance of the hamster, where the viewer has probably already guessed it would be. An ingenious idea and a conspicuously neat and pleasing execution.

Fiona Ross (review date August 1990)

SOURCE: Ross, Fiona. *School Librarian* 38, no. 3 (August 1990): 102.

[*Can You Find Sammy the Hamster?*] has everything I look for in a children's picture book: colourful, lively illustrations; large, clear typography strategically placed; brief text; attractive endpapers; and stout binding. A lovely book with the simple storyline of search and find for use as a first reader for small children or as a stimulus for slow readers.

GLAD RAGS (1990)

Don Pemberton (review date July 1991)

SOURCE: Pemberton, Don. *Magpies* 6, no. 3 (July 1991): 32-3.

Joan Lingard is expert at mapping the nuances of tension in and between families. In this book [*Glad Rags*], a stand-alone sequel to *Rags and Riches,* she intertwines two insiders' accounts of a lively and likeable unconventional family in Edinburgh. As they tell the story in alternating chapters, Sam (short for Samantha) and her brother Sebastian share an amused tolerance for their mother Isabella and father Torquil, their indomitable granny Ina McKetterick and other members of the clan who live in an isolated croft in the Orkneys and a rundown castle in Argyll.

Little ever goes to plan in this family. The warm and zany mother Isabella scorns materialism and so makes little money from her second-hand clothes dealing; Torquil the father is a charming and unreliable layabout. It is little wonder, then, that their relationship is volatile and they make problems for their two children. Particularly, Seb and his girlfriend Viola fall out of friendship when her better-off parents suspect Seb of stealing their antique compass, and even more when Torquil's carelessness lets thieves in to rob Viola's father's safe. Then there are other problems: father's joblessness, Sam's uncertain relationship with her boyfriend Ric, the yobbos who say that Seb's friend Hari has "shit-brown" hands, granny's double pneumonia, the expense of maintaining grandfather's leaking castle.

Somehow, these difficulties are untraumatic. Sam and Seb are so sure of each other, so reliably sane and well balanced, that they control the vagaries of their world. Through them, Joan Lingard gives us a realistic Edinburgh with warmth and wit. Her light-hearted storytelling here is consummately assured.

Books for Keeps (review date November 1992)

SOURCE: *Books for Keeps* 240, no. 77 (November 1992): 25.

[*Glad Rags*] is a follow-on from *Rags and Riches* told alternately by Seb and Sam, offspring of a dizzy second-hand clothes dealer mother and an unreliable aristocratic father. Their varied, incident-filled lives take in an assortment of unusual characters—a battle-axe granny, a mad grandfather with a decaying castle and their own school mates.

Joan Lingard's skill is in making the whole thing sound not just lively but also quite plausible and in inducing the reader to want to keep turning the pages.

BETWEEN TWO WORLDS (1991)

Zena Sutherland (review date December 1991)

SOURCE: Sutherland, Zena. *Bulletin of the Center for Children's Books* 45, no. 4 (December 1991): 98.

Gr 7-9. In a sequel to *Tug of War* Lingard [in *Between Two Worlds*] brings the Petersonses, a Latvian refugee family, to Canada. Fleeing the aftermath of World War II, they have been sponsored by a Toronto family; all their plans are sadly changed when Father becomes ill and the Petersonses' hosts move to another part of the country. It is up to the young people in the family to earn money and to try to find a place to live and stay united. Lingard does as good a job of building a convincing, solid tale of adjustment and adaptability here as she did of describing the tension and courage of displaced persons in Europe. Particularly astute are the many ways in which the young people are shown to adopt new friends and new interests while remembering old bonds with affection.

Margery Fisher (review date January 1992)

SOURCE: Fisher, Margery. *Growing Point* 30, no. 5 (January 1992): 5639.

The Petersons [in *Between Two Worlds*], driven from Latvia in the war years and suffering a bleak existence as displaced persons, are encouraged when they find a sponsor offering them a home in Toronto and a university place for Lukas Petersons, a classics Professor before war ruined his life. Then disaster struck. Lukas had a heart attack at the very minute of their arrival in the hospitable city and his sponsor had to go to a post elsewhere. The years of hardship and separation seemed once more to threaten the family. Lodgings had to be found. Hugo took a job on a building site and his twin sister Astra went to a family as a babyminder, only to find herself exploited by her self-centred, hectoring employer; young Tomas battled at school with inadequate English and the half-understood taunts of his schoolfellows and out of school with deliveries for a Polish grocer. The ups and down of the young people and their parents are chronicled with sympathy but without sentiment and the city folk of 1948, with their unexpected kindnesses and hurtful prejudice, are set against the courage and enterprise of the Petersons who earn a place for themselves slowly and painfully in a society very different from that of their homeland.

Hanna Zeiger (review date January 1992)

SOURCE: Zeiger, Hanna. *Horn Book Magazine* 68, no. 1 (January 1992): 99.

(Older). The Petersons family, whose flight from Latvia in World War II was detailed in *Tug of War*, have come to Canada to start a new life [in *Between Two Worlds*]. When their father has a severe heart attack on the day they arrive, the eighteen-year-old twins, Astra and Hugo—and even young Tomas—must get laborious and menial jobs. As with other displaced people they meet, life is a struggle to keep going while setting aside a little money for a better life. The story ends on a hopeful note as the family is able to buy land on which to build their own home.

Marcus Crouch (review date February 1992)

SOURCE: Crouch, Marcus. *Junior Bookshelf* 56, no. 1 (February 1992): 32.

We first met the Petersons, flotsam and now jetsam of world war, in *Tug of War.* Now they are washed up on the shores of Canada, part of a horde of displaced persons and lucky to have found a sponsor who will accept responsibility for them in a new world. There their luck ends. First Lukas, their father, has a heart attack and is taken, not to their new home, but to hospital. Then the Frasers, their kind protectors and sponsors, confess that their own plans have changed and they have to move to a new job. There is no place for the hapless Latvians in their plans, and they must become lodgers of Mrs. Craik, who smiles but not with her eyes. The Petersons, who have survived Hitler and the camps of Europe, still find Mrs. Craik hard to bear, but they are survivers. They also work hard, and gradually pull themselves out of the abyss by their own efforts and the help of new friends. Fate still has a few tricks up its sleeves. By a stroke worthy of Thomas Hardy the convalescent Lukas, dressed in the new coat which is

the pride and joy of the family, visits the park and disturbs a skunk! It is not all gloom. Hugo finds a girl-friend and finds that he can do without her. Astra's social life opens up and she sees a distant future. Tomas makes friends in school and profits from his open nature. A sequel which must come will be happier.

Joan Lingard turns no blind eye to the difficulties of strangers in a new country. The Petersons suffer some hostility, more indifference. Post-War Canada wants to get on with life, not to be reminded of the past. Problems of language and custom—Tomas gets into trouble about St. Valentine's Day!—are almost as great as those of money and shelter. Their energy and persistence demand that we must admire the Petersons. I found, most reluctantly, that I did not care for them overmuch. They engage sympathy rather than affection. But *Between Two Worlds* is a remarkable piece of historical writing, and all details of late-40s Toronto convince. Ms Lingard keeps the pulse of her story beating insistently, its complex strands separate and each equally important. As a technical exercise in narrative it could hardly be bettered. As a novel it falls a little short—at least with some readers—through lack of involvement. These entirely admirable people should matter as much to us as they clearly do to their creator.

Verna LaBounty (review date September-October 1992)

SOURCE: LaBounty, Verna. *Book Report* 11, no. 2 (September-October 1992): 49-50.

Gr 8-12. World War II has just ended, and 18-year-old twins Astra and Hugo, their parents and younger brother Tomas arrive in Canada, refugees from war-torn Latvia [in *Between Two Worlds*]. When their father suffers a heart attack and their sponsoring family moves, the twins take responsibility for the family. At the same time, Hugo worries about a marriage commitment he made to a girl in Europe, but finally they both realize the long distance relationship will not work and they agree to set each other free. Meanwhile Astra meets a young man. By the end of the book, the family has saved enough money to buy land and plans to build a house. Sequel to *Tug of War,* this gentle story of family values can be recommended to students who enjoy *Anne Frank: the Diary of a Young Girl* and *The Upstairs Room.* It will show readers what happened to many people after the war and can provide insight into the problems of today's homeless and of refugees from Cuba, Haiti and Southeast Asia. *Recommended.*

📖 *MORAG AND THE LAMB* (1991)

Marcus Crouch (review date April 1991)

SOURCE: Crouch, Marcus. *Junior Bookshelf* 55, no. 2 (April 1991): 57-8.

Joan Lingard's pleasant picture-book [*Morag and the Lamb*] is set firmly in the real world. Russell and his dog Morag go to stay with Grandma and Grandpa in the country. It is lambing time, and boy and dog both take to heart the instruction 'You mustn't worry the sheep'. While Russell goes for a ride on the trailer Morag mopes along the dry-stone wall. Here she finds a lamb entangled in brambles. What does a good dog do? Morag enjoys a small triumph. The tiny story is told with just the right emphasis, and Patricia Casey's drawings capture the drama and the charms of the scene with equally quiet success.

Books for Keeps (review date May 1992)

SOURCE: *Books for Keeps* 66, no. 74 (May 1992): 11.

Russell and his dog Morag stay with Grandma and Grandpa at lambing time [in *Morag and the Lamb*]. Russell is puzzled why everyone says his dog must not 'worry the sheep', and when he goes off to the fields Morag is left behind. From the garden she hears bleating on the other side of the wall and soon discovers a lamb caught in a thorny bramble bush. Morag helps to rescue the lamb and the farmer explains to Russell what 'worry the sheep' actually means. Stunning illustrations and a really satisfying story make this ideal for 4-7 year-olds.

📖 *HANDS OFF OUR SCHOOL!* (1992)

R. Baines (review date February 1993)

SOURCE: Baines, R. *Junior Bookshelf* 57, no. 1 (February 1993): 22.

At the school Katy McCree attends in the Scottish Highlands the roll is down to fourteen pupils and there is a danger of closure [in *Hands Off Our School!*]. Linked with a project for the school magazine, Katy tells the story of this threat and of measures to combat it devised by the children and adults of Glen Findie.

Together the pupils of the school prepare a letter for the Director of Education, and this is followed by an improvised meeting of the whole community in the village hall. Eventually, after a coach trip to Edinburgh, an appearance on television and a visit from the Director of Education himself, the campaign to save the school succeeds.

Occasionally Joan Lingard's ten year old narrator speaks in a distinctly adult style, but the author uses her to present a current social problem simply and sympathetically. The book is enhanced by Mairi Hedderwick's deceptively unsophisticated drawings.

Margaret Campbell (review date February 1993)

SOURCE: Campbell, Margaret. *School Librarian* 41, no. 1 (February 1993): 16.

A slice of Scottish Highland life is here [*Hands Off Our School!*] recorded with verve by Katy McCree, one of the fourteen pupils at a one-teacher primary school threatened with closure. Odd sentences about the history of the school, built in 1880, are thrown in with details of the yellow plastic bucket in the corner to catch the rain when the roof leaks. Comments by the teacher writing 'Small is beautiful' on the blackboard are interspersed with the children's chat. They visit their neighbours to record a survey of the glen; the local councillor and her dog visit the school; parents attend a protest meeting; heavy snow blocks the road and Katy is nearly lost; the school wins *The Scotsman* school magazine competition. Finally a coachload from the glen travels to Edinburgh with a petition and the Director of Education in person visits the school. All this activity is tellingly illustrated, warts and all, in black and white by Mairi Hedderwick. A book to amuse all ages from five upwards.

📖 *NIGHT FIRES* (1993)

Linda Newbery (review date February 1994)

SOURCE: Newbery, Linda. *School Librarian* 42, no. 1 (February 1994): 22.

Set in an unnamed Eastern European police state, this simply told but vivid story [*Night Fires*] will give younger secondary pupils a clear idea of the pressures of life under a totalitarian regime.

Lara and Nik, inhabitants of an orphanage, leave its bleak confines for the uncertainties of a life on the run. After meeting a wounded dissident student, Oscar, they find themselves involved in plans for the revolution, delivering messages and leaflets. A particularly strong episode is where Nik, sent to find a student leader, realises that Stefan has been arrested and that the young man who befriends him is a police spy. Subsequent events—the peaceful revolution in the city square, the finding of Nik's father when the jail is opened, and the epilogue told by Lara—are a little anti-climactic by contrast.

However, this is a very readable story which brings home the hardships of curfews, separations, food shortages and constant surveillance in a world in which no one can be readily trusted. A book to widen the awareness of young readers.

John Murray (review date November 1994)

SOURCE: Murray, John. *Magpies* 9, no. 5 (November 1994): 33.

Lingard has written several novels about war and civil war and their effects on people; here [in *Night Fires*] she extends her interest in social and political themes to include Eastern Europe in the late 1980s when one after another of the seemingly indestructible regimes established in the aftermath of World War II collapsed. Lara and Nik are among the oldest children in a state-run orphanage in a central European country (Czechoslovakia?) that is taking its first fearful steps towards defying the authorities. The director of the orphanage and his assistant have already sensed their danger and run away, leaving Nik and Lara free to go to the city to find out what is happening. There they find themselves committed to helping the dissidents. They put their own lives in danger; they find friends as well as encountering that most despicable outgrowth of state terrorism, the *agent provocateur*.

The story is fast-moving and conveys something of the fear and distrust of living under a totalitarian regime, though not so well as Elizabeth Lutzeier's *The Wall* written in 1991 about the reunification of Germany. The very speed and busyness of the narrative may be the reason for that; there is little time for creation of atmosphere or characterisation beyond fairly simple levels but younger readers may, therefore, find *Night Fires* more accessible as a result.

Books for Keeps (review date January 1996)

SOURCE: *Books for Keeps* 22, no. 96 (January 1996): 12.

State brutality and corruption is rife but cannot suppress totally the spirit of the ordinary man and woman who will strive constantly for freedom [in *Night Fires*]. Nik and Lara, two orphans on the run, become involved with the underground movement in this fast, deftly plotted thriller set not a million miles away from the Eastern Block.

One of the most approachable political novels of recent years that's certain to provoke some deep discussion.

CLEVER CLIVE AND LOOPY LUCY (1993)

Books for Keeps (review date July 1994)

SOURCE: *Books for Keeps* 18, no. 87 (July 1994): 7.

This '2 books in 1' format always appeals and these two stories [*Clever Clive and Loopy Lucy*] have been very popular. Joan Lingard brings a twist of the unusual to an everyday situation. Clever Clive amazes everyone, including himself, when he can suddenly and most uncharacteristically provide an instant answer to any question he's asked. Loopy Lucy loves doing cart-wheels. One day she loops over a high wall into a new and magical garden which others see only as a piece of wasteland used to dump rubbish. These are both stories to be read and re-read, delightfully and helpfully illustrated, to be shared with children or ideal for the child who is in the early stages of solo reading.

SULKY SUZY AND JITTERY JACK (1995)

Andrew Kidd (review date March 1997)

SOURCE: Kidd, Andrew. *Books for Keeps* 244, no. 103 (March 1997): 20.

These two stories in the 'Flipper' series [*Sulky Suzy and Jittery Jack*] are ideal for younger and less able readers in terms of content and their level of difficulty. The very topical *Sulky Suzy* deals with a girl who dreams of a lottery jackpot so that the family will not have to move house and she will not have to leave her friends behind. Suzy's family never win a penny on the lottery. Will the magic pen that Suzy sends away for change their luck?

Jittery Jack is the story of a new boy at school who does not seem to be able to settle in and be accepted by his peers. Discovering a previously hidden talent for vaulting changes everything and Jack jumps up the popularity table.

Both stories have mainly three-quarter page black and white illustrations, some with additional speech bubbles. The intended reader is not, therefore, overfaced by the amount of text to read. I find the 'Flipper' format irritating (the reader has to flip the book upside down to read the second story). This gimmick works against everything young children are taught about how to turn the pages in a book from front to back.

LIZZIE'S LEAVING (1995)

Geraldine Brennan (review date 1 September 1995)

SOURCE: Brennan, Geraldine. *Times Educational Supplement* 242, no. 4131 (1 September 1995): 24.

Joan Lingard's Lizzie is looking for a better life too [in *Lizzie's Leaving*], but her grasp on reality is more feeble than La Vaughn's or Jolly's. Lizzie seeks out Mark, the father who deserted her mother before she was born. She sees Mark as an escape from boisterous family life with her mother and stepfather, and goes to live in his more sophisticated household. Mark is fantasy fodder—down to his thick dark hair and crinkly-eyed smile, straight out of a teen romance. He takes his "new" daughter to expensive restaurants and flatters her, but when it comes to meeting Lizzie's needs he cannot match the kind but ordinary newsagent who has helped to bring her up.

Lizzie's Leaving charts the erosion of Lizzie's fantasy, exposed in letters home, her sister Alice's diary and straight narrative. The cracks appear too slowly. Lizzie comes over as a shallow, naive, misguided creature, a much less sympathetic character than sharp, witty Alice, who would catch the next train home if Mark and his cold-hearted yuppie wife treated her as a free au pair, as they do Lizzie.

Alice's struggles with her shyness hold more interest than Lizzie's predictable traumas and her position at the heart of a friendly community is part of the past that Lizzie has exchanged for isolation *chez* Mark. Her passage through misery and anger is touching but the plot becomes increasingly fragile and the sitcom-style ending smacks of desperation.

Val Randall (review date September 1997)

SOURCE: Randall, Val. *Books for Keeps* 71, no. 106 (September 1997): 30.

Lingard has always reliably entertained—most notably with her Kevin and Sadie titles (the human face of Northern Ireland's troubles). This new novel [*Lizzie's Leaving*] tells the story of Lizzie's departure from what she sees as the insoluble problems of home and family (mother, stepfather and stepsiblings) to live with her real father and his family. Inevitably, she inherits a whole new set of problems.

Lizzie's journey from exhilaration to pragmatism is wholly absorbing: there is something very satisfying about unravelling a master storyteller's thread. This is a rich and rewarding book for Year 9 readers and beyond.

A SECRET PLACE (1998)

Sandra Bennett (review date spring 1999)

SOURCE: Bennett, Sandra. *School Librarian* 47, no. 1 (spring 1999): 46.

Eleven-year-old Maria hasn't seen her father Antonio for two years, since her parents separated [in *A Secret Place*]. She is amazed when he appears at her school playground one lunch-time. Events move quickly, and soon Maria and her little brother Carlos have flown to Spain with Antonio. However, the excitement Maria feels at being back in Spain with her father begins to give way to anxiety. Antonio takes the children to stay with their ancient Aunt Teresa in an isolated mountain village. The village is picturesque, with its terraces of white-walled and red-roofed buildings, but it begins to feel like a 'white prison' to Maria. The villagers seem to know everything that Maria does, and when she tries to call her mother from the one public telephone in the village, this is quickly revealed to Aunt Teresa. However, when Maria's parents are unable to reach a compromise over the custody of the children, Aunt Teresa unexpectedly helps Maria to find a solution that will please everyone.

This is a convincing portrayal of family conflict. Each character is sympathetically presented and the use of a first-person narrative makes the novel accessible and immediate. One to recommend to readers of 11 upwards.

Robert Dunbar (review date September 1999)

SOURCE: Dunbar, Robert. *Books for Keeps* 246, no. 118 (September 1999): 27.

The children described on the cover of Lingard's novel [*A Secret Place*] as being 'far from home' are six-year-old Charlie and his eleven-year-old sister

Maria. They live in Edinburgh with their Scottish mother, who for two years has been separated from their father, now a flamenco dancer in his native Spain. When one day he appears unexpectedly at the children's school and takes them away with him to his 'secret place', they—and the reader—become caught up in a story of conflicting claims, attachments and loyalties. Lingard writes a pleasantly readable story, essentially a variation on the adventure and chase genre, with the bonus of some attractive local colour in the Spanish scenes.

DARK SHADOWS (1998)

Adele Geras (review date 30 October 1998)

SOURCE: Geras, Adele. *Times Educational Supplement* 124, no. 4296 (30 October 1998): 10.

"When you move into the sun, shadows shorten," says Jess at the end of this intelligent and moving new novel [*Dark Shadows*], set in Belfast. The author is well-known for her Kevin and Sadie books, which also deal with the pressures teenagers feel, living in a divided community.

In this book, Jess, a Catholic, meets her Protestant cousin Laurie for the first time. The two branches of the family haven't spoken since Jess's father married a Catholic, Maeve O'Shea. A shared interest in music brings the girls together, and with Neal, Jess's cousin, they decide to enter a song-writing competition.

This is the simple framework Joan Lingard uses to tell a more complicated story which involves lies, bombing, kneecapping, joy-riding, bullying, playing truant and many combinations of discord, love and friendship.

The end is full of hope, with the families going together to listen to their children's music, but it comes after a near-tragedy.

Lingard grew up in Belfast and you can hear the accent in the dialogue. You also learn words like "mitching" for playing truant. For someone with such an economical, plain style, however, the author is somewhat over-generous with her exclamation marks, but this is nit-picking.

Robert Dunbar (review date January 1999)

SOURCE: Dunbar, Robert. *Books for Keeps* 124, no. 114 (January 1999): 27.

Like much of the young adult fiction dealing with the Ulster 'troubles' this novel [*Dark Shadows*] chooses

to focus on a representative from each side of the conflict and, through a series of events, to take them closer to mutual understanding. The novelty here is that the protagonists are girl cousins, long separated by a family feud but now brought together by a chance meeting and a shared involvement in music. Lingard brings her usual assured and sympathetic touch to the presentation of her heroines' experiences and is particularly good in contrasting the entrenched stubbornness of an older generation with the more open tolerance of a younger one. She is, however, wise enough to avoid the euphoria of easy, or imminent, total reconciliation, a stance which—sadly—gives her novel a pleasing credibility.

TOM AND THE TREEHOUSE (1998)

Karen Yeomans (review date summer 1999)

SOURCE: Yeomans, Karen. *School Librarian* 47, no. 2 (summer 1999): 89.

Tom is adopted and has always considered himself special [in *Tom and the Treehouse*], as his parents had chosen him above anyone else. However, after talking to his friend Sam he begins to have doubts. His 'unreal mother' tries to console him, talking to him about his adoption and how much they love him. Then, after his 8th birthday, his parents tell him that they are going to have a baby. Preparations for the new arrival begin to take over the household and Tom decides to build a treehouse. When the baby is born Tom feels very mixed-up and retreats to his treehouse more and more. Then something happens and he saves his sister's life and suddenly comes to realise how much his mother and father really do love him. This touching story explores sensitively the feelings of jealousy and isolation that a young child in this situation might feel. The short chapters, interspersed with delicate line drawings, make it an ideal book for young readers aged 7 to 9 making the transition from picture books to story books.

THE EGG THIEVES (1999)

Michael Thorn (review date 26 November 1999)

SOURCE: Thorn, Michael. "Feeding the Reading Fever." *Times Educational Supplement Primary* 14, no. 4352 (26 November 1999): 35.

The Egg Thieves by Joan Lingard has a brilliantly cinematic and action-packed opening, as Lecky Grant tries recklessly to intercept a gang of osprey egg thieves in their getaway car. Schoolfriend Nora McPhee, whose father runs the village post office, has an idea who the suspect is. A superb adventure story for years 2 to 4 with illustrations by Paul Howard.

NATASHA'S WILL (2000)

Tricia Adams (review date spring 2001)

SOURCE: Adams, Tricia. *School Librarian* 49, no. 1 (spring 2001): 47.

The McKinnon family live in a large house in Scotland running a bed and breakfast guest house after the death of their aged Russian benefactor, Natasha [in *Natasha's Will*]. Natasha's only living relative appears to claim his inheritance—the McKinnon's home, for though the family had been promised the house, no will has been found. The heir knocks down Sonia McKinnon with his car as he leaves the house and she is left in a coma. During her time in hospital we watch as the heir moves closer to legally claiming his inheritance, and we see Natasha's story unfold in Sonia's dreams as we are transported to Russia during the 1917 Revolution. The path to find the will is ingeniously hidden and we rush to read through the book and try to solve the clues before Sonia comes home and must learn she is to lose her home. A thoroughly gripping read which will appeal to good readers from year 6 upwards.

FURTHER READING

Criticism

Rolston, Bill. "Escaping from Belfast: Class, Ideology, and Literature in Northern Ireland." *Race and Class* 20, no. 1 (summer 1978): 41-62.
      Discusses *The Twelfth Day of July*.

Alvin Schwartz
1927-1992

American author of books for adults and children.

For more information about Schwartz and his works, see *Children's Literature Review,* Volume 3.

INTRODUCTION

Best known for his work in American folklore and humor, Alvin Schwartz has published more than fifty books for children. Many of his titles compile tall tales, tongue-twisters, wordplay, riddles, and American and British folklore. Also a master of the grotesque, Schwartz has delighted children with his frightening short stories, most popularly the Scary Stories series.

BIOGRAPHICAL INFORMATION

Schwartz was born April 25, 1927, in Brooklyn, New York, the son of Harry Schwartz, a taxi driver, and Gussie (Younger) Schwartz. He attended City College (now of the City University of New York) from 1944-45 and served in the U.S. Navy from 1945-46. He earned his M.S. in journalism from Northwestern in 1951 and worked as a newspaper reporter and professional writer during the 1950s. He married Barbara Carmer, a learning disabilities specialist, on August 7, 1954, and in the 1960s became a freelance writer. He was a professor of English at Rutgers University from 1962-1978 and began his career as an author in 1963. Schwartz, whose works are extensively researched, has said that one of his guiding principles for writing is to approach his subject matter with a sense of humor and "learn everything I can about the genre."

Schwartz died March 14, 1992, in Princeton, New Jersey.

MAJOR WORKS

Illustrating Schwartz's love of America's linguistic past, *Chin Music* (1979) is an extensively documented compilation of folk terminology used be-

tween 1815 and 1950. Antiquated terms like "Knowledge box" (school) and "killcow" (bully) appear side-by-side with more outrageous choices like "discumgalligumfricated" (surprised). *School Library Journal* 's Daisy Kouzen called the book a "reservoir of American life" but cautioned that its references to rural life might make it "alien to metropolitan youth. Perhaps a less academic and more thoughtful approach might have helped bridge the gap." *Flapdoodle* (1980) is another attempt by Schwartz to retain continuity with America's folk past. One *Kirkus Reviews* contributor said of the book's whimsical and often nonsensical assortment of visual jokes, tricks, silly rhymes and spoonerisms, "it swarms with kid-tested absurdity that keeps them moving." Schwartz's books are highly conducive to reading aloud. A collection of forty-six delightfully challenging phrases, *Busy Buzzing Bumblebees and Other Tongue Twisters* (1982) challenges readers of any age to rapidly recite such tricky phrases as "Pete's pop shops for chops in chop shops." *And the Green Grass Grew All Around* (1992) compiles rhymes, riddles, silly and serious poems, and nonsense. Schwartz's absurd and pun-filled story collections *There is a Carrot in My Ear* (1982) and *All of Our Noses are Here* (1985) build on his explanation that "a noodle is a silly person" to present ridiculous events that run the gambit from Mr. Brow's run-in with his underwear to Grandpa's attempt to hatch a baby horse.

Schwartz puts the art of predicting the future into appealing terms for children in *Telling Fortunes* (1987), a well-documented volume that explains how objects and actions like crystal balls, tea leaves, omens, and palm reading fit into the process. The author makes history and legend his purview in *Gold and Silver, Silver and Gold* (1988), whose tales of hidden riches include stories about El Dorado and Captain Kidd. Half of the accounts in Schwartz's original collection are documented fact, while the rest rely on folklore and fancy. Written, it would seem, with Halloween parties and campfire gatherings in mind, the Scary Stories books feature humor and spookiness as well as extensive bibliographies and source lists for curious literature students. Ghoulish tales from British legend and folktales from the American south come together in *Ghosts! Ghostly Tales From Folklore* (1991). *Horn Book*'s Maeve Visser Knoth noted that Schwartz's choice of stories reflects his gift for recognizing what will motivate children to learn to read," and a *Booklist* reviewer commended Schwartz for recording the stories "just as children might tell them instead of rewriting them into literary tales."

CRITICAL RECEPTION

Reviewers generally regard Schwartz's compilations of riddles, tall tales, scary stories and wordplay as a treasure-trove of American and British language and heritage. Critics tend to remark on his gift for delivering entertaining content in a carefully documented format. Sylvia Vardell of *Language Arts* wrote that Schwartz "has done for folklore for children in the United States what the Grimm brothers did in Germany, Perrault did in France, and Joseph Jacobs did in England."

AWARDS

Schwartz received New Jersey Institute of Technology awards in 1966, for *The Night Workers*, 1968, for *The Rainy Day Book*, 1969, for *University; The Students, Faculty, and Campus Life at One University*, 1972, for *A Twister of Twists, A Tangler of Tongues*, 1977, for *Kickle Snifters and Other Fearsome Critters Collected from American Folklore*, 1980, for *When I Grew Up Long Ago: Family Living, Going to School, Games and Parties, Cures and Deaths, a Comet, a War, Falling in Love, and Other Things I Remember; Older People Talk about the Days When They Were Young*, 1981, for *Chin Music: Tall Talk and Other Talk*, and 1987, for *Ten Copycats in a Boat and Other Riddles and Tales of Trickery from the Land of Spoof*. He was placed among the American Library Association notable book citations in 1967, for *Museum: The Story of America's Treasure Houses*, 1982, for *The Cat's Elbow and Other Secret Languages*, 1983, for *Unriddling: All Sorts of Riddles to Puzzle Your Guessery*, and 1984, for *In a Dark, Dark Room and Other Scary Stories*. He was named to the *New York Times* Outstanding Book citations in 1972, for *A Twister of Twists, A Tangler of Tongues*, and in 1973, for *Tomfoolery: Trickery and Foolery with Words*. He recieved a National Council of Teachers of English citation in 1972, for *A Twister of Twists, a Tangler of Tongues*, and in 1975, for *Whoppers: Tall Tales and Other Lies Collected from American Folklore*. In 1972 and 1973, he was awarded the American Library Association and National Endowment for the Humanities bicentennial book for *The Unions: What they Are, How They Came to Be, How They Affect Each of Us*, and *Central City/Spread City: The Metropolitan Regions Where More and More of Us Spend Our Lives*, respectively. Schwartz was given "Notable Children's Trade Book in the Field of Social Studies" citations, National Council for the Social Studies and the Children's Book Council in 1973, for *Central City/Spread City*, 1974, for *Cross your Fingers, Spit in Your Hat: Superstitions and Other Beliefs*, 1975, for *Whoppers*, 1979, for *Chin Music*, and 1980, for *Flapdoodle: Pure Nonsense from American Folklore*. He received a "Book of the Year" citation from the Child Study Association of America, in 1973, for *Witcracks: Jokes and Jests from American Folklore*, 1974, for *Central City/Spread City and Cross Your Fingers, Spit in Your Hat*, 1975, for *Whoppers*, and 1979, for *Tales of Trickery from the Land of Spoof, There is a Carrot in My Ear and Other Noodle Tales, In a Dark, Dark, Room*, and *Ten Copycats in a Boat and Other Riddles*. He also received "Children's Choice" citations from the International Reading Association and Children's Book Council, 1975, for *Cross Your Fingers, Spit in Your Hat*, 1976, for *Whoppers*, 1977, for *Kickle Snifters and Other Fearsome Critters*, and 1981, for *Ten Copycats in a Boat and Other Riddles. Kickle Snif-*

ters and Other Fearsome Critters was named one of *School Library Journal* 's Best Books of the Year in 1976; *Witcracks* was chosen one of New York Public Library's Books for the Teen Age in 1980, and *Cross Your Fingers, Spit in Your Hat,* in 1980, 1981, and 1982. *In a Dark, Dark Room and Other Scary Stories* was selected as a Notable Children's Book by the Association for Library Services to Children in 1984, and Ohio Buckeye Children's Book Award, Washington Library Media Association, Virginia Children's Book Award, New Jersey Library Association, all in 1986. Also in 1986, Schwartz received both the Ohio Buckeye Children's Book Award from the State Library of Ohio; and the Colorado Children's Book Award for *Scary Stories to Tell in the Dark;* and the Arizona Young Readers Award from Arizona State University, in 1987, for the same title. In addition to these awards, Schwartz was honored for his body of work by Rutgers University School of Communications, Information and Library Studies in 1986.

More Scary Stories to Tell in the Dark [reteller] (juvenilia) 1984

All of Our Noses are Here and Other Noodle Tales (children's book) 1985

Tales of Trickery from the Land of Spoof [reteller] (juvenilia) 1985

Telling Fortunes: Love Magic, Dream Signs and Other Ways to Learn the Future [reteller] (juvenilia) 1987

Gold and Silver, Silver and Gold: Tales of Hidden Treasure (juvenilia) 1988

I Saw You in the Bathtub and Other Folk Rhymes (children's book) 1989

Ghosts!: Ghostly Tales from Folklore (children's book) 1991

Scary Stories, No. 3: More Tales to Chill Your Bones [reteller] (juvenilia) 1991

And the Green Grass Grew All Around: Folk Poetry From Everyone (juvenilia) 1992

Stories to Tell a Cat (juvenilia) 1992

*

PRINCIPAL WORKS

Trickery and Foolery with Words (children's book) 1973

Stores [editor and compiler] (children's book) 1977

When I Grew Up Long Ago: Family Living, Going to School, Games and Parties, Cures and Deaths, a Comet, a War, Falling in Love, and Other Things I Remember: Older People Talk About the Days When They Were Young [compiler] (young adult) 1978

Chin Music: Tall Talk and Other Talk (juvenilia) 1979

Flapdoodle: Pure Nonsense from American Folklore [compiler] (juvenilia) 1980

Ten Copycats in a Boat and Other Riddles [reteller] (children's book) 1980

Scary Stories to Tell in the Dark [compiler] (juvenilia) 1981

Busy Buzzing Bumblebees and Other Tongue Twisters (children's book) 1982

The Cat's Elbow and Other Secret Languages (juvenilia) 1982

There is a Carrot in My Ear and Other Noodle Tales [compiler] (children's book) 1982

Unriddling: All Sorts of Riddles to Puzzle Your Guessery [reteller] (juvenilia) 1983

Fat Man in a Fur Coat and Other Bear Stories [compiler] (children's book) 1984 (Reteller)

In a Dark, Dark Room and Other Scary Stories (juvenilia) 1984

AUTHOR COMMENTARY

Alvin Schwartz and Sylvia Vardell (interview date April 1987)

SOURCE: Schwartz, Alvin, and Sylvia M. Vardell. "Profile: Alvin Schwartz." *Language Arts* 64, no. 4 (April 1987): 426-32.

[In the following interview, Vardell explores Schwartz's writing styles.]

Who has done for folklore for children in the United States what the Grimm brothers did in Germany, Perrault did in France, and Joseph Jacobs did in England? Alvin Schwartz, that's who! Schwartz, himself, would call this comparison a "whopper," "gally flopper," or a "tall tale," but many critics, teachers, and readers of all ages are finding his collections of tongue twisters, jokes, riddles, rhymes, scary stories, tall tales, wordplay, conundrums, noodle tales, puns, superstitions, secret languages, nonsense, memoirs, wisecracks, and outright lies rich and delightful sources of language and literature. His work is unique and distinctive in the field of children's literature, in the breadth of types and topics covered, as well as in the variety of purposes and audiences which might be appropriate. Each book is thoroughly and meticulously researched, with background notes and sources cited and complete bibliographies included. Together, these collections represent an impressive gathering of folklore for children which Alvin Schwartz characterizes as "a living tradition . . . the experience of the human race . . . something remarkable and continuous" (Schwartz 1977).

Schwartz has been recognized by School Library Journal, the American Library Association, the National Endowment for the Humanities, the National Council of Teachers of English, and the National Council for the Social Studies. In the *New York Times Book Review,* William Cole claimed Schwartz "elevated foolishness to a form of art." *Horn Book* (February 1984) said, "If the current generation grows up with a knowledge of traditional humor, it may well be because of Alvin Schwartz's many volumes of humorous American folklore." His work has been adapted to audio cassette form by Caedmon and Listening Library and supplemented with teacher's guides by Lippincott Publishing Company.

This New York native, born April 25, 1927, has been writing for children since 1966, (with *The Night Workers*), and collecting folklore since the very successful *Tongue Twisters* appeared in 1972. His background also includes degrees from Colby College and Northwestern University, extensive experience as a journalist and editor, and service in the U.S. Navy in World War II. He is the son of a taxi driver, married to an educator, and the father of four grown children.

Schwartz's extensive interviewing and rigorous research has culminated in over three dozen works. His collections of folklore are wonderful teaching tools; as a source of oral-based literature, they are suitable for children of all ages. In the following interview, which took place at the NCTE convention in Philadelphia (November 1985), Schwartz discusses openly his approach to writing and research, his own evolution as an author, and his views on humor, children, and works in progress.

[Vardell]: Can you briefly describe the process that you go through in a typical book or if you have several projects going on at one time?

[Schwartz]: I overlap my work—sometimes I'm working on three things at once, and I do that for practical reasons. One of the reasons is that I might "block" or simply become very bored with what I am doing if I work with it too intensively. Then I will move to something else, and in the process, my mind clears when it comes to the first project.

Basically, what I do with every book, is learn everything I can about the genre. This will involve a lot of reading and scholarly books and journals and sometimes discussions and scholarly folklorists. I do a lot of my work at Firestone Library at Princeton University. I live about a half mile from there, and this is one of the reasons we live in Princeton. It's really a fine library. In the process of accumulating everything on a subject, I begin setting aside things that I particularly like. What's interesting is that eventually patterns emerge. What I'm looking for is not only what I like, but things that typify the genre. So there is a range of material and there always will be. In working with "scary story" material, one finds five or six or seven typologies. I was not aware of this with *Scary Stories* until I began searching the material and putting it together. Sometimes I will go so far as to study the structure of an item to see how it works, because this is important in making selections and it's also interesting to people to understand this, I think.

Then having done the research, I begin putting the book together. If there is writing involved, then that comes next. Generally, one of the short books, an "I Can Read" book, takes me six months to do, about half the time in research and half the time in writing. The writing is very important to me. Everything I write is read aloud three or four times in the bathroom because the acoustics are so good. I'm listening to the way the sounds link up and work together, so I will lock myself in the bathroom and read the book aloud and put big red circles around those things that are not working in terms of sounds. Since a lot of this material is going to be *told,* the sounds are important. But, what I'm also after here, when I'm dealing with tales, are stripped down tales—right down to the essentials, because traditionally, storytellers will take such a tale and embellish it themselves. I want them to be able to do this. Now I've discovered that professional storytellers are using my stuff. And librarians use it in this way, I hope. They should be. After all, every time you sing a folksong, it changes. That's essentially what I do.

The older books take a long time. They generally take a year or more. A book I did called *Fat Man in a Fur Coat and Other Bear Stories* was an experiment. I began, for the first time, using mixed media. I was using folktales and some poetry, including an Abraham Lincoln poem. I used some journalism—I developed the story on the air force research using bears. There is some historical material in the book and there's hyperbole and so on. The idea was to use all of these media to reflect the nature and texture of the varied relationships, fanciful and otherwise, that we have with bears.

Sort of a bear anthology?

More of a social history, I thought. That sounds grandiose, but that was what I had in the back of my mind.

Sometimes it's all very easy. When I did **The Cat's Elbow and Other Secret Languages,** I was brash enough to sign a contract without really looking to see what there was. I assumed, well, there just had to be stuff, and I could just find it. I became quite nervous after three months because I was finding very little. And then one day I was on C Floor of Firestone Library, staring at a very brief reference to secret languages in the *New York Folklore Journal* which referred me to a science magazine from 1890, which referred me to a defunct German folklore publication, which was published in the 1890s! The editor had an interest in secret languages, and he had made periodic requests of his readers for secret languages they knew. There was a trove of material there. I found all that in one morning! So I hired some graduate students who translated this stuff from the Old Norse and Swahili and Chinese and so forth. I think there are nine or ten of these secret languages which ended up in the book, including the title "The Cat's Elbow." I discovered on an airplane ride what it actually meant. It's from the German. I was riding out to Sacramento, and the man sitting next to me taught German literature at Wake Forest University. He said, "What are you working on?" And I told him. He said, "You know what that means? The 'cat's elbow' means the funny bone." The Germans refer to the funny bone as "the cat's elbow." So when I got off the plane I called my editor in New York. They were putting the book together, and we worked it into the text.

Of course, everyone always wants to know what got you interested in folklore, particularly in writing and collecting?

So far as the writing is concerned, there is a practical matter here as well as a matter of interest. When I began writing kids' books, they were concerned basically with the kinds of things that fascinated me as a journalist. This was in the 1960s and I initially was concerned with social issues and American institutions and things of that sort. I did books ranging from how public opinion functioned and formed to a book on the labor movement and how it functioned.

The market for them was really supported by the funding from the Elementary and Secondary Education Act in 1965. When that funding began to die in the early 1970s, I realized that this was not a practical avenue. I liked to do these books, but I was not going to support myself and have the freedom that I had gained, if I continued to write them, at least as many.

Well, I've always been interested in wordplay. I decided I was going to pursue this. I did a book of tongue twisters and in the process of collecting this material (being a journalist, I naturally decided to find some expert resources), I determined who the President of the American Folklore Society was and I called him up. He happened to be in the folklore department at the University of Pennsylvania, actually, and I've used that department ever since as a resource. He has followed my work and been very helpful. Many folklorists across the country have also been cooperative. That's what happened. The first book was a national best-seller. My feeling was, my goodness, if this is the response, I certainly must pursue this! And that's what happened.

I think there have been, thus far, including the "I Can Read" material, probably nineteen or twenty collections. Although they deal with a range of subjects, basically there are two or three kinds of books involved One is a kind of distillation of all the material associated with a particular genre—riddles, jests, poetry—which provides, basically, a sense of the genre, what the genre is. Second, when I'm dealing with tales, often I try for a synthesis of the variants of basic motifs. In one instance, I might stack twenty or thirty variants of a tale that I like and create my own version. In other cases where there are motifs, but there really aren't any decent versions, I will construct my own, using the traditional construct.

What kinds of criteria do you keep in mind when you put those things together and choose the best for children? Is there anything specific that guides you?

No, no, no—just gut, really—all those books contain things that I like, and I think I have fairly good taste. I don't know why, but what I like kids apparently respond to also. In the early days—the **Tomfoolery** material and the material in **Witcracks** and so on, and belief material such as **Cross Your Fingers**—I would try the stuff on my kids or I'd ask them questions about how they used riddling or trickery. The one criterion that I do use now for the material for younger children is asking myself "Do they know enough—have they had enough experience to understand this, and what kind of an effect will it have on them?" So, I do do that. But basically again, it's a question of whether I like it or not.

That's pretty basic. You mentioned the "I Can Read" books. How did you get involved in those?

That was my agent's idea, actually. And it was a good idea. There's a very large market there, and I've discovered something which is more important than that in many ways, and that is—it's a wonderful audience. I just love working with the younger children. They are very responsive. I had a lovely experience in Tulsa of doing a story and having them ask me to do it *all* over again *right away*. So that was very nice. What I am trying to do is essentially deal with all of the folklore genres all over again, on a level they can enjoy.

What's next? What kinds of projects are you working on now?

Well, I'm working on several things actually. I'm finishing up a second "I Can Read" book of scary material called **Ghosts!** which is very, very interesting material. I'm finishing a book of treasure tales, which are really an interesting form in American literature.

What is a treasure tale?

Treasure tales recount the experiences of people who are looking for treasure that has been hidden in some way. But most treasure tales—in at least American literature—follow a particular structure, and the treasure is not often found. So the emphasis is on the excitement of the hunt rather than on the actual recovery of a treasure. Anyway, this stuff is really interesting. I'm also doing an anthology of folk poetry.

Any particular kind of poetry?

Varieties of things. I'm going to follow the kind of patterning I did with **Unriddling,** which was to present varieties of the riddle. And there is a lot of intriguing material out there I am having fun with.

As you are researching, is that how ideas are generated? One thing sort of connects with another?

Sometimes that way. Sometimes—in reading something—it strikes me that an idea might be possible. I write myself a note and drop it in a little box on my work table, and then maybe once a month I empty the box and I look to see what I've got. Most of it I

throw away. If something seems possible, I begin collecting material. I have folders on everything that vaguely interests me.

Somethings may dead end and others may prove productive?

Oh, yeah. I have an interest in horses, for example. And I have a son who is a newly minted Ph.D., a political scientist. He was doing a lecture on the role of the horse in rulership of various kinds and so I was pleased that he turned to me to see what I had.

There's a lot of humor in a lot of the books. Is that on purpose, or is that part of folklore?

In part, that's me. Oh, of course, a lot of the stuff is very funny, and when dealing with hyperbole we are dealing with essentially an American form. If you look in the introduction to **Whoppers,** there is an interesting explanation of our interest in this form and how it really emerged. It exists throughout the world, but it emerged in a peculiarly American form, I think, during the frontier days. When people were confronted with so much, they simply had to make themselves bigger and stronger through their tales, to deal with it. But, the humor I use does, I think, reflect me. I'm not very—what's the word I'm looking for—I'm not socially forthcoming in many ways, but I do love things that are funny. So I have a great time when I'm dealing with something that's funny—much of this is ironic material.

Do you find that kids pick up on this? Is that a favorite aspect of theirs also?

Yep, yep, yep. Although, one of the things I've been doing is using material that once was regarded as material for adults, and I've discovered that children have gotten so sophisticated that it works. And the material itself is acceptable, whereas, maybe twenty or thirty years ago, it wouldn't have been. If you asked me for an example, I couldn't give you one. It's just a general impression I have of what I've been doing and what's been happening.

Do you have any advice for teachers along this line? About adults working with kids?

Well, in terms of working with the kinds of material that I use, I would certainly suggest that they look to *themselves* as a resource. They know a lot of folklore, as much as anybody else, if they stop and think about it. And they should go back to the generation that precedes them, their relatives and older friends.

The kids, after all, are also authors of this stuff, and that's really something when you think about it. There's something remarkable about all these people who don't see themselves as especially talented as having created all this wonderful material. This, to me, is very exciting. I think it can be reinforcing for kids who are having problems—problems with self-confidence—to understand that folklore is something that unknown ordinary people have created as expressions of some of their innermost feelings. It's really very important. They need to know this.

Reference

Schwartz, A. "Children, Humor and Folklore." *Horn Book Magazine.* (June 1977): 281-287 and (August 1977): 471-476.

Alan Schwartz and Leonard S. Marcus (interview date June 1988)

SOURCE: Schwartz, Alan, and Leonard S. Marcus. "Night Visions: Conversations with Alvin Schwartz and Judith Gorog." *The Lion and the Unicorn* 12, no. 1 (June 1988): 44-62.

[*In the following interview, Marcus probes into Schwartz's scary story genre.*]

"Scary stories" is the informal designation generally applied to a range of children's fiction with sources as diverse as supernatural and surrealist fantasy, black humor, and the cautionary tale. Among the current American writers who have contributed significantly to the genre is Alvin Schwartz.

Alvin Schwartz is the author or adapter of a long shelfful of books for young readers, including four folk tale collections in the "scary" vein: *Scary Stories to Tell in the Dark, More Scary Stories to Tell in the Dark: Collected and Retold from Folklore, In a Dark, Dark Room,* and the forthcoming *Ghosts!* A former reporter, Schwartz brings to his work a journalist's respect for clear, crisp prose and solid background research, and a keen sense of his audience.

Schwartz lives in Princeton, New Jersey, and the following interview is based on a conversation recorded in his home on January 13, 1988:

INTERVIEW WITH ALVIN SCHWARTZ

[*Marcus*]: *How did you start writing books for children?*

[Schwartz]: I was about 36 or 37 years old when I began. I had a background in journalism, had worked as a newspaper reporter for quite a few years and

then left, as my family enlarged, and went into public relations. I moved to upstate New York, had three jobs in rapid succession, hated them all, then came down here to Princeton, where I went to work for a research corporation. I couldn't stand that, either. So one day, I said, look why don't I do this half time and do everything else I want to do in the other time? And I did that for two more years. In that period I had written a few adult books, which were essentially guide books for parents. Along the way I had acquired an agent. I was very anxious to resume what I had been doing in journalism, and in the late sixties there was an opportunity to produce children's non-fiction books for the library market on all sorts of subjects that fascinated me. I did six books for Dutton. The first, called *The Night Workers,* was a photographic essay. A photographer here in town did the pictures. I did a book on public opinion, how it forms and functions, and then began a number of other books on American institutions—one on labor unions, one on museums, one on city planning, another on politics. I was really having a good time until the Federal funding for this type of library book began to run out. I have always had a good sense of humor and an interest in word play. So my editor at Dutton, Dorothy Briley, who had meanwhile left and gone to Lippincott, and my agent and I all talked about it and I said I would like to do a book of tongue-twisters and maybe some other things that would be folkloric. Dorothy said go ahead, and, being a journalist, the first thing I did in that connection was to determine who was the president of the American Folklore Society. It turned out to be Kenny Goldstein, who teaches at the University of Pennsylvania. He is a very generous man and to this day he is quite helpful. I use his personal library and he gives me all kinds of advice. I went down to the Library of Congress and began working there too. One thing led to another and *Witcracks* became a national best-seller. To this day it sells very well. We brought out a second volume, which also did well. We had a wonderful contract with Lippincott. They had to put ten percent of everything that came in into promotion. So these books were being advertised for the adult audience. There were commercials on the New York radio stations. They were given a lot of attention. Authors crave that! So then I decided that this was very nice. So I would continue to do this. I liked the freedom. Being a journalist, I began to learn a lot about folklore.

In the early 1980s, my agent suggested that we begin bringing some of the material down for younger children. Since Harper had acquired Lippincott, I had become a Harper author. So the idea was to try some books for Harper's "I Can Read" series.

By then, you had already published the first "Scary Stories" collection?

That's right. That came out in 1981 under the Lippincott imprint, though it was really published by Harper. This was right after the merger.

Not long ago, I heard a panel discussion sponsored by the Authors Guild in which a number of children's librarians and booksellers all said that the genre for which they get the most requests is "scary stories." I was surprised and struck by that. Why do you think it is?

I think the essential reason is that stories of this kind enable people to explore the outer edges of their experience. Death, the unknown, strangeness, things that are not explainable and cannot be explained. You have to provide your own explanation. Traditionally, stories have served this function.

But there's more to it than that because you then must ask yourself about horror tales, for example—particularly the ones that are so popular in dormitories where freshmen women live. These are basically cautionary tales. The "babysitter legend," for example, in which a babysitter is sitting there and somebody calls her on the telephone repeatedly and in some versions these people are actually murdered. All of these stories, and there are scads of them, are really saying: "Watch out. The world's a dangerous place. You are going out on your own soon. Be careful." One of the most popular stories in the two "Scary Stories" books is a tale that I call "High Beams" in which a girl goes to a basketball game at night by herself. She lives out in the country and drives back alone and there is a car following her and periodically the other driver will turn up his beams. She can't understand what is going on, and she becomes progressively more frightened. As it turns out, there was somebody sitting in the back seat. He had slipped in when she left and each time he rose up to assault her the guy in the car in back of her turned on his high beams. It's a story told all over.

So, she's afraid of the wrong person.

Exactly. That's where the story ends. Again, this cautionary material. "Watch out." It appears in a dozen different versions. There is the whole business of this being fun, like visiting a strange country where strange things happen but nothing's going to happen . . .

. . . because it's just a story.

It's just a story. People like that. There's no danger. It's what the English call "having a gentle or a good fright." It's like having a good cry. This is what Hitchcock says and I think he's right.

Psychologists say that there are other factors at work also. There is the business of a young child having a great many anxieties that are rather nebulous, and there is a need to have something concrete to hang them on so that they can be more easily mastered. Scary stories function in that way too.

What would you say is the age range of your "I Can Read" book **In a Dark, Dark Room***?*

The publisher says four to eight. That's on the low side. I would guess six to 10 or 11. One of the most popular stories in the book is the one about the woman whose head falls off when the ribbon she wears around her neck is taken off. Some kids think the story is very funny, and so do I. Others think it's scary. I spoke in an elementary school once and the entire fifth grade walked in with green ribbons around their necks, which pleased me.

Isn't it odd how one person's joke can be another person's nightmare?

Yes, it's because the context is different from one person to the next. I find that children, for example, are more apt to find the ribbon story funny than parents are. Parents are very protective.

What are they afraid of?

I am not certain. Of course, it is a very scary thing to think that your head might fall off! And we do get letters. I don't see most of them, fortunately. My editors deal with them. Every letter is answered and the point is made that this is traditional material and that, in addition, it has developed a lot of interest in reading.

Children think a good deal about their bodies and how they are changing. To have your head fall off is a very dramatic, exaggerated version of what a child may actually fear.

This may be further fueled, if that is the case, by television experiences. I read that by the time a kid is 16 he or she has seen 18,000 television murders. That's a lot of murders. I've read that, no matter what we write, life itself is more horrible and fiction cannot match it. I believe that.

Have you ever found that when you tell a story to kids they are more frightened by it than you thought they would be?

No. Not at all. Usually it's the other way. The children in my audiences usually already know the stories. They ask for their favorites. They regard the material in part as game material—the "jump stories" or "startle stories," for example, in which someone in the story is made to jump with fright, and also the ones with the awful ending or the nonendings that permit you to use your own imagination as to what might happen. Most of them love these things. The younger kids particularly like them because the stories give them a feeling of being older and more grown up. It is new material for them.

Perhaps some children like the stories expressly because they know their parents would disapprove of them.

There have been efforts to ban these books now and then. I wasn't surprised.

Where?

The wonderful story involves Colorado. One day there were two parallel articles in one of the Denver papers. One piece, which appeared on the front page, announced that **In a Dark, Dark Room** had won the Colorado Children's Book Award which is a prize voted on by the children themselves. Next to it was a story about a suit that parents in Jefferson County, Colorado, which is the largest suburban Denver county, were bringing to have the book removed from the library.

On what grounds?

On the grounds that it was inappropriate material.

What sort of objection was being raised?

I'm told that a Christian fundamentalist group was responsible for it. I am pleased to have that kind of attention. It was ironic and pleasing that, at the same time, their ideas were rejected by the children.

Mark Twain was delighted when Huckleberry Finn was banned in Boston. He said it would be good for 20,000 in sales.

Oh, yes. And the kids were thinking: "What's all the fuss about?"

What criteria of appropriateness, if any, do you consider valid in working with scary stories for children? What, more specifically, is the process of adjusting, or, as you say, of "bringing down," such material for younger readers?

I think that the one guiding criterion involves the possibility that younger kids might confuse fantasy with reality, that they won't be able to step back from it and say: "This is really a story," or "This is really happening." But I have also realized that I cannot do a book of this kind if I keep using that as a screen. So it becomes a question of intuitively deciding what I would like my seven-year-old to read. I have discovered with my work that I think pretty much the way kids reading the books do. So I do it intuitively.

Clearly, these books are made books in that, in the "I Can Read" ones, for example, I'm taking six stories or poems that have to work together and I have to carefully select the elements so that they relate to each other and provide some forward movement, variety, and counterpoint. So, there's an artistic involvement. We wanted some funny stuff and some scarier material. We were very very lucky to have Dirk Zimmer to illustrate **In a Dark, Dark Room** because Zimmer combines both these qualities in his work.

Let me ask you specifically about violence.

I try to avoid violence, even in the books for older children.

A good deal of violence is implied in many of the stories.

Yes, but it is not explicit. I'm talking about gore. Infanticide, for example, is a theme in American folklore and European folklore as well. There is an Ozark folktale that Vance Randolph recorded, and which has been reported elsewhere, in which a man in his youth goes away and travels and becomes quite successful. His parents are quite poor. He comes back one night after many many years have elapsed and he looks completely different. He thinks he will therefore surprise them. He has come back with a lot of money and he wants to give it to them. They have an inn and he takes a room there for the night. They don't recognize him and he thinks that in the morning he will announce that he is their son. Well, they murder him during the night for his money. It's a marvelous story but I would not put it in one of my books. It really upsets me. This kind of thing I avoid.

Tell me a little more about how you gather the material for your books.

I will probably stack up several hundred stories before I select 20 or 30 for a collection and then after I have gotten them all I begin looking for more. The retelling is also time-consuming. It takes a lot of time.

Each book has a list of sources in the back. The stories come from all over. A few stories have come directly from children I've spoken with. "The Ghost with the Bloody Fingers" came from the Indiana University collection, but I have also heard the story independently. "The Viper" is a story that I heard twice in the same week, first from a kid in Philadelphia, then from a folklorist who teaches at Temple. Mostly, I do archival research, which principally involves the collections amassed by the students in various folklore departments, who are required to collect the stuff.

In all of my books what I'm doing basically is presenting adult material in a way that children can understand. Children are so sophisticated these days that it works for them.

Sophisticated in what way?

In terms of their life experiences or maybe simply their life experiences through the media. What fascinates me is that with the scary material, you'd think they would be jaded. But they're not. They're refreshed. The values involved in the stories really appeal to them, the themes are so traditional, the searching and trying to understand, that they are not the least bit jaded. The stories are a treat to them. They are also reassuring.

It seems to me that scary stories often touch on matters that in other types of children's fantasy are considered taboo.

I think so. For example, we have some cannibalism in the books. People don't see it as cannibalism but it is. The most overt example is the story "Wonderful Sausage," which is about a butcher who is a sort of

prototypical Sweeney Todd. There is a fragmented version of it from New Orleans, and there is the song that I learned when I was a kid in Scout camp, "Dunderbock and the Sausage Machine." What happens is that Dunderbock makes sausage from dogs and cats and one day the machine slips or falls and he goes into the machine himself. This is the end of it: "His wife had the nightmare. / She walked right in her sleep. / She grabbed the crank, gave it a yank, / And Dunderbock was meat." It's an old camp song, really. But the cannibalism is there.

Some of the stories, although not overtly erotic, deal obliquely with sexuality and related matters: for example, the stories about going out on a date and having it end in a horrific way.

Yes. These, again, are cautionary tales. For my third "Scary Stories" collection, I have been thinking about including a story called "The Boyfriend's Death," which is about a teenage boy and girl who go out and park, as we used to call it when I was growing up. It's a Fifties story. The boyfriend discovers when it's time to leave that they don't have any gas. So he says well I'll get some. While he's away the girl falls asleep and is awakened by a scraping sound. The boyfriend has been murdered in a ghastly way by somebody. He's been hung upside down, and in the morning she's awakened by the police. The police come and fetch her. And she's asked not to look behind her because something dreadful has happened. But you see I would not describe what it was, I would leave that to the reader's imagination.

Sometimes I suppose an illustration can be helpful in bringing forward a suggestion that you don't want to be too explicit about in the text.

One could illustrate that story by simply having the girl look back and not showing what she sees. Stephen Gammell has made a very important contribution to these books because he has such a wild imagination.

His drawings are very intense.

Yes. We would never consider having him do a book for the "I Can Read" group.

*With all the attention being given in the news and elsewhere to the kidnapping of children and to child abuse, do you think that the context in which scary stories are read is changing in any way? For example, in **In a Dark, Dark Room**, there's the story about a man who gives a child a ride home at night. The man is a stranger to the child. So it's about a situation that every child is being told to avoid.*

My editor and I talked about that and my feeling was that this is a traditional story and so we should use it. The man in the story is a very benign man as it turns out.

And it's told from his point of view, so you identify with him and not with the child. Did you intentionally frame the story that way, with a view to making it less frightening?

No. That's the way the story is told. All of the so-called "vanishing hitchhiker stories" are told form the point of view of the person who encounters the ghost. They wouldn't work as stories the other way round. There's a balancing that is involved. I have to be very careful not to get in the way of the material. I try to understand the genre I am working in and how it functions.

For my new "I Can Read" book, *Ghosts!,* there was an English story that I liked very much but I thought the material wasn't right for younger children, so I recast it in terms they would understand. Let me explain what I mean. The original story is about the ghost of a dreadful old man who haunts his daughter because he doesn't like her new husband. He does things like rising up out of the pond while they're swimming—a lot of funny things like that. But the material was a little too old for the "I Can Read" group. Still, I thought, I would love to use it because in the end the couple corners the ghost and puts him in a little green bottle, which is a standard procedure for disposing of ghosts.

I didn't realize there were standard procedures for such things.

Oh, there are. Ministers are specialists in them—especially Anglican ministers. So, I thought, what can we do? We'll have a girl who has a run-in with the class bully and turns the bully in. The bully says, "I'm going to get you for this!" But he dies before he has a chance to, and he comes back and haunts her and is absolutely dreadful, just as the old man in the other story is. There are a lot of funny things in the new version that gives the illustrator an opportunity to exercise his talent. In the end because of the false bravado that the ghost exhibits, he also is trapped in a bottle and the bottle is closed. The last line of the story is: "If you ever find a green bottle on the beach, don't open it!" So, that's an example of bringing down a story to a level that younger kids can respond to.

*In your introduction to **Witcracks,** you say that a new kind of sick humor developed in the 1950s. You say that this grew out of "the great changes which were taking place and how anxious they made us feel about our lives." What changes did you have in mind?*

Most of all, what I was thinking about was the existence of the atomic bomb and our anxiety over how much longer we were all going to be alive.

And that filtered down into children's awareness?

Yes. It was expressed in a variety of ways, in many of which anxiety was couched in terms of hostility. Ethnic humor has a similar basis, in feelings of being threatened over one's space and one's status. The jokes are always the same.

A lot of the humor that is circulating today on television and elsewhere is very nasty humor.

Yes, it's the same thing again.

You have said in another interview that you think folklore has special value for children who have problems with self-esteem. What did you mean by that?

These stories allow children to feel that they have something to contribute, because this is their material. They helped to create it. In effect they are shaping it. The knowledge that one is contributing to a body of literature, which is so old and so new, and so sustaining and so stabilizing, should be reassuring and enhancing. The stories aren't made up by professionals. They're made by ordinary people, including children, who are meeting their needs by creating the stories that they need.

TITLE COMMENTARY

📖 *STORES* (1977)

Andd Ward (review date May 1977)

SOURCE: Ward, Andd. *School Library Journal* 23, no. 9 (May 1977): 65.

Gr 3-6— In an easy, readable narrative [*Stores*], Schwartz describes the workings of nearly 40 kinds of stores in a typical American town. Beginning in the wee hours with the opening of a bakery and an Italian restaurant (where the owner begins cooking enough spaghetti sauce for 200 people at 6 a.m.) he gives interesting glimpses into a ice cream store, a shoe repair shop, a kennel, a bank, etc. The pleasant photos and personalized text which is chock full of extras (e.g., how to read medicine prescriptions; a recipe for "The Big Bux" banana split) make this far more entertaining than typical career information guides.

WHEN I GREW UP LONG AGO: FAMILY LIVING, GOING TO SCHOOL, GAMES AND PARTIES, CURES AND DEATHS, A COMET, A WAR, FALLING IN LOVE, AND OTHER THINGS I REMEMBER: OLDER PEOPLE TALK ABOUT THE DAYS WHEN THEY WERE YOUNG (1978)

Nancy J. Schmidt (review date January 1979)

SOURCE: Schmidt, Nancy J. *School Library Journal* 25, no. 5 (January 1979): 62-3.

Gr 9-12—This collection of excerpts from interviews with 156 elderly Americans who grew up between 1890 and 1914 [*When I Grew Up Long Ago*] provides a panorama of the commonplaces of life at the turn of the century. The book is arranged in 32 topical sections that cover such things as family life, food, housing, dress, school, games, songs, employment, stories, church, love, death, holiday celebrations, punishments, and responses to Halley's Comet and the San Francisco Earthquake. Directions are provided for playing games, scores for singing songs, and recipes for making favorite foods and home medical remedies. Each excerpt is identified by date and place; most are presented in the language spoken by those interviewed. The author provides brief editorial comments and explanations when necessary, and in the final chapter outlines his methods of research and selection. This is a unique, personalized introduction to the American past that will arouse the interest and curiosity of many young readers.

CHIN MUSIC: TALL TALK AND OTHER TALK (1979)

Daisy Kouzel (review date November 1979)

SOURCE: Kouzel, Daisy. *School Library Journal* 26, no. 3 (November 1979): 94.

Gr 6-8—This compendium of folk words and phrases [*Chin Music*] is as "queerisome" as a "snallygaster." It consists of 69 pages of perfectly ordinary terms,

alphabetically arranged, for each of which the author provides a goodly number of equivalents from American folk speech. Plus, there are 31 pages of explanations, sources, bibliographies, and acknowledgments, making this a smallish dog wagging a rather large and ponderous tail. Some of the terminology might get a smile out of a few young sophisticates, but one wonders at the average reaction to "Killcow" for bully, "Nimshy" for girl, "Knowledge Box" for school, and similar tomfoolery. Some of the words show signs of having been originated by some 19th-Century writer and anthologized into spurious authenticity. Was there a person who ever said "discumgalligumfricated" instead of "surprised"? As the French say, *n'exagerons rien*. The book covers the period 1815-1950, with rural America the predominant locale, and many references to animals and small town situations, making it alien to metropolitan youth. Perhaps a less academic and more thoughtful approach might have helped to bridge the gap, and withal evoke the interest of today's young readers in this reservoir of American life.

FLAPDOODLE: PURE NONSENSE FROM AMERICAN FOLKLORE (1980)

Publishers Weekly (review date 14 November 1980)

SOURCE: *Publishers Weekly* 218, no. 20 (14 November 1980): 55.

Here are a dozen delightful diversions [in *Flapdoodle*] selected by the master humorist whose *Witcracks, Tomfoolery* and other anthologies of folklore are prized as a relief from sane and sober reality. Schwartz presents poems and stories that make no sense at all except to readers looking for the chance to shake off cares and *have* that "good day" everyone orders. What fun to meet a fellow who tells us: "I knocked at the maid and the door came out. She asked could I eat a glass of buttermilk and drink a crust of bread and cheese. I said, 'No thank you. Don't mind if I do.'" Then he meets a bark who dogs at him. The tall tales are sympathetically, skillfully illustrated by [John] O'Brien's drawings. *(All ages)*

Kirkus Reviews (review date 15 December 1980)

SOURCE: *Kirkus Reviews* 48, no. 24 (15 December 1980): 1572.

"Do you want to see a funny looking ape?" (Hold a mirror up to the person.) "Do you want to hear a dirty joke? A horse fell in the mud." Schwartz's source notes indicate that children are still passing along these timeless groaners, as well as the "visual jokes" that bloomed in the early Sixties ("Pull the skin behind the corners of each eye and call, 'Mama, Mama! You pulled my ponytail too tight!'") and such ancient put-downs as "Sally bum-bally / Tee-ally, go-fally / Tee-legged, tielegged, / Bow-legged Sally." This latest clutch of tomfoolery is filled out with some limericks, punch-liners, doubletalk, and pure flapdoodle, about a boy who drowns in a dry creek and a woman whose children are all orphans—"Except for one tiny tot / Who lived across the street / In a house on a vacant lot." If this lacks the rapscallious rusticity that flavors many Schwartz collections, [*Flapdoodle*] still swarms with the kid-tested absurdity that keeps them moving. *8-10.*

Booklist (review date 15 January 1981)

SOURCE: *Booklist* 77, no. 10 (15 January 1981): 701.

"I feel more like I do now than I did when I came in," "Did you hear the one about the bed? . . . It hasn't been made up yet," "Plums or figs? Pigs, fleass," are but three wonderful examples of the mischievous tomfoolery Schwartz supplies in this latest collection of nonsense culled from American folklore [*Flapdoodle*]. Visual jokes, wordplays, spoonerisms, pronunciation rhymes, and other whimsical parodies to amuse and delight are included. Humorous line drawings extend the wit for lovers of folklore or casual browsers. Source notes and a bibliography are appended. *Gr. 4-8.*

Horn Book Magazine (review date February 1981)

SOURCE: *Horn Book Magazine* 57, no. 1 (February 1981): 61-2.

Illustrated by John O'Brien. In earlier books the collector has celebrated many different types of American folklore: tongue-twisters, wordplay, jokes, tall tales. His latest work [*Flapdoodle*] is a crazy-quilt assortment of nonsense "made up by a lot of ordinary people like you and me." Included are samples of spoonerisms, doubletalk, visual jokes, tricks, silly rhymes, and shaggy dog stories. The introduction states that some of the folklore is old, and some of it new; children may be surprised to find several of the jokes and rhymes currently very much alive in the schoolyard. Nearly every page of the entertaining book is decorated with a suitably absurd line drawing. Notes, sources, and bibliography.

Marsha Hartos (review date August 1981)

SOURCE: Hartos, Marsha. *School Library Journal* 27, no. 10 (August 1981): 71.

Gr 5-6—The folklorist presents more old-fashioned humor to modern youngsters, and it is worth passing along. The title [*Flapdoodle*] is a colloquial word for "nonsense." There are poems, jokes (including a few limericks), visual tricks (such as the old trick of pulling an imaginary needle and thread through the fingers) and stories. There are suggestions for using these witticisms on unsuspecting friends. Background material describes some of the curiosities mentioned, such as mummers, the Lone Ranger, Betty Boop and spoonerisms. The format is attractive, with medium-size print on ivory stock and droll line drawings. This kind of humor, which kids have always liked, gives a feeling of continuity with the past. As usual, Schwartz adds complete notes on sources, and the bibliography indicates which books are of interest to young readers.

TEN COPYCATS IN A BOAT AND OTHER RIDDLES (1980)

Horn Book Magazine (review date December 1980)

SOURCE: *Horn Book Magazine* 56, no. 6 (December 1980): 638.

Illustrated by Marc Simont. Early elementary-grade children are usually ardent devotees of riddles and with very little encouragement will gladly read them aloud to anyone obliging enough to listen. For such enthusiasts the dedicated collector of wit and wisdom from the oral tradition presents twenty-eight puzzlers in an easy-to-read text [*Ten Copycats in a Boat and Other Riddles*]. For example, "Ten copycats were sitting in a boat, and one jumped out. How many were left? None. They were all copycats." Not the least of the book's engaging qualities are its design and illustration: Dark bluish type beautifully matches droll, lively, and often dramatic drawings washed with a variety of colors.

SCARY STORIES TO TELL IN THE DARK (1981)

Leslie Burk Chamberlin (review date January 1982)

SOURCE: Chamberlin, Leslie Burk. *School Library Journal* 28, no. 5 (January 1982): 81.

Gr 3-8—This folklore collection [*Scary Stories to Tell in the Dark*] is unusually good. True to the genre, the stories contained are suitable for telling, particularly at Halloween and around the campfire. Contemporary and humorous stories are blended with spooky ones. The scholarship in the source notes and bibliography will be useful to serious literature students. Although the cover art is not charming, it hints at the peculiarly macabre, shadowy black-and-white illustrations inside. The stories are not unbearably grotesque; they are suitable even for the low elementary grades.

Booklist (review date 1 May 1990)

SOURCE: *Booklist* 86, no. 17 (1 May 1990): 1697.

From "The Ghost of the Bloody Fingers" to "The Hook" and "The Big Toe" (tales for which campfires are made), Schwartz offers a collection of stories [*Scary Stories to Tell in the Dark*] from American folklore. Besides sending a chill up the reader's spine, this and its sequel, *More Scary Stories to Tell in the Dark,* provide students with models of scholarship—careful documentation, lists of sources, and useful bibliographies.

American Libraries (review date March 2002)

SOURCE: "*Scary Stories* Stay Put." *American Libraries* 33, no. 3 (March 2002): 25.

The superintendent of the Cedar Rapids, Iowa, school district agreed with the recommendation of a materials review committee to retain Alvin Schwartz's *Scary Stories to Tell in the Dark.* Lew Finch's decision was in response to a challenge from the parents of a 6-year-old 1st-grader enrolled at Kenwood Elementary School who had borrowed the book from the school's media center in December.

The boy's mother, Esther McCandless, said in the January 20 *Cedar Rapids Gazette,* "At first I got mad at him for bringing it home because we don't tell scary stories at our home. Then I got mad that the school would allow him to even check it out." McCandless, who explained that her son was prone to nightmares, had sought either the book's removal or its circulation being restricted to children in upper grades.

PTA Reconsideration Committee member Adam Witte told the *Gazette* January 24 that he "didn't find the book to be anything but upfront to having fun with stories that we tell one another." But fellow committee member and Metro High School student Mykael Willis countered that *Scary Stories* "scared the tar" out of her as a youngster and recommended shielding K-2 students from it. Access to the book was upheld in a 9-1 vote.

📖 THE CAT'S ELBOW AND OTHER SECRET LANGUAGES (1982)

Peter Neumeyer (review date August 1982)

SOURCE: Neumeyer, Peter. *School Library Journal* 28, no. 1 (August 1982): 122.

Gr 3 Up—Funny, exuberant Alvin Schwartz is a lucid teacher, clearly describing 13 secret languages and codes (example: I=*Ob*-i; love=1-*ob*-ov-*ob*-e, etc.) and demonstrating them with riddles and jokes ("'E-b ful-care th-wi at-th e-knif,'" said Tom S. cuttingly). The languages become progressively more difficult in the book [*The Cat's Elbow and Other Secret Languages*], and by the seventh, "Sa-La," you-lou-sou may-lay-say have-lave-save trou-lou-sou ble-lle-sle. The proverbial children of all ages will find the book irresistible. The ink illustrations are vintage [Margot] Zemach—mainly crazy, jittery, jumping animals, pictorially punning on the text. The mandarin mutts for the Chinese Sa-La language—to cite merely one illustration—occupy their pictorial space with a perfection worthy of study. The book's manufacture—the shape, the cover with its graceful mouse-tailed silver cat—is exemplary and elegant. Also, Schwartz has provided instructive and entertaining notes, and answers to the sometimes very difficult language puzzles. The bibliography of scholarly sources is welcome, for this book predictably will encourage the curious to follow through, perhaps to learn more about Boonville lingo, a secret language used by a whole California town between 1880 and 1930.

Junior Bookshelf (review date October 1989)

SOURCE: *Junior Bookshelf* 53, no. 5 (October 1989): 231.

An import from North America. *The Cat's Elbow* is one of the most unusual books I have seen this, or any year. Alvin Schwartz collects languages for children: thus we are initiated into Pig Latin; Iggity; Ku; Obby-Dobby; Eggo-Peggo; Ip. Schwartz introduces each new language, offers detailed examples, and then sets practice riddles. Margot Zemach's pleasing line drawings add to the sense of nuttiness. It is all rather cracked yet makes sense in an odd-ball way.

For example: take the 'Ziph' language in which "after each vowel add the letter 'g', then repeat the vowel". Thus we see that *elephant* becomes *ege-l-ege-ph-aga-nt.* And what is more there is half a page of practice for such extravagance.

It could become a cult, it could develop a wide readership. I must give it a whirl back at school— "id-sa M-o-t S. ly-i-craft." Mm.

📖 BUSY BUZZING BUMBLEBEES AND OTHER TONGUE TWISTERS (1982; NEW EDITION, 1992)

Hazel Rochman (review date 1 April 1992)

SOURCE: Rochman, Hazel. *Booklist* 88, no. 15 (1 April 1992): 1460.

Gr. 1-3. Newly illustrated in wild, cheerful watercolors and with a multicultural cast, this 1982 collection of tongue twisters [*Busy Buzzing Bumblebees and Other Tongue Twisters*] is perfect for beginning readers. The participatory nonsense forces repetition ("Just say it three times as fast as you can"), as well as concentration on small differences ("Swim, Sam! Well swum, Sam!"). From the oldies about seashells to newly invented twisters ("Pete's pop shops for chops in chop shops"), there's sheer joy in words and their strangeness.

Nancy A. Gifford (review date June 1992)

SOURCE: Gifford, Nancy A. *School Library Journal* 38, no. 6 (June 1992): 111.

K-Gr 3—A newly illustrated version [*Busy Buzzing Bumblebees and Other Tongue Twisters*] of the 1982 collection. It still contains 46 easy-to-read tongue twisters that can be enjoyed both by beginning readers and by more advanced fans of the genre. [Paul] Meisel's colorful pen-and-ink and watercolor illustrations often add a different twist to the humorous tangling phrases, and his style is brighter and more detailed than the original. It's an attractive new edition, but the old one is still quite serviceable.

Horn Book Guide (review date fall 1992)

SOURCE: *Horn Book Guide* 3, no. 2 (fall 1992): 318.

K-3. Illustrated by Paul Meisel. I Can Read series. This collection of forty-six tonguetickling phrases [*Busy Buzzing Bumblebees and Other Tongue Twist-*

ers] has been updated by a new illustrator's whimsically detailed illustrations. It is unfortunate to note, however, that while one twister is illustrated with an environmentally aware canvas-bagtoting shopper, another twister portrays "nine nice night nurses"—all female—supervised by one male doctor.

📖 THERE IS A CARROT IN MY EAR AND OTHER NOODLE TALES (1982)

Kirkus Reviews (review date 1 March 1982)

SOURCE: *Kirkus Reviews* 50, no. 5 (1 March 1982): 274.

Schwartz's noodle tales, drawn from diverse folk sources, are really jokes that culminate in a final punchline—except for the sixth and last which strings together a collection of one-liners about going to bed. (A sample: "I am taking my ruler to bed. I want to know how long I sleep.") Schwartz casts all the anecdotes to feature the Brown family, pictured as cheerful humans with rodent-like profiles, who start out by cooling off in a swimming pool that hasn't yet been filled with water. Next, young Sam and Jane Brown, camping out, elude a swarm of mosquitoes only to be visited by fireflies. "'Oh, no!' Sam groaned. 'They are back! And now they are looking for us with flashlights.'" The title line [*There Is a Carrot in My Ear*], from a vaudeville exchange, is spoken by Jane, who is puzzled by the development because "I planted radishes." And so it goes, in brisk, easy-to-read words and sentences: trusty nuggets that give beginning readers some periodic reinforcement.

School Library Journal (review date 1 May 1982)

SOURCE: *School Library Journal* 28, no. 9 (1 May 1982): 78.

Gr 2-4—*There Is a Carrot in My Ear and Other Noodle Tales* is a collection of six stories from sources (as the author's note informs us) as diverse as American "Little Moron" stories, ancient Greek tales and vaudeville pieces. Explaining in his foreword that a "noodle is a silly person," reteller Alvin Schwartz goes on to introduce the noodly Brown family and reveal their various foibles: "swimming" in a pool with no water, fearing that fireflies are mosquitoes with flashlights, trying to hatch a pumpkin, taking a ruler to bed to find out "how long I sleep," etc. Most of the stories don't appear in other beginning noodle collections and will provide laughs for readers who catch the puns and absurdities the stories hinge on. The drawings by Karen Ann Weinhaus, washed in shades of red and yellow, show funny, pointy-probosciced folk blissfully unaware of their own goofiness.

Publishers Weekly (review date 21 May 1982)

SOURCE: *Publishers Weekly* 221, no. 21 (21 May 1982): 77.

Schwartz has regaled older readers with anthologies of folklore; now he gives a collection of six absurdities to the I-Can-Read audience [in *There Is a Carrot in My Ear*]. Weinhaus's color cartoons ably depict the goofiness perpetrated by the "noodles," as Schwartz dubs silly types like the Browns, who act out "Little Moron" and other old jokes. Little Sam and Jane Brown think that a host of fireflies are mosquitoes, searching for them with flashlights. A sly grocer sells Grandpa a pumpkin, passing it off as a horse egg, and Grandpa sits on it dutifully, waiting for the baby horse to hatch. Et cetera, and et cetera—unfortunately for the grownups whom young funsters will surely repeat the sallies to, over and over. *(4-8)*

Booklist (review date 15 June 1982)

SOURCE: *Booklist* 78, no. 20 (15 June 1982): 1372.

Drawing on noodle folklore of American and European origins, Schwartz concocts six funny stories about a family of very silly people [*There Is a Carrot in My Ear*]. Whether it's Grandpa's attempt to hatch a baby horse, Mr. Brown's run-in with his underwear, or Sam and Jane's altercation with a most unusual mosquito, the stories are short, simply stated, and lavishly laced with hilarity—the kind that cry to be read alone or aloud over and over again! [Karen] Weinhaus' cartoon drawings are bright and perky and lend just the right degree of silliness.

📖 *UNRIDDLING: ALL SORTS OF RIDDLES TO PUZZLE YOUR GUESSERY* (1983)

Carol Hurd (review date March 1984)

SOURCE: Hurd, Carol. *School Library Journal* 30, no. 7 (March 1984): 164-65.

Gr 4 Up—The multitude of children who love riddles will realize that until reading this book [*Unriddling*] they had merely scratched the surface in cracking their riddle jokes. Schwartz presents many types, including chapters of droodles, rebus riddles and letter riddles. The range of new, familiar and long-forgotten riddles is splendid, and should not be limited to the elementary grades. Amusing black-and-white sketches are found on almost every page and add to the fun. In addition, notes, sources and a bibliography give a brief history of riddles and a guide for further study of this fascinating subject. Schwartz has compiled many other entertaining books such as *Tomfoolery* (1973), *Witcracks* 1973) and *Whoppers* (1975). My "guessery" is that this new one will be another favorite.

📖 *MORE SCARY STORIES TO TELL IN THE DARK* (1984)

Cathryn A. Camper (review date February 1985)

SOURCE: Camper, Cathryn A. *School Library Journal* 31, no. 6 (February 1985): 79.

Gr 4 Up—A book guaranteed to make your teeth chatter and your spine tingle with fear [*More Scary Stories to Tell in the Dark*]. Not since Schwartz' first collection of ghost stories (*Scary Stories to Tell in the Dark*) has there been a collection of horror stories as well suited for children. He has wisely chosen to record the stories just as children might tell them instead of rewriting them into literary tales. Most of the stories are short and perfect for kids to tell aloud. The collection includes humorous ghost stories, and even a song, complete with musical notation. [Stephen] Gammell's eerie drawings are excellent: they give realistic definition to the ghouls he's illustrating and at the same time create a mood. The inclusion of footnotes and sources further elucidate the stories and help remind readers that these are, indeed, only stories. Buy two; like the ghouls it contains, this book will tend to disappear.

Carolyn Angus (review date January 1992)

SOURCE: Angus, Carolyn. *Kliatt Young Adult Paperback Book Guide* 26, no. 1 (January 1992): 52.

The scary stories collected from American folklore and retold by Schwartz include tales of ghosts, monsters, vampires, graveyards, practical jokes gone awry, and weird happenings of every unimaginable kind [in *More Scary Stories to Tell in the Dark*]. Irving's voice is whispery, breathless, chilling, or filled with blood-curdling laughter as appropriate for each tale, but always clear and distinct. The pacing is just right, and eerie music at the beginning or end of each tale provides a nice transition, adding to the mood but never overwhelming the storyteller's voice. The listener is given just enough time to take a deep breath before being plunged into the next spinetingling story. Irving's readings are superb, making these ghostly anthologies perfect chillers and frightening good fun.

FAT MAN IN A FUR COAT AND OTHER BEAR STORIES (1984)

Maria Salvadore (review date December 1984)

SOURCE: Salvadore, Maria. *School Library Journal* 31, no. 4 (December 1984): 86.

Gr 5 Up—A convincing portrayal of bears as truly extraordinary, intelligent, sometimes humorous animals who have been misunderstood and abused by most yet revered and respected by many. Schwartz includes 50 stories [in *Fat Man in a Fur Coat*]—old and recent, true and tall—and intermingles straight factual material on the animals. This collection is not for the faint of heart or the very sensitive. The big fellow "rassled" and killed by Uncle Lemmie on a dark Vermont road turns out to be a bear. James Clyman recorded what Jedediah Smith, a 19th-Century trapper and explorer, looked like after an unexpected encounter with a grizzly, and how he stitched up Jedediah's ear and scalp wounds. Though animal training certainly has progressed, performing bears were once trained to "dance" by being placed onto a red-hot slab of stone. This unusual look at bears is extended by numerous expressive, softly rendered black-and-white illustrations reminiscent of Steven Gammell in mood and style. The sources, notes and bibliography are comprehensive, a characteristic of Schwartz, and as interesting as the stories themselves.

Junior Bookshelf (review date June 1990)

SOURCE: *Junior Bookshelf* 54, no. 3 (June 1990): 144.

There is not much of Pooh or Yogi Bear in these pages [*Fat Man in a Fur Coat*] which, with the exception of a few tall 'shaggy-bear' stories, are made up of anecdotes about bears in the wild and, sadly, the barbarous ways in which Civilization has treated them. The emphasis is on North America, although the bears of Europe and Asia get a mention. Alvin

Schwartz's retellings are commendably brief but not over-entertaining. He is best taken in small doses with long pauses for reflection. Lovers of these great, powerful and largely admirable beasts will find the book invaluable. If it appeals to the general reader this will be because of David Christiana's masterly illustrations, soft pencil-drawings laid most effectively on the page and capturing the majesty, the terror and the occasional humour of their subjects with the surest of touches. Here is an artist who deserves a large page, better paper and a more varied theme.

TALES OF TRICKERY FROM THE LAND OF SPOOF (1985)

David Gale (review date January 1986)

SOURCE: Gale, David. *School Library Journal* 32, no. 5 (January 1986): 70.

Gr 4-6—The practical jokes, hoaxes and parlor tricks Schwartz describes lose something in the retelling—mostly, these are pranks for which "you had to be there." The 22 stories [of *Tales of Trickery from the Land of Spoof*] relate April Fools' jokes, regional tales, traditional stories, puzzles and more. A few will be familiar, yet even those that are fresh are marred by a lackluster style. Although copious notes and sources are included, rarely do they convey a sense of *when* these pranks took place. The extensive bibliography lists adult titles almost exclusively, the only exceptions being one out-of-print title and four Schwartz titles. The elegant design of this slim book—open and clean looking with lots of white space and peppered with attractive pen-and-ink drawings—is in opposition to the more low-brow content. Children may be amused by some of these tricks, and they may be inspired to try some trickery themselves, but overall they will feel slighted by this collection.

ALL OF OUR NOSES ARE HERE AND OTHER NOODLE TALES (1985)

School Library Journal (review date May 1985)

SOURCE: *School Library Journal* 31, no. 9 (May 1985): 107.

Gr 1-4—Five more noodle stories [*All of Our Noses are Here*] from around the world (with sources cited) join Schwartz's earlier collection, *There Is a Carrot*

in My Ear & Other Noodle Tales. As the foreward notes, "Most noodles are kind and loving people. But they have very few brains." The family of noodles here proceeds to demonstrate these facts. From a variation on the "Six Foolish Fishermen" tale to a talking "dead" boy to a human turned into a donkey, these stories of gullible goofs will keep children giggling. The pointed-nosed family shown here adds a calm absurdity to the stories, and although neither the tales nor the softly colored illustrations are as broadly comic as Allard and Marshall's "Stupids," it's clear that they share a cuckoo's nest in the same family tree.

Booklist (review date 15 May 1985)

SOURCE: *Booklist* 81, no. 18 (15 May 1985): 1340.

Schwartz has taken five Noodlehead stories from several countries and simplified them for the easy-to-read set [in *All of Our Noses are Here*]. The funniest story concerns a family of five who go boating and then are unsure if they have all gotten home. Only after a wise fisherman advises them to stick their noses in the ground and count the holes are they convinced they're all safe and sound. Some of the stories end abruptly, but there is enough humor to keep burgeoning readers' interest. [Karen] Weinhaus' weirdlooking people, with their extended noses and pin-drop eyes, deftly capture the Noodle concept.

📖 *TELLING FORTUNES: LOVE MAGIC, DREAM SIGNS AND OTHER WAYS TO LEARN THE FUTURE* (1987)

Booklist (review date 15 September 1987)

SOURCE: *Booklist* 84, no. L (15 September 1987): 153.

Gr. 4-6. Schwartz, who successfully explained superstitions in *Cross Your Fingers, Spit in Your Hat,* now examines another subject that fascinates kids: how to foretell the future [in *Telling Fortunes*]. Among the items covered are omens, love magic, tea leaves, card and palm reading, dream and death signs, crystal balls, and astrology. Woven throughout are historical tidbits, anecdotes, and folk beliefs that add substance to the text. Although he makes the point that these methods can be misleading, it is obvious that Schwartz sees nothing wrong with these forms of fortune-telling, considering them fun. Readers are sure to agree. Well-executed pen-and-ink drawings

pepper the pages and provide visual interest. The extensive source notes and expanded bibliography evince Schwartz' interest in research. Readers wanting to delve further into the topic will find the bibliography of great help.

Denise A. Anton (review date October 1987)

SOURCE: Anton, Denise A. *School Library Journal* 34, no. 2 (October 1987): 135.

Gr 3 Up—All of us, adults and children alike, occasionally wonder what our future holds. [*Telling Fortunes*] is an excellent compilation of fortune-telling beliefs, traditions, and folklore which emphasizes the fun to be had in trying each method. With his customary thoroughness, Schwartz has amassed an amusing catalog of both familiar and little-known methods of fortune-telling. Included are such standbys as astrology, crystal-gazing, and the reading of cards, palms, and tea leaves; as well as fortune-telling with a raw egg, omens involving animals and everyday objects, ways to determine who loves whom, and even a "cootie catcher." Procedures and step-by-step directions are included when necessary, enabling readers of all ages to become amateur fortune-tellers. The simple pen-and-ink drawings are competent yet fail to match the often light-hearted text. As with his other works, Schwartz' thorough notes, list of sources used, and related bibliography are indispensible for both readers and librarians. This welcome addition to both school and public library collections is destined to become a hit.

📖 *GOLD AND SILVER, SILVER AND GOLD: TALES OF HIDDEN TREASURE* (1988)

Publishers Weekly (review date 23 December 1988)

SOURCE: *Publishers Weekly* 234, no. 26 (23 December 1988): 82-3.

Schwartz carefully assembles facts, fiction and folklore around a fascinating subject for children: the finding of buried treasure [in *Gold and Silver, Silver and Gold*]. In the now-familiar style of Schwartz's *Fat Man in a Fur Coat* and *Tales of Trickery,* the book is documented with extensive explanatory notes and an inclusive bibliography. The text is well-paced as it touches on the various aspects of treasure: shipwrecks, pirates, abandoned mines, Indian legends, buried booty, maps, codes, secret signs, ciphers and more. He doesn't neglect fictional treasures, mentioning Robert Louis Stevenson's *Treasure Island* and Edgar Allan Poe's *The Gold Bug,* nor does he stint on the technologies that have aided inveterate treasure hunters—the diving bell, metal detectors, submarines, scuba gear. [David] Christiana's soft black-and-white drawings and decorations enhance the text, offering readers a treasure trove of information they'll return to again and again. *Ages 10-Up.*

George Gleason (review date 1 February 1989)

SOURCE: Gleason, George. *School Library Journal* 35, no. 6 (1 February 1989): 107.

Gr 6 Up—Twenty-eight brief, true tales of treasures buried, sunk, sighted, sought, found, haunted, and some still hunted [in *Gold and Silver, Silver and Gold*]. These are new-world treasures, chiefly in the United States (New England to California), some in the Caribbean (Spanish galleons laden with gold, silver, and jewels) and in Central and South America. Most of these treasures, treasure-hiders, and treasure-finders have been described in books, newspapers, and magazines, but they are fun to read about again. Schwartz acknowledges his sources in an excellent bibliography and notes that if pursued, they will lead to many more treasure tales. Of particular interest to some is information about ways in which people have hidden treasures and left codes, ciphers, and signs for finding them again. One page is given to a cipher that is unsolved, and the treasure still undiscovered. Charcoal sketches are more decorative than informative, not that they're very decorative. Fascinating stories that will embed themselves in readers' minds.

Carolyn Phelan (review date 1 March 1989)

SOURCE: Phelan, Carolyn. *Booklist* 85, no. 13 (1 March 1989): 1196.

Gr. 4-8. From tales of El Dorado to the childhood memories of buried coins Schwartz found in an empty lot, from Captain Kidd's treasure to the salvaging of rich cargo from sunken ships, from truth to fiction through a no man's land of conjecture and legend that lies somewhere in between, this book [*Gold and Silver, Silver and Gold*] covers a lot of ground in a thoroughly entertaining manner. Although Schwartz does not always differentiate between history and legend while telling these tales of hidden wealth, his excellent appended notes and sources clarify a great deal while providing intriguing glimpses behind the scenes. In addition to the pirate tales one might expect, there are more unusual chapters. One describes the hunt that absorbed read-

ers of Kit Williams' *Masquerade,* which led one seeker to the buried, bejeweled golden rabbit the author had made. Another tells of a fortune supposedly hidden in Virginia 150 years ago and still sought today. The inclusion of an unsolved cipher giving directions to buried gold and silver should keep young code fanatics busy for some time. [David] Christiana's fine-textured pencil drawings lend an air of mystery and drama that heightens the book's appeal. An excellent work on a high-interest subject, this will be a natural for booktalks.

Philip Morrison and Phylis Morrison (review date December 1989)

SOURCE: Morrison, Philip, and Phylis Morrison. *Scientific American* 261, no. 6 (December 1989): 149.

His title [*Gold and Silver, Silver and Gold*] rings like pieces of eight in an ironbound chest; this talented author can write no wrong for good readers young or old. Half of the tales here are true and documented (not every time from sources quite as primary as one might hope for); the rest are legends mixing fact and fancy, one a folktale echoed (or echoing) Chaucer. A chapter on codes, maps and signs, a few diving bells and minisubs, the grand "silver reef" from the broken galleon searched out for 19 years through old archives and in untiring dives—all justify this as a book of mathematics, technology and the worth of evidence.

One true tale of treasure in Boston Harbor is hard to top. Edward Rowe Snow heard that a lighthouse keeper, perhaps an old pirate, had maybe once buried a treasure on one of the harbor islands. An old fisherman recalled that a man from Canada had spent two weeks searching on Great Brewster and had left a note. The note was mislaid but turned up after six years. Finally Snow searched where the note had hinted, but on Middle Brewster instead. (Yes, there are four Brewster islands; New Englanders are parsimonious with names, too.) Only a dull old book was found in the old house—not much use. But a clever librarian found that page 101 had been pricked with 15 pinholes. The letters they designated spelled out nine strange words; read backward—hardly a challenging code—they began: gold is due east of trees . . . , and then said where. Months of searching with a metal detector on the right Cape Cod island eventually brought Snow a box of 316 gold coins, among them pieces of eight. The mysteries of who and how and when and why remain.

📖 *I SAW YOU IN THE BATHTUB AND OTHER FOLK RHYMES* (1989)

Denise Wilms (review date 1 March 1989)

SOURCE: Wilms, Denise. *Booklist* 85, no. 13 (1 March 1989): 1199.

Gr. 1-3. Schwartz offers an amusing assortment of folk rhymes, chosen for their simple vocabulary and brevity, that have entertained children over the years [in *I Saw You in the Bathtub and Other Folk Rhymes*]. Some will be familiar ("I scream, / You scream, / We all scream / For ice cream!"), others not; all are fun and trip easily off the tongue—"My father is a butcher, / My mother cooks the meat, / I'm a little hot dog / That runs down the street." Backed by color pen drawings in [Syd] Hoff's customary cartoon style.

Janie Schomberg (review date 1 May 1989)

SOURCE: Schomberg, Janie. *School Library Journal* 35, no. 9 (1 May 1989): 101.

K-Gr 3—A collection of 41 folk rhymes [*I Saw You in the Bathtub and Other Folk Rhymes.*], visually interpreted in Hoff's trademark style of humorous watercolor illustration. The "Foreword" and the source note at the end both add simple background information about the rhymes and encourage children to write their own rhymes. Children will appreciate the humor of the rhymes, the rhythms, and the illustrations. Another "I Can Read" hit.

📖 *GHOSTS! GHOSTLY TALES FROM FOLKLORE* (1991)

Publishers Weekly (review date 5 July 1991)

SOURCE: *Publishers Weekly* 238, no. 29 (5 July 1991): 64-5.

No stranger to this genre, Schwartz (*Scary Stories to Tell in the Dark*; *In a Dark, Dark Room*) assembles his spirited collection of mildly spooky stories and verses from such sources as a British legend and a Southern folktale [in *Ghosts!*]. The subjects range from an invisible but beloved cat ("Susie died a year ago. But she comes back to visit now and then") to the specter of a school bully (as intimidating in death as in life) to a tongue-twisting incantation to banish ghosts. The tales in this I Can Read book rely as much on whimsy as on chills, a combination that seems tailor-made for Chess's (*Tommy at the Grocery Store*; *A Hippopotamusn't*) friendly, funny, ever-mischievous art. *Ages 4-8.*

Mary Lou Budd (review 1 September 1991)

SOURCE: Budd, Mary Lou. *School Library Journal* 37, no. 9 (1 September 1991): 249.

K-Gr 2—Those familiar with Schwartz's ability to produce the best of scary tales for young readers will find this newest addition [*Ghosts! Ghostly Tales from Folklore*] to be a hit. The sentences are short with a manageable vocabulary, even for those kindergarteners who can tackle the challenge of an early reader. The text is complemented with primitive watercolor illustrations executed in attractive pastels; while the facial expressions are given a semblance of ghoulishness, the total effect is one of enticement (and even humor) rather than of horror. While these stories are not as heart-thumping as those in Schwartz's *In A Dark, Dark Room,* this will nevertheless provide a fun introduction to the "ghostly" genre, and give children a chance to check out a "scary" book. Appended is a page on the origins of the tales and legends.

Hazel Rochman (review 15 September 1991)

SOURCE: Rochman, Hazel. *Booklist* 88 (15 September 1991): 168.

Gr. 1. "There was a big old house where nobody lived . . ." The simplicity of the easy-reading text [in *Ghosts! Ghostly Tales from Folklore*] and the comically sinister pictures are perfect for these old stories that draw you right into the suspense without spelling everything out. As a wary brother and sister go through an empty, dusty, haunted house, we see the ghastly hand on the door before they do. The story ends with the boy whispering to his stricken sister the scariest words of all: "But what is that behind you?" Chess can draw kids as horrible as your worst fantasy: in one story, the bully Victoria "suddenly got sick and died," but she returns as a ghost to haunt her victim everywhere, at his school desk, in the night shadows, in the kitchen appliances. Some ghosts are slobs, like the three eating buttered toast ("They had butter on their fists / Running down their wrists / Butter on their sheets / Running down their feet"). From graveyards to bedrooms, there's a sense of the world as a deliciously scary place, where you can get control—maybe. In the best folklore tradition, the stories encourage participation with lots of repetition ("I want my teeth. Give me back my teeth") and good-naturedly gruesome joy.

Maeve Visser Knoth (review date September-October 1991)

SOURCE: Knoth, Maeve Visser. *Horn Book Magazine* 67, no. 5 (September-October 1991): 607.

Illustrated by Victoria Chess. Young readers will delight in Alvin Schwartz's newest collection of frightening folk tales [*Ghosts! Ghostly Tales from Folklore*], beginning with the double-chinned ghosts floating across the front cover and ending with the tombstone that closes the book. Schwartz's choice of stories reflects his gift for recognizing what will motivate children to learn to read. Victoria Chess's illustrations balance the scary stories by introducing many humorous touches. Her rotund characters, complete with beady eyes, verge on the macabre and are deftly suited to the subject matter. Source notes included.

▥ *SCARY STORIES, NO. 3: MORE TALES TO CHILL YOUR BONES* (1991)

Publishers Weekly (review date 9 August 1991)

SOURCE: *Publishers Weekly* 238, no. 36 (9 August 1991): 58.

In this third book of a series [*Scary Stories, No. 3*], Schwartz continues to successfully mine legend and folklore for spooky tales. Here, ghost stories about such traditional subjects as witches, ghosts and severed hands join such offbeat entries as "Running Wild," a legend about a girl raised by wolves in 1830s Texas, and "The Trouble," a documented case of a family pestered by a poltergeist. Gleefully gory, the stories—bolstered by Gammell's eerily impressionistic drawings—are engaging, and may spark the interest of reluctant readers who drag their feet at meatier works. Extensive source notes at the end are intriguing, showing how stories are handed down over the years—one of the tales dates back to ancient Rome. *Ages 9-up.*

Molly Kinney (review date 1 November 1991)

SOURCE: Kinney, Molly. *School Library Journal* 37, no. 11 (1 November 1991): 132-33.

Gr 3-5—Scary Stories, No. 3 is here! And it was worth the wait. Schwartz has once again created a crowd pleaser with these 25 short stories that include

everything from confronting death to jump tales. There are six major categories of gore with one to eight concise tales in each to delight horror lovers. The selections are straightforward and to the point, allowing readers to put their imaginative skills to full use. The book is well paced and continually captivates, surprises, and entices audiences into reading just one more page. [Stephen] Gammell's gauzy, cobwebby, black-and-white pen-and-ink drawings help to sustain the overall creepy mood. To complete the picture, source notes explain the origins of each story; a comprehensive bibliography includes materials for adults and children. This will be a well-used addition to all collections. Children who have read and reread and reread Schwartz's other books will appreciate this new offering. Teachers will use it in their classrooms as a readaloud. Storytellers will make these tales part of their repertoires. Definitely a first-purchase consideration.

Horn Book Magazine (review date November-December 1991)

SOURCE: *Horn Book Magazine* 67, no. 6 (November-December 1991): 749.

(Intermediate) Illustrated by Stephen Gammell. Some of these short tales [*Scary Stories, No. 3*] are spooky enough or grisly enough to chill the bones; others are silly and are sure to elicit a chuckle or a groan. Like other attractive collections assembled by Schwartz, the book is enticing. The anecdotal tone suggests that these unnerving events just might have happened, and many of the stories combine traditional themes with contemporary settings. Powerful dreams and odd visitations of death abound, eerily depicted in Stephen Gammell's grotesque sketches. As always, the author's notes on each story identify sources and variants, including movies and novels based on these ideas. Brief storytelling hints are appended to some stories, and an inviting bibliography is included.

Paula F. Rohrlick (review date January 1992)

SOURCE: Rohrlick, Paula F. *Kliatt Young Adult Paperback Book Guide* 26, no. 1 (January 1992): 22.

Twenty-six short, spine-tingling folktales are collected here from various sources and retold by Schwartz, in this third book [*Scary Stories, No. 3*] of his popular series. The stories range from creepy to hair-raising to funny, and they are sure to please Y As who love the macabre. They are meant to be read aloud, and instructions to the reader are given (e.g., "as you say the last line, grab one of your friends.") The grotesque, shadowy b/w drawings by Gammell add to the spooky mood. An appendix of notes and sources gives background information and origins of the tales (and often reassurances that the events described could never happen!). Perfect for Halloween, and appealing to reluctant readers, too.

AND THE GREEN GRASS GREW ALL AROUND: FOLK POETRY FROM EVERYONE (1992)

Kirkus Reviews (review date 1 April 1992)

SOURCE: *Kirkus Reviews* 60, no. 7 (1 April 1992): 472.

Not since Carl Withers's *A Rocket in My Pocket* (1948) has there been such a grand compilation of familiar (and unfamiliar) rhymes and chants from the children's own tradition: riddles, games, wishes and taunts; poems about love, food, school, or animals; parodies, nonsense, and stories [in *And the Green Grass Grew All Around*]. Schwartz organizes them by topic and/or form and provides all kinds of fascinating supporting material: an engagingly conversational introduction; general explanatory notes plus full item-by-item sources, many of which are intriguing in themselves ("Avik Roy, age 13, Detroit . . . 1986"; "Editor's recollection, Ten Mile River Boy Scout Camp . . . 1940"), or which give alternate versions; even an occasional tune. In b & w pen and watercolor, Truesdell's marvelous characters dance across the generously broad pages, peering inquisitively at the hilarious goings-on or gleefully joining in the shenanigans. It's hard to imagine a child who wouldn't greet this treasure trove with enthusiasm. Extensive bibliography (items "of interest to young people" are starred); index. *4+.*

Hazel Rochman (review date 1 May 1992)

SOURCE: Rochman, Hazel. *Booklist* 88, no. 17 (1 May 1992): 1598.

Gr. 3-6, Younger for Reading Aloud. Understand, rubber band? The late Alvin Schwartz has left a joyful legacy in this collection of folk poetry for everyone to share. He put together 300 of his favorites—chants and teases, wishes and warnings, jokes and riddles, skip-rope rhymes and stories, fun and games [in *And the Green Grass Grew All Around*]. [Sue] Truesdell's exuberant multicultural cartoon drawings on every page express the farce and the essential sociality of the encounters, whether kids are throwing food, mothers are yelling, or alligators are doing the boogie-woogie. For some rhymes, Schwartz included simple musical notation that emphasizes how much these lines are meant to be performed and sung. There are lots of parodies ("On top of spaghetti"); as Schwartz said, we often learn the irreverent version before we hear the originals. Many rhymes are about the U.S., ranging from verses about immigration and work ("When I first came to this land, / I was not a wealthy man") to street chants. There are also the universal rhymes that kids all over the world seem to learn from each other. As always, Schwartz's scholarship is unobtrusive and stimulating, with detailed notes at the back about sources and variants for any child or adult who's curious to find out more. His chatty introduction celebrates the ordinary people who made up these rhymes "in their everyday language to meet their everyday needs." With the Opies' *I Saw Esau,* illustrated by Sendak, children's folk poetry this spring has come in like a lion.

Publishers Weekly (review date 25 May 1992)

SOURCE: *Publishers Weekly* 239, no. 24 (25 May 1992): 56.

The late folklorist Schwartz (*Scary Stories to Tell in the Dark*) compiled more than 250 familiar folk poems for this volume [*And the Green Grass Grew All Around*], including such seldom-recorded favorites as "Just plant a watermelon on my grave" and "Liar, liar, pants on fire." Folk rhymes are not "literary," suggests Schwartz, but are "intended to be spoken or sung or performed in some other way" and have been passed down through generations of children. The poems are arranged loosely according to topic (People, Food, School, Wishes—and Warnings, Love and Marriage, etc.) rather than according to kind (jump-rope rhymes, camp songs, parodies, nursery rhymes, street rhymes), and their histories are explained in a 30-page listing of source material. The size and format of the book, with its amusing black-and-white cartoons, call to mind collections of poetry by Silverstein or Prelutsky; and though the book is significant for its archival qualities, its exuberance and good fun should make it welcome in home libraries as well. *All ages.*

Lee Bock (review date June 1992)

SOURCE: Bock, Lee. *School Library Journal* 38, no. 6 (June 1992): 135.

Gr 3 Up—A marvelous book [*And the Green Grass Grew All Around*] that is sure to become a classic if children have any say in the matter. Schwartz has gathered sassy, funny, scary, and slightly naughty children's folk poetry heard on schoolgrounds and wherever else kids are having fun. Adults who stew over the appropriateness of Roald Dahl's books or Shel Silverstein's poetry may have concerns here, but kids will love having all their underground playground rhymes in one volume. Scores are included for "On Top of Spaghetti," "Mine Eyes Have Seen the Glory / Of the Closing of the School," and other songs. It's hard to imagine illustrations better suited to the book's silly, energized tone than [Sue] Truesdell's big-eyed, animated, and humorous characters. Given plenty of white space, they tumble, goof, and guffaw across the pages, in ideal tandem with the poetry. These drawings may be in black and white, but readers will never pick up a more colorful book. Of additional interest to many people, adults in particular, are the "Notes" in the back on folk poets and poetry; "Sources" that trace the selections' origins are also helpful. Read this outrageous volume before it is shelved; once the kids discover it, it will always be checked out.

Horn Book Magazine (review date July 1992)

SOURCE: *Horn Book Magazine* 68, no. 4 (July 1992): 460-61.

(Intermediate) Illustrated by Sue Truesdell. Move over your copies of Shel Silverstein and Jack Prelutsky and make room for Alvin Schwartz's collection of folk poetry [*And the Green Grass Grew All Around*]. Full of vigorous, swinging rhythms and funny, often nasty, sentiments, the pages are filled with well-known rhymes as well as new discoveries. Sources range from university and folklore archives to the contributions of people of all ages, including the editor's own recollections of childhood. There are rhymes children use for choosing up sides, clapping hands, and jumping rope. Parodies of nursery rhymes include "Mary had a little lamb, / A little pork, a little ham." There are old songs as familiar as "On Top of Spaghetti." There are rhymes for autograph albums, including several versions of "Roses are red," and nonsense rhymes for all occasions. In many instances the music for the poems is included, making it impossible to keep from singing a bar or two or even from humming for the rest of the day. Sue Truesdell's cartoon drawings dance and tumble

across the pages as a perfect accompaniment to the rhymes they illustrate. Notes about folk poetry, sources, an extensive bibliography, and an index of first lines are included. A wonderful collection for reading, singing, and laughing out loud, this book is strongly recommended for sharing in groups so that everyone can rediscover old favorites—and the reader won't feel silly singing alone.

Horn Book Guide (review date fall 1992)

SOURCE: *Horn Book Guide* 3, no. 2 (fall 1992): 323.

K-3 Illustrated by Sue Truesdell. Full of vigorous, swinging rhythms and funny, often nasty, sentiments, the pages are filled with well-known rhymes as well as new discoveries [*And the Green Grass Grew All Around*]. There are rhymes children use for choosing up sides, clapping hands, and jumping rope, as well as parodies of nursery rhymes and nonsense verse for all occasions. In many instances the music for the poems is included. Truesdell's cartoon drawings dance and tumble across the pages. A wonderful collection.

STORIES TO TELL A CAT (1992)

Stephanie Zvirin (review date 15 December 1992)

SOURCE: Zvirin, Stephanie. *Booklist* 89, no. 8 (15 December 1992): 734.

Gr. 3-6. Though you'd never know it by looking at the fetching dust jacket (a perky green parrot sits atop the head of a friendly looking marmalade cat), this collection of cat stuff [*Stories to Tell a Cat*] isn't for children who want to read about cuddly critters. In fact, the late Schwartz's first story reads very much like a horror tale. So do several others in the roundup of cat stories and poems that folklorist Schwartz adapted from a variety of sources. But even though Schwartz's cats rarely purr sweetly, they are certainly an intriguing lot. In "Make-Believe Cats," for example, cats sketched on a screen spring heroically to life to save a boy from rats; and in "The Fastest Cat on Earth," a funny takeoff on the familiar fable about the tortoise and the hare, a self-satisfied feline meets its match in a clever crab. As usual, Schwartz conscientiously included source notes, which also make interesting reading.

Margaret Chathman (review date March 1993)

SOURCE: Chathman, Margaret. *School Library Journal* 39, no. 3 (March 1993): 200.

Gr 3-5—Fourteen folktales, stories, and poems about cats now cast for telling *to* cats, with notes on origins and a bibliography of sources [in *Stories to tell a Cat*]. In most cases, this results in an easy delivery and a contemporary American locale. The rewriting works well in such tales as "The Cat Came Back," and "The King of the Cats," but leaves others, such as "The Nest," rather flat. "Once There Was a Cat," a snippet of description of the Cheshire Cat from *Alice in Wonderland,* is so formless that it might have been better if it had disappeared entirely. [Catherine] Huerta's graceful gray wash and pencil drawings add a touch of humor, and they sit well in the invitingly open format. Felines are always popular, but this volume falls into the category of nice-but-not-necessary.

Additional coverage of Schwartz's life and career is contained in the following sources published by the Gale Group: *Contemporary Authors,* **Vols. 13-16R, 137;** *Contemporary Authors New Revision Series,* **Vols. 7, 24, 49, 86;** *Literature Resource Center; Major Authors and Illustrators for Children and Young Adults,* **Eds. 1, 2; and** *Something about the Author,* **Vols. 4, 56, 71.**

Philip Turner
1925-

(Full name Philip William Turner; also wrote under the name Stephen Chance) English novelist, playwright, and short story writer.

INTRODUCTION

Philip Turner, an ordained Anglican priest, is noted for his writing of both ecclesiastical plays and novels for children. His books for children often take place within ecclesiastical settings, while chronicling the adventures of young boys. His books have been translated into several languages, including Japanese and German.

BIOGRAPHICAL INFORMATION

Turner was born in Rossland, British Columbia, Canada, the son of Christopher Edward (a clergyman) and Emma (Johnston) Turner. He returned with his family to England when he was six months old. He grew up in the English industrial town of Leeds, where his father was the vicar of a large parish. At the outbreak of World War II, Turner's father was moved to a different parish, this time in the countryside. It was this countryside that would inspire Darnley Mills, the fictional setting of Turner's children's novels.

After serving a brief stint in the Royal Navy during the war, Turner enrolled at Oxford University to study English. While at Oxford, he was greatly influenced by two of his professors: J. R. R. Tolkien and C. S. Lewis. While studying at theological college, Turner married Margaret Diana Samson, with whom he had three children. Ordained a priest of the Church of England in 1951, he has filled several positions, among them curate in Leeds, from 1951 to 1956; priest-in-charge, Crawley, Sussex, from 1956-1962; vicar of St. Matthews, Northampton, from 1962-1966; and chaplain of Eton College, Windsor, England, from 1973-1975. He also worked for the British Broadcasting Corp., Midland Region, Birmingham, from 1966 to 1970, as a religious broadcasting organizer, and as a teacher of English and di-

vinity at Briar Mill High School, Droitwich, England, from 1971–1973. He continues to serve as a part-time instructor of history at Malvern College, a post he began in 1975.

Turner began writing ecclesiastical plays in the 1950s, but it wasn't until the 1960s that Turner started writing books for children. His first and most notable series of books was the Darnley Mills series, which centers on the fictional countryside village of Darnley Mills. In his later years, Turner continued the Darnley Mills series, as well as several works of juvenile fiction featuring the main character Septimus, under the pseudonym Stephen Chance. He continues to take ultimate solace in Christianity, the countryside, and his peaceful cottage in North Wales.

MAJOR WORKS

Turner's most famous books are found in the series focusing on the inhabitants of Darnley Mills—an English village near an old Benedictine abbey. Unlike many series, Turner's works are not linked to a specific character or characters. Although many of the books describe the adventures of three modern boys—David, Arthur, and Peter—in the town and the area surrounding it, others relate tales of the First World War and Victorian times in the same setting. This series comprises the books *Colonel Sheperton's Clock* (1964), *The Grange at High Force* (1965), *Sea Peril* (1966), *Steam on the Line* (1968), *War on the Darnel* (1969), *Devil's Nob* (1970), *Powder Quay* (1971), and *Skull Island* (1977).

One major work of Turner's was in collaboration with illustrator Brian Wildsmith, *Brian Wildsmith's Illustrated Bible Stories* (1969), for which Turner provided the writing. It depicts well-known stories from both the Old and New Testaments, including the stories of Adam and Eve, Noah's Ark, Moses, David and Goliath, through to the life of Jesus and the carrying of His message into all the world. Turner has also written for younger children, notably a charming story of two runaway piglets, *Wig-wig and Homer* (1969).

CRITICAL RECEPTION

Critics laud Turner's ability to bring religious stories to life in an approachable way for younger readers. His writing skill, reports a reviewer for *Horn Book Magazine,* is reflected in his "ability to use an ecclesiastical setting for an interesting adventure story for boys." Of *Colonel Sheperton's Clock,* Zena Sutherland in the *Bulletin of the Center for Children's Books* wrote: "The plot is admirably constructed, but the charm of the book lies chiefly in the deft humor of dialogue and endearingly distinctive characterization." Critics have also noted that his writings are ones of substance, which will not be quickly or easily forgotten.

AWARDS

Turner was awarded the Carnegie Medal for best children's book published in United Kingdom, by the Library Association in 1966, for *The Grange at High Force.*

PRINCIPAL WORKS

The Darnley Mills Series

Colonel Sheperton's Clock [published as *The Mystery of the Colonel's Clock* (1984)] (children's fiction) 1964

The Grange at High Force [published as *The Adventure at High Force* (1984)] (children's fiction) 1965

Sea Peril (children's fiction) 1966

Steam on the Line (children's fiction) 1968

War on the Darnel (children's fiction) 1969

Devil's Nob (children's fiction) 1970

Powder Quay (children's fiction) 1971

Dunkirk Summer (children's fiction) 1973

Skull Island (children's fiction) 1977

Other Major Works

Brian Wildsmith's Illustrated Bible Stories (children's book) 1969

Wig-wig and Homer (children's fiction) 1969

Rookoo and Bree (children's fiction) 1979

The Candlemass Treasure (children's fiction) 1988

Under pseudonym Stephen Chance

Septimus and the Danedyke Mystery (juvenile fiction) 1971

Septimus and the Minster Ghost [published as *Septimus and the Minster Ghost Mystery* (1974)] (juvenile fiction) 1972

Septimus and the Stone of Offering [published as *The Stone of Offering* (1977)] (juvenile fiction) 1976

Septimus and the Spy Ring (juvenile fiction) 1979

GENERAL COMMENTARY

M. J. Board (essay date September 1979)

SOURCE: Board, M. J. "Children's Writers: Philip Turner." *School Librarian* 27, no. 3 (September 1979): 209-14.

[*In the following essay, Board examines the philosophy behind Turner's books.*]

Philip Turner has a self-acknowledged penchant for trains and for writing about them: mechanical things are to him objects for admiration—and manipulation. Turner started writing for children—frequently about trains and other mechanical things—as a relief from the almost insoluble problems he encountered as a priest of the Church of England. In children's books he felt he could offer a few solutions and create a better world than the one the children saw in the course of their real lives (see 'Philip Turner' in *Junior Bookshelf,* Vol. 30, No. 3, June 1966).

With such a conception of his literary calling it is no wonder that Turner's books offer his young readers primarily an escape into a world which is beneficent but largely free from the tensions of reality. Turner's world is also nostalgic—'a little behind the times' he calls it—and romantic, being peopled by types who exhibit fewer complications than non-literary personalities. It is consequently not quite the striven-for good of the genuine world he succeeds in creating, but an easier probity in which the heroes' successes are achieved with the minimum expenditure of concern.

THE CHORISTER STORIES

Yet *Colonel Sheperton's Clock* (1964), the first of a series set in the imaginary Darnley Mills, shows us a positive side to Turner. In these chorister stories the church and its traditions are never far away—the boys sing in the choir, they scour dusty church records, they lead the verger a merry dance round the clerestory and finally they thwart the theft of the church roof lead—for Turner is conscious of heritage. He introduces his readers, for example, to the beauty of ecclesiastical buildings and in the middle of one particularly boyish escapade he has Arthur, one of the chorister heroes—farmer's son and junior man-of-action though he is—give half his attention to 'the lovely melody of a Bach chorale which (crept) shyly down the corridor'.

Colonel Sheperton's Clock also introduces the minor character types who are to people the sequels to this story and whom Turner often distinguishes by amusing ideolects: 'Saturday,' (Old Charlie) said, 'at two pip emma sharpish, I wants you confetti-throwing limbs of Satan on parade. For why? There's a wedding. I shall expect you promptitudinally . . . with brooms ready for off . . .'.

Colonel Sheperton's Clock also contains a feature somewhat uncharacteristic of Turner which gives this book the edge over its successors, the 1966 Carnegie medal awarded to *The Grange at High Force* notwithstanding: the poignant yearning of the crippled David, the carpenter's son of the chorister trio, to lead the same active life as his friends, and the ensuing glimpse which Turner offers of the inner consciousness of one of his characters, suggests, unusually, that all is not for the best in the best of all possible worlds—and the book is the better for it.

In contrast *The Grange at High Force* (1965) is characterised by a certain genteel cosiness. David's lameness having been cured, nothing now seems to disturb the even tenor of the three protagonists' lives. Public-spiritedly they help to restore a derelict church, they engage once more in a piece of ecclesiastical detective work and they rescue an old lady snowbound on the isolated moors. However, as if to prove that boys will be boys, they destroy an apparently worthless pianola with Peter's replica of a Roman ballista and, supported by those two overgrown schoolboys, the retired Admiral Beauchamp-Troubridge and his faithful retainer Guns Kelly, they chauvinistically sink the *Bismark*—a hastily constructed raft—with the Admiral's antique cannon.

In typical Turner fashion mechanical devices and engineering contrivances abound: ranges, trajectories, the point-by-point destruction of the targets, the intricacies of Peter's homemade tricycle and his pyrotechnic skills in clearing the snow-blocked road. In fact, Turner tends to offer difficulties the heroes can easily solve by mechanical contrivance as an alternative to the often insoluble problems which are characteristic of genuine human behaviour.

Such romanticism is also well illustrated in another way, as the little group sing evensong in the newly restored chapel and the Admiral's alsatian patters in to sit peacefully throughout the service.

A similar tendency is also evident in the chronological setting of *Sea Peril* (1966) which, ostensibly set in the fifties and sixties, is permeated rather by an atmosphere of the twenties and thirties. Lady Bridgebolton is driven by her elderly butler in a cabriolet, no less, while Bos'n Jake's, the ship's chandlers, with its store of corned beef and ship's biscuit, has a place in the nineteenth rather than the twentieth century.

Turner's love of tradition takes the more negative form of nostalgia in *Sea Peril.* Indeed the physical anachronisms of this book point up the ossified values inherent in Turner's stories as a whole and indicate why he is unable to use the three youths to explore for his readers the evolving attitudes of the modern world.

The fourth of the chorister stories *War on the Darnel* (1969) offers further evidence of Turner's romanticism. 'The three irrepressible heroes', as they are described in the blurb, are again distinguished by their powers of contrivance: they convert their punt into a miniature battleship and, in the unimpeachable cause of Christian Aid, attack with the precision of marine commandos 'that shower from St Mark's' who hold Ballast Island. While smoke charges float down the Darnel and Arthur diverts the foe with pre-recorded battle noises, David swims in to sabotage the net blocking the channel.

It is all strongly reminiscent of Dieppe or D-Day. But there is one major difference—no one gets hurt in the war on the Darnel and so no one has any real cause for fear. And however complex and apparently dangerous the incidents of the battle, the effect on the reader is muted by Turner's portrayal of his characters' responses. Peter's fear at the height of the storm in the estuary, for example, is conveyed only in the stylised and inadequate '(he was) deathly pale' and 'sick at heart'.

MECHANICAL DEVICES

When Turner interrupted the chorister stories with *Steam on the Line* (1968) and its sequel *Devil's Nob* (1970) he chose for his setting the mid years of the nineteenth century when the imaginary Devil's Back and Darnley Mills Light Railway was converting from horse and gravity to steam. Young Taffy Hughes's love of horses arouses a twinge of sympathy for the Messianic Elijah who prophesies doom and destruction on a land sullied with steam. Yet in spite of the suspicions of Taffy and his schoolfriend Sarah, it is not Elijah who causes the landslip on the line but Henry Jenner, the local coach proprietor, and his drunken accomplice Geordie Bill. In Turner's gentle world, however, there is no room for villainy: Jenner, suitably contrite, ships aboard a cargo boat and Geordie Bill disappears after a fleeting appearance half-way through the book.

Characteristically, hearts of gold there are aplenty. Dublin Pat, a brawny Irish navvy, befriends Taffy and Sarah in their efforts to discover the saboteurs. Owing much to the music hall Irishman, Dublin Pat complains virtuously, after throwing an offending coachman through the taproom window; 'Oi've niver heard such language. Not since Mickey McFeeney the miller from Mullarney dropped the millstone on Father McNulty's toe—and him with the terrible corns.'

A similarly amusing but faintly factitious note, whose antecedents lie perhaps in the children's comic, is to be found in a number of amusing incidents in the story, such as when the slowly moving slate truck carrying an embarrassed and apprehensive Taffy—should he raise his cap or not?—gently butts the magenta-clad Sir Henry in the 'back end'.

The calculated contrivance of such incidents and such characters is significant—Turner's picture of the England of railway mania is an orderly one in spite of the confusions of the reality. In Turner's story everyone knows his place and when Dublin Pat is invited to a meal with the carpenter's family he surreptitiously and romantically copies their table manners.

In the equally ordered world of *Devil's Nob,* Taffy overcomes, as easily as the choristers have overcome their mechanical problems, the financial obstacles which prevent him marrying his childhood sweetheart. So in the last few pages he is able to slip the engagement ring on Sarah's finger. Such a tendency to manipulate his characters to fit his romanticism prevents Turner once more from using the hero as one who is sensitive to the changes of time. It is, for example, not Taffy who responds to Elijah's tirade but Turner. Indeed Taffy is not allowed a response at all: '(Taffy) gave up the speculation without realising that he had touched on something that

was beginning to change the world. For a few immemorial skills which had lasted hundreds—thousands—of years were giving way to new skills and ever more of them.'

Powder Quay (1970) continues the presentation of an orderly and cosy world in which all know and keep their places, whether at morning service in the parish church, in relations between master and servant, or in life aboard ship. More firmly in the field of adolescent fiction than the railway novels, *Powder Quay* has as hero a sixteen-year-old midshipman whose growing love for the orphaned daughter of a well-to-do family is traced.

Dickie, exhibiting the usual uncomplex virtues of Turner's heroes, sticks to his captain's side until he is wounded, hastens back as soon as he has sufficiently recovered and, in spite of exhaustion, steers a sure course with his boatload of survivors.

The familiar avuncular adults recur—the warm-hearted Captain Rolleson and the faithful Leading Seaman Hassock, a former coachman with the family—and the broad strokes of the characterisation are paralleled by the equally unsubtle and coincidental nature of the plot.

WARTIME ENGLAND

This ordered cosiness, however, is apparently replaced in *Dunkirk Summer* (1973)—in which the critical events of 1940 match the changes taking place in the eighteen-year-old hero—by some of the problems of the genuine world.

During his eighteenth year Andy becomes more conscious of his responsibilities—to his landlady, to the sea cadets, to the heritage of Darnley Mills parish church and above all to the other sex, represented by a sixth-former at the local girls' grammar school with whom he falls in love. In consequence he breaks away from a smutty-minded adolescent attitude to girls personified by his sixth-form companion, Archie, whose favourite reading—behind his set books—is the then topical *No orchids for Miss Blandish.* And Turner portrays with further clear-sightedness David Lambert, the subaltern son of the rector. We do not see the young officer in uniform, he avoids the subject of war in mealtime conversation, he is emaciated, has retreated through France smashing his equipment en route and when he does talk about his wartime experiences it is with a disparaging cynicism. Furthermore he advises Andy against volunteering for such things as the Dunkirk evacuation, which the protagonist had tried to join, and he warns, in contradiction of what was apparently a wartime slogan, 'You won't take one with you'.

But disappointingly this hard cynicism with which Turner begins to look squarely at wartime England is not maintained: the rector, for example, comments sentimentally, 'Well, whatever happens at least we've lived to see the country find its soul'; and the suggestion at one point that war is hideous—Andy is roused to fury on discovering that a younger schoolboy has looted the glove of the incinerated German airman—is quickly undermined by Turner's somewhat flaccid, '(Andy) suddenly felt old and tired'.

BACK TO THE CHORISTERS

Having touched however lightly on the world as we know it in *Dunkirk Summer,* Turner reverts in *Skull Island* (1977) to the characteristic avuncular adventure with the three chorister heroes, now in their late teens. Supervised by the Admiral and Guns Kelly, and accompanied by Peter's war-widowed Aunt Caroline, they explore the uninhabited Gethsemane Island to discover how Caroline's pilot husband had died. So once more the chorister heroes are offered an adventure at second hand. The avuncular Admiral provides an exciting and worthy opportunity for the boys to display their steadfastness, ingenuity and understanding: Arthur goodnaturedly accepts the leader's decision that he is not to be in the initial landing party and offers a silent sympathy to Caroline on the return from her husband's grave; David collapses before he will voluntarily delay the expedition by revealing his illness; and Peter's mechanical expertise is amply demonstrated.

The heartiness of the earlier chorister stories is evident once more and so too is the school-story invective: '"Arthur Steaming Ramsgill," said (Peter) with the utmost seriousness, "you're a turnip suffering from an attack of wireworm . . ."' Turner's tendency to the romantic and stereotyped rather than the precise presentation of character is also present: 'Arthur (was) like a cavalier, he went gaily through life broadcasting a general impression of total indestructibility.' And Guns Kelly sees the world through 'blue . . . far-seeing eyes'.

Indeed Guns Kelly perhaps best of all illustrates Turner's failure to see the world through the eyes of his characters and to attribute his own romantic conceptions to the people who inhabit his fictional world: 'Words like "love", "affection", "loyalty" did not exist in his vocabulary and he would have been blasphemously disbelieving if anyone had tried to point out that they governed his life.' But the sentimental accolade for Turner's fiction should be awarded to the incident in *Skull Island* in which the Admiral regards the sick and feverish David: 'The Admiral looked down at the pale, drawn face under the dark hair. He was thinking, "This is the sort of son I would have liked had things turned out differently." A line of poetry stabbed his memory like a knife—"Little son, do not die".'

THE JUSTIFICATION

How far are we justified in offering fiction such as Turner's now considerable output to children and young people? The weaknesses in Turner—his sentimentality, his character stereotypes, his undemanding language and his failure to see the world through the eyes of his protagonists—have been outlined, while on the credit side can be listed his feeling for permanence and tradition, the excitement of some of his narrative detail and the deliberately unexotic nature of his settings. But perhaps Turner's most obviously characteristic feature—his catalogue of technical details—suggests a more positive critical standpoint for his juvenile readers: these 'crusonnades' are concerned with the kind of initiative which overcomes obstacles in a technological society. They provide a vicarious opportunity for young readers to experience tests of physical but predominantly mental stamina in a world which seeks to protect its young from such challenges. Moreover, the boys' efforts, initiatives and even subterfuges are all in such obviously good causes—a Roman signal tower is discovered, the anguish of an elderly lady assuaged and the funds of a charity increased—that Turner in effect indicates to the adventure-starved youth of the twentieth century that it is possible to have an exciting time and even to cooperate with likeminded adults in the pursuit of legitimate, even admirable social ends. Turner is perhaps best regarded as a fictional exponent of that phenomenon of the mid twentieth century, the Duke of Edinburgh Award Scheme.

TITLE COMMENTARY

COLONEL SHEPERTON'S CLOCK (1964); REPUBLISHED AS *THE MYSTERY OF THE COLONEL'S CLOCK* (1984)

Richard Robinson (review date 13 November 1964)

SOURCE: Robinson, Richard. *New Statesman* 68, no. 1757 (13 November 1964): 752.

Colonel Sheperton's Clock, set in a Northumbrian mill-town, has a better plot than the average Mayne and many kindred felicities, particularly with schoolmasterly mannerisms. One of the boys has to stay in after school and write out 50 times 'I must not play foolish entomological jokes on members of the staff.' And how admirably Maynish is 'The bells suddenly stopped, so that he had to check his shout and it came out as a whisper with too much air round it.' The absorbing work of solving the mysterious death of a vanished colonel of 1914, through a scrap of old newspaper and some amateur archaeology, is only interrupted for the dot-and-carry 10-year-old hero to go and have a leg shortened in hospital; he learns to use it in a last-minute adventure with some lead-thieves which is pure bonus.

Library Journal (review date 15 November 1966)

SOURCE: *Library Journal* 91, no. 20 (15 November 1966): 5774.

Colonel Sheperton's Clock by Philip Turner is the first American edition of a book published in England in 1964. It is the story of boyish pranks in a town on the moor dominated by its parish church, whose architecture tells the story of 1000 years of English history. David and his friends, Arthur and Peter, delight in exploring the forbidden top stories of this ancient building and on one occasion come across a 1914 newspaper clipping about a certain Colonel Sheperton whose grandfather clock has stood, uncalled for, in David's family's carpenter shop since that date. The boys' curiosity is aroused and after much investigation they find that the colonel was a British spy before World War I and that he had sent the clock to be repaired just hours before he was murdered. After all these years, David discovers the secret concealed in the clock and sees that Colonel Sheperton is posthumously given the recognition he deserved. The mystery is less important than the lively adventures of three very British boys. Recommended for additional purchase.

Saturday Review (review date 12 November 1966)

SOURCE: *Saturday Review* 49 (12 November 1966): 51.

Published in England in 1964, **Colonel Sheperton's Clock** is the first book written for young people by Philip Turner, whose **The Grange at High Force** won the British Library Association's Carnegie Medal. It is a remarkably balanced book, giving a vivid picture of a town in the north of England, of the continuity of generations, and the curiosity of boys anywhere. David, Peter, and Arthur are in the

All Saints choir, and while they are illicitly investigating the clerestory passages, they come across an old newspaper article that excites their imagination. With the help of various adults, they pursue the clues that lead to their discovery of an unknown act of espionage in World War I and to the realization that Colonel Sheperton was an unsung hero of that conflict. The story line is deftly handled; the dialogue and characterization are superb. Ages 10-13.

Junior Bookshelf (review date February 1986)

SOURCE: *Junior Bookshelf* 50, no. 1 (February 1986): 31-2.

The Mystery of the Colonel's Clock (originally **Colonel Sheperton's Clock,** 1964) was the first of Philip Turner's 'Darnley Mills' stories. His second won a Carnegie Medal. This belongs, perhaps, to the William Mayne tradition, in its quirky characters, its concern for a real setting as a vital ingredient in the story, and in its consciously fine writing. Many of its qualities are characteristic of this writer, the character of David for example. This is one of the most honest portrayals of a handicapped child, quite free of sentimentality. It is a good story too, and one which introduces in the most natural and unpedantic way some of the techniques of historical enquiry. (The boys research, half a century after the event, the fate of a British secret agent at the outbreak of the First World War.) There are surely many things here to appeal to today's children, not least the excellence of the writing, in, for example:

> '. . . like an enormous scythe cutting through grass, the swish of the great moorland wind running free across the high places of the world, and carrying with it like debris on a flood, the far cry of the sheep and the sad mewing of the curlew.'

The Dawlish book is without illustrations. In the Turner, Philip Gough's fine drawings have been replaced by new illustrations from Bridget Bone, which are adequate but not a patch on the original pictures.

📖 *THE GRANGE AT HIGH FORCE* (1965)

Margery Fisher (review date July 1965)

SOURCE: Fisher, Margery. *Growing Point* 4, no. 2 (July 1965): 539.

The Grange at High Force, sequel to **Colonel Sheperton's Clock,** is another mystery-adventure involving a statue of the Virgin lost from an old church, a cannon from one of Nelson's ships and a snowstorm which causes crisis in many households. In the centre of action the three boys (David the carpenter's son, Peter from the Vicarage, Arthur from the hill farm) nose about, determined to find the lost statue but equally determined to enjoy their new friend the retired Admiral, who knows how to make gunpowder. Not for everyone, this tale of Northern hills, for it is moderately sophisticated in language and attitude, but for the child who likes action with a little elegance, who enjoys meeting in books odd and arresting personalities, and who will accept a basis of sturdy moral value.

Robert Bell (review date December 1965)

SOURCE: Bell, Robert. *School Librarian* 13, no. 3 (December 1965): 370-71.

It is always gratifying to meet a junior novel [*The Grange at High Force*] which, besides having an exciting and fast-moving plot, is certain, through its setting, to stimulate the interest of young readers in things of value, without any conscious attempt on the author's part but simply through his own sincerity and enthusiasm. Frederick Grice, among others, is a past master at this, and the Rev. Philip Turner, in this his second book, shows this quality in abundant measure. The main plot deals with the tracing of a lost statue which once stood in a niche in the church, and the solving of this mystery involves the Rector's son and his friends in delving into Church history and parish records in a way which brings these things vividly to life and makes them quite absorbing. There is, besides, a profusion of other incident which keeps the interest and excitement at a high level throughout. Some of the adult characters may seem at first acquaintance to be rather made-to-measure (grumbling old verger, irascible organist, eccentric maiden lady and retired Admiral who is still a boy at heart) but they are excellently portrayed and quite convincing. The youthful conversation and sense of fun are absolutely genuine. The book is beautifully produced and illustrated, and is highly recommended.

Saturday Review (review date June 1967)

SOURCE: *Saturday Review* 50 (June 1967): 36.

High Force is a tiny English hamlet where Folly Grange [in *The Grange at High Force*] has been rented to a briny and gregarious retired admiral who is interested in ships, firearms, boys, and mysteries,

and who has ample opportunity to indulge his interests when he meets the local version of the Three Musketeers. David, Peter, and Arthur are hot on the trail of a statue of the Madonna, long missing from an old church. The statue is found, but it is less through the boys' efforts than through the capricious gratitude of an elderly woman. The plot is sturdy enough, but it is in the lively characterization and distinctive writing that the great charm of the book lies. Ages 11-14.

Helen B. Crenshaw (review date August 1967)

SOURCE: Crenshaw, Helen B. *Horn Book Magazine* 43, no. 4 (August 1967): 472-73.

Illustrated by W. T. Mars. The ability to use an ecclesiastical setting for an interesting adventure story for boys [*The Grange at High Force*] is a skill displayed here by the minister-author. "Operation Bird's Nest" means getting rid of the pigeons in the Darnley Church (a homemade ballista of uncertain aim has been fired near the church windows; the resulting broken window has given entry to the pigeons). Not only does the occasion begin the story in an attention-compelling fashion, but it introduces three inventive boys and a few local characters of Darnley Mills, including eccentric Miss Cadell-Twitten, a nature lover. A multitude of events follows—the brakes on one boy's bike fail on a steep hill; the three boys meet a retired admiral and his servant Guns Kelly; target practice for the ballista and the antique cannon of the admiral is arranged; Miss Cadell-Twitten and other well-meaning citizens interfere. The exciting climax takes place in a howling snowstorm. Humorous touches, fascinating details, and a mystery are only three ingredients of this Carnegie Medal winner.

Margery Fisher (review date January 1986)

SOURCE: Fisher, Margery. *Growing Point* 24, no. 5 (January 1986): 4569.

In the parish church of Darnley, once a monastic foundation, a statue of the Virgin was removed by eighteenth century improvers [in *The Grange at High Force*]. Three schoolboys, one the son of the incumbent, resolve to find it and replace it in the niche empty for so long. A treasure—hunt drawn to a triumphant conclusion and a fine picture of a community in northern moorland.

SEA PERIL (1966)

Junior Bookshelf (review date August 1966)

SOURCE: *Junior Bookshelf* 30, no. 4 (August 1966): 257.

This chronicle of youthful exuberance [*Sea Peril*] has some of the characteristics of Mr. Turner's Carnegie Medal winner *The Grange at High Force,* and is the third story about Peter Beckford, Arthur Ramsgill and David Hughes and their activities in Darnley Mills.

The serious element in the plot is supplied by a search for a Roman signal station but the bulk of the story is full of the hilarious adventures and misadventures that Philip Turner handles so expertly: a punt converted into a bicycle-driven paddle-boat; a lively running quarrel with the owner of an expensive motor-launch; a battle with the local lady of the manor; a perilous rescue in a turbulent stream.

All good fun, plenty of teenage slang, a parade of unusual and captivating characters—not an award winner but well above the average children's book in conception and execution.

Pamela Royds (review date December 1966)

SOURCE: Royds, Pamela. *School Librarian* 14, no. 3 (December 1966): 347-48.

The reverend Philip Turner has established himself as a writer with a high standard. This [*Sea Peril*], the latest book about Peter, Arthur and David, is structurally the best of the three. Peter's engineering flair and David's skill as a carpenter are used to convert a derelict punt into a paddle-driven, bicycle-pedal-powered cabin cruiser. In this uncertain craft the boys spend an adventurous summer half-term holiday afloat. Other characters play minor parts; an irascible river-hog in a motor-cruiser, the school history master searching for a Roman signal tower, an archetypal dowager duchess and her grand-daughter. There are minor plots; Arthur's captaincy of the Northern Schools' cricket team, the insanitary Castle Hanger drains, but all have a bearing on the main adventure.

Philip Turner's boys are individuals, and single-minded as only boys can be. The gently mocking schoolboy humour in their dialogue has a freshness and authenticity that strikes again and again. Only in the narrative are there lapses into repetitiveness and cliché.

It is pleasant to be reminded in this admirable story that boys in a small country town can, and do, lead full lives without benefit of television.

Zena Sutherland (review date January 1969)

SOURCE: Sutherland, Zena. *Bulletin of the Center for Children's Books* 22, no. 5 (January 1969): 86.

A sequel to *Colonel Sheperton's Clock* and *The Grange at High Force* [*Sea Peril*], those delightful books about England's substitute for Athos, Porthos, and Aramis. Peter, Arthur, and David are as inventive, articulate, and engaging a trio here as ever as they plan, construct, and operate a bicycle-powered punt and go exploring on the river. Their varied adventures are enjoyable, but it is the characters of the boys and their friends (plus a few eminently detestable enemies) that give the story its zest and color.

STEAM ON THE LINE (1968)

Barbara Willard (review date May 1968)

SOURCE: Willard, Barbara. "Important Grown-Ups." *New Statesman* 75, no. 1941 (May 1968): 693-94.

Philip Turner's *Steam on the Line* is set in the author's Darnley Mills in earlier days. The little local railway is to be mechanised. To young Taffy, whose father works for the company, steam is a miracle. Taffy is bold enough to play a hero's part when the line is threatened, child enough to weep for the loss of 'the wise horses who needed no orders'. But he and young Sarah, his constant and brave companion, are not even half the story. There is not a nonentity in the cast. The swift, poetic plot is creamy with characters like Taffy's father; Miss Grant, the schoolmistress; the eccentric Sir Henry Bridgebolton; Dublin Pat and Round Annie. A very re-readable book.

Junior Bookshelf (review date June 1968)

SOURCE: *Junior Bookshelf* 32, no. 3 (June 1968): 191.

Based on the development of a light railway serving a lonely quarry, and on the rivalry the prospect of a passenger service occasions with other local interest, this is a delightful book [*Steam on the Line*] from cover to cover. Taffy and Sarah, the children involved, are gay, adventurous and enterprising and further than usual from the improbable. Their family background is not the least attractive element of the tale. The local society too has a fair share of attention and produces a variety of attractive characters, of all ages. It is a thoroughly satisfactory as well as an entertaining tale, attractively illustrated.

Robert Bell (review date July 1968)

SOURCE: Bell, Robert. *School Librarian* 16, no. 2 (July 1968): 221.

To readers of the Rev. Philip Turner's previous novels, Darnley Mills will have become a familiar setting. In this one [*Steam on the Line*] he takes us back to the advent of the age of steam and imagines its effect upon the Devil's Back and Darnley Mills Light Railway, and upon the community. To the quarry owners and railway engineers it promises prosperity, to the proprietor of the horse-drawn coach company it constitutes a threat, to the eccentric prophet-like hermit it typifies the machinations of the forces of evil, and to young Taffy and Sarah it brings the thrills and excitement which have captured the imagination of subsequent generations of children.

The author exploits this with all the verve, humour and imagination we have come to expect from him. The story is excellently conceived and presented, the characters colourful and convincing, and the pace unflagging.

Virginia Haviland (review date April 1969)

SOURCE: Haviland, Virginia. *Horn Book Magazine* 45, no. 2 (April 1969): 175.

Illustrated by Gareth Floyd. Although this Victorian story [*Steam on the Line*] has a particularly English quality of setting and characters (many of whom use country speech), its plot and theme have universality of significance; for they are related to the economic and social implications of the Industrial Revolution at the advent of the steam railroad engine. The treatment has strength, vividness, and dramatic appeal. The new developments of "The Devil's Back and Darnley Mills Light Railway" serving the slate quarry and, eventually, passengers—and the sabotage attempts—are followed through the eyes of David and Sarah, whose fathers work for the railroad and the quarry. A broad cast of characters and homely details of family and school life make the story unusually

realistic. The David of the author's three earlier books is grandson of the David who in this story risks his life to prevent a wreck on the new train's first passenger run.

◫ *WIG-WIG AND HOMER* (1969)

Junior Bookshelf (review date December 1969)

SOURCE: *Junior Bookshelf* 33, no. 6 (December 1969): 375-76.

A whimsical tale [*Wig-wig and Homer*] of two piglets who escape to seek their fortunes. The intellectual Homer has been sold by the Professor to a boorish farmer who lashes him to a cart to his great indignation. The pink pig Wigwig is escaping from a fate called bacon, she does not know what bacon is but it does not sound very nice. They journey in search of the wise woman and after many adventures fulfil their destiny on Sanctuary Island.

The under 11's will enjoy the pathos and humour of the story, which is much more suited to the gentle world of Philip Turner than his other more robust stories for older boys have been. Graham Humphreys has wedded the black and white illustrations to the text with a masterly stroke, and manages to make the reader see things as the pigs would have seen them.

Kirkus Reviews (review date 15 September 1970)

SOURCE: *Kirkus Reviews* 38, no. 18 (15 September 1970): 1038.

"I am shaped like a sugared almond, and the oyster is my destiny." It sounds mysterious but the sequence is somewhat predictable and the actual revelation has no punch. Wigwig the pig, mindful of a fate beyond fried trotters, leaves the farm and embarks on a search for a safer life [in *Wig-wig and Homer*]. Homer, a polysyllabic pig equally reluctant to become bacon, is her companion in a series of skimpy episodes with Lone Badger (an open door policy), sly John Fox, and the Wise Woman who cares for animals missing wings or limbs or sight. On Christmas Eve the truth is revealed: Wigwig is to be queen of Sanctuary Island, with an oyster shell crown. Some of the animals are nearly allegorical and the prose has hints of deeper concerns but the action is minimal, the tension slight. Unlike the author's earlier books (about Peter, Arthur and David), some of the humor may be lost to American children—e.g. errors in a rhyme about Guy Fawkes Day—because it depends on the ignorance of the animals. No truffle—just a trifle.

📖 *WAR ON THE DARNEL* (1969)

Margery Fisher (review date October 1969)

SOURCE: Fisher, Margery. *Growing Point* 8, no. 4 (October 1969): 1397.

An old locomotive is discovered in *War on the Darnel* but this is only one thread in a complex pattern. The first part of this story concerns a formal but harmless battle (mud hurled from a homemade ballista) between boys blocking the estuary route by Ballast Island and the three friends of the Darnel stories who are bent on taking the short cut to visit their friend the Admiral. The token battle is resolved in time for both sides to join a rescue party when storm and flood threaten the Bridgebolton almshouses and the engine coveted by a rich American, descendant of the man who first drove it on the branch line. The link with *Steam on the line* will attract readers who are prepared to accept the rather self-conscious slang and generally old-fashioned tone of this writer's holiday adventures.

David Churchill (review date December 1969)

SOURCE: Churchill, David. *School Librarian* 17, no. 4 (December 1969): 405.

Although difficult to assess, this story [*War on the Darnel*] undoubtedly offers a good read for any boy in the lower half of the secondary school. In an age of piped and canned pleasure it portrays groups of boys engaged actively in doing things that are interesting and ingenious, if at times misguided. The slang they talk will no doubt be enjoyed by the child reader and, not being carefully contemporary, may avoid dating the book too soon. One group of boys has seized control over a narrow waterway and is exacting tolls towards a Christian Aid collection from all who pass. A rival group (our heroes), also collecting for Christian Aid, equips its pedal boat with diabolical weapons and attacks to force the passage. The story develops from this to describe how the groups of boys join forces to fight flood danger threatening some almshouses. Apart from the brave but uncomfortable attempts to capture the private talk of lively, intelligent, intimate school boys, the language is at a mature level. The book has action, spirit and humour and is well worth considering.

Kirkus Reviews (review date 1 December 1969)

SOURCE: *Kirkus Reviews* 37, no. 23 (1 December 1969): 1267-268.

Two wars actually [in *War on the Darnel*], on that formidable Darnley Mills estuary that's been the scene of prior adventures-for-adventures'-sake with Peter and Arthur and David. One's an exuberant mini-battle in which the trio takes on a competitive group of fund-raisers for Christian Aid who've taken over a mid-river island to collect tolls from passing punts. The crew of *Sea Peril II* won't stand for the piracy (or the threat that the pirates may amass more than they did); Peter-alias-Einstein masterminds an involved bit of mud-slinging (not the figurative kind) based on differential calculus and after endless preparatory machinations the trio triumphs. Next case—defensive—against the storm interrupting their return to shore: with retired Admiral "Trouty" and his millionaire American Colonel friend they rescue the thwarted pirates and some flooded almshouse old-folk, and save imperious Lady Bridgebolton's bridge . . . whereupon said Colonel is permitted to run his sentimental railroad (that's a sub-plot) across her veddy proper property. They're a busy bunch in a quite busy book, typically Turning a nice phrase now and then between dialects and in-jokes. As the Admiral says in one of the story's rare reflective moments: "This is what it had all been for—the fear, the death, and the fighting. That two groups of riotous boys might engage in hilarious and harmless battle on an English river." Well carry on then boys—for whomsoever will run with you rollicking motley. *11-13.*

Zena Sutherland (review date February 1970)

SOURCE: Sutherland, Zena. *Saturday Review* 53 (February 1970): 45.

The three musketeers of Darnley Mills, Peter, David, and Arthur, ride again [in *War on the Darnel*], this time deploying their bicycle-powered home-made boat against a rival party of boys who have established themselves at a judicious point on the river and demand a toll. The river piracy is for a Worthy Cause, but our stalwarts cannot spurn the challenge. They plan and execute extremely complicated and ingenious naval and quasi-naval maneuvers that result in a hilarious battle-royal. Very, very British in the nicest way: the boys rattle along in precocious fashion, the policeman and the retired naval men just escape being typed, the humor is best-boys'-school, and the book is full of action without seeming too busy. Ages 10-13.

Junior Bookshelf (review date April 1970)

SOURCE: *Junior Bookshelf* 34, no. 2 (April 1970): 109.

Liberally spattered with robust schoolboy slang (a selection of the language really used by young men, Wordsworth might have said?) and even the odd mild obscenity, *War on the Darnel* shows once again that Philip Turner can write with gusto, pace and virtuosity: there are likely to be few dull moments in a book that can offer "I'll thump your teething troubles through the back of your flaming neck" alongside "For Jane the morning stretched empty as the Sahara desert to the distant oasis of lunch-time".

His plot has the right ingredients to maintain persistent discord: battles between two rival gangs of boys, a struggle to open a disused railway line, a storm that threatens life and property. The three boys who have appeared in Philip Turner's earlier books have lost none of their enterprising and energetic zest: they build boats, invent strange weapons and fight with the cunning and courage of commandos . . . and all for Christian Aid!

Zena Sutherland (review date June 1970)

SOURCE: Sutherland, Zena. *Bulletin of the Center for Children's Books* 23, no. 10 (June 1970): 168-69.

5-9. [*War on the Darnel* is] a sequel to *Colonel Sheperton's Clock* and several other delightful books about three lively English boys whose ingenuity and curiosity afford them—and the reader—the pleasures of some fascinating capers. Here they engage in a mighty battle with another set of boys who have set up a river barricade and are asking a fee in the name of charity. The trio are all for the charity, but their spirits cannot resist the challenge, and they organize a counter-attack that is complicated, funny, clever, and successful. The characterization is good, the dialogue even better, and the setting firmly British.

📖 *BRIAN WILDSMITH'S ILLUSTRATED BIBLE STORIES* (1969)

Publishers Weekly (review date 10 February 1969)

SOURCE: *Publisher's Weekly* 195, no. 6 (10 February 1969): 75.

(*4-Up*) Your reviewer has obviously no way of knowing what theologians will think of this collection of Bible stories [*Brian Wildsmith's Illustrated Bible Stories*]. As a grandmother, *I* know I can hardly wait to read them to Jessie, my six year old granddaughter, from cover to cover from the first chapter, "God Made Everything," with its lines filled with wonder—"from the small snail with his fragile house on his back to the tawny lion, king of the jungle and needing no house, God made them all" to the last chapter, "In the End," and its last line filled with compassion—"So be it, Lord Jesus. The grace of the Lord Jesus be with you all." I can hardly wait to share Brian Wildsmith's pictures with Jessie, pictures aglow with the wonder and the majesty of the words.

Saturday Review (review date 10 May 1969)

SOURCE: *Saturday Review* 52 (10 May 1969): 54.

Brian Wildsmith is a winner of the Greenaway Medal, and his distinctive paintings make this book [*Brian Wildsmith's Illustrated Bible Stories*] a thing of beauty, brilliant in the use of color and imposingly dramatic in interpretation. Philip Turner, an ordained minister, is a Carnegie Medal winner and his adaptations are brief, pungent stories that deftly combine biblical mood and contemporary language, giving the most familiar stories a depth and continuity that make the book simple enough for the very young and meaningful enough for older children. *Ages 5-12.*

Commonweal (review date 23 May 1969)

SOURCE: *Commonweal* 90, no. 10 (23 May 1969): 301.

Contemporary children would probably prefer this book [*Brian Wildsmith's Illustrated Bible Stories*] with its livelier biblical syntax for up-to-date language and baroque imagery calculated to arouse a sense of wonder. The dynamic illustrations are sophisticated enough to be provocative. *10 and Up.*

Margaret Meek (review date June 1969)

SOURCE: Meek, Margaret. *School Librarian* 17, no. 2 (June 1969): 216.

When Arthur Mee's *Children's Bible* was the accredited form of holy writ for the young, parents and teachers were absolved from the need to choose a 'suitable' version of the Bible. Now there are many, not all of them designed for Christians only. [*Brian Wildsmith's Illustrated Bible Stories*] is a combination of prize winners, yoked to make a striking presentation of the Scriptures for the under-twelves.

Philip Turner has selected the theme of man's moral growth and his increased awareness of God. The force of the textual critics and demythologizers is strong; the walls of Jericho don't fall down, for example, and Jonah isn't to be found. Some incidents—the flood, David, the nativity—have fired narrator and illustrator alike. Goliath is a true giant, the prophets speak out strongly, the temptations in the wilderness are memorably set: 'the heat haze shimmered over the desert, the lizard flicked across the rock.'

Brian Wildsmith's drawings are shot through with light, leaving space for the child's imagination to fill the interstices of iconic outlines. I suggest that prospective buyers should look at Noah, Elijah and Palm Sunday and compare this version with those that come from Taizé.

Commonweal (review date 21 November 1969)

SOURCE: *Commonweal* 91, no. 8 (21 November 1969): 253.

Man's faith in God is highlighted in these chronologically arranged Bible stories [***Brian Wildsmith's Illustrated Bible Stories***], skillfully and dramatically retold by a winner of the Carnegie Medal. The stunning paintings make this a book to treasure. *8-14.*

Janet Ann Ingraham (review date July 1990)

SOURCE: Ingraham, Janet Ann. "Bible Stories for Children: Israelites, Miracles, and Us." *Catholic Library World* 62 (July 1990): 300-01.

The bold, emphatic paintings in ***Brian Wildsmith's Illustrated Bible Stories*** display a strikingly different artistic interpretation from the soft, reserved offerings of the Petershams. Philip Turner's compact retelling of the entire Bible in colloquial, easy language attempts to make God accessible and presents difficult events and ideas straightforwardly, with neither gloss nor overexplanation. Wildsmith's illustrations combine simple black outlines with a density of bright color. The variety in placement of text and pictures is attractive but the prominence of the lavish illustrations may hinder readers from appreciating the worthy narrative.

📖 *DEVIL'S NOB* (1970)

Junior Bookshelf (review date October 1970)

SOURCE: *Junior Bookshelf* 34, no. 5 (October 1970): 310.

The Darnley Mills Light Railway and the local characters for whom it is directly or indirectly the chord of existence and interest have already proved a happy

inspiration for Mr. Turner and seem likely to do so until he has brought all the existing children—possibly their children as well—to adult status. This time [in *Devil's Nob*] the indomitable Taffy Hughes, now an apprentice carpenter at the slate quarry, is used to help illustrate the little-appreciated dangers of work of such a kind in the nineteenth century, and the railway figures largely in the perils as well as the fun of life among the prosperous but still poor community of Darnley. Taffy's developing prowess as a fisherman is part of the fun; Lister's plea for antiseptic surgery is part of the peril. Both illustrate the author's happy knack of turning to account some aspect of his period which not only establishes the period without labouring it but provides an incidental "wonder" which we now accept without remembering the revolution which preceded its acceptance. Taffy's rescue of Sarah Thurgood is an incident which should long linger in the reader's memory and here again Mr. Turner makes expert use of technical details to prolong the suspense. Although Taffy and Sarah have reached an understanding one hopes Mr. Turner will not bring them to the altar precipitately. As children they have been wholesome and courageous; but they have a long way to go; for their sakes as well as the readers' they should be allowed to take their time.

Robert Bell (review date December 1970)

SOURCE: Bell, Robert. *School Librarian* 18, no. 4 (December 1970): 458, 461.

The darnley mills light railway and the Devil's Back slate quarry in the latter part of the nineteenth century again provide the setting for Philip Turner's new novel [*Devil's Nob*], which I think is much his best to date, and illustrates his growing stature as a children's author. It has greater depth than his previous books, excellent as they are. The workings of the quarry are described in more detail and the social conditions of the work-people more graphically portrayed. Most successful of all, the burgeoning of the love between apprentice Taffy Hughes and his childhood friend Sarah Thurgood is very beautifully and sensitively done and is an object lesson in the way in which this element should be treated.

There are thrills and adventure a-plenty, and the climax is the race, for a wager of a thousand guineas, between the steam engine *Taffy*, driven by Sir Henry Bridgebolton, and Sir Josiah on his horse Black Prince. Here the author skates on the edge of melodrama, as he sometimes does, with the baronets' dialogue peppered with 'demmit' and 'stap me.' This merely adds to the fun, however, and in no way detracts from the quality of the book, which is recommended strongly for both boys and girls in the upper eleven-to-fourteen range.

Publishers Weekly (review date 26 March 1973)

SOURCE: *Publishers Weekly* 203, no. 13 (26 March 1973): 70.

(12-Up) High-voltage action and romance, plus beautiful writing, lift this novel [*Devil's Nob*] far above the ordinary. Its setting is Victorian England, where life was hard for the working man and his family. The hero is Taffy Hughes who works as a carpenter's apprentice at the Devil's Slate Quarry. The boy is in love with Sarah, a motherless girl saddled with the care of her sick father and her brothers and sisters. Their future looks bleak until the boy makes a friend of an influential member of the community. Taffy's manhood is put to the test in some grueling adventures, the most riveting of which describe his efforts to find Sarah when she is lost in a storm on top of sinister Devil's Nob. Help is given to Sarah's family, in the form of an undemanding job for her father and the two lovers are united at last.

Childhood Education (review date October 1973)

SOURCE: *Childhood Education* 350, no. 1 (October 1973): 30.

Taffy and Sarah of **Steam on the Line** (1968) are now grown and much in love [in **Devil's Nob**]; but poverty and Sarah's motherless family impede their marriage. The book's Victorian mores are remote, as is the English mining town setting. The action (quarry accidents and a race between a locomotive and a horse) is absorbing, however, with keen tension and suspense. *Ages 12 Up.*

◫ *POWDER QUAY* (1971)

Ann Thwaite (review date 5 March 1971)

SOURCE: Thwaite, Ann. "Not as Good as Tolstoy." *New Statesman* 81, no. 2085 (5 March 1971): 312.

For the most part, then, it is praise. But, as Philip Turner has won a Carnegie Medal in the past, and therefore something of a reputation, I should warn potential readers that his new book, *Powder Quay* is a disappointment. Set in 1914, with Midshipman Richard Bridgebolton out to prove himself a man, the story could be moving and exciting, but is not. Richard is a dull boy and Emma, the girl he kisses in the shed on Powder Quay, is a cardboard figure, in spite of her puckish smile. Even the sinking of HMS *Grangemouth* never comes to life. It's almost as if Mr Turner has taken too careful a note of an earlier criticism of one of his books: 'He isn't as effective as he could be if he thinned his texture by half.' The texture of the new book is too thin to warm us.

Times Literary Supplement (review date 2 April 1971)

SOURCE: "The Good Old Days." *Times Literary Supplement* no. 3605 (2 April 1971): 385.

The author of *Powder Quay* (which is set in the first few months of the First World War) does not aim at pastiche any more than the author of *The Henchmans*; yet its approach seems basically different. Richard Bridgebolton, a 16-year-old midshipman, comes home for Christmas leave. On the same train is Leading Seaman Hassock (in former life "Uncle Bob", his father's coachman). The Flanders massacre has already touched the village. The girl Emma, staying at Dick's home, has just lost her father, the Colonel (he was also Richard's godfather); Stationmaster Hughes ("Mr. Taffy") who runs the neglected local line almost singlehanded, has lost his only son. An idyllic if wintry Boxing Day expedition with Emma is brought to an end by Richard's recall to Scapa Flow. There, in action, his ship is destroyed and—hauled from the sea by Hassock—he finds himself in an open boat with several other survivors, two of them wounded—one a midshipman friend, the other a rating. Naturally, the boy assumes command, and (with plenty of discreetly-conveyed advice from Hassock) he gets the boat back through the notorious Hellrace to Powder Quay. There, Mr. Taffy and Emma discover them. Richard is awarded the Albert Medal; Hassock (after a generous word from Richard) is made petty officer. Reading the lesson in church, at Easter, Richard feels at one with his 500 years of valiant warrior ancestors whose memorials are all around.

The story is told with a close and insistent meticulousness. There is something curious, though, about the author's stance as he presents his noble and gallant gentry and his rough or semi-comic crowd characters, the under-servants and ratings. (*Flambards,* on this point, provides an enlightening contrast.) Of course, on Christmas Day, the household staff did stand at the foot of the stairs, "in descending order of importance", to receive their gifts; of course, in church, the congregation was divided, women on one side, men on the other; the bootboy and the scullery maids at the back, the families of the rector and the agent at the front. Segregation did not extend; to be sure, to the gentlefolk in the pews; Richard and Emma indeed shared a prayerbook. Most memorable, though, of many vignettes is that of the junction station on that first Christmas leave. Richard is ushered into the first-class waiting room with its blazing fire; but Hassock is left out in the snow; the lower-grade waiting rooms are (for economy) kept locked. To be sure, the boy kindly invites the older man inside. But what makes a reader uneasy about these passages is something indulgent and difficult to define. Can it be sheer nostalgia?

Children's Book Review (review date June 1971)

SOURCE: *Children's Book Review* 1, no. 3 (June 1971): 94.

Philip Turner's second book [*Powder Quay*] set in the Darnley Mills area describes the experiences of a midshipman in 1914-15 and his maturing friendship with the daughter of a neighbouring family.

Of particular merit is the portrayal of the boy's feelings when, after an explosion, he commands a boatload of wounded survivors including men older and wiser than himself who look to him for guidance. The discomfort and dangers of warfare are contrasted with the ease and order of life for the well-to-do at home, for whom the social pattern is as yet unchanged. The two worlds make sudden contact when Richard lands his companions at Powder Quay.

The book is written in an easy, graphic style which helps make characters and incidents alive. The happy ending and the lightness with which grief and fear are presented prevent this being a deeply moving book, but it is thoughtful and sincere, the writer's values clear but not paraded. *Twelve Up.*

Robert Bell (review date September 1971)

SOURCE: Bell, Robert. *School Librarian* 19, no. 3 (September 1971): 266.

The setting [in *Powder Quay*] is again the Darnley Mills area, which will be familiar to readers of the author's previous novel *Devil's Nob,* but this story

has a greater depth and seriousness. The period is the first world war, and young Midshipman Richard Bridgebolton, on Christmas leave, spends an idyllic day with his young friend Emma sailing down river to Powder Quay. The day becomes even more perfect for them when they realize their love for each other. Richard is recalled to his ship, which is sunk in an engagement with the enemy, and he leaves his boyhood behind when he takes charge of a boatload of the surviving crew and brings them back to Powder Quay, so recently the scene of his happiness but now with a grimmer significance in his life and that of Emma.

Mr Turner goes from strength to strength. This is a very fine story, full of exciting adventure and with great depth of feeling and understanding. It cannot fail to be a winner.

DUNKIRK SUMMER (1973)

Margery Fisher (review date May 1973)

SOURCE: Fisher, Margery. *Growing Point* 12, no. 1 (May 1973): 2162-164.

Philip Turner always tells a vigorous story but his plots are never wholly supported by character or idiom. Perhaps he tries too hard to be in with the young. His youths and girls chatter away in terms unexceptionable as to date and phrase but somehow their speeches sound as though they had been laboriously constructed from dictionaries of slang. The characters have none of the quirks or inconsistencies of, say, characters in stories by John Gordon or Nina Bawden. And this matters. It means that *Dunkirk Summer,* like the rest of the tales set in Darnley Mills, have the air of being historical exercises rather than novels. This new book starts with a flashback when Andy Birch, on a corvette somewhere in the Atlantic early in 1941, recalls the summer of Dunkirk, when he and his coarse-grained chum Archie were evacuated from London and their school twinned with the Alice Bridgebolton school for girls. Andy's first meeting with Patricia Lambert was unusual; she saw him spying on the VIth Form history lesson through a trapdoor in the classroom ceiling. The incident began a friendship that grew into love as the two of them, with Archie, listened to news of Dunkirk and heard of the loss of their cadet training barge, which the Colonel had gallantly taken across Channel, watched a German 'plane crash in flames, busied themselves with buckets when the church tower was set alight by incendiary bombs. Details are accurate and well chosen, incidents varied and appropriate, plot neatly brought to an open end, but the final impression is one of academic tidiness, of a faint priggishness, of a curious lack of red corpuscles.

A. R. Williams (review date August 1973)

SOURCE: Williams, A. R. *Junior Bookshelf* 37, no. 4 (August 1973): 277-78.

Unlike *Carrie's War*, **Dunkirk Summer** does concentrate upon the impact of war on young people; on Andrew Birch, the Londoner evacuated to Darnley Mills, and Patricia Lambert, another sixth-former and a member of the local girls' school which Andrew's school has to share. One faint resemblance to *Carrie's War* lies in the mode of introducing Andrew and his story through his day-dreaming, off duty, as Ordinary Seaman Birch. Mr. Turner does not avoid, any more than he sensationalises, the realities of war which made themselves felt occasionally in Darnley: the crashed enemy aircraft whose pilot Andrew could not rescue; and a finely composed incident during Andy's and Pat's firewatching spell when Pat's father's church was nearly destroyed. Through these and other actualities of war, including Andy's attempt to join his local sea-scout leader in a trip to Dunkirk, Mr. Turner threads the growing tension of the affection ripening between boy and girl, never salacious and never soppy, frankly physical but never permissive. How far this author or Miss Bawden really convey the ambience of that particular summer to anyone who did not live through it, it is impossible to say. One feels that Mr. Turner, at any rate, had a very good try.

C. E. J. Smith (review date September 1973)

SOURCE: Smith, C. E. J. *School Librarian* 21, no. 3 (September 1973): 269.

Hilaire Belloc defined the craft of writing as 'the production in the reader's mind of a certain image and a certain emotion'. The ability to do this is possessed in full measure by both these writers. Philip Turner's story [**Dunkirk Summer**] of Andrew Birch and Patricia Lambert, sixth-formers during the summer of 1940, caught up in preparations for the evacuation from Dunkirk, the consequences of the Battle of Britain, the fire-raids of the Luftwaffe, and their growing love for each other, moved me deeply. Admittedly, this is the period of my own adolescence

and personal memories intrude, but the writing is so clear and strong that I am sure it will move youngsters equally. If you know Mr Turner's other Darnley Mills books, then you will know that characterization is deep, action swift, and emotion true.

📖 *SKULL ISLAND* (1977)

Gerald Haigh (review date 10 February 1978)

SOURCE: Haigh, Gerald. "Mysteries to Solve." *Times Educational Supplement* no. 3270 (10 February 1978): 24.

Authenticity of background, too is the hallmark of **Skull Island**—which; despite its title and cover, is much more than a Blyton-style mystery yarn. Philip Turner has written an excellent story about an uninhabited island where a Swordfish crashed during the war. The pilot's friend and his widow return there with some young companions, and an intriguing story with many levels and nuances unfolds. Turner is a sensitive and perceptive writer as well as an old salt-horse sailor, and the combination works very well. Karen was particularly taken by the way that Bible names and references are woven into the story, something which adds an evocative quality to this often moving book.

D. A. Young (review date June 1978)

SOURCE: Young, D. A. *Junior Bookshelf* 42 no. 3 (June 1978): 162-63.

Three separate strands are cleverly woven into the tale of an uninhabited island off the Shetlands [in **Skull Island**]. Two generations happily join forces in an attempt to solve a wartime mystery. Richard Goddard of the Fleet Air Arm had gone submarine hunting at the start of a convoy to Russia and disappeared without trace into 'a rock-lined cloud'. So Richard's friend Admiral Sir John Beauchamp-Troubridge V.C., D.S.O., R.N. (rtd) decides to sail his converted Thames barge to this inhospitable rock in search of the crashed Swordfish and an end to the speculation about Richard's fate. Three schoolboys make up his crew. Richard's widow comes along to cook and the Admiral's man, Guns Kelly, provides the professional element in the expedition.

They find the Swordfish and much else besides including evidence of the time when the island had been inhabited. The characters are well-drawn and sufficiently delineated to catch the reader's interest on their own. The narrative, despite its complications, is neatly told and it is pleasant to meet people who can get on together and respect each other across the so-called generation gap. I liked it.

Margery Fisher (review date July 1986)

SOURCE: Fisher, Margery. *Growing Point* 25 no. 2 (July 1986): 4647.

When *Skull Island* was first published nearly ten years ago Philip Turner's three schoolboy heroes had already enjoyed four adventures in the intervals of cricket matches and church festivals and were at the beginning of further education and adult life. Brought up to date a little in practical details and idiom, the book still has the cheerful holiday atmosphere and the steady concern for human beings which are hallmarks of this author, who remains closer to Ransome in his approach than to many writers of his '60's vintage. The journey to an island inhabited only by wild goats, reminiscent of both Rockall and St. Kilda, is one more interesting journey with their friend the Admiral as far as David, Peter and Arthur are concerned, but for the old man and for David's Aunt Caroline it is a quest into the past. Caroline's husband had died when his plane hit the peak of Gethsemane Island during the war many years earlier; the Admiral, leading a convoy at the time, had not been able to investigate and still feels responsible at least for the paucity of information about the tragedy. The adults approach the island with apprehension as the boys view it with explorative zeal; the remains of an old settlement claims their interest as the crashed aeroplane is uppermost in the minds of their elders. It is the confident amalgamation of adult and young reactions to a deserted place that gives this book its depth and ballast and ensures that it can still be read as a novel where character matters as much as action or locality.

DECISION IN THE DARK (1978)

Marcus Crouch (review date June 1979)

SOURCE: Crouch, Marcus. *Junior Bookshelf* 43 no. 3 (June 1979): 174.

It is a long time since Philip Turner first delighted us with his tales of young people in the Durham countryside, and he has not stood still. His new book [*Decision in the Dark*] is quite different. He has taken eight unsolved problems, some of the *Marie Celeste* school, others of a more general nature, and instead of retelling them with his own interpretations he has invented parallel stories designed to realise the wonder and suspense latent in their themes. They range in time from a human tragedy of the Roman withdrawal from the Wall to a bomber raid over Berlin, in place from a ruined chapel in Ireland to a canal 'cut' in the Midlands. The stories are exciting, provocative, agreeably inconclusive. Mr. Turner's object is not to solve problems but to make you think, and he achieves this most effectively in this stimulating collection.

Margery Fisher (review date September 1979)

SOURCE: Fisher, Margery. *Growing Point* 18 no. 3 (September 1979): 3579.

The author of these 'Tales of Mystery' [*Decision in the Dark*] offers explanations or extra possibilities of actual events. For example, in 'The Site at Corvoricum' he suggests that the dig is haunted because of an ancient conflict between pagan and Christian belief; in 'The Maybury Disaster of 1866' he gives a plausible reason for a shocking railcrash: another story is based on the riddle of the deserted lighthouse on the Flannan Islands. A lively, concrete style and congenial subject-matter should commend this collection to Secondary School libraries.

ROOKOO AND BREE (1979)

M. Hobbs (review date December 1979)

SOURCE: Hobbs, M. *Junior Bookshelf* 43, no. 6 (December 1979): 342.

It is a measure of the unevenness of this, in the end, lively and amusing fantasy [*Rookoo and Bree*] that it appears to begin in serious fashion with the education and launching from the nest of a collared dove, in an uneasy mixture of careful ornithology and anthropomorphism ("Thank you for all you have done for me since I was an egg"!). It comes as a surprise to find Rookoo, her wing damaged by a cat, being saved by the great shire horse Bree and healed by the Wise Woman who can talk with animals—we are back in the world of *Wigwig and Homer*. Before we meet the pigs, however, Rookoo has several dangerous adventures, and the Wise Woman is turned out of her cottage in the forest. She sends Rookoo and Bree, with the blind donkey, the one-winged Canada Goose and the one-legged herring gull who are her "family", to Queen Wigwig on Sanctuary Island, and as soon as Rookoo journeys to the pigs, the story becomes funny, fast and exciting: we are prepared to suspend disbelief. The observation of natural sights and animal behaviour is close throughout the book, and the homely comparisons vivid, but the images, to which young readers will readily relate, are outside the experience of the young dove with whom we are being asked to identify. Perhaps Philip Turner is trying to do too many things together this time.

THE GOOD SHEPHERD (1986)

Stephen Barber (review date February 1987)

SOURCE: Barber, Stephen. *School Librarian* 35, no. 1 (February 1987): 39.

[*The Good Shepherd*] is a retelling of the parable of the lost sheep from St. Luke's gospel amplified to picture-book length. It would be suitable for reading to, but not by, infants. It is, however, really a vehicle for the hazy and prickly illustrations of Bunshu Iguchi, which amplify the story more successfully than does the text. The parables are not as easy to expand as they may seem. The whole is over-lavish for what it offers but may serve a purpose in presenting an important story for the first time.

Marcus Crouch (review date December 1986)

SOURCE: Crouch, Marcus. *Junior Bookshelf* 50 no. 6 (December 1986): 220.

In an effective picture-book [*The Good Shepherd*] Philip Turner brings together the message of the 23rd Psalm and the parable of the Good Shepherd. He tells his story through the voice of the errant lamb, adequately though with no special eloquence. The words provide a useful vehicle for Bunshu Iguchi's very fine paintings. These represent a compromise between the Japanese and European traditions which I think most people will find totally satisfactory. The big double-spreads are full of the smell of the desert and of new pastures. The colour control is beautifully restrained and the reproduction is admirable, the more so because of the textured paper used. Satisfactory books with a religious aim are still thin on the ground, and here is a welcome addition to the range.

THE CANDLEMASS TREASURE (1988)

E. Colwell (review date August 1988)

SOURCE: Colwell, E. *Junior Bookshelf* 52, no. 4 (August 1988): 202.

Philip Turner was awarded the Carnegie Medal for his second book, *The Grange at High Force*. Since then he has written a number of adventure and mystery stories for young people, the last of them in 1979.

It is pleasant, therefore, to welcome a new story after this interval. This mystery [*The Candlemass Treasure*] has the added interest of a treasure hunt for which six clues must be solved. Readers too can try their skill in company with the young people in the story. Here is an example of the complicated clues: 'Coal mine ESEWSE.000000 and drop the perpendicular to Mayfair C Cheops'. Solving the clues leads the young people on a visit to a prison and culminates in a journey to the Isle of Lindisfarne.

The characters in the story are contrasts—a retired undertaker who becomes the guardian of two teenagers (half Indian and half Korean), a delightfully eccentric countrywoman and a 'proper' villain, Ferrety Ferris, who uses electronic devices to eavesdrop on the treasure seekers. The climax is both exciting and amusing.

Philip Turner has not lost his skill as a storyteller and has combined mystery and adventure in a modern setting. Incidentally social problems are an integral part of the story, for there is the generation gap between the young people and their guardian and the question of racial prejudice is very real in their experience.

Elizabeth Finlayson (review date November 1988)

SOURCE: Finlayson, Elizabeth. *School Librarian* 36, no. 4 (November 1988): 146.

Three engaging characters dominate this absorbing adventure [*The Candlemass Treasure*]: a teenage brother and sister, orphans of mixed racial descent, and their guardian, an elderly gentleman. Their efforts to recover family jewels involve a battle of wits with an evil crook—Ferret by name and ferret by nature—and a struggle to unravel the clues whose solution will reveal the whereabouts of their inheritance. Besides the clues, there are maps; and the traditional ingredients of a good thriller—shady characters, double-crossers, good guys—combine to provide a satisfying and exciting read.

The question of bereavement, approached in a forthright manner, is treated sensibly and sympathetically. The other problem which besets the children is race. They grapple with the paradox of feeling 'as English as anyone else' and yet of having absolutely nothing apart from their 'funny faces' to show who they are. Less philosophically and more practically, they both fear and experience persecution. Both dilemmas are sensitively explored. Again, the reader, along with the characters, is obliged to scrutinise received ideas on morality, to recognise shades of grey as well as blacks and whites. The honest, compassionate crook is not necessarily a contradiction in terms. Finally, the writing—now lyrically descriptive, now chillingly dramatic—is consistently excellent.

Margery Fisher (review date November 1988)

SOURCE: Fisher, Margery. "Making Things Happen." *Growing Point* 27, no. 4 (November 1988): 5062-067.

It is impossible not to be concerned about the two young people central in *The Candlemass Treasure* who set themselves to work out clues to their lost inheritance. Half Indian, and half Korean, Farah and Murray have lived with their co-guardians, Charles Candlemass a retired funeral director and old Colonel Murray, since their parents died in a car crash. A letter from a repentant conman in prison offers them elaborate clues to the whereabouts of jewels stolen from their father; they are hampered in their search by the malicious attentions of unpleasant Mr. Ferris who is also on the track of the treasure and who is sometimes ahead of them with solutions to book reference, anagrams and map figures. East Anglia and Holy Island serve as background to chases, escapes and encounters and a climax on a tidal causeway brings to a conclusion a fast-moving tale with a very firm 'Crime does not pay' moral. The boy and girl also offer the author the chance to make one or two anti-racist comments but though, like the rest of his books for the early 'teens, this one has a strong educational flavour, the variety of settings and characters makes for exciting reading.

Additional coverage of Turner's life and career is contained in the following sources published by the Gale Group: *Contemporary Authors,* **Vol. 25-28R;** *Contemporary Authors New Revision Series,* **Vols. 11, 27;** *Literature Resource Center;* *Something about the Author,* **Vols. 11, 83;** *Something About the Author Autobiography Series,* **Vol. 6; and** *St. James Guide to Children's Writers,* **Vol. 5.**

Elizabeth Winthrop
1948-

(Full name Elizabeth Winthrop Mahony) American author of children's fiction, picture books, and young adult novels.

INTRODUCTION

Elizabeth Winthrop was one of the first children's book authors to address the subtler nuances of human relationships. The characters in both her picture books and her young adult novels are confronted with the issues of family relationships, gender identity and bias, communication skills, friendship, and loyalty. The themes are the same, although the characters and settings in her novels are more complex and sophisticated than those in her picture books. The young adult novel *A Little Demonstration of Affection,* published in 1975, was a break-through book in that it delved into issues of physical affection and sexuality. *The Castle in the Attic* (1985), her most popular book, addresses concepts of independence and maturity, as does its sequel *The Battle for the Castle* (1993). Her picture books take up similar important personal issues. For example, *Lizzie and Harold* (1986) is about what constitutes friendship, and *Tough Eddie* (1984) and *Dumpy La Rue* (2001) are both about sex role stereotypes.

In an interview for the Internet Public Library Winthrop said, "When people ask me where I get my ideas, my answer is always 'from inside myself,' even when I'm writing about ducks and dolls and miniature knights in armor, I'm writing about myself because a writer takes all her . . . fears and worries and angers and puts them inside her characters."

BIOGRAPHICAL INFORMATION

The only girl in a family of six children, Winthrop is the daughter of the late political journalist Stuart Alsop, as well as the niece of President Franklin D. Roosevelt. Her childhood in Washington, D.C., was a major inspiration for her writing. The Alsop family lived in the city in a large ramshackle house with an acre of woods and a stream and a family atmosphere

that encouraged creativity and a love of reading. In the evenings, she and her siblings, along with her father and mother, would read aloud from Shakespeare with everyone taking parts. Books were everywhere, and "reading was like breathing." Winthrop's interest in writing was inevitable. As a child she attended a Roman Catholic girls' school, which she later described as an extremely repressive environment, and after school she kept a journal and composed stories. She spent her summers at her grandmother's home with a cousin who was a painter, and together they wrote and illustrated stories. She wrote her first book at age 12, but lost it on the bus.

In the tenth grade Winthrop began attending boarding school at Miss Porter's School in Connecticut, a less restrictive environment where "We were allowed to talk!" After graduation from Miss Porter's, she attended Sarah Lawrence College where she experienced complete freedom from the restrictions of her

CLR Cumulative Nationality Index

AMERICAN

Aardema, Verna 17
Aaseng, Nathan 54
Adams, Adrienne 73
Adkins, Jan 7, 77
Adler, C(arole) S(chwerdtfeger) 78
Adler, Irving 27
Adoff, Arnold 7
Alcott, Louisa May 1, 38
Aldrich, Bess Streeter 70
Alexander, Lloyd (Chudley) 1, 5, 48
Alger, Horatio 87
Aliki 9, 71
Allard, Harry 85
Anderson, Poul (William) 58
Angelou, Maya 53
Anglund, Joan Walsh 1
Armstrong, Jennifer 66
Armstrong, William H(oward) 1
Arnold, Caroline 61
Arnosky, James Edward 15
Aruego, José (Espiritu) 5
Ashabranner, Brent (Kenneth) 28
Asimov, Isaac 12, 79
Atwater, Florence (Hasseltine Carroll) 19
Atwater, Richard (Tupper) 19
Avi 24, 68
Aylesworth, Jim 89
Aylesworth, Thomas G(ibbons) 6
Babbitt, Natalie (Zane Moore) 2, 53
Bacon, Martha Sherman 3
Ballard, Robert D(uane) 60
Bang, Molly Garrett 8
Barron, T(homas) A(rchibald) 86
Baum, L(yman) Frank 15
Baylor, Byrd 3
Bellairs, John (Anthony) 37
Bemelmans, Ludwig 6
Benary-Isbert, Margot 12
Bendick, Jeanne 5
Berenstain, Jan(ice) 19
Berenstain, Stan(ley) 19
Berger, Melvin H. 32
Bess, Clayton 39
Bethancourt, T. Ernesto 3
Bishop, Claire Huchet 80
Block, Francesca Lia 33
Blos, Joan W(insor) 18
Blumberg, Rhoda 21
Blume, Judy (Sussman) 2, 15, 69
Bogart, Jo Ellen 59
Bond, Nancy (Barbara) 11
Bontemps, Arna(ud Wendell) 6
Bova, Ben(jamin William) 3
Boyd, Candy Dawson 50
Brancato, Robin F(idler) 32
Branley, Franklyn M(ansfield) 13
Brett, Jan (Churchill) 27
Bridgers, Sue Ellen 18
Brink, Carol Ryrie 30
Brooks, Bruce 25
Brooks, Gwendolyn (Elizabeth) 27

Brown, Marcia (Joan) 12
Brown, Marc (Tolon) 29
Brown, Margaret Wise 10
Bruchac, Joseph III 46
Bryan, Ashley F. 18, 66
Bunting, Eve 28, 56, 82
Burch, Robert J(oseph) 63
Burnett, Frances (Eliza) Hodgson 24
Burton, Virginia Lee 11
Butler, Octavia E(stelle) 65
Byars, Betsy (Cromer) 1, 16, 72
Cabot, Meg 85
Cadnum, Michael 78
Caines, Jeannette (Franklin) 24
Calhoun, Mary 42
Cameron, Eleanor (Frances) 1, 72
Carle, Eric 10, 72
Carter, Alden R(ichardson) 22
Cassedy, Sylvia 26
Catalanotto, Peter 68
Charlip, Remy 8
Childress, Alice 14
Choi, Sook Nyul 53
Christopher, Matt(hew Frederick) 33
Ciardi, John (Anthony) 19
Clark, Ann Nolan 16
Cleary, Beverly (Atlee Bunn) 2, 8, 72
Cleaver, Bill 6
Cleaver, Vera (Allen) 6
Clifton, (Thelma) Lucille 5
Climo, Shirley 69
Coatsworth, Elizabeth (Jane) 2
Cobb, Vicki 2
Cohen, Daniel (E.) 3, 43
Cole, Brock 18
Cole, Joanna 5, 40
Collier, James Lincoln 3
Colum, Padraic 36
Conford, Ellen 10, 71
Conrad, Pam 18
Cooney, Barbara 23
Cooper, Floyd 60
Corbett, Scott 1
Corcoran, Barbara (Asenath) 50
Cormier, Robert (Edmund) 12, 55
Cox, Palmer 24
Creech, Sharon 42, 89
Crews, Donald 7
Crutcher, Chris(topher C.) 28
Cummings, Pat (Marie) 48
Curry, Jane L(ouise) 31
Curtis, Christopher Paul 68
Curtis, Jamie Lee 88
Cushman, Karen 55
Dalgliesh, Alice 62
Danziger, Paula 20
Daugherty, James (Henry) 78
d'Aulaire, Edgar Parin 21
d'Aulaire, Ingri (Mortenson Parin) 21
Davis, Ossie 56
Day, Alexandra 22
de Angeli, Marguerite (Lofft) 1
DeClements, Barthe (Faith) 23

DeJong, Meindert 1, 73
Denslow, W(illiam) W(allace) 15
dePaola, Tomie 4, 24, 81
Diaz, David 65
Dillon, Diane (Claire) 44
Dillon, Leo 44
Disch, Thomas M(ichael) 18
Dixon, Franklin W. 61
Dodge, Mary (Elizabeth) Mapes 62
Domanska, Janina 40
Donovan, John 3
Dorris, Michael (Anthony) 58
Dorros, Arthur (M.) 42
Draper, Sharon M(ills) 57
Dr. Seuss 1, 9, 53
Duke, Kate 51
Duncan, Lois 29
Duvoisin, Roger (Antoine) 23
Eager, Edward (McMaken) 43
Ehlert, Lois (Jane) 28
Emberley, Barbara A(nne) 5
Emberley, Ed(ward Randolph) 5, 81
Engdahl, Sylvia Louise 2
L'Engle, Madeleine (Camp Franklin) 1, 14, 57
Enright, Elizabeth (Wright) 4
Epstein, Beryl (M. Williams) 26
Epstein, Samuel 26
Estes, Eleanor (Ruth) 2, 70
Ets, Marie Hall 33
Feelings, Muriel (Lavita Grey) 5
Feelings, Tom 5, 58
Ferry, Charles 34
Field, Rachel (Lyman) 21
Fisher, Aileen (Lucia) 49
Fisher, Dorothy (Frances) Canfield 71,
Fisher, Leonard Everett 18
Fitzgerald, John D(ennis) 1
Fitzhugh, Louise (Perkins) 1, 72
Flack, Marjorie 28
Fleischman, (Albert) Sid(ney) 1, 15
Fleischman, Paul 20, 66
Forbes, Esther 27
Foster, Genevieve (Stump) 7
Fox, Paula 1, 44
Freedman, Russell (Bruce) 20, 71
Freeman, Don 30
Fritz, Jean (Guttery) 2, 14
Frost, Robert (Lee) 67
Fujikawa, Gyo 25
Gaberman, Judie Angell 33
Gag, Wanda (Hazel) 4
Gaines, Ernest J(ames) 62
Galdone, Paul 16
Gallant, Roy A(rthur) 30
Gammell, Stephen 83
Gantos, Jack 18, 85
Garden, Nancy 51
Gauch, Patricia Lee 56
Geisel, Theodor Seuss 53
Geisert, Arthur 87
George, Jean Craighead 1; 80
Gibbons, Gail (Gretchen) 8

Nationality Index

Nationality Index

CLR-89 Title Index